UPHOLSTERY

in America & Europe
from the Seventeenth Century
to World War I

Editor
  Edward S. Cooke, Jr.

Editorial Consultants
  Susan L. Paxman
  Regina Ryan

UPHOLSTERY

*in America & Europe
from the Seventeenth Century
to World War I*

by

Edward S. Cooke, Jr.   Jonathan L. Fairbanks   Jane C. Nylander

Peter Thornton   Robert F. Trent   Margaret Swain

Brock Jobe   Wallace Gusler   LeRoy Graves   Mark Anderson

Morrison H. Heckscher   Andrew Passeri   Patricia Chapin O'Donnell

Jeffrey Munger   Linda Wesselman Jackson   C. A. Burgers

Florence M. Montgomery   Elisabet Stavenow-Hidemark

Martha Gandy Fales   Jan Seidler Ramirez   Anne Farnam

Richard C. Nylander

A BARRA FOUNDATION BOOK

W. W. Norton & Co.

New York · London

Printed in the United States of America.
Typeset, printed and bound by Meriden-Stinehour
Meriden, Connecticut and Lunenburg, Vermont.
Book and jacket design by Carl Zahn.
ISBN 0-393-02469-5.

W. W. Norton & Company, Inc.
500 Fifth Avenue, New York, N.Y. 10110

W. W. Norton & Company Ltd.
37 Great Russell Street, London WC1B 3NU

Contents

Introduction   11

JONATHAN L. FAIRBANKS
Katharine Lane Weems Curator
American Decorative Arts and Sculpture
Museum of Fine Arts, Boston
and
JANE C. NYLANDER
Director
Strawbery Banke

Upholstered Seat Furniture in Europe,
17th and 18th Centuries   29

PETER THORNTON
Director
Sir John Soane's Museum

17th-Century Upholstery in Massachusetts   39

ROBERT F. TRENT
Curator
Connecticut Historical Society

The Turkey-work Chairs of Holyroodhouse   51

MARGARET SWAIN
Textile Historian
Edinburgh, Scotland

The Boston Upholstery Trade, 1700–1775   65

BROCK JOBE
Chief Curator
Society for the Preservation of New England Antiquities

The Technique of 18th-Century
Over-the-rail Upholstery   91

WALLACE GUSLER, LEROY GRAVES, and
MARK ANDERSON
Department of Conservation
The Colonial Williamsburg Foundation

18th-Century American Upholstery Techniques: Easy Chairs, Sofas, and Settees   97

MORRISON H. HECKSCHER
Curator
Department of American Decorative Arts
Metropolitan Museum of Art

Evidence from the Frame of a Late
18th-Century Sofa   112

EDWARD S. COOKE, JR.
Assistant Curator
American Decorative Arts and Sculpture
Museum of Fine Arts, Boston
and
ANDREW PASSERI
Upholstery Consultant
Museum of Fine Arts, Boston

Richard Wevill, Upholsterer   114

PATRICIA CHAPIN O'DONNELL
Decorative Arts Consultant
Philadelphia, Pennsylvania

French Upholstery Practices of the
18th Century   121

JEFFREY MUNGER
Assistant Curator
European Decorative Arts and Sculpture
Museum of Fine Arts, Boston

Beyond the Fringe: Ornamental
Upholstery Trimmings in the
17th, 18th, and Early 19th Centuries   131

LINDA WESSELMAN JACKSON
Decorative Arts Consultant
Lenox, Massachusetts

Some Notes on Western European
Table Linen from the
16th through the 18th Centuries   149

C. A. BURGERS
Keeper of Textiles
Rijksmuseum, Amsterdam

18th-Century American Bed and
Window Hangings   163

FLORENCE M. MONTGOMERY
Textile Consultant
Department of American Decorative Arts
Metropolitan Museum of Art

Bed and Window Hangings in
New England, 1790–1870   175

JANE C. NYLANDER
Director
Strawbery Banke

Contents

Swedish Royal Curtains from the Early 19th Century   187

ELISABET STAVENOW-HIDEMARK
Curator
Textile Department
Nordiska Museet, Stockholm

F. A. Moreland's *Practical Decorative Upholstery*   197

MARTHA GANDY FALES
Decorative Arts Consultant
Brunswick, Maine

Drapery Documents in the Study Exhibition   207

JANE C. NYLANDER
Director
Strawbery Banke

The Re-Dressing of a Boston Empire Sofa   223

JAN SEIDLER RAMIREZ
Research Curator
The Hudson River Museum of Westchester

The A. H. Davenport Company of Boston: Notes on the Upholsterer's Trade in the Late-19th and Early 20th Centuries   231

ANNE FARNAM
Director
Essex Institute

Spring Seats of the 19th and Early-20th Centuries   239

EDWARD S. COOKE, JR.
Assistant Curator
American Decorative Arts and Sculpture
Museum of Fine Arts, Boston
and
ANDREW PASSERI
Upholstery Consultant
Museum of Fine Arts, Boston

Upholstery Documents in the Collections of the Society for the Preservation of New England Antiquities   251

RICHARD C. NYLANDER
Curator of Collections
Society for the Preservation of New England Antiquities

Acknowledgements

TEN YEARS in production, this book is the result of many people's ideas and labors. Some contributed to the 1979 Conference on Historic Upholstery and Drapery from which these essays evolved, others played important roles in the preparation of these essays for publication, and many were involved during the entire process. Plans for the conference began back in 1976 with the convening of a planning committee that consisted of Diane Pilgrim, Curator of Decorative Arts at the Brooklyn Museum and then President of the Decorative Arts Society, Jane Nylander, then Curator of Textiles and Ceramics at Old Sturbridge Village, and Jonathan L. Fairbanks, Curator of American Decorative Arts and Sculpture at the Museum of Fine Arts, Boston. Jan Seidler, then the Assistant Curator of American Decorative Arts and Sculpture at the Museum of Fine Arts, wrote a successful grant application to the National Endowment for the Arts (NEA).

The financial assistance of the NEA and the cooperative efforts of many individuals and institutions ensured a rich, multi-faceted program. In addition to the authors included in this volume, many others made invaluable contributions to the landmark conference. We would like to acknowledge the help and participation of Marilynn Johnson, Richard Cheek, Philip Curtis, Samuel Dornsife, Wilson Faude, Margaret Fikioris, R. Craig Miller, Adriana S. Bitter and Paul Tiralla of Scalamandre, Murray Douglas and Carmi Dennis of Brunschwig and Fils, John Morse of F. Schumacher, Sally McGeough of McGeough, Robinson, and Edith Campbell of Clarence House. Staff at the two sponsoring institutions, the Museum of Fine Arts, Boston and Old Sturbridge Village, also played prominent roles in the success of the conference. From the Museum, we would like to thank Ellen Abernathy, Michael Brown, Karen Guffy, Sarah Olson, the late Mary Quinn, Joy Cattanach Smith, Robert Walker, and Carol Warner, Department of American Decorative Arts and Sculpture; Christina Corsiglia and Anne Poulet, Department of European Decorative Arts and Sculpture; and Joanna Hill, Catherine Kvaraceus Hunter, and the late Larry Salmon, Department of Textiles. Those at Sturbridge Village who made important contributions include Donna K. Baron, David L. Colglazier, John Obed Curtis, Madeline Jolin, Henry E. Peach, Margaret Piatt, Caroline Sloat, and Frank White. We also wish to acknowledge Jan Fontein, Director of the Museum of Fine Arts, Boston, and Crawford Lincoln, President of Old Sturbridge Village, for their leadership and support of a trailblazing conference.

The selection of certain papers presented at the conference and the preparation of these manuscripts for publication in a single volume intended for a wide audience including museum professionals, conservators, craftsmen, decorators, and the general public has depended upon the work of many others. Those at the Museum of Fine Arts include Rachel Camber, Paula Kozol and Gillian Wohlauer, Department of American Decorative Arts and Sculpture; Victoria Jennings, Department of Prints, Drawings and Photographs; Janice Sorkow, Department of Photographic Services; and Carl Zahn, Office of Publications. In transforming slide presentations into publishable essays that comprise a balanced, coherent volume, we were extremely fortunate to have the considerable editorial skills of Regina Ryan Publishing Enterprises. Sue Paxman of Editorial Associates, Inc., copy edited the text. Most importantly, we must recognize the unfailing encouragement and support of Robert McNeil, President of the Barra Foundation. Without his interest and involvement, this volume would not have been possible and the information presented at the conference considerably less accessible.

EDWARD S. COOKE, JR.

Introduction

WITHOUT A DOUBT, the most visually dominant decorative elements of a historic room are its window treatments, bed hangings, table coverings, and furniture upholstery. From the seventeenth through the nineteenth centuries, all these trappings were the domain of the upholsterer. This master craftsman coordinated matters of interior decoration in much the same way that an interior designer does today. Although richly carved furniture is most valued by present-day collectors, the most expensive furniture in the past was that which was upholstered. Before the twentieth century, most people acknowledged the importance of upholstered furniture. For example, the English poet William Cowper, in 1804, summarized the evolution of seating forms from common bench to fashionable upholstered sofa:

> The growth of what is excellent; so hard
> T'attain perfection in this nether world.
> Thus first necessity invented stools,
> Convenience next suggested elbow chairs,
> And luxury th'accomplished sofa last.
>
> "The Task" in *The Poetical
> Works of William Cowper*
> (London: George Routledge and Sons,
> 1854), p. 190

Twenty years ago, it was standard museum practice to send out historic furniture in need of reupholstery to commercial shops. At that time, neither upholsterers nor curators paid much attention to the process. Rarely did they take care to remove the existing materials so as to discover whether anything remained of the original covering fabric, foundation materials, or nailing. Few took the time or the trouble to search for or photograph the small bits of fabric, original nail marks, or other small clues that could shed light on an object's past history or that could even be integrated into the new upholstery treatment. Indeed, commercial upholsterers were required by law to remove all old material from the frame and to reupholster only with new materials. (Those few curators who felt that the original elements should be saved and integrated with new covering only occasionally found upholsterers willing to bend the law.) Even the appropriate type of covering fabric was not always fully researched, the choice of fabric often depending upon the decorative needs of the moment. As a result, succeeding scholars and craftsmen have found it extremely difficult to reconstruct with accuracy the original shape and appearance of historic upholstered furniture and drapery.

It is hard to estimate how much important information has been lost due to past practices. Further, it is now clear that the vast majority of upholstered antique furniture and drapery purported to have been restored in authentic period style does not, in fact, possess the proper historic appearance.

In the late 1960s, there were only a few inquisitive scholars who conducted serious research into historic textiles and their proper use in upholstery and drapery. The pioneering work of these scholars raised the consciousness of other scholars and curators who began to think in terms of internal materials, contour, and finish fabric in addition to carving and inlay. As the rigorous examination of furnishing fabrics in seventeenth- and eighteenth-century homes began to reveal considerable variety in textile materials and use, the old clichés of silk damask drapes for formal parlors and blue-and-white checked linen for country rooms began to be questioned.

While these scholars and curators uncovered significant new manuscript and pictorial documentation, they still lacked any real understanding of how the textiles were actually cut out, assembled, and shaped. This limitation was due to three factors. First, written period sources are generally silent about trade practices. Secondly, much invaluable empirical evidence had, by the late 1960s, been either lost or hidden out of sight, buried beneath subsequent coverings. Finally, few scholars went beyond the more usual art historical sources to examine carefully the evidence of the artifact itself as a means of extrapolating original practices. As a result, in their zeal to re-create accurate historic interiors, they frequently used awkwardly hung swags, incorrectly hung bed draperies, and strangely stuffed furniture.

As data about historic upholstery and drapery materials and techniques has accumulated, scholars, conservators, and craftsmen have recognized the need to question formerly held assumptions about period upholstery practices and to collaborate in reconstructing the shapes, proportions, fabrics, hardware, foundation materials, and methods of assembly. The advantages of interaction among scholars, conservators, and craftsmen led the Decorative Arts Society to organize a forum that would bring together people from these different fields to exchange results and to chart future directions. The four-day symposium, which took place March 21 through 24, 1979, brought together over two hundred museum curators, upholsterers, conservators, interior designers, collectors, and historians. The forum included talks, special exhibitions, workshops, and opportunities for informal interaction and constructive dialogue. The conference also led, ultimately, to this collection of essays derived from some of the papers presented there.

The two exhibitions mounted in conjunction with the conference were extremely revealing. One was organized by the Museum of Fine Arts and included samples of historic upholstery materials salvaged from English and American furniture dating from the late seventeenth through the late nineteenth centuries. The other exhibit, organized at Old Sturbridge Village, displayed historic American drapery, principally window and bed hangings, from the early eighteenth century through the nineteenth century.

An unusual and very influential part of the conference was the demonstration of upholstery and drapery methods by master craftsmen at Old Sturbridge Village. Andrew Passeri, a Boston master upholsterer with fifty years experience, demonstrated nineteenth-century techniques of tufting and spring tying. Wallace Gusler and Albert Skutans of Colonial Williamsburg demonstrated eighteenth-century upholstery methods. Charles Anello of the Metropolitan Museum of Art offered a session on early nineteenth-century practices and the stitching of a "French edge." Ernest LoNano, a decorator who does a great deal of restoration work, demonstrated methods and materials of drapery and festoon work. Unfortunately, it is difficult to recapture

the special character of the exhibitions and workshops; however, in an effort to convey this added dimension, we have included several annotated pictorial essays on these exhibitions and workshops.

The following combination of informative essays and pictorial case studies is intended to assist a diverse audience, from contemporary upholsterers to those curators and decorators who may be called upon to guide a craftsman in reupholstering period furniture or creating period draperies. This volume is meant not only to provide a readily available summary of the actual conference, but it is also intended as a source book for the future for those who were not fortunate enough to attend the original conference. It is our hope that the publication of these papers in one volume will assist this wide audience. Much about upholstery and drapery has been learned and published since the 1979 conference, due in part to the stimulus of that event; nevertheless, the papers from that conference remain key documents.

JONATHAN L. FAIRBANKS
Katharine Lane Weems Curator
of American Decorative Arts and Sculpture
Museum of Fine Arts, Boston

JANE C. NYLANDER
Director
Strawbery Banke

June 1986

Plate 1 (*see* fig. 17)
Leather great chair, Boston, 1660–1680.
Maple and oak; leather with brass nails; original upholstery
foundation; modern cushion.
Courtesy, Museum of Fine Arts, Boston.

Plate 3 (*see* fig. 249)
Side chair, probably Portsmouth, New Hampshire, 1760–1770.
Mahogany; original green harateen fabric and upholstery.
Courtesy, Society for the Preservation of New England Antiquities.
Photograph by J. David Bohl.

Plate 4 (*see* fig. 87)
Easy chair, New England, 1730–1790.
Walnut and maple; original upholstery and worsted covering.
Courtesy, Brooklyn Museum. Henry Batterman Fund.

Plate 5 (*see* fig. 88)
Easy chair, Newport, 1758.
Walnut and maple; original upholstery with Irish stitch and
embroidered needlework covering.
Courtesy, The Metropolitan Museum of Art. Gift of
Mrs. J. Insley Blair.

Plate 6 (*see* fig. 114)
Detail of wall hanging or bed cover, Lyon, France, 1786.
Reboul et Fontebrune. Courtesy, Museum of Fine Arts, Boston.
Gift of Mrs. Helen Howard Hudson Whipple and
Mrs. Alice Wayland Hudson White.

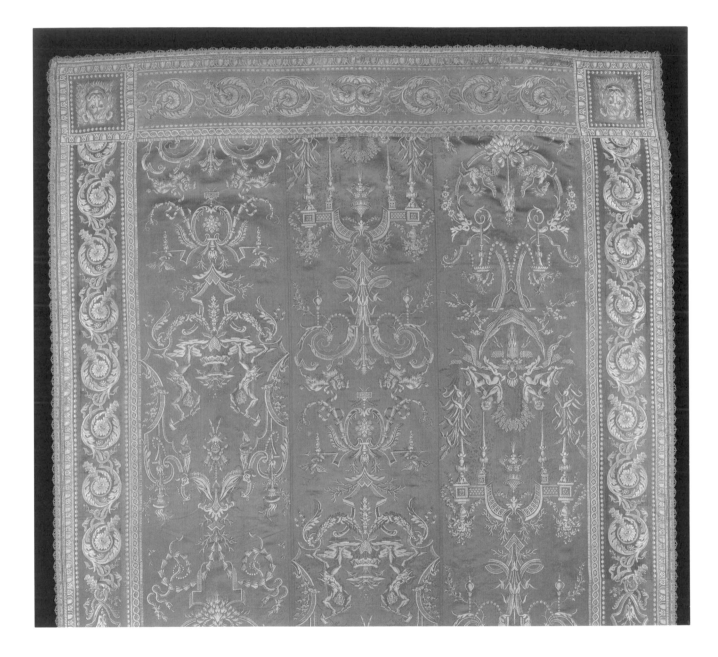

Plate 7 (*see* fig. 123)
Detail of bed valance, English materials, 1720–1735.
Calendered cheney with wool tape, lined with buckram.
Courtesy, Essex Institute. Photograph by Richard Cheek.

Plate 9 (*see* fig. 156)
Detail of valance, c. 1790–1795.
Block-printed cotton with polychrome cotton fringe, tape heading,
and cotton-covered gimp.
Courtesy, Society for the Preservation of New England Antiquities.
Photograph by J. David Bohl.

Plate 10 (*see* fig. 196)
Window drapery, early nineteenth century.
Stamped blue wool with floral designs, blue and yellow wool braid
and fringe, tan cotton linings.
Courtesy, National Society of the Colonial Dames of America in the
State of New Hampshire. Photograph by Henry E. Peach.

Plate 11 (*see* fig. 197)
Window drapery, England, c. 1810.
Block-printed glazed yellow, red, and brown cotton.
Courtesy, Old Sturbridge Village. Photograph by Henry E. Peach.

Plate 12 (*see* fig. 201)
A swag and a tail or cascade, England, c. 1825–1830.
Roller-printed glazed cotton in a chinoiserie design with red, green,
and yellow wool tapes; and spool fringes covered with yellow silk.
Courtesy, Old Sturbridge Village. Photograph by Henry E. Peach.

Plate 13 (*see* fig. 208)
Lambrequin, c. 1850–1860.
Red silk brocatelle with tassels.
Courtesy, Society for the Preservation of New England Antiquities.
Photograph by Henry E. Peach.

25

Plate 14 (*see* fig. 209)
Detail of drapery panel, Boston, c. 1865.
Green and cream silk lampas with pink flowers, lined with white china
silk. Original silk cords and tassels.
Courtesy, Society for the Preservation of New England Antiquities.
Photograph by Henry E. Peach.

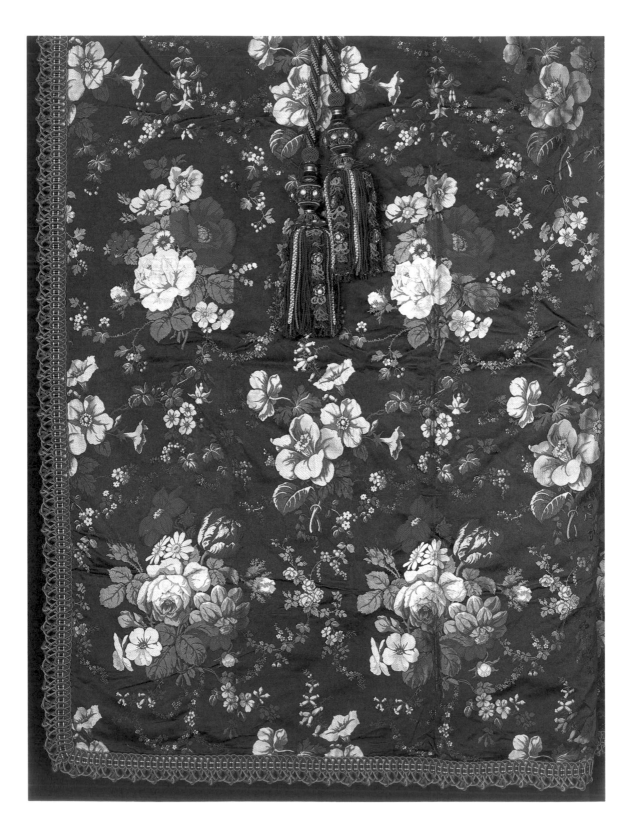

Plate 15 (*see* fig. 223)
Empire sofa, Boston, c. 1825–1835.
Mahogany, birch, yellow poplar, oak; modern upholstery.
Courtesy, Museum of Fine Arts, Boston. Gift of Colonel and Mrs.
Thomas R. West.

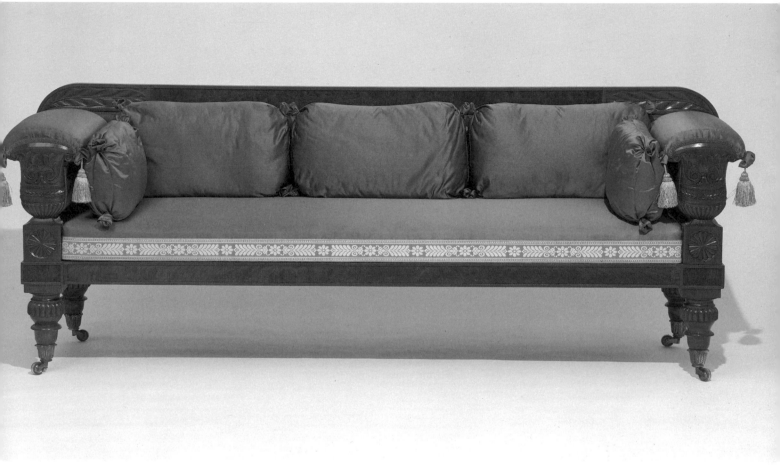

Upholstered Seat Furniture in Europe, 17th and 18th Centuries

Peter Thornton

UNTIL the beginning of the seventeenth century, the usual way to make a seat comfortable was to lay a cushion on it. Although in the medieval period a few especially grand chairs were provided with fixed padding, upholstery as we understand the term evolved only after 1600.[1] All upholstery techniques, with the possible exceptions of certain stitched edges and of springing, had been developed before 1700. Continental craftsmen were the leading innovators in upholstery at that time, and there is no reason to suppose that any peculiarly English techniques existed before then. Indeed, many of the upholsterers working for the English Crown before 1700 had French names, suggesting that the chief practitioners of this new trade in England were foreign. Certainly, the most notable advances in upholstered comfort were made in Paris by craftsmen working for discriminating and fastidious customers like the Grand Dauphin and a small group of aristocratic women who appreciated the sense of well-being that comfortable surroundings could evoke.

It is a simple matter to pile padding on a seat and secure a cover over it with nails around the edge; however, the padding is apt to distort rapidly. When something more elaborate is required, a way must be devised for securing the padding in the right position. This is especially true when chair backs are to be padded. Early attempts to secure padding depended on quilting, an embroidery technique involving lines of stitching in parallel or diamond patterns (fig. 1), and occasionally, notably in Italy and Spain, in more complicated fish scale patterns. As the padding became thicker and firmer, upholsterers turned for guidance to saddlers who long before had solved the problems of securing padding that was subject to much more rough treatment than chair upholstery.[2] Simple chairs with padded seats that seem to have been stitched after a saddler's system are illustrated in Dutch and Flemish pictures of about 1625 (fig. 2).

By that time, the back stool (fig. 3) had been developed. It was to become the most common type of chair of the seventeenth century in all but the most humble circles, and it remained in production well into the eighteenth century. The basic conformation, as shown in figure 3, was always the same whatever the quality of the individual chair. The status or cost of such chairs depended on the richness of the textile covering and trimming and the amount of decoration on the visible wooden parts — that is, the legs and stretchers. (The uprights to the back were normally covered.) The techniques used on these back stools were rudimentary,

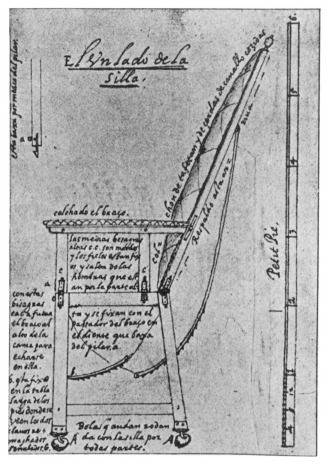

1. Drawing of the invalid chair of Philip II of Spain (d. 1596) from Henry Havard, *Dictionnaire de l'Ameublement et de la Décoration Depuis le XIIIe siècle jusqu'à nos jours* (Paris: Ancienne Maison Quantin, 1887–1889) vol. III, p. 686, fig. 503. Note the reference to quilted padding of taffeta with horsehair sewn in ("Colchon de tafetan y de cerdes de cavallo cozidas").

as was characteristic of all upholstery work throughout the seventeenth century. The upholsterer provided grand effects by using rich materials and masses of expensive trimming.

In England during the second half of the seventeenth century, large numbers of backstools of this type were covered with specially woven panels of Turkey work, a woven fabric imitative of Turkey carpets and exported widely. (*See* the discussion of Turkey work in Margaret Swain's essay in this volume.) Even more chairs of this sort were covered with leather. The nailing patterns of both versions could be decorative, sometimes incorporating round-headed nails of two different sizes.

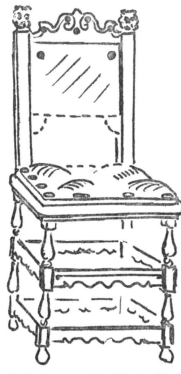

2. Sketch of a Flemish Chair, c. 1625, with stitched padding in velvet. Based on a painting in the London art market in 1969. Drawing by the author.

4. "Great Chair," England, c. 1625. Original red velvet on back, with line of fringe indicated by unfaded band. Crown copyright, Victoria and Albert Museum, London.

3. Painting by Gesina ter Borch (1631–1690), Netherlands, 1672. Notice the back stool. Courtesy, Rijksprentenkabinet, Amsterdam.

Toward the end of the seventeenth century, all chairs, including the upholstered back stool, developed taller backs and, in England, remained tall until about 1740. The gap between the padded seat and the padded back rest gradually dwindled away and was gone by 1700. There was, however, no essential difference between the upholstery of back stools in the seventeenth century and that of chairs produced during the first third or so of the eighteenth.

In Europe and England a set of back stools was often accompanied by a scaled-up version with arms. These upholstered armchairs, called "great chairs," would have been occupied by the highest-ranked person in the company on any given occasion. The arms were at first close-covered with material (fig. 4) but were later left bare (fig. 5).

The easy chair, that huge and accommodating confection, often fitted with wings or cheeks, seems to have

5. *The Lying-in*, by Mathys Naiveu (1647–1721). The painting shows an enlarged armed back stool or great chair in a late seventeenth-century Dutch interior. Note uncovered outside back, domed seat, double-banked trimming, and nailing around back. Courtesy, Stedelijk Museum, Leiden.

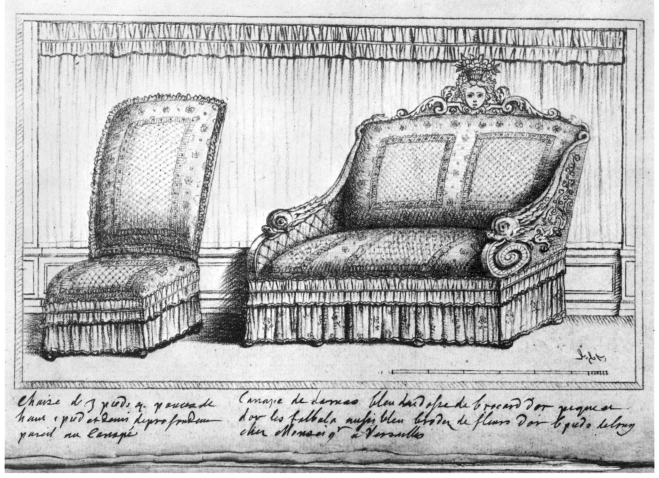

*chaise de 3 pieds 4 pouces de
haut 1 pied et demi de profondeur
pareil au canapé*

*Canapé de damas bleu doublé de brocard d'or piqué a
d'or les falbala aussi bleu broder de fleurs d'or b pieds de long
chez Monseigr à Versailles*

6. Sketch of sofa and chair in the Dauphin's apartment at Versailles,
late seventeenth century. The fashionable chunky silhouette was
achieved by pleated skirting that hid the legs. Courtesy, Bibliothèque
de la Conservation, Château de Versailles.

been developed from the invalid chair and the "sleeping-chair" rather than from the standard armchair.[4] Indeed, it was apparently in this area of chairmaking that truly comfortable upholstery was first developed. Easy chairs were seen in luxurious Parisian apartments by the 1690s (fig. 6). The great sofas of the period were merely double-seated versions of these easy chairs. These upholstered forms were at first to be found primarily in bedchambers and *grands cabinets* which were semi-formal rooms, rather than in the more formal withdrawing rooms and *salons*.[5]

The great comfort of these late seventeenth-century easy chairs and sofas came with the use of huge, down-filled seat cushions set in wells formed by rolls of padding in the underseat. For padding backs, horsehair was used because of the ease with which it could be secured in place by stitches. The invalid chair of Philip II of Spain had a back padded with horsehair (fig. 1), and the bill for some chairs made for Charles II of England in 1660 and 1661 included the item "curled haire to fill the chaire backs."[6] Horsehair became a common back stuffing around 1670, but only in the eighteenth century was horsehair used all over chairs.

32

During the seventeenth century, a certain squaring of edges was achieved by piping and other forms of trimming. The technique of building stiff upright sides seems not to have been devised until well into the next century, although such details have not yet been fully studied. The seat of one back stool, from about 1630 (fig. 7), was presumably meant to have vertical sides, but the means to retain them were clearly lacking. Most seats and backs with fixed padding remained rounded until well after 1700.

The covering material of easy chairs and sofas had to be fixed because the shapes of the furniture made it virtually impossible for the covers to be removable and still be neat and trim; however, the contemporary great chairs commonly had slipcovers of expensive material, one for the seat and one for the back. These slipcovers were made to fit tightly by means of hooks and eyes at the corners of the seat and at the sides of the lower back (fig. 8). This practice was in favor for high style furniture until 1730, whereafter the expensive covers tended to be fixed and protected with a loose cover.

Chairs with caned seats and backs comprised an important part of chair production in England and Holland in the second half of the seventeenth century. In France, caning was not adopted to any great extent until after 1715 but then became popular and remained so through mid-century. The English fashion for caned chairs declined in this same period, only to be revived in the 1760s and later. In England, caned chairs in the seventeenth century were almost invariably provided with cushions and in the later eighteenth century with fitted squabs. (Cushions are bag-like; whereas squabs are square-edged, shaped like small mattresses.) The French went one better and fitted both seat and back with squabs, which were tied on with ribbons (fig. 9). There appears to be no English parallel for this French practice before the Regency period of the early nineteenth century. In Holland, rush-seated chairs with turned members and various forms of ladder-back chairs were also often provided with such padded overlays.[7]

While for the most part the stylistic evolution of English seat furniture in the eighteenth century is widely understood, the development of the chief upholstery treatments merits further examination. By the 1690s, a few chairs with walnut backs carved in open-work patterns were fitted with upholstered seats. Some had slipcovers with deep fringes or actual skirts, which made their silhouettes much more chunky than is generally realized. One sees this in engravings by the emigré

7. Back stool, England, c. 1630. Worsted cover, with original silk appliqué and now deformed squared padding. Note sheathed uprights to back and unsheathed or "raw" legs. Crown copyright, Victoria and Albert Museum.

8. Grand Chair, probably Paris, c. 1670. Slip-over brocaded silk covers with fringe, secured by hooks and eyes; natural-colored top canvas underneath. Crown copyright, Ham House, Victoria and Albert Museum.

9. *Portrait of Marquis de Mirabeau*, 1743, by J. A. J. Camelot (1702–1766). Behind the Marquis is an eighteenth-century French caned chair with a tied-on squab on its back (and presumably another on its seat). Courtesy, Musée du Louvre.

French designer Daniel Marot who worked for William III, the Prince of Orange who became King of England in 1688. (For an example, *see* figure 141.) The chair with a wooden openwork back and a padded seat came to be the most common form of seat in polite circles throughout the eighteenth century both in England and in places influenced by English practice.

More comfortable was the direct descendant of the back stool with its fully upholstered back and seat. This type of chair, which period documents continued to call a back stool, remained popular until the 1760s. The painter Zoffany illustrated several in some of his conversation pieces. A less common version, popular from about 1720 to 1745, had a wooden frame around the upholstery of the back.

The exceptional comfort of the French *fauteuil*, an upholstered armchair, was appreciated by traveling English *milords*, and the form was imitated in England.

The English "French chair," however, with its relatively short legs and padded armrests, never really acquired the comfort of the French original. The French *fauteuil* usually had a fat down cushion that was set either on interlaced webbing or on a padded seat. The tops of these cushions came almost level with the arms of the chair; however, we have no evidence that these "French chairs" were ever in England provided with cushions. Instead they relied solely on a padded seat. Indeed, although the subject requires more study before we can be certain, the padding seems to have been rather thin and firm. (There were, of course, English easy chairs with fitted cushions that were derived, as the *fauteuil* was, from the extremely comfortable, late seventeenth-century French easy chair.)

Padding on eighteenth-century English furniture in general seems not to have been very thick and only slightly domed, judging from engraved designs of seat furniture and other contemporary pictures as well as analysis of surviving furniture. Because of the thinness of the padding, it may have been that English upholsterers were the first to develop ways of stiffening the vertical sides of upholstered seats. Certainly, squared edges became popular in England well before they did in France. In England, squared edges continued the line dictated by the rectilinear chair frames that were common by the 1750s. In France, where the *fauteuil* with cushion remained popular, upholsterers continued to use rounded padding even when squared structures for chairs had been introduced in the 1770s under the renewed influence of classicism. Squared padding seems to appear in France only in the 1780s.

The stiff edges were formed in this way: Padding was compacted at the edge by stitching from the side diagonally upward and drawing the padding toward the sides (fig. 10). This formed a well or trough in the center of the seat that then had to be filled with a second lot of padding, rather like the cushion in the well of an easy chair seat. (For detailed photographs of this process, *see* figures 68–80 in the essay by Gusler, Graves, and Anderson in this volume.) The top canvas, which covers the padding on the seat, at first comprised a top section with separate vertical side sections stitched together in a seam along the top edges of the seat. This created a weak point where strength was required. Later, perhaps about 1775, the top and side canvas was made of one piece of material. The top edge, where there had been a seam, was now defined by a line of blanket stitch.

The upholsterer could keep the visible top cover in place on the padding with a few quilting stitches. To

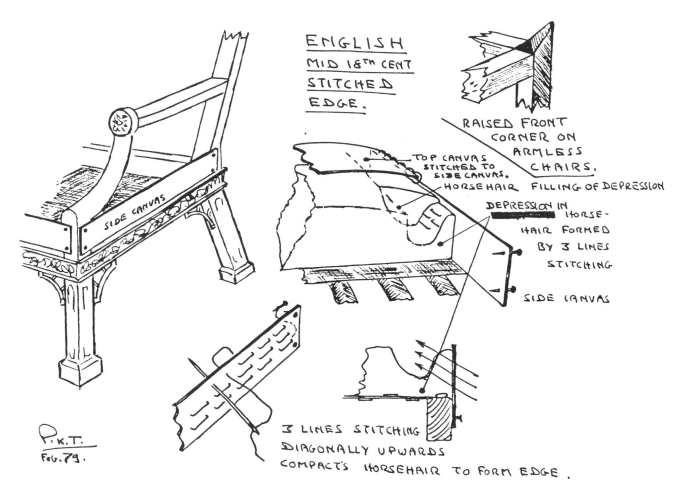

ENGLISH
MID 18TH CENT
STITCHED
EDGE.

RAISED FRONT
CORNER ON
ARMLESS
CHAIRS.

SIDE CANVAS

TOP CANVAS
STITCHED TO
SIDE CANVAS.

HORSEHAIR   FILLING OF DEPRESSION

DEPRESSION IN   HORSE-

HAIR FORMED

BY 3 LINES

STITCHING

SIDE CANVAS

3 LINES STITCHING
DIAGONALLY UPWARDS
COMPACTS HORSEHAIR TO FORM EDGE.

P.K.T.
Feb. 79.

10. Sketch, by the author, of an armchair with stitched edge, England, mid-eighteenth century. Based on investigations of old upholstery at the Victoria and Albert Museum.

spread the strain on the covering canvas caused by the stitch pulling down through thick padding, he used tufts of thread. A tuft was originally a small wad of unspun silk or wool. The French called this *capiton* hence *capitonné* or buttoned. (Buttoning with actual buttons was a nineteenth-century development.) In the eighteenth century, a bunch of silk or linen threads in an appropriate color was the usual tuft. Spread out, the tuft became a decorative feature, and some were quite elaborate, with looped threads forming a sort of rosette. The degree of indentation in tufting was much less deep in the eighteenth century than in the nineteenth. Because eighteenth-century silks were woven at a width of

nineteen to twenty-one inches, wide chair backs and seats had to have seams toward the sides. If the tufting was pulled too deep, it distorted the seams in an unsightly manner. When wider materials became available, tufting could be set deeper but the practice was, by then, to use buttons which took the strain better.

Tufting was first developed for thickly padded squabs and mattresses, where quilting was inadequate. Tufting was certainly in use by the 1680s for the long squabs of Parisian daybeds. There are also tufts in the padded seat, under a cushion, of an English sofa at Lyme Park that dates from about 1700.[8] Although the French also used the technique for squabs, they do not seem to have

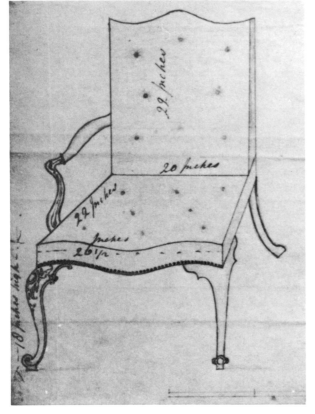

11. Design for an armchair with tufting, England, mid-eighteenth century. The high setting of the top central tuft follows the bowed top rail. Courtesy, The Metropolitan Museum of Art.

adopted tufting for chair padding until late in the eighteenth century. We believe, however, that tufting became customary in English "French chairs" (fig. 11) and padded back stools in the 1750s.[9]

The proper positioning of tufting on a chair back required a good eye. A chair with a straight horizontal crest rail usually had three tufts in a straight line about six inches below the top; while a chair with a bowed or arched top edge often, but not invariably, had the central tuft set higher. There were usually two more rows below. With an armchair, the tufts near the roots of the arms might be set further in toward the center (fig. 11). When a chair is reupholstered, the original tufting pattern of a chair back can often be determined by looking for the threads of old tufting embedded in the padding of the reused chair back.

Close-nailing, the use of nails to secure the edges of the cover fabric, also became a decorative feature. Pat-

terns of nailing were more complicated and ornamental than is generally realized. The rectilinear chair frames already mentioned above also dictated rectangular patterns of nailing at the corners of the seat rails. Curving patterns that followed the lines of armrest supports or scrolled back legs were also known. Careful study of old nail holes will usually reveal the pattern that was originally used on a chair.

Another means of increasing the comfort of seats was the use of springs in upholstery foundations. Although it is usually thought that springs were first introduced in the nineteenth century because they were so widely used at that time, in fact springing of some sort was used on a few pieces of seat furniture in the second half of the eighteenth century.[10] W. Stengel, a German scholar, claims to have found documents that show that certain pieces of sprung seat furniture were to be found in Berlin as early as 1765.[11] In France, in 1770, Madame Victoire, the daughter of Louis XV, said to a friend that there was no need to fear that she would follow her sister into a nunnery; she loved her armchair too much. The friend noted that it was fitted with springs.[12] We have no idea what these springs were like; they could have been of the flat metal sort used for carriages. Or they might have been similar to the spiral springs used on the exercising chair known in England as a "chamber horse" (fig. 12). This chair had a seat that bounded up and down on between two and four tiers of spiral springs with boards between. A bill for a chamber horse from 1791 refers to the use of thirteen pounds of wire.[13]

The above survey demonstrates that the student of upholstery must carefully study the evidence that survives on the actual furniture itself in order to determine its original appearance. Such an analysis helps to correct the inadequacies of the more traditional sources such as design books, bills or ledgers, and paintings. Renderings of furniture in popular design books of the period, however, are so conventionalized that they reveal only the general look. Period documents are helpful for the identification of the materials used for upholstery at various times but tell us little about techniques or finished look. Contemporary paintings and engravings reveal a great deal but, of course, are not invariably accurate. Modern books illustrating antique furniture are virtually useless because the upholstered seat furniture in the photographs rarely sports its original covering. Often the padding has also been reshaped so that this too distorts the form.[14]

However, the student must be aware that investigating ancient upholstery to reveal the techniques used is

CHAMBER HORSE

12. "Chamber-Horse" or exercising chair, illustrated in Plate 22 of Thomas Sheraton's *The Cabinet-Maker and Upholsterer's Drawing-Book* (London: T. Beasley, 1802).

like archeological excavating and must be done with an understanding of the original techniques. There is often far more evidence than modern professional upholsterers have generally learned to recognize. Such "archeology" can tell us not only the original covering material but a good deal about the actual shape of the padding, the tufting, the nailing patterns, and thus the total appearance of the piece of furniture. This information, in turn, helps us gain an idea of the designer's or maker's original intentions.

NOTES

In my studies in this field, I have benefited enormously from the knowledge and support of my colleagues, Elizabeth Clinton (now Lady White), and Frances Collard. I am indebted to the Marc Fitch Fund for the help it has given over the years to the Department of Furniture and Woodwork at the Victoria and Albert Museum. I also gratefully acknowledge the advice and help given me by Heather Gilbey, Carole Thomerson, and Dorothy Holley.

1. Upholstery is used here in the modern sense, but it must be borne in mind that upholsterers in the past were commonly engaged to provide *all* the textile components of a room. This upholstery might comprise not simply the padding on seat furniture but also wall hangings, bed hangings, window curtains, *portières*, screens, table coverings, and floor coverings. During the period 1625 to 1870, when unity in decorative schemes was demanded, it was to a large extent the upholsterer who achieved this unified effect by means of color, materials, and design. *See* John Fowler and John Cornforth, *English Decoration in the Eighteenth Century* (London: Barrie & Jenkins, 1974); Peter Thornton, *Seventeenth-Century Interior Decoration in England, France & Holland* (New Haven: Yale University Press, 1978); and Thornton, *Authentic Decor: The Domestic Interior, 1620–1920* (New York: Viking Press, 1984).

2. In fact, it was a court saddler who, in the mid-seventeenth century, provided the Crown Prince of Sweden with padded chairs that were stuffed with reindeer hair. *See* William Karlson, *Stat och Vardag i Stormaktstidens herremanshem* (Lund: A.-b. P. Lindstedts universitetsbok- handel, 1945), p. 281.

3. Back stools are popularly called "farthingale chairs," but the term does not occur in English inventories of the period. *See* Thornton, *Interior Decoration*, p. 186; and the essay by Swain in this volume.

4. Thornton, *Interior Decoration*, pp. 195–202.

5. On the question of formality and privacy, *see* Thornton, *Interior Decoration*, pp. 10, 14–23, 296; and Mark Girouard, *Life in the English Country House: A Social and Architectural History* (New Haven: Yale University Press, 1978), especially pp. 128–35.

6. Thornton, *Interior Decoration*, p. 360, n. 147.

7. They were made in large quantities and widely exported. In English inventories, they sometimes appear as "Dutch chairs."

8. Thornton, *Interior Decoration*, fig. 203 (sofa), fig. 304 (day bed).

9. The daybeds by Benjamin Goodison at Longford Castle, c. 1740, have tufted squabs. *See* Ralph Edwards, *The Shorter Dictionary of English Furniture: From the Middle Ages to the Late Georgian Period* (London: Country Life, 1964), under "Couches, " fig. 13.

10. Samuel Pratt took out a patent for spiral wire springs in England in 1825 but a German registered a patent for springs in 1823.

11. W. Stengel, *Alte Wohnkultur in Berlin und der Mark im Spiegel der Quellen des 16.–19. Jahrhunderts* (Berlin: B. Hessling, 1958), p. 144. Stengel claimed that he knew a reference (presumably in a Berlin area newspaper or other document) to a spring sofa dated November 13, 1766; while on October 7, 1769, the *"Englische Stuhlmacher"* Funke was drawing attention to *"ein perlfarben gepolstertes Kanapee mit Bild-hauerarbeit, Springfedern und Vergoldung"* (a pearl-colored, upholstered sofa with carving, springs, and gilding). Because German chairmakers who produced seat furniture in a vaguely English style called themselves *"English chairmakers"* Funke's German nationality is not in question. Stengel also mentions a bill of 1772 for an upholstered chair in which the springs are itemized. Presumably this chair was also a Berlin product.

12. Henry Havard, *Dictionnaire de l'Ameublement et de la Décoration Depuis le Xiiie siècle jusqu'à nos jours* (Paris: Ancienne Maison Quantin, 1887–1890), under *"Elastique."*

13. Records of the Gillows firm, December 1791, Westminster Public Library, London.

14. For example, of two hundred chairs illustrated in Edwards's *Shorter Dictionary of English Furniture*, only the following are still upholstered in their original covers and therefore presumably may also have their original padding more or less in shape. *See* figures 6, 22, 23, 44, 46, 47, 50, 52, 58, 72, 78, 86, 88, 89, 90, 91, 92, 94, 102, 135.

13. Russia leather chair, Boston, 1660–1680. Maple and oak with ball turnings and red stain; Russia leather with brass nails; original upholstery foundation and marsh grass stuffing. One of two surviving Boston chairs of this form covered in Russia leather (the other is illustrated in figure 22), this example retains almost all of its vasiform turned feet. The rear posts are relieved at the bottom by chamfers on the front faces. Extremely large square pegs secure the joints. Courtesy, The Henry Francis du Pont Winterthur Museum.

17th-Century Upholstery in Massachusetts

Robert F. Trent

IN THE seventeenth century, leather chairs were the characteristic seating furniture of prosperous people living in English and American urban centers, according to probate inventories and prints.[1] Despite the fact that these commonplace decorative art objects yield important information, they have yet to receive much scholarly attention.[2] For example, in Great Britain, where these chairs still survive in the hundreds, only three different sets have been dated and documented.[3] This essay will discuss upholstered chair frames made in New England before 1695, when the high-backed, early Baroque chair frame was introduced. In addition, the essay will describe the original upholstery foundation and covering of a typical Boston leather chair.

The Frames

The frames of Boston seventeenth-century leather chairs (figs. 13 and 14) are closely related to those of upholstered chairs made all over northern Europe in the first half of the century (fig. 15). These chairs were lined up around the walls of rooms by the half-dozen or more as part of the rigid decorative schemes favored during the seventeenth century (fig. 16). Not surprisingly, the composition of each chair form was based on an overriding concern for the appearance of the front. It was intended that the chairs be seen head-on. The decorative impact of the coverings was also very much in the forefront of seventeenth-century minds. Chair coverings included leather, Turkey work, or green serge.

Like their joined, paneled contemporaries, upholstered chairs of the seventeenth century were conceived of as architecture in miniature, small exercises in geometry, and their rectilinear frames reinforce this aspect of their designs. The key compositional elements are (1) the width and depth of the seat, (2) the seat height, (3) the overall height of the back, and (4) the relative size of the upholstered back panel and the space underneath it. (*See* Appendix A of this essay for a table of measurements of surviving chairs and Margaret Swain's article in this volume.)

The width and depth of the seat and the height of the seat from the floor establish the center mass of the entire chair. The seats often are quite high, between eighteen and twenty inches. The overall height of the back completes the basic outline of the frame. The compositional element subject to the greatest change was the relationship between the upholstered back panel and the space below it. Through the manipulation of these two areas, the composition of a chair could be made more squat or more vertical. The variations of

14. Leather chair, Boston, 1660–1680. Oak and maple with ball turnings (turned front feet and bottom section of rear legs are missing) and dark brown stain; leather with brass nails; original upholstery foundation and marsh grass stuffing. The prime enemy of leather coverings is dehydration, which promotes drastic shrinkage and brittleness. The back of this example has shrunk to the point where it has torn itself apart under the pressure of the upholstery foundation. Almost all the trim strip around the seat has fallen away. Note how the leather of the seat comes only halfway over the seat rails and how the corners of the seat are folded forward. Note also the turnings of this frame compared with those on the chair shown in figure 13; the great similarity suggests that Boston turners worked in a very consistent fashion. Courtesy, Museum of Fine Arts, Boston.

15. Leather chair, England, 1650–1680. Oak with ball turnings and brown stain; scored leather with brass nails; original upholstery foundation (with later reinforcements) and marsh grass stuffing. The leather of the chair has a deeply impressed, large-scale diapered surface, commonly seen on European examples. It is single nailed, with sheathed uprights, an open outback, and stitched seat foundation. The double-stuff stitching is oval in contour. Courtesy, Colonial Williamsburg Foundation.

design during the latter part of the seventeenth century strongly suggest that all the possibilities were explored.

An important factor in the appearance of these chairs was the use of cushions on the seats (fig. 17). Unlike the thin pads seen on period room chairs in museums (on which no one sits), seventeenth-century cushions were heavy and rounded in form, with their bulk partially or wholly obscuring the gap between the chair seat and the back panel. Cushions for armchairs, which usually had lower seats than side chairs from the same set, were heavier. The authoritative appearance of the armchair and the thick cushion indicated the high status of its sitter.[4]

Massachusetts leather chairs display substantial variation in the treatment of these compositional elements. This diversity is difficult to explain because it is commonly believed that most early American upholstered seating furniture was made by a small number of Boston craftsmen, although a few "maverick" chairs are tentatively assigned to New York because of their histories of ownership (figs. 18–20).[5] The Massachusetts variations may reflect an eagerness to follow each and every vagary of the much larger London upholstery trade. There was little, if any, time lag between the introduction of a new London fashion in the upholstered chair frame and its adoption in Boston.

Among the Massachusetts side chairs, some have seats as small as 17⅞ inches wide by 14⅞ inches deep, while others have seats as large as 20¼ inches wide by 16⅞ inches deep. Backs range from 16 to 23 inches in height. The size of the back panel in relation to the space underneath it can vary from the panel being smaller than the space, to the panel and the space being roughly equal in size, to the panel being two and a half times as large as the space.

Chairs with extremely large, high back panels were made after 1680 (*see* figs. 37 and 38), perhaps reflecting a desire to update the design of the upholstered chair in response to the new French style of high backed chairs that were first made for Louis XIV's court only a few years earlier in about 1675 (fig. 8).[6] Such chairs remained popular into the eighteenth century perhaps because their back height made them compatible with the high-backed, Baroque-style cane and bannister-back chairs that were introduced in Massachusetts in the 1690s. As late as the 1720s, Turkey-work chairs, a form that often had tall backs, were described as "new" in some New England probate inventories.[7] (Chairs covered with Turkey work were ordered for use in government buildings in England as late as the 1730s, but the

16. *Le Cordonnier*, engraving by Abraham de Bosse (1602–1676), Paris, c. 1640. A *haut bourgeois* parlor closely following fashionable Italian influence at Louis XIII's court with rows of upholstered back stools along the wall, tapestry wall hangings, elaborate bed hangings, a center table with carpet, and a *lit de repos*, or day bed, with fixed bolster and heavy cushion trimmed with tassels and braid. One chair has been pulled into the center of the room. All the sumptuous textiles would have harmonized, even though they were not all of the same fabric. The parlors of many wealthy Boston merchants looked much like this, though a little less grand. Courtesy, Museum of Fine Arts, Boston.

17. Leather great chair, Boston, 1660–1680. Maple and oak with ball turnings and brown stain; leather with brass nails; original upholstery foundation and marsh grass stuffing. The wide frame and square arms are typical of English upholstered armchairs at mid-century. The chair first belonged to Dr. Zerubbabel Endicott, a chirurgeon of Salem, Massachusetts. The down cushion, covered in wine-colored silk velvet and matching silk cord and tassels, is a modern reconstruction based on one in England at Knole, Sevenoaks, Kent. Courtesy, Museum of Fine Arts, Boston.

18

19

18. Sealskin chair, Boston or New York City, 1660–1680. Maple and oak with ball-and-hollows and vase turnings and red stain; sealskin with brass nails; original upholstery foundation and marsh grass stuffing. Hair hides such as sealskin are vellums and are cured by drying on frames and by working alum into the inner surface of the hide. Hair hides are unsuited for covering a stuffed foundation because they are inflexible and brittle. The use of sealskin as an upholstery covering was therefore unusual. This purportedly belonged to a member of the Saybrook Colony in Connecticut, Lady Alice Apsley Boteler, also known as "Lady Fenwick." More likely it was first owned by her brother-in-law, John Cullick, or another relative. Courtesy, Old Saybrook Historical Society, Saybrook, Connecticut.

19. Leather chair, possibly New York City, 1660–1680. Red oak (by microanalysis) with vase and barrel turnings and great heels; leather with brass nails; original upholstery foundation and marsh grass stuffing. Similar in appearance to Dutch and Flemish chairs of the 1630s and the Holyroodhouse chairs purchased in London in 1668 (see figure 31). Owned by the Amsden family of Suffield in the upper Connecticut River Valley, it was probably made in New York and brought to Connecticut via water. The trim strip around the seat is missing, as is most of the upholstery of the back. Courtesy, Pocumtuck Valley Memorial Association, Deerfield, Massachusetts.

20. Leather chair, possibly New York City, 1660–1680. Oak and black ash (by microanalysis) with ball-and-disc turnings and red stain; leather with brass nails; original upholstery foundation and marsh grass stuffing. This extremely heavy, crudely fashioned, and atypically upholstered chair has little in common with Boston examples. It displays double pegging at all joints and double nailing around the seat. The rear posts are sheathed by two pieces of leather, each held by brass nails; the outback is also covered by a separate piece of leather brass-nailed to the sides of the rear posts. These highly irregular treatments suggest the hand of a saddler or a cordwainer rather than that of a professional upholsterer. The chair was found on Long Island. Courtesy, John Hall Wheelock Collection, East Hampton Historical Society, East Hampton, New York. Photograph by Joseph Adams.

21. Serge chair, Salem, Massachusetts, 1680–1695. Oak, maple, and black ash (by microanalysis) with reel-and-ball turnings and red stain; modern green twilled serge, with silk galloon, fringe, and brass nails. One of two known Salem chairs of this form, this one has been restored from a heavily altered frame. Between 1685 and 1695, Salem supported the only New England upholsterer of the seventeenth century to reside outside Boston. This reconstruction gives us our only three-dimensional idea of what the many cloth-covered chairs listed in New England inventories might have looked like. Courtesy, Museum of Fine Arts, Boston.

20

21

stylistic attributes of their frames are not known.[8])

Various ornamental turnings were used on Massachusetts leather chairs. Boston chairmakers employed virtually all of the turned elements in use in England, including the early vasiform and ball and the later reel and twist turnings (figs. 21 and 22). The single exception was the columnar ornament of which none has yet been identified as a Massachusetts product. Reel and twist ornaments were probably introduced into the Massachusetts design vocabulary after 1665 and were often associated with the high-backed version of the leather chair.[9]

Upholstery Foundations

The "foundation" of a chair's upholstery is defined as all materials not meant to be visible on the finished chair. Insofar as the low-backed chair form is concerned, the foundation consists of girt webbing, sackcloth, stuffing, and double-stuff stitching. The seventeenth-century Massachusetts upholsterer had a narrow range of foundation materials available to him. Webbing and sackcloth were mostly made of linen even though it was not ideally suited for the purposes of support because it stretched easily. (During the nineteenth century, cotton linings of various kinds were introduced, and jute webbing began to be used because, although it didn't last as long as linen, it was far more resilient.) As the underside view of the Massachusetts leather chair illustrated in figure 23 suggests, the upholsterer began by tacking three strips of webbing to the top surfaces of the seat rails, two from front to rear and one from side to side. Some side chairs have two webbing strips running from side to side instead of only one. The Endicott leather great chair shown in figure 17, the only known New England armchair of the low-backed upholstered form, has five webbing strips in all, three from front to rear and two from side to side, presumably because its frame is much wider than that of a side chair. The webbing strips are made of tightly woven linen and average one and three-quarters inches in width.

Once the interwoven webbing strips were tacked in place, a piece of sackcloth—a coarse, nubbly, loosely-woven linen cloth, similar in appearance, though not in substance, to jute burlap—was laid over them and tacked to the top surfaces of the seat rails. (It is visible between the webbing strips in figure 23.) Because the webbing strips are widely spaced, the sackcloth takes up much of the stress exerted upon the seat. On the backs of these leather chairs, where the upholsterer used no webbing strips, the sackcloth formed the sole founda-

22. Russia leather chair, Boston, 1675–1695. Beech with twist turnings; Russia leather with brass nails; original upholstery foundation and marsh grass stuffing. One of five known New England examples with twist turnings, all of which are made entirely of either beech or maple, this chair and the one in figure 13 are the only two known New England chairs covered in Russia leather. As with their English prototypes, the twist ornament of New England chairs was fashioned through laborious use of a round rasp. Seating furniture with twist ornament came into fashion at Charles II's court about 1670, which accounts for the late date range assigned this New England version. Courtesy, North Andover Historical Society, North Andover, Massachusetts.

tion layer. The sackcloth of the back panel is often far lighter in weight than that used in the seat. Sometimes a light canvas was used instead.

Together, the webbing and sackcloth form the support for stuffing. Although by the 1660s European upholsterers were using horsehair, tow, and other materials,[10] seventeenth-century Massachusetts chairs invariably were stuffed with grass. In the Endicott great chair, spike grass (*Distichlis spicata*), a native of the drier sections of marshes on the Atlantic and Gulf coasts, was used (fig. 24).[11] Bunches of grass, arranged parallel to the front seat rail, covered the seat and back of the chair. The bunches were shaken and packed to produce heavy, round-shouldered contours with slight domes that were quite flat by European standards. The ends of the grass were tucked over the seat and back rails to protect the leather coverings from chafing against the sharp edges of the frame.

Massachusetts seventeenth-century upholsterers never used a lining over the stuffing, even though their European contemporaries often used cotton, linen, or woolen linings, especially over horsehair stuffing. Massachusetts Turkey-work chairs were not lined because the upholsterers relied on the tough linen or hemp warp and weft of Turkey work to resist the tendency of the grass to poke through. Linings were not used on leather chairs for similar reasons. This seventeenth-century technique persisted into the eighteenth-century. For example, Massachusetts leather chairs in the high-backed early Baroque style—popular from 1695 to 1725—still had their leather coverings applied directly over the stuffing. Only on easy chairs and other cloth-covered chairs made after 1695 did Massachusetts upholsterers use linings.

In order to prevent the grass stuffing from shifting under the weight of a chair's occupant, upholsterers placed a series of stitches at the center of the seat, a technique now called double-stuff stitching. On Massachusetts examples, the stitches are usually made in a rectangle, but on many English, Dutch, and Scandinavian examples, the stitches form an oval (fig. 15). Made with heavy, loosely spun linen line, the stitches pass through the layers of webbing, sackcloth, and stuffing, binding them together. On leather chairs, the stitches often pass through the leather covering as well, with dire consequences for its structural integrity. Because the center of the seat is a prime stress point and because the stitches weaken the leather, the seats of leather chairs are often found to have collapsed directly over the stitching.

23. Detail, underside of figure 14. The three webbing strips and sackcloth of a typical Boston chair with the double-stuff stitching touched in white to make it clearer. An end of one of the webbing strips was clipped off at some point, but its location is apparent from the shadow that it left behind. These coarse linen materials were often woven in two shades of brown, which here have faded considerably. The stress exerted upon the sackcloth by the weight of the chair's occupants has distorted it a great deal. Also visible in this view are the joiner's scribe marks for cutting the tenons of the stretchers and seat rails. Courtesy, Museum of Fine Arts, Boston.

24. Marsh grass removed from the Endicott great chair (fig. 17). This *Distichlis spicata*, or spike grass, was taken out of the outback of the chair to relieve pressure on the fragile leather covering. The presence of mature "fruits," or seedheads, indicated that the grass was harvested between August and October. It was evidently stored in bunches of fistful size and used as needed. The crimped ends of the grass are the result of its having been tucked around the edges of the back posts to protect the leather covering. By using a large blunt needle called a "regulator," the upholsterers could adjust the position and compaction of such grasses to a wide range of desired contours and softness or firmness. Courtesy, Museum of Fine Arts, Boston.

Upholstery Leathers

Gilded and tooled leathers were the most prestigious leather upholstery covers, but they were extremely expensive and rarely used in Massachusetts. Rather, Massachusetts chairs were covered with either of two principal kinds of leather: Russia leather imported from Russia via London and "neat" or "calf" leather from local hides. (For a unique use of a third kind, sealskin, *see* figure 18.) Russia leather—goat or calf hides that underwent a complex curing process—was a product of northern Russia. The hides were first steeped in rye or oat flour and then soaked in vats of willow, poplar, or larch liquors. After these initial steps, the hides were soaked in a mixture of birch tars and seal oil and hammered in two directions. The hammering broke down the fibers of the hides, released the oils contained in them, and produced a hard, resilient surface that made the hides far more durable. Because of the treatments with oils and the hammering, Russia leather shrank far less than other varieties of leather and stayed free from rot and insects.[12] The hammering also created a faint, regular diamond pattern that was extremely attractive (fig. 25). Sometimes the hides were even treated with brasilwood dyes, giving them red or purple hues.

So desirable was Russia leather that European tanners tried to imitate its diamond surface pattern. They scored their leather, passed it through rollers, or scorched it with hot metal plates. Many chairs identified in probate inventories as Russia leather chairs may, in fact, have been covered in one of these imitations. No Massachusetts chair has been found covered with an imitation, however, while many European chairs have been (figs. 15 and 26).[13]

Massachusetts leather, often referred to as "neat" or "calf" to distinguish it from the higher quality Russia leather, was a soft-dressed cattle hide. Contrary to popular belief, these earlier domestic leathers were not "full substance" hides but were skived down to about one-third their original thickness, partly to eliminate skinning flaws and partly to make the hides to be used for upholstery more supple. Massachusetts leathers were cured by soaking them in vats of oak bark distillates for as long as eighteen months.[14]

It is difficult to tell exactly what color or surface luster these hides had when new because they are always dehydrated when found and their original color consequently bleached out. Once they are conserved by washing, chemical neutralization, and treatment with leather dressing (*see* Appendix B), they turn a uniform dark brown color and develop a glossy surface. In the

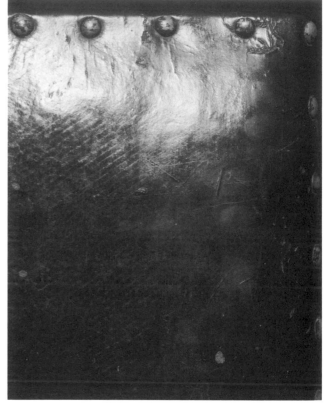

25. Detail, Russia leather on an early eighteenth-century New York chair. The regularity and faintness of the fine diamond or diapered surface has led some to contend that it could not possibly have been produced by hand-hammering wet pliable hides. It is probable, however, that large-scale production of Russia leather for export encouraged any number of economizing measures, including planchets or hammers mounted on frames and connected to a self-advancing bed much like that used in a sawmill. Certainly, mechanized treatment of leathers today makes possible highly regulated surface treatments. Courtesy, Museum of Fine Arts, Boston.

26. Detail, back panel of an English leather chair. This is typical of what is believed to be an English scored, pressed, or scorched imitation of genuine Russia leather. Made of calf leather, the diapered or crosshatched patterns are much larger in scale and more deeply impressed than the faint, small dicing seen on Russia leather (*see* figure 25). It may be a mistake to make this clean-cut distinction between the two varieties of leather, but it is probable that the two or three varieties were also confused during the period. Courtesy, Colonial Williamsburg Foundation.

nineteenth century, some early chairs received coats of a dark green lacquer on their original upholstery leathers. (The chair in fig. 13 was so treated.) The green lacquer was intended as a preservative. Unfortunately, it is difficult to remove without damaging the leather.

Leather Coverings

The techniques used to attach leathers to the frames were straightforward and are therefore easily discerned. The seats and backs were not cut precisely to size before being laid over the grass stuffing because the leather was laid dry and stretched in place and because it was difficult to judge how much the leather might be distorted as it was stretched.

Two methods were employed to treat the edges once the leather was in place: masking rough edges of the seat with trim strips and trimming the edges of the back with a cutting knife. On the seats, separate trim strips of leather, about one and one-quarter inch wide, were used. The covering was first drawn over the seat rails and tacked in place halfway down; the appearance of its rough edges is shown by the chair in figure 14, which has lost much of its trim strip. The front corners of the seat customarily were folded rather than cut and sewn; curiously, the folds invariably were formed with the pockets facing forward, making them far more conspicuous than they would have been if placed facing the sides. At the rear of the seat, the covering was cut and folded under to fit around the rear posts, with a long central flap drawn over the rear seat rail.

The trim strips ran around all four sides of the seat frame. On the front and sides, the top edge of the trim strip was garnished with ornamental brass nails set an inch and a half apart, while the bottom edge was held with identically spaced iron tacks. (Note the seventeenth-century distinction between nails and tacks. Thus, if a period document contains a reference to "double nail'd" chairs, it means that the chairs were decorated with two rows of decorative brass nails, not iron ones.) On the rear seat rail, only iron tacks were used. This extreme parsimony in nailing is not often seen in English work, where double and triple brass nailing on all edges is not uncommon. On Boston and New York leather chairs of the early Baroque period (1705–1725), double nailing was used, but it appears to have remained an optional feature. When Mrs. Mercy Oliver of Cambridge, Massachusetts, died in 1710, the appraisers of her estate distinguished between different decorative nailing finishes and different leathers of the chairs in her "Great Lower Room." They listed:

½ Doz Rushia chairs double nail'd @ 10/6
six Dit to calf 9/6
4 leather chairs single nail'd 8/[16]

The second method of treating edges, the clever use of a cutting knife, was used on the back (fig. 27). The back cover was secured along the bottom edge of the stay rail, or lower rail of the back panel, with iron tacks. The leather was then stretched vertically, brought over the top of the crest rail, tacked to the backside of the crest rail, and then trimmed to a narrow lip about one-half inch in width. The leather was stretched from side to side in a similar manner and brought just around the sides of the posts, where it was tacked and trimmed as on the upper edge.

In order to divert attention from the many small iron tacks used to secure the edges, the front surface of the back was garnished with one row of brass nails. They ran along the edges of the bottom and sides and along the upper edge of the heavy bevel on the crest rail. Again, English examples often display far more generous double or triple nailing on the backs.

Boston leather chairs, like many European examples, had no leather over the rear surface of the upholstered back panel. On chairs with open outbacks, the sackcloth that forms the foundation for the back's upholstery is exposed inside the rear of the frame. One Boston example (fig. 27), however, has a lining inside the outback made of dark green, lightweight canvas or duck. This was most likely an optional feature.

It is important to note that in the Anglo-American upholstery tradition (as opposed to the Iberian tradition and Dutch practices stemming from Spanish influence), brass nails were reserved for ornamental effects and were not generally used to keep leather seats and backs in place. Spanish leather chairs, by contrast, often have slung leather seats and backs secured exclusively by large brass nails or *bullions*, an English term of the period (fig. 28). Nails used in England and America were much smaller, with plain cast brass heads of low profile. The undersides of the heads were left rough, both as an economy measure as well as to augment the grip of the nails in the upholstery covering. The tapered shanks of the nails were also made of brass. On stripped frames, the shanks of broken-off brass nails and the impressions of the brass heads help to identify the original nailing patterns.

This brief description of Massachusetts's earliest upholstered chairs is perhaps sufficient for the purposes of those craftsmen who are covering old frames or fabricating new chairs for historic houses. These leather

27. Detail, outback of Boston leather chair in figure 14. The open outback is masked by a lining of dark green canvas or duck. The tack holes where the duck was attached to the front surface of the frame are clearly visible; it was displaced by the pressure of the shrinking leather cover. Underneath the duck is a layer of fine, lightweight canvas, forming the foundation for the grass stuffing. Note the trimmed edges of the leather cover at the top and side. The grass stuffing of the seat can be seen through the tear in the leather, where it has collapsed over the double-stuff stitching of the upholstery foundation. Courtesy, Museum of Fine Arts, Boston.

chairs, however, still have much to tell us about craft technology and design sense in the seventeenth century. A fuller treatment would deal with the various coverings and valuations cited in probate inventories, the makers themselves (insofar as they can be identified), a far more detailed study of the wooden frames, and a thorough investigation of the stylistic development that resulted from the interplay of local craft traditions and new designs from London.

28. Leather chair, Spain, 1650–1700. Walnut, with shaped front stretcher (feet lost); tooled leather with brass nails and bullions. This is a characteristic Iberian chair with heavy leather seat and back that function as slings and require no upholstery foundation or stuffing. The Dutch chairs upon which the chairs in figures 19 and 31 were modeled were based on similar Spanish prototypes but only began to receive stuffed seats in the 1620s or so (fig. 2). The chair in this figure most likely belonged to Governor William Wanton of Rhode Island (1670–1733), although it is traditionally assigned to his son, Governor Joseph Wanton (1750–1780). Courtesy, Trinity College, Hartford, Connecticut, on loan to the Wadsworth Atheneum.

Appendix A:
Measurements of Leather Chairs (in inches)

	Overall Height	Width at Seat	Depth at Seat
WINTERTHUR (fig. 13)	36	18	15¾
MFAB (fig. 14)	32½	17¾	14⅞
WILLIAMSBURG (fig. 15)	35¾	18⅜	16¼
ENDICOTT (fig. 17)	38	23⅝	16¼
OLD SAYBROOK (fig. 18)	36¾	18¾	15½
DEERFIELD (fig. 19)	36⅝	17¾	14⅞
EHHSA (fig. 20)	34	17¾	18
SALEM (fig. 21)	41¾	9	16¾
NORTH ANDOVER (fig. 22)	35½	18½	18½
TRINITY COLLEGE (fig. 28)	35	16½	14½

	Height at Seat	Height of Back Panel	Front Leg Stock
WINTERTHUR	19⅞	5¹¹⁄₁₆	1⅝ x 1⅝
MFAB	16⅜	8¾	1⅞ x 1⅞
WILLIAMSBURG	20¾	9¼	1¾ x 1¾
ENDICOTT	15¼	15	1⅝ x 1⅝
OLD SAYBROOK	20	9⅛	1¾ x 1¾
DEERFIELD	20½	9⅛	1⅝ x 1⅝
EHHS	18⅝	9⅛	1⅞ x 1⅞
SALEM	19½	11¾	1½ x 1½
NORTH ANDOVER	20½	9	1¾ x 1½
TRINITY COLLEGE	15⅞	9½	1⅜ x 1¾

Appendix B: Conservation of Endicott Chair Leather Covering

The leather was first cleaned with five applications of Neutrogena Soap, a mild soap that contains no harsh detergents. The soap was applied with a brush and water and the lather wiped off with a sponge so that the dirt would not be pushed into the leather after each application.

Saddle soap of a soft brown variety was then applied ten times with a brush and water. After every five applications, the leather was sponged off to remove dirt. After the tenth application, no discoloration of the suds could be seen, an indication that the leather was clean and the pores open.

The leather was then allowed to dry slowly. Afterwards, British Museum Leather Dressing, a standard solution of lanolin, beeswax, and oil of cedar leaf dissolved in hexane, was applied eight times to the leather. (The lanolin restores the oils lost through dehydration, beeswax gives body and luster, and oil of cedar leaf discourages pests.) In this case, five cc. of 1 percent potassium lactate were mixed with five-hundred cc. of British Museum Leather Dressing. (Potassium lactate neutralizes sulphur compounds in the leather that might contribute to its deterioration.) The first two applications were made with a brush. A soft rag was used to polish and wipe off the excess, and the leather was allowed to set three days between applications.

After the leather had been wiped with a damp cloth, the third and fourth applications were made with a soft cloth. All the other applications were made each day and the leather polished the following day. The leather used for repair was cleaned and saddle-soaped just as the leather on the chair itself was; however, only four applications of Leather Dressing were used on this piece of leather. Leather Dressing should be applied to the chair every six months, until such time as the leather is thoroughly saturated with beeswax.

MERVILLE E. NICHOLS
*Senior Conservator
Research Laboratory
Museum of Fine Arts, Boston*

July 7, 1978

NOTES

1. Peter Thornton, "Back-stools and Chaises à Demoiselles," *Connoisseur* 93, no. 744 (February 1974): 99–105.

2. For studies that forward the relatively new attitude towards the examination of common artifacts rather than the grandest or oddest examples, *see* Henry Glassie, *Folk Housing in Middle Virginia* (Knoxville: University of Tennessee Press, 1975); Robert F. Trent, *Hearts & Crowns: Folk Chairs of the Connecticut Coast, 1720–1840* (New Haven: New Haven Colony Historical Society, 1977); Robert Blair St. George, "Style and Structure in the Joinery of Dedham and Medfield, Massachusetts, 1635–1685," *Winterthur Portfolio* 13 (1979): 1–46; and Robert Blair St. George, *The Wrought Covenant: Craftsmen and Community in Southeastern New England, 1620–1700* (Brockton: Brockton Art Center and Fuller Memorial, 1979).

3. For the best sources now in print on English back stools, *see* Percy MacQuoid, *A History of English Furniture: The Age of Oak* (London: Lawrence & Bullen, 1904), pp. 174–90; R. W. Symonds, "Charles II. Couches, Chairs and Stools, 1660–1670," *Connoisseur* 93 (January 1934): 15–22; Symonds, "Part II, 1679–1680," *Connoisseur* 93 (February 1934): 86–95; Thornton, "Back-stools"; Pauline Agius, "Late Sixteenth- and Seventeenth-Century Furniture in Oxford," *Furniture History* 7 (1971): 72–86 and fig. 24b; Swain, "The Furnishing of Holyroodhouse in 1668," *Connoisseur* 194, no. 780 (February 1977): 122–30; and the essay by Swain in this volume. Agius and Swain give two of the dated and documented sets of English leather chairs; the third is given in Victor Chinnery, *Oak Furniture — The British Tradition* (Woodbridge, Suffolk: Baron, 1979), p. 519, fig. 4:245. For the most recent American literature, *see* Robert F. Trent, "A History for the Essex Institute Turkey Work Couch, *Essex Institute Historical Collections* 113, no. 1 (January 1977): 29–37; Robert F. Trent, "The Endicott Chairs," *Essex Institute Historical Collections* 114, no. 2 (April 1978): 103–19; and Robert F. Trent, "Two Seventeenth-Century Salem Upholstered Chairs," *Essex Institute Historical Collections* 115, no. 1 (January 1980): 34–40.

4. Peter Thornton, *Seventeenth-Century Interior Decoration in England, France & Holland* (New Haven: Yale University Press, 1978), pp. 180–82, 192–96.

5. On Boston's upholstered chair craftsmen, *see* Benno M. Forman, "Boston Furniture Craftsmen 1630–1730," unpublished ms., 1969, especially Chap. XI, "The Upholders, Upholsters, and Upholsterers of Boston, 1665–1723."

6. Peter Thornton, "The Parisian Fauteuil of 1680," *Apollo* 101, no. 156 (February 1975): 102–107.

7. For example, Mrs. Mary Prout, a widow of New Haven, Connecticut, owned at her death in 1724, "6 new Turkey work chairs" worth fourteen shillings apiece. *New Haven County Probate District*, vol. 5 (1719–1730), p. 191. Microfilm of original book on file at the Connecticut State Library, Hartford, Connecticut.

8. R. W. Symonds, "English Cane Chairs: Part I," *Connoisseur* 127 (April 1951): 8–15. *See also* Margaret Swain's article in this volume.

9. Symonds, "Charles II," pp. 86–89.

10. Thornton, *Seventeenth-Century*, pp. 128–29.

11. The writer thanks Dr. Bernice Shubert, Arnold Arboretum, Harvard University Herbarium, Cambridge, Massachusetts, for identifying the grass. Five "fruits," or seedheads, have been deposited at the Herbarium as record specimens. *See also* M. L. Fernald, ed., *Gray's Manual of Botany*, 8th ed., (New York: American Book, 1950), p. 131.

12. John J. Waterer, *Leather in Life, Art and Industry* (London: Faber & Faber, 1946), pp. 167–68.

13. Thornton, *Seventeenth-Century*, pp. 119–23.

14. John J. Waterer, *A Guide to the Conservation and Restoration of Objects made wholly or in part of Leather* (New York: Drake, 1972), pp. 6–17.

15. The writer thanks the late Benno M. Forman, Winterthur Museum, for calling to his attention the nineteenth-century date of such green lacquers.

16. *Middlesex County Probate District, Old Series (1649–1855)*, Middlesex County Courthouse, Cambridge, Massachusetts, Vol. 12A, p. 191.

The Turkey-work Chairs
of Holyroodhouse

Margaret Swain

ONE of the most misunderstood materials in decorative
arts studies has been Turkey work. Many people have
mistakenly thought it to be a form of needlework,
wrought by either amateurs or professional craftsmen.
In fact, Turkey work consisted of colored worsted yarns
that were knotted onto a hemp base during weaving.
These yarns were then cut to produce an even pile. A
second confusion that has arisen regarding Turkey work
is the period in which it was produced. Turkey-work
chairs were listed in large numbers in seventeenth-century inventories, and many examples of the fabric have
survived; however, few of these examples can be dated.
Past studies have tended to date its manufacture beginning in the late sixteenth century and extending to the
mid-seventeenth century. More recent documentary
and material evidence reveals that Turkey work continued to be woven into the early eighteenth century.

Six Turkey-work chairs from Holyroodhouse, the
royal residence in Edinburgh, provide important information about this confusing upholstery cover. It has
been assumed that these six examples formed part of the
furniture of the Stuart kings, especially of Charles I,
who was crowned at Edinburgh in 1633. Early dates
were assigned to these chairs because this chair type is
usually associated with the first half of the seventeenth
century; however, recent documentary research has
revealed that four chairs with covers *en suite* (one of
them is illustrated in figure 29), which are noticeably
higher in back and seat than the other three (figs. 30 and
31), can be dated to 1685. The three in figures 30 and 31,
which have covers of various patterns, were made in
1668.[1]

A brief survey of Holyrood's history in the seventeenth century shows that caution must be exercised in
assuming that any furniture now there was in the palace
before the restoration of Charles II in 1660. In the first
half of the seventeenth century, Holyrood was neither
well furnished nor well maintained. After the King of
Scots succeeded Queen Elizabeth as James I of Great
Britain in 1603, the king and courtiers moved to London, and the furnishings in his Scottish palaces were
not renewed. When James returned for a single visit in
1617, old beds and tapestries had to be repaired hastily.
For the Scottish coronation in 1633 of James's son,
Charles I, certain furnishings were brought from London. Charles I only returned once to Holyrood in 1641,
a defeated and discredited king, and no other reigning
British monarch stayed at Holyrood until Queen Victoria began to use the palace on her way to and from
Balmoral some two hundred and fifty years later.[2]

29. Turkey-work chair, London, 1685. Oak frame with twist turnings
and "Greate Heeles"; polychrome woolen yarns knotted on linen or
hemp warp and weft, with vestiges of black woolen background (now
perished); upholstery foundation renewed. One of four similar chairs,
survivors of four dozen bought for the new council chamber of
Holyroodhouse. The chairs were supplied with green baize cases.
Courtesy, Royal Palace of Holyroodhouse, Edinburgh. Copyright
reserved.

31. Turkey-work chairs, London, 1668. Oak frames with baluster turnings. Left: polychrome flowers on black background, of which vestiges remain. Right: back has rows of polychrome flowers, heartsease, and rose on blue ground; seat has a similar design on dark brown ground. Upholstery foundations renewed. Part of the consignment of 1668. Note the similarity of these frames to that of figure 19. Courtesy, Royal Palace of Holyroodhouse, Edinburgh. Copyright reserved.

30. Turkey-work chair, London, 1668. Oak frame with ball turnings and "Great Heeles." Polychrome woolen floral designs with vestiges of black woolen background (now perished) and remains of polychrome worsted fringe around the seat and lower edge of the upholstered back panel; upholstery foundation renewed. One of two similar chairs, survivors of a consignment of several dozen bought for the use of the Privy Council of Scotland at Holyroodhouse. Courtesy, Royal Palace of Holyroodhouse, Edinburgh. Copyright reserved.

In the 1640s, during the Civil War, the palace suffered a great deal of damage. Cromwell's troops were billeted there and accidentally set the palace on fire. Some ineffectual repairs were made, leaving the roof by no means watertight. In spite of its dilapidated condition, the palace was used as the meeting place for both the Privy Council of Scotland, the body of advisors to the king, and the Lords of Session, the High Court of Judges in Scotland. Apartments in the palace were granted to various officers of state, such as the Lord Privy Seal, to use as their Edinburgh residences if their own houses were several days' journey from the capital. They furnished these apartments themselves.

In the late 1660s, the Commissioner (Secretary of State) for Scotland, the Earl of Lauderdale, looked into suitable furnishings for both the council and sessions chambers. He wrote a letter from London dated March 17, 1668, to the Commissioners of the Treasury. In this letter, he refers to the furnishings that he had priced, and he asks for final approval and cash to be sent for payment: ". . . for all must be bought for ready money." The furnishings included tapestries, a crimson velvet chair of state with matching cushions and carpet, a silver mace "of the bignes[s] they use them here" [i.e., at Whitehall], a clock, an embroidered panel with the king's arms, a full-length portrait of the king by "Mr. Lillie" [Sir Peter Lely], a carpet for the council table, and, what interests us here, Turkey-work chairs. He wrote: "You will see the price of your Turky Chaires, such as we choised for the best. At St. Bartholomeo's we were ask't six shillings a piece more for the very same..."[3]

What price was finally paid for these chairs is not known, as no itemized bill survives; however we do know that the chairs, at most six dozen of them, were bought and shipped by sea to Edinburgh. On the voyage, one chair was damaged and later had to be repaired by the Scottish craftsman, James Somerville. He also made loose covers of red "Bazill" leather for three dozen of the chairs (Bazill or Basil refers to the tanning process.). His bill of July 29, 1668, shows:

6 doz Reid Bazill skinns at 16sh ye doz	£04	16	0
More for making of 3 doz of slips	00	18	0
More for whangs [thongs] to tie them	00	02	0
more for mending of a chair that was			
broken as it came from London	00	01	0
(Scots)	£05	17	0[4]

Slip covers of leather are unusual but may have been ordered in this case to render chairs with different Turkey-work designs uniform.

Although Somerville's bill refers to making slips for only three dozen chairs, the evidence indicates that more than three dozen Turkey-work chairs may have been bought in London in 1668. Seventeen years later, in 1685, the household inventory lists one hundred and twenty chairs of which four dozen had just been bought in London that year for the newly built council chamber.[5] This means that six dozen were already there at Holyrood House. The fact that no other bills survive from the seventeen years after 1668 suggests that all six dozen were bought in London in 1668.

According to a detailed invoice dated March 1685, for furnishings bought in London, the new chairs cost fifteen shillings sterling each. There was also "one great turkey chair" bought at the same time that cost two pounds five shillings, and two carpets, presumably also of Turkey work, one of them nine yards long and six and a half yards wide. The chairs and armchair came supplied with cases (loose covers) of green baize at three shillings each.[6]

It is to Lauderdale's credit that while he was commissioner, he not only refurnished the council chamber but he also persuaded the king to order the rebuilding and expansion of Holyrood into its present elegant form around a quadrangle. The new structure included a handsome council chamber and a splendid Baroque royal suite of rooms. The palace now became fit for royalty again, and from 1679 to 1682 the king's brother, the Duke of York (later James II), occupied the newly built palace as king's commissioner, having succeeded Lauderdale.

The afore-mentioned inventory of 1685 makes it clear that the Turkey-work chairs and all the furniture remaining in the royal wardrobe at Holyrood were reserved for the use of government officers—judges and members of the Privy Council of Scotland. This practice continued until 1707 when the Act of Union united the Scottish and English parliaments, and the Privy Council of Scotland was abolished. Nevertheless, the Turkey-work chairs continued to be used. They were carried to Parliament House to be used by the judges and to various churches on official occasions and were used for ceremonies at Holyrood, such as the election of representative Scottish peers to the House of Lords. However, no more chairs were bought, and the number dwindled. An inventory taken in 1714 noted only twenty-eight carpet chairs in the Session House "whereof nine are laigh [low] back'd, the other 19 newer fashioned. But [they have] old carpets [i.e., Turkey-work covers]."[7] Today only six chairs survive undamaged.

Taking this documentation and the study of the forms together, it is reasonable to make certain assumptions about the dates of the surviving Turkey-work chairs. The four with similar covers (*see* fig. 29) are the "newer fashioned" chairs bought in 1685. These are higher in the seat and back,[8] reflecting the taste for chairs with elongated backs like those imported from France and Holland from the 1670s on.[9] The swept "Greate Heeles," rather than straight rear legs, are another later feature.[10] The functional rectangular shape of earlier chairs is, however, retained. The chairs with lower backs and straight rear legs in figures 30 and 31 can be accepted as survivors of the consignment bought in 1668.

Chair Frames

This type of rectangular chair, with a horizontal padded back panel leaving a space between back and seat, is often known today as a "farthingale" chair because of the padded bustle or "farthingale" that supposedly could be accommodated by the space below the armless back. The term farthingale, however, is a fanciful misnomer and should be avoided. It is certainly not a period term.

Further, the chairs at Holyrood were certainly bought, not for the use of women wearing farthingales but for men on public business. A number of sets of chairs of similar shape but covered in leather were also bought for the use of men: Some that still survive were bought for the (all-male) college of Christ Church, Oxford, in 1692.[11] Another set, of which ten survive, was bought in 1688 for Bishop Leighton's library at Dunblane soon after its foundation, for the sole use of ministers.[12] These leather-covered back stools, like the related Turkey-work chairs, continued to be made throughout the whole of the seventeenth century.[13]

Turkey Work

Turkey work, the covering of the upholstery of the Holyrood chairs, was long considered to be a type of needlework and in fact, given a suitable canvas, it is easy to produce a tolerable imitation of it by using a cut looped stitch. However, the late scholar C. E. C. Tattersall in his *The History of British Carpets* (1934) offered convincing proof that it was woven on a loom, with the pile knotted during weaving in the same way as that of genuine Turkey carpets. His view is now generally accepted. Although several pieces of Turkey work are traditionally said to have been made by amateurs—in particular two cushions in the chapel of Wadham College, Oxford, piously ascribed to the Foundress Dorothy Wadham (who died in 1610), and a table carpet dated 1710 belonging to the Company of Merchants of the City of Edinburgh, said to have been made by the pupils of the Merchant Maiden Hospital—these traditions seem to have arisen in the period when Turkey work was still thought to have been made with a needle. Another example of work incorrectly attributed to amateurs is a floor carpet, now at Mount Vernon, dated 1746 and signed "Ann Nevill Parnel Nevill." This carpet was described by Tattersall as the work of two sisters sitting at one loom with a line of demarcation on it.

Recent examination, however, suggests that the carpet has been cut down from a larger, professionally made one and that the line represents a join.[14] However romantic these stories, the close similarities in some of the designs of surviving Turkey work strongly suggest that Turkey work was the product of professional weavers, probably working in one center in England. They produced both chair covers and carpets of similar designs. The early carpets have a much finer count than the coarse and durable chair covers on the Holyrood chairs, which average thirty-five to forty-seven knots to the square inch. This heavier weave seems to have been used on chairs and cushions.

The identity of this center is not yet known though some evidence points to Norwich. In 1588, the inventory of Robert Dudley, Earl of Leicester, listed "A Turquoy carpett of Norwiche work, in length ij yards, in breadth j yard quarter."[15] This reference and others like it have given rise to the belief that Turkey work was a Norwich product and, because Norwich sheltered a large colony of refugee weavers, mainly from the Netherlands, that the Turkey work might also be a Dutch product. The Norwich theory is strengthened by the existence of a set of twelve Turkey-work cushions bearing the city arms of Norwich; in 1651, they were presented by the mayor for the comfort of aldermen using Blackfriars Hall in Norwich as a council chamber. Although the gift is noted in the treasurer's accounts, no clue is given as to where the cushions were made. The Norwich theory is weakened by the existence of other surviving armorial Turkey work, notably twelve cushions at Oxford. (*See* Appendix B for dated and documented examples.) There is also a set of a dozen chair seats bearing the arms of Stanhope, a Yorkshire family, mounted on slip seats of mahogany chairs of the 1740s.[16] Furthermore, no documentary evidence has yet come to light in Norwich itself to suggest extensive manufacture of Turkey work in that city.

Several English Turkey-work carpets survive. The Duke of Buccleuch owns four, one bearing the arms of Montagu and the date 1585.[17] Another, now in the Strangers Hall Museum, Norwich, bears the arms of a Norfolk family with the date 1571.[18] A carpet thought to be English has recently come on the market. Like the Buccleuch carpets, it duplicates an oriental design but has the initials *M E G I L K* incorporated for its owner John Lyon, second Earl of Kinghorne and tenth Lord Glamis and his first or second wife, Margaret Erskine or Elizabeth Maule.[19]

Turkey work has been generally thought to date from

the end of the sixteenth to the middle of the seventeenth century; however, a petition from the woolen industry to the king dated about 1698 sought the prohibition of the manufacture and sale of cane chairs, stools, and couches in order to protect the English Woolen Manufacture, particularly its Turkey work. Although the woolen industry was not above exaggerating numbers when lobbying its case, this document shows clearly that Turkey-work covers were still important in the last decade of the seventeenth century. The petition declared the following:

I. THAT before the aforesaid [cain] *Chairs, Stools,* and *Couches,* were generally made and used; there were yearly made and Vended in this Kingdom above five thousand dozen of *Set-work,* (commonly called *Turkey-work Chairs,* though made in *England*) . . .

IV. Great Quantities of these Chairs were Vended and sent yearly beyond the Seas. *But since* Cain Chairs, Stools, *and* Couches, *which generally the* Frames *are made of* French Walnut, *and the Seats of* Indian Canes, *are become so much in use; the Consumption of Wool the Growth of this Kingdom,* Silk, *and* Russia Leather, *which is the Product of Wool, is greatly decreased; and above 50,000 of His Majesties Subjects formerly Employed in the Manufactury thereof, have lost their Employments, to the Ruine of them and there numerous Families.*[20]

Certainly Turkey-work chairs were not immediately discarded when cane chairs became fashionable. The two types flourished happily in the same houses. For example, Randall Holme, in his book *Academy of Armoury,* published in 1688 but probably written earlier, noted the following:

Things necessary for and belonging to a dineing Rome . . . A turky table cover, or carpett of cloth or leather printed. Chaires and stooles of Turky work, Russia or calves Leather, cloth or stuffe or of needlework. Or els made all of Joynt work or cane chaires.[21]

Two years later, in 1690, the high dining room of Hamilton Palace was furnished with two dozen carpet chairs, four tables, and three table carpets. The room led into the duchess's drawing room, which had "a dozen of kain chairs & a carpet for the floor."[22]

The continued popularity of Turkey work helps to explain the selection of Turkey-work chairs for the council chamber at Holyrood in 1685. It would be a mistake to regard this purchase as an old fashioned choice. On the contrary, as Lauderdale's letter of 1668 makes clear, the Scottish Council was determined to order the exact same furnishings as those at Whitehall, even the same size of mace. The 1685 chairs were no

doubt replicas of those supplied to the committee rooms in the House of Commons and the House of Lords.

R. W. Symonds' own notes on the purchase records for furnishings of Whitehall, now preserved at the Henry Francis du Pont Winterthur Museum, reveal the extent to which Turkey work continued to be used at Whitehall. A brief summary shows that from 1704 to 1733, there was a surprising number of Turkey-work chairs and table carpets ordered for various committee rooms:

1704–1705
House of Commons *Committee Room:* 4 doz Turkey work chairs at 13 shillings each
3 armchairs at £1.5.0 each
Turkey work carpet £6.10

1709–1710
Court of Wards: 1 doz Turkey work chairs
1718
House of Lords
Princes' Room: 2½ doz at £ 9.10 per doz
2 Russia leather folding stools for clerks 9 shillings each
Lord Great Chamberlain's Room: 1 doz Turkey work chairs
1 Turkey carpet £9.5
Bishops' Room: ½ doz Turkey work chairs and Turkey carpet £12
Lord Privy Seal's Room: ½ doz ditto and carpet . . .
Robe Room: 1 doz ditto and carpet . . .
Earl Marshall's Room: ½ doz Turkey work chairs . . .
Black Rod's Room: 1 doz Turkey work chairs . . .
House of Commons Committee Room: 4 dozen Turkey work chairs . . .

Thus, in 1718, a total of 11½ dozen chairs was purchased together with three armchairs and two folding stools. Single chairs cost thirteen shillings or fifteen shillings and sixpence. In 1722, 11½ dozen more were bought for various rooms, the cost as before. In the period 1729 to 1733, no less than 13½ dozen single Turkey-work chairs were bought at twenty shillings each, together with three armchairs and eight carpets. Only in 1733 is there a purchase of one dozen "fine walnuttree cane chairs" for the speaker's room, costing sixteen shillings each.[23]

The prices paid for the single Turkey-work chairs bought for Whitehall—thirteen shillings or fifteen shillings sixpence, rising to twenty shillings in 1729—are comparable to the fifteen shillings apiece paid for the Holyrood chairs in 1685. The price makes it probable that the Whitehall chairs were of the same functional shape with horizontal back. There is, however, an armchair with elongated back, on loan to the Victoria and Albert Museum from the Exchequer Department, that has Turkey-work upholstery, but this upholstery may not be original to the frame.[24]

Turkey-work Chair Covers

The frames and cover material of the six Turkey-work chairs at Holyrood indicate that the frames were made to fit the covers. Even in matching sets of Turkey-work covers, there is significant variation in the dimensions of the covers. This is perhaps difficult for the modern mind to appreciate, being accustomed to the precision of contemporary manufacturing processes, but the simplicity of the rectangular structure made it easy to adjust the back panel to the selvage of a particular piece of Turkey work. This is borne out by the four Holyrood chairs with similar covers (*see* figure 29), whose width is not uniform as it would have been if the frames had been made first, but varies between eighteen and a half and twenty-one inches. So neatly were the frames made to fit the covers that the deterioration of the selvages has caused the covers to gape in places. It should also be kept in mind that these chairs were sold, not by joiners or chairmakers, but by upholsterers who supplied all the chairs to the Houses of Parliament, as listed above.[25]

An English tall-backed chair of about 1690–1700, in the carved style usually associated with cane seats and backs, survives with part of its original Turkey-work cover still in place (fig. 32). The cover and upholstery foundation on the seat were renewed in leather in the late nineteenth century, but the Turkey-work back is intact. The bottom and side selvages remain, an indicator that the frame was made to fit the cover. The original brass nailing is present, and numerous fragments of a polychrome worsted galloon trimming survive underneath the nails (fig. 33). The upholstery foundation of the back was removed at some point, but a handful of the marsh grass stuffing remains tucked around a slot cut in the crest rail. The upholsterer pulled the cover material through this slot. (This technique is also found on New York leather chairs of this period. Because the tacking and nailing patterns for a leather chair closely parallel those indicated by this example, it may be that many chair frames now covered in leather were originally covered in Turkey work.)

Recognition of the practice of making frames to fit Turkey-work covers has enabled us to document the widespread exportation of such covers. One handsome pair, now at Aston Hall, Birmingham (fig. 34), have English covers with a recognizably English design

32. Turkey-work chair, London, 1690–1700. Beech frame with *s*-scroll carving and twist turnings. Turkey work: sixty knots per square inch; polychrome woolen floral design with vestiges of black woolen background (now perished) and remains of polychrome worsted galloon trim. The standard pattern of Turkey work has here been adjusted to fill a vertical format, as has the pile that falls "down" as it should. The original Turkey-work seat cover was probably trimmed with matching fringe. Courtesy, Museum of Fine Arts, Boston.

mounted on walnut frames that were probably made in Florence, Italy. Because the frames were obviously made to fit the covers, the covers were apparently exported and the completed chairs brought back to England.

Other examples of exported English Turkey-work covers can be found in Sweden and Norway. One in the Nordiska Museum in Stockholm (233.607) belonged to

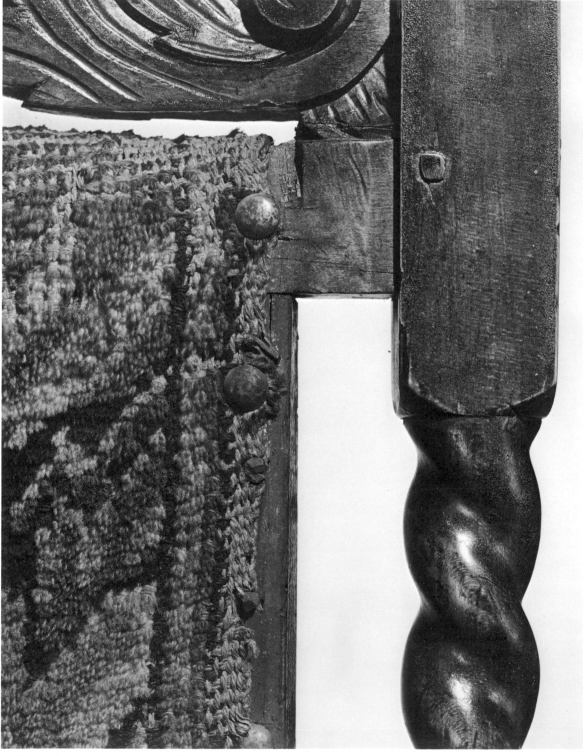

33. Detail of upper right hand corner of figure 32.

34. Turkey-work chairs, Italy, 1600–1640. Walnut frames, with columnar turnings. English Turkey work: rows of polychrome flowers with stems on white background dotted with black; guilloche border, galloon trim and silk fringe; original upholstery foundations and marsh grass stuffing. Traditionally from the Davanzati Palace, Florence, Italy. Now at Aston Hall, Birmingham, England. Courtesy, Aston Hall.

the distinguished tapestry scholar, Dr. John Böttinger, and has a design related to that of figure 29. In the Kunstindustrie Museum, Oslo, there are two beechwood chairs with Turkey-work covers. One (OK 2256) has the shorter back of the 1668 Holyrood chairs; the other (OK 2817)—which came from Öyestad Church on the southeast coast of Norway, an area with many trade links to Britain—has the taller back and covers that are reminiscent of the 1685 Holyrood chairs. Yet another, in a private collection in Norway, has a cover design the same as the chair on the left in figure 31. Future research will undoubtedly uncover many more English Turkey-work covers that were exported during the period to be placed on frames made all over Europe.

Indeed, it was probably the accepted practice, unless one resided in or visited London, to buy Turkey-work covers and have the stools or chairs made up later. The 1601 household inventory of Hardwick Hall in Derby-

shire lists "twelve Covers for Stooles of turkie work" stored in the Low Wardrobe.[26] In Scotland, "A Note of such things as were left in the house of Caerlavrock [Caerlavrock Castle, Dumfriesshire] at my Lord's departure in the year of God 1640" includes the following:

> A great wrought bed, a sute of Cloth of Sylver Chaires and stools to be made up and an embroidered Canaby of Gray Sattin to be made up too . . . 7 covers of Turky work for Stules and a Cushion . . ."

Also listed were three Turkey-work stools that had already been made up.[27]

For those living in colonial America, the import of completed Turkey-work or leather chairs would have been expensive and hazardous, whereas rolls of Turkey-work covers and carpets would have been simple to transport. That this, in fact, was the case is borne out by

35. Turkey-work couch, Boston, 1697/98. Maple and oak with ball turnings. Polychrome flowers on black background (now perished), with vestiges of polychromed worsted fringe around the seat; original upholstery foundation and marsh grass stuffing. Made for John Leverett of Boston, later president of Harvard College. In the inventory of Leverett's wife's first husband, Thomas Berry, the covering was listed as "Turkey Work for a Couch 16/." In Leverett's inventory of 1724, the couch was listed as part of a suite: "12 Large Turky Chairs and Couch £9." Originally the couch possessed wings or "falls" like those of the famed couch at Knole, Sevenoaks, Kent. Courtesy, Essex Institute. Photograph by Mark Sexton.

the work of the American textile scholar Linda Baumgarten, who found quantities of Turkey-work listed in Boston inventories from the last half of the seventeenth century,[28] and also by the evidence provided by the remarkable Essex Institute Turkey-work couch, the cover of which was inventoried in 1697 as "Turkey Work for a Couch 16/" (fig. 35).[29] The cover of the couch has a design similar to those on the chairs brought for Holyrood in 1685 (*see* figure 29) and suggests a common place of origin and date for these and for other similar covers. The design has been extended to fit a couch by the time-honored English method of simply repeating the pattern two or three times to fill the space. The Essex Institute Turkey-work couch is the only known surviving couch in which the cover and the frame made for it are intact. The few other examples of Turkey-work couches known to the writer are not reliable sources to document the practices of the period. At Aston Hall, Birmingham, a Turkey-work cover has been mounted on a different frame than the original.[30] In the Sir William Burrell collection, Glasgow, there are two couches with identical covers. One (14/219) has six repeats of the pattern, three on the back and three on the seat, as on the Essex Institute couch. Another (14/218) has only two repeats on the back and seat respectively; however, documentation exists that suggests Sir William pieced together single chair covers in 1931 to fit bare couch frames. In his *Purchase Book* of that year, he listed a "17th cent. stuff back oak settee to put on 6 of my Turkey Knot seats." In fact, only four of the "Turkey Knot seats" were used for one of the couches (14/218). Two unmounted covers of similar pattern remain (29/217–218). A similar cover has been used to cover an oak stool (14/30).[31] Modern Turkey-work borders and knotted woolen fringes were purchased to finish the couch.

Design

With so few Turkey-work covers dated or documented, it would be presumptuous to attempt to assign a date to any given design or to try to trace a development. It is possible, however, to make a broad classification of two groups based on central design, background, and border in the hope that future scholars will be able to add to our knowledge.

The design on one of the early Holyrood chairs (fig. 31, right) and also the design on the back covers of the Aston chairs (fig. 34) show an affinity with the needlework design of the period, the rows of flowers—rose, heartsease, and marigold—on samplers, for example. A chair now at the Metropolitan Museum of Art, New

36. Turkey-work chair, Boston, 1660–1680. Maple and oak with ball turnings; polychrome flowers on black background (now perished); original upholstery foundation and marsh grass stuffing. This is an early short-backed version. It is 37¼ inches in height. In the inventory of Thomas Berry, taken in 1697, six such chairs were called "old-fashioned," and the same chairs were called "small" in John Leverett's inventory of 1724. This confirms the stylistic progression of chair frames suggested by the documentation of the Holyrood examples. Traditionally said to have been owned by Roger Williams, founder of Providence in the Rhode Island Colony. Courtesy, The Metropolitan Museum of Art. Bequest of Mrs. J. Insley Blair.

York (fig. 36), has covers of the same floral design as one of the Holyrood chairs bought in 1668 (fig. 30). The frame, moreover, is the same height (thirty-seven inches) as the Holyrood chair but is of red oak and maple instead of English oak, indicating that it was made for its imported cover in New England, probably in Boston. It retains its original upholstery foundation and marsh grass stuffing.

The Aston chairs have, in addition, a white background powdered with black dots as if to emulate fur—ermine or miniver—and, on the back panel, a guilloche border. Similar backgrounds and borders can be found on examples with a different central motif. This "miniver" background, used with the arms of the Cavendish family, is found on the Turkey-work cover of a stool at Hardwick Hall. This cover may have been cut down from a table carpet. An unmounted set of covers at Colonial Williamsburg (1954–375) features an inter-

37. Turkey-work chair, Boston, 1680–1700. Maple and oak with ball turnings; polychrome flowers on black background (now perished); original upholstery foundation and marsh grass stuffing. This chair has a height of 43¾ inches. Similar high-backed chairs were valued in Thomas Berry's inventory of 1697 at thirty shillings each, and the same chairs were referred to as "large" when listed *en suite* with John Leverett's Turkey-work couch in his inventory of 1724 — yet another confirmation of the stylistic progression offered by the Holyrood chairs. The design of the cover is the mirror image of that on the 1685 Holyrood chair in figure 29. Courtesy, The Metropolitan Museum of Art. Bequest of Mrs. J. Insley Blair.

38. Turkey-work chair, Boston, 1680–1700. Maple and oak with ball turnings; polychrome flowers on black background (now perished); upholstery foundation renewed, with modern galloon around seat. Note the geometric design of the selvage on the sides of the back cover. Courtesy, New York State Education Department, Albany.

laced strapwork design on a miniver background. The one-piece cover of an armchair at the Victoria and Albert Museum (W30–1923) — a cover not original to the chair but most likely cut down from a table carpet — has a similar strapwork design with a guilloche border identical to that on the Aston chairs.

The four taller chairs at Holyrood bought in 1685 (*see* figure 29) belong to another group of later examples with crowded naturalistic flowers — rose, tulip, daffodil, and pea pod — and a black ground, which has usually perished due to the iron mordant used in dyeing the wool. All of these elements appear in the same arrangement on a chair made in Boston in the last two decades of the seventeenth century (fig. 37). Another Boston chair of the same period has similar covers (fig. 38). The chair has been rewebbed, but the covers are original. The same pattern is repeated three times along the width of the seat and back of the Essex Institute couch,

which retains its original upholstery foundation and marsh grass stuffing (fig. 35). It seems likely, therefore, that the 12 Turkey-work chairs (now lost) that originally accompanied the Essex Institute couch resembled those in figures 37 and 38.[32]

A variation of this later crowded floral design with black ground appears on a set of six chairs, one of which is at Colonial Williamsburg (1954–374), four of which are at the Brooklyn Museum (25.814.1–4), and another of which is at the Victoria and Albert Museum (W63–1926).[33] The same design appears on a set of unmounted covers at the Royal Scottish Museum (1956–1267), and, even more remarkably, surrounds the arms of Stanhope on the slip seats of a set of twelve mahogany chairs made around 1740.[34] The design has strong affinities with a table carpet in the Victoria and Albert Museum (T132–1924) bearing the arms of Molyneux impaling those of Rigby (a Lancashire family) and the date 1672.[35]

The three similar chairs at Holyrood have slight variations in the design, as if the weavers did not work from a cartoon but instead wove the patterns from memory in the same way as Hebridean knitters produce their patterns today. Often the design is reversed, or even reversed and partially inverted from example to example. Two English chairs on loan to the Royal Ontario Museum, Toronto, have similar covers mounted on slightly different frames; the covers appear to be original to the frames. The chairs, however, have been provided with new upholstery foundations, and in the process, the covers of the backs have been replaced upside down so that the pile goes up instead of down. They have been embellished with modern yellow braid in place of the original fringe.

Appendix A:
Measurements of Turkey-work Chairs (in inches)

	Overall Height	Width (seat)	Depth (seat)	Height (seat)
Fig. 29	41½	18¼	18	21½
Fig. 30	37	20	17	19
Fig. 31 (left)	36½	19¼	16¾	19
Fig. 31 (right)	37	19	17	19½
Fig. 36	37¼	19⅝	16⅞	20½
Fig. 37	43¾	19⅞	16¾	16⅞
Fig. 38	42	19¾	17¾	19

	Height of Back Panel	Front Leg Stock
Fig. 29	15½	1⅝ x 1⅝
Fig. 30	11½	1¾ x 1¾
Fig. 31 (left)	11	2 x 2
Fig. 31 (right)	10½	2 x 2
Fig. 36	10½	1⅝ x 1⅝
Fig. 37	17	1⅝ x 1⅝
Fig. 38	17¾	1¾ x 1¾

Appendix B:
Dated or Documented Turkey-work Covers and Cushions

1450—Panel (Colonel Parker). Tattersall suggests this should be 1540.

1581—Carpet. Arms of Montagu. The Duke of Buccleuch, Boughton.

1649—Chair back and seat. Victoria and Albert Museum (W428–1896).

1651—Cushions (twelve). Arms of the City of Norwich, England, given by the mayor. Norwich Cathedral and Strangers Hall Museum.

1666—Cushions (twelve). Arms of Sir Richard Sutton and of Bishop Smyth of Lincoln. A bill survives. Brasenose College, Oxford.

1667—Cushions (twenty). Arms of Matthew Wren, Bishop of Ely. In Pembroke College Chapel, Cambridge.

1668—Chairs (four). Bought in London for Holyroodhouse. (*See* figures 30 and 31.)

1672—Carpet. Arms of Molyneux impaling Rigby. Victoria and Albert Museum (T132–1924).

1685—Chairs (four). Bought in London for Holyroodhouse. (*See* figure 29.)

1697—Couch. Made in Boston for John Leverett (1662–1724). Essex Institute, Salem, Massachusetts. (*See* figure 35.)

NOTES

1. Since this paper was written, two more Turkey-work chairs have been located at Holyrood, making eight in all. The frames of both are damaged, one even being in two pieces. On the other frame, the covering is intact and identical to that seen in figure 30, though it lacks the woolen fringe (Inv. No. 3307).

2. Charles II was crowned at Scone, Perth, not at Edinburgh. George IV held a reception at Holyrood in 1822 but stayed with the Duke of Buccleuch at Dalkeith Place.

3. Scottish Record Office (hereafter S. R. O.), GD90/2/93. The letter is quoted in full in Margaret Swain, "The Furnishing of Holyroodhouse in 1668," *Connoisseur* 194, no. 780 (February 1977): 122–23. For a description of the appearance and use of a chair of state and its appurtenances, *see* Peter Thornton, "Canopies, Couches and Chairs of State," *Apollo* 100, no. 152 (October, 1974): 292–99.

4. S. R. O., E28/74/4.

5. S. R. O., E/35.

6. S. R. O., E28/33 3/4 1/1.

7. Ms. 5725, National Library of Scotland. The inventory is also quoted in A. F. Stewart, "The Plenishing of Holyrood House in 1714," *Proceedings of the Society of Antiquities of Scotland* 62 (1927–1928): 181–96.

8. The height of the taller chairs is forty-one and one-half inches as compared with thirty-seven inches for the lower-backed chair. *See* Appendix A.

9. Peter Thornton, "The Parisian *Fauteuil* of 1680," *Apollo* 101, no. 156 (February 1975): 102–07.

10. For this period term, *see* R. W. Symonds, "Charles II. Couches, Chairs and Stools, 1660–1670. Part II," *Connoisseur* 93 (February 1934): 95.

11. Pauline Aigus, "Late sixteenth- and seventeenth-century furniture in Oxford," *Furniture History* 7 (1971): 72–86 and pl. 24B.

12. *Bannatyne Miscellany* (Edinburgh, 1855), III: 250.

13. Leather-covered back stools with rectangular frames, often today called "Cromwellian chairs," have been mistakenly dated to the middle of the seventeenth century. For a discussion of this chair form, *see* Peter Thornton, "Back-stools and Chaises à Demoiselles," *Connoisseur* 185, no. 744 (February 1974): 99–105.

14. *See* C. E. C. Tattersall, *A History of British Carpets* (Benfleet, Essex: F. Lewis, 1934), pp. 51–57; Mildred B. Lanier, *English and Oriental Carpets at Williamsburg* (Charlottesville: The University Press of Virginia, 1975), pp. 3–12, for a discussion of Turkey work. I am grateful to Harrison M. Symmes for information regarding the Nevill carpet at Mount Vernon, Virginia.

15. J. O. Halliwell, *Ancient Inventories* (London: 1854), p. 147.

16. Karin M. Walton, *The Golden Age of English Furniture Upholstery 1660–1840* (Leeds: Temple Newsam House, 1973), no. 14.

17. Tattersall, *British Carpets* pls. II-IV.

18. I am indebted to John L. Nevinson, for notifying me of this carpet, and Pamela Clabburn, for confirmation.

19. Sotheby's, London. April 17, 1980, no. 149.

20. Quoted in R. W. Symonds, "Turkey Work, Beech, and Japanned Chairs," *Connoisseur* 93 (April 1934): 221–22. In reference to the term *Set-work* used in the petition, Peter Thornton has drawn my attention to an inventory of 1624 that lists *Set-work* and *Turkey work* as if they were two different textiles. In the case of the petition, however, the terms were clearly intended to be synonymous.

21. Randall Holme, *Academy of Armoury* (1688; reprint, London: Roxburgh Club, 1905), Bk. III, Ch. XIV, p. 15.

22. Hamilton Papers, 126/8/8. I am indebted to the Duke of Hamilton for permission to quote from this inventory.

23. Symonds Papers, The Henry Francis du Pont Winterthur Museum Libraries, Winterthur, Delaware, 75 x 64.14. I am grateful for permission to quote from these papers.

24. A chair of this form belongs to the Company of Merchants of the City of Edinburgh and may originally have been the master's chair. *See* Swain, "The Furnishing of Holyroodhouse," p. 127, no. 6.

25. Symonds, "Turkey Work," pp. 223–24.

26. L. Boynton, "The Hardwick Hall Inventories of 1601," *Furniture History* 7 (1971): 41.

27. S. R. O., Nithsdale Family Papers, 505/21.

28. Linda Baumgarten, "The Textile Trade of Boston, 1650 to 1700" in Ian M. G. Quimby, ed., *Arts of the Anglo-American Community in the Seventeenth Century* (Charlottesville: The University Press of Virginia, 1975), pp. 219–74.

29. Robert F. Trent, "A History for the Essex Institute Turkey Work Couch," *Essex Institute Historical Collections* 113, no. 1 (January 1977): 29–37.

30. M. Woodall, "Furniture at Aston Hall," *Antiques Collector* 31 (April 1960), fig. 8.

31. I am indebted to Alison Lindsay and the staff of the Textile Conservation Department of the Burrell collection, Glasgow, for allowing me to examine these objects and papers.

32. Trent, "Essex Institute Turkey Work Couch," p. 35.

33. Lanier, *Williamsburg*, pp. 10–11; Marvin D. Schwartz, *American Interiors 1675–1885* (Brooklyn: The Brooklyn Museum, 1968), fig. 4 and pl. II; Ralph Edwards, *English Chairs*, 3rd ed. (London: Her Majesty's Stationery Office, 1970), p. 19 and pl. 12. The Brooklyn and the Williamsburg examples all originated with the American collector Luke Vincent Lockwood, who purchased them from a dealer in London in 1925. The covers have been altered to fit over sprung seats.

34. Walton, *Golden Age of English Furniture Upholstery*, no. 14.

35. Tattersall, *British Carpets*, p. 48.

39. *Unidentified Woman* (once thought to be Mrs. Thrale), oil painting
by John Singleton Copley. New York, 1771. Los Angeles County
Museum of Art. Photograph, courtesy, Hirschl & Adler Galleries.

The Boston Upholstery Trade, 1700–1775

Brock Jobe

"Mr. Chippendale would be proud" proclaimed a recent advertisement for a furniture manufacturer.[1] Pictured above the announcement was a large reproduction mahogany sofa in the Chippendale style with straight, molded legs and a serpentine crest. Although Thomas Chippendale might have recognized the frame, he certainly would not have understood the upholstery. Deeply tufted in a diamond pattern, the sofa was more reminiscent of the Victorian passion for bulging, spring-stuffed contours than of eighteenth-century upholstery practices. In his well-known *Gentleman and Cabinet-Maker's Director* (third edition, 1762), Chippendale depicted crisp, angular contours, often accented with rows of polished brass nails.[2] For additional comfort, he recommended that sofas "have a Bolster and Pillow at each End and Cushions at the Back, which may be laid down occasionally . . ." as is shown in John Singleton Copley's portrait of an unidentified woman painted in New York in 1771 (fig. 39).[3]

The use of Victorian upholstery contours on an eighteenth-century form is symbolic of a major dichotomy in decorative arts scholarship. While knowledge of colonial cabinet- and chairmaking rapidly grows, that of the related craft of upholstery does not. The perishable nature of textiles and the everchanging state of fashion have led to the reupholstery of most American seating furniture and almost all beds; yet, much can be learned of the trade through examination of period documents and careful study of those objects that retain some of their original upholstery.

This essay focuses on the upholstery craft in one American city, Boston, between the years of 1700 and 1775. It begins with a brief review of the role of the upholsterer in England and then discusses Boston upholsterers—their number, business practices, and economic level within the community. Finally, it examines the materials and construction methods used by New England upholsterers.

In England during the first half of the eighteenth century, the upholstery trade was one of the most lucrative and prestigious crafts. Robert Campbell, author of *The London Tradesman*, an informative report on English crafts published in 1747, ranked the upholsterer above all other furnituremaking artisans. The master of a large shop, noted Campbell,

employs Journeymen in his own proper Calling, Cabinet-Makers, Glass-Grinders, Looking-Glass Frame-Carvers, Carvers for Chairs, Testers, and Posts of Bed, the Woolen-Draper, the Mercer, The Linen-Draper, several Species of Smiths,

and a vast many Tradesmen of the other mechanic branches.[4]

Upholsterers provided an assortment of household goods and services to customers. They made beds, curtains, and upholstered seating furniture; retailed a wide variety of dry goods and textiles; arranged funerals and supplied coffins and drapery; appraised estates; and auctioned secondhand wares. More importantly, they served as interior decorators who completely outfitted homes with appropriate furnishings. They became, in essence, arbiters of taste for their customers. "I have just finished my House," wrote Campbell, assuming the role of the typical client, "and must now think of furnishing it with fashionable Furniture. The Upholder [sic] is chief Agent in this Case: He is the Man upon whose Judgement I rely in the Choice of Goods."[5] English upholstery shops, like their counterparts on the continent, reflected an air of gentility and elegance far removed from the dingy environment of woodworking establishments of the day. Compare, for instance, illustrations of a chairmaker's workroom (fig. 40) and an upholsterer's facility (fig. 41) both from Diderot's *Encyclopédie*. In England, upholstery was an urban trade with most of the large shops located in London. In America upholsterers' workrooms were also concentrated in the major cities. The reasons for this are obvious. Only in urban areas could upholsterers easily obtain the variety of imported materials necessary to their trade, attract a sufficient number of wealthy clients to assure steady employment, and find the specialists needed for the many ancillary tasks crucial to the craft.

In Boston, forty-four individuals are known to have practiced the upholstery trade between 1700 and 1775. The great majority came from well-established, local families of the middle and upper strata of society. For example, David Mason, who practiced the trade from 1726 to 1746, was descended from an affluent line of seventeenth-century Boston merchants. The upholsterer William Gray, who worked in the third quarter of the eighteenth century, was the son of a prominent ropemaker. William's brother, Harrison Gray, served on the governor's council and held the post of treasurer for the Massachusetts Bay Colony. Another brother, John Gray, amassed a significant fortune as a merchant in the town. At least seventeen other upholsterers came from families whose wealth and reputations were similar to those of the Mason and Gray families. Prominent Boston families clearly considered the upholstery trade a suitable profession for their children.

40. View of a chairmaker's shop from Denis Diderot, ed., *Recueil de Planches, sur les Sciences, les Arts Libéraux, et les Arts Méchaniques* (Paris, 1771), vol. 2, "Menuisier en Meubles, Sieges" section, pl. 1. Courtesy, Society for the Preservation of New England Antiquities Library. Photograph by J. David Bohl.

41. View of an upholsterer's shop from Denis Diderot, ed., *Recueil de Planches, sur les Sciences, les Art Libéraux, et les Arts Méchaniques* (Paris, 1771), vol. 9, "Tapissier" section, pl. 1. In the lower left corner of the picture, the master of the shop shows an upholstered armchair to a client. Above and to the right four seamstresses work at a table. Courtesy, Society for the Preservation of New England Antiquities Library. Photograph by J. David Bohl.

Although not all were successful, upholsterers could profit greatly in their trade. Thomas Fitch, the most prosperous upholsterer in early eighteenth-century Boston, left a personal estate of over £3000 at the time of his death in 1736.[6] William Gray, Samuel Grant, who trained with Fitch, and William Downe, a contemporary of Fitch's, assembled comparable fortunes and gained social and political status as well. Downe, Fitch, and Grant served as selectmen and Gray as auditor.

After young men had completed their apprenticeships, they could attempt to establish their own upholstery business if they had the means for the requisite "considerable Stock to set up with."[7] Unlike furnituremakers, who needed only a few tools, lumber, glue, nails, and brassware, upholsterers required a substantial inventory of both imported and local materials. Imported cloth alone called for an investment of at least several hundred pounds. At the start of his career in 1728, Samuel Grant acquired goods costing over £600 to stock his shop.[8] Like many young Boston tradesmen, Grant lacked the necessary capital to make such immense purchases outright and therefore drew on his ties within the community to receive goods on credit. He benefited both from his family's prominence as successful shipwrights as well as the stature of his former master, Thomas Fitch.

Once in business, Boston upholsterers combined the activities of craftsmen and merchants. They supervised the fabrication of beds and seating furniture in their shops and continually acquired a variety of imported goods for their own use or for sale. Two important documents—the trade card of Ziphion Thayer (fig. 42) and the ledgers of Samuel Grant[9]—provide insight into the day-to-day intermingling of the commercial and craft aspects of the trade.

Thayer's card, published in 1765, identifies thirty-three types of imported goods.[10] Although the list does not include every sort of import used by Boston upholsterers, it does give an accurate impression of the range and popularity of certain upholstery materials and other furnishings. Sconce and pier looking-glasses head the list. Like other Boston upholsterers, as well as general merchants, print sellers, and japanners, Thayer vended imported looking-glasses.[11]

Next, the trade card names several stylish imported upholstery fabrics: yellow worsted damask, crimson moreen, yellow and green harateen, cheneys, prints, check furniture, and (after listing a variety of other goods) horsehair seating. The damask, moreen, harateen, and cheney described by Thayer were worsteds—

42. Trade card of Ziphion Thayer, drawn and engraved by Nathaniel Hurd. Boston, c. 1765. Courtesy, Worcester Art Museum.

fine, closely woven fabrics composed of long, tightly twisted wool threads. Throughout the colonial period, worsteds remained the most popular upholstery textile in Boston. Samuel Grant used them for over eighty percent of the bed hangings that he sold between 1730 and 1760.

Worsted damasks were the costliest of the group. Thayer's yellow damask probably resembled the fabric on an easy chair made for the patriot John Hancock (fig. 43). Some wealthy New Englanders acquired more luxurious damasks made from a combination of silk and worsted fibers or from silk alone. During the 1760s, Samuel Moffatt of Portsmouth, New Hampshire, outfitted his "Yellow Cham[be]^r with bed hangings and window curtains of silk and worsted damask."[12] A Newburyport family selected a similar fabric for their grandest bed. (*See* figure 146).

Thayer's listing of moreen, harateen, and cheney in that order reflected their respective popularity in the year 1765. Moreen was the most fashionable, having

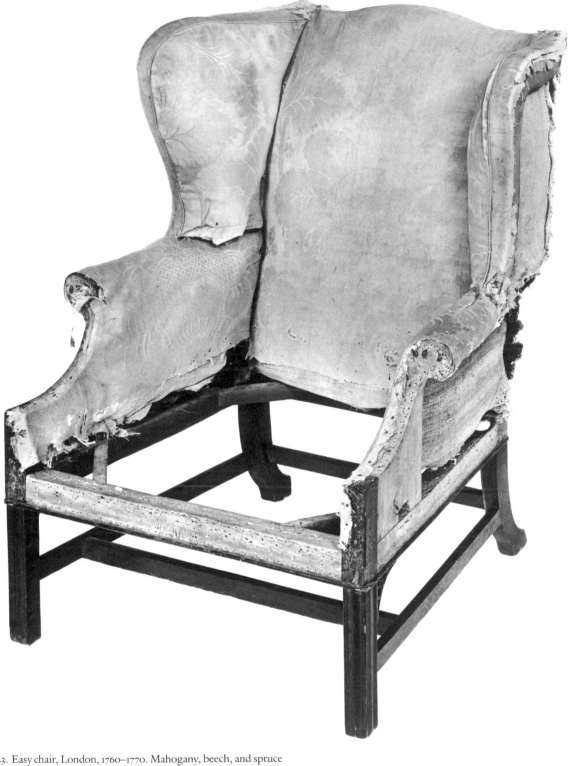

43. Easy chair, London, 1760–1770. Mahogany, beech, and spruce
with original yellow worsted damask on the back, wings, and arms.
This chair belonged to John Hancock of Boston and probably is the
yellow damask easy chair listed in the "Great Chamber" in Hancock's
estate inventory of 1794. The room also contained a sofa, ten chairs, a
bed, and window curtains—all covered in yellow damask. Courtesy,
New England Historic Genealogical Society. Photograph by Richard
Cheek.

44. Detail of chair seat, Portsmouth, New Hampshire, or York, Maine, 1760–1775. Mahogany chair frame, white pine corner blocks, and black walnut and birch seat frame, with original harateen or moreen upholstery. This seat is from a chair (*see* figure 249) that is part of a set originally acquired by Jonathan Sayward of York, Maine. Another set of chairs owned by Sayward retain the same covering. In both cases, the original green color of the fabric has faded to blue. Courtesy, Society for the Preservation of New England Antiquities. Photograph by Richard Cheek.

been recently introduced into Boston.[13] Harateen, on the other hand, had been available since at least 1710 and cheney since the middle of the seventeenth century.[14] Today, differences in the three are difficult to determine. Documented samples of moreen (*see* figure 144) and harateen (*see* figure 145) are virtually identical. Both feature watering, a finishing technique intended to impart the look of more expensive silk moiré. Watered worsteds were created by folding the ribbed fabric face to face, winding it onto a roller, and rolling it beneath huge blocks of stone. The weight crushed the thicker weft threads and, in the process, impressed a wavy surface on the cloth. Additional decoration was often applied to the fabric by means of an engraved metal cylinder that embossed a design onto the surface of the fabric. One common pattern has a meandering line, another depicts flowers and butterflies, and on occasion, both patterns ornament the same fabric (fig. 44). Documented samples of cheney have not survived; yet, contemporary descriptions of the cloth clearly establish

its relationship to moreen and harateen as well as to another similiar worsted, camlet.[15]

After worsteds, Thayer named prints and check furniture. Both were lightweight materials made of linen, cotton, or a combination of the two. Prints, as the term implies, were printed or stamped with a pattern transferred in dye by either a carved wooden block (*see* figure 148) or an engraved copper plate (fig. 45). The latter technique, borrowed from printmaking, made it possible to fashion extremely precise lines and to suggest subtle effects of light and shade. The introduction of copperplate printing in the 1750s sparked new interest in printed textiles, and by the last quarter of the eighteenth century, prints had become very popular.

Check furniture refers to plain woven cloth with stripes of color in both the warp and weft. The colors varied considerably as did the size of the checks. Boston upholsterers often used the material for slipcovers. In 1756, Samuel Grant billed a local merchant for "bottom[in]g" (upholstering the seats) six walnut chairs with crimson harateen and making "6 check cov^{er} [s] for ditto."[16] These covers, such as those in figure 46, protected the more expensive harateen from wear and, in all likelihood, were only removed for special occasions. Grant sometimes made bed hangings of check (*see* figures 150, 151, and 193), a less expensive alternative to worsted examples. In 1759, Major George Scott paid £10:1:2 [L.M.] for a bed hung in green harateen, £8:7:5 [L.M.] for a "furniture check bed."[17]

Thayer ended his list of upholstery fabrics with horsehair seating (also called haircloth) — a durable cloth woven with a weft of hairs from the manes and tails of horses on a warp of linen or cotton. This 1765 reference and a newspaper advertisement in the same year are the earliest known instances of horsehair's use in Boston.[18] After the American Revolution, demand for this material increased dramatically, and for much of the nineteenth century horsehair remained the standard covering on seating furniture. The most common pattern and color was a plain black in a satin weave. Patrons, however, could also select from striped or diaperwork examples in such colors as red and green as well as black (fig. 47).

Thayer's list does not include leather, the most common chair covering at that time. Only imported goods appear in the advertisement, and, by the 1760s, leather was rarely imported. During the first quarter of the century, "Russhia" leather had been a fashionable import but afterwards became more difficult to obtain; instead, upholsterers turned to "New England" leather.

45. Slipcover for an easy chair cushion, probably England, 1761–1770.
Copper-plate printed linen and cotton cloth with woolen and cotton
fringe. This cover is part of a set of upholstery items that includes bed
curtains and three seat covers for side chairs (one of which is at the
Winterthur Museum). The set was found in New England early in
this century. Its prior history is unknown. Courtesy, Colonial Williamsburg Foundation.

46. *Sergeant-at-Arms Bonfoy, His Son, and John Clementson, Sr.*, oil
painting by John Hamilton Mortimer. England, 1770–1775. Courtesy,
Yale Center for British Art, Paul Mellon Collection.

70

47. Side chair, Portsmouth, New Hampshire, 1765–1780. Mahogany with original horsehair upholstery. Private collection. Photograph, courtesy, Elizabeth R. Daniel Antiques.

Samuel Grant, for example, relied on two Boston tanners for native leathers made from goat-, seal-, and calfskins. The color of the leather depended on the type of skin: Seal was an off-white, goat slightly darker, and calf a rich brown. All were occasionally dyed black or red and sometimes polished with wax.[19]

An assortment of trimmings follows the list of fabrics on the trade card. None-so-pretties and bed laces were decorative tapes used as edging for bed curtains and easy chairs. (*See* figures 94 and 123). Fringes were a more expensive embellishment for trimming upholstery.

Made of silk or worsted, they came in many sizes and designs. In 1705, the Boston upholsterer Thomas Fitch asked his London agent to send a "green worsted shag [fringe], inch [deep] and edging speck'd wth crimson and white enough for a rais'd bed."[20] Fringes were a fashionable form of decoration throughout the seventeenth and early eighteenth centuries. By the 1720s, however, their use had declined, and not until the Revolutionary era did interest in fringes revive. (For examples of original fringe on eighteenth-century upholstery, *see* figures 121, 124, 146, and 149.) The next items, line and tassels, served a myriad of purposes, both decorative and utilitarian. For certain types of hangings, they were needed to raise or lower the curtains. Occasionally, they were merely suspended from a bed valance for decoration.[21]

After trimmings, Thayer listed feathers. Boston upholsterers, like their fellow craftsmen in other communities, used thousands of pounds of feathers, primarily for stuffing mattresses and loose cushions. Demand for this material remained high throughout the colonial period. Thomas Fitch, writing to a rural client in 1706, noted, "it is allways in my way to buy feath[ers]. If therefore now or at any time Y[o] See meet to Send me Yo[er] feath[ers] or give me offer of them I will allways allow Y[o] the heigh of the market."[22] Local farmers filled much of the demand even though imports from distant towns found a ready market in Boston. The captain of one Boston vessel was instructed to return from a voyage to Virginia and the Carolinas with "goose duck & Swan feathers."[23]

The cost of feathers was substantial. During the 1730s, Samuel Grant charged between three and four shillings per pound for feathers. A fully outfitted bed needed almost sixty pounds of feathers to fill the mattress, bolsters, and pillows. The total charge for such a quantity of feathers exceeded ten pounds. In comparison, the frame for the bed, called a bedstead in the eighteenth century, cost only about three and one half pounds.[24]

The trade card next names bed ticking—a plain or striped linen from England, Scotland, or Holland—and then quilts, rugs, coverlets, and blankets. All were essential bed furnishings, and Boston upholsterers stocked them in large supply. In 1751, Thomas Baxter had in his shop 28 bed rugs, 11 bed quilts, 36 counterpanes and coverlets, 107⅞ yards of bed ticking, and 158 pairs of blankets of varying sizes.[25]

After bedding, Thayer advertised canvas and crewels, two common materials used by women to create geometric patterns or colorful scenes in needlework. Examples of both appear on a remarkable easy chair retaining almost all of its original upholstery. (*See* figures 88 and 90.) The front is worked in a geometric flame-stitch pattern, called "Irish stitch" during the colonial period. The back features an exotic landscape design, wrought in crewel, of running deer and soaring birds. The woman responsible for this extraordinary needlework probably stitched each section on an embroidery frame and then called upon an upholsterer to mount the completed panels onto the easy chair. Samuel Grant served a similar function for the Scollay family in 1756 when he stuffed "7 Seats cov^d wth needle work."[26]

The list of upholstery goods concludes with four small but necessary items: girt web, brass nails, tacks, and curtain rings. Girt web, a narrow linen strip often coarsely woven in a herringbone pattern, served as the first layer of support for seating furniture. (*See* figures 62 and 84.) Brass nails were a major decorative element for upholstery throughout the colonial era. They not only imparted a dazzling appearance to an object but emphasized the crisp contours characteristic of that period's upholstered seating furniture. British manufacturers offered a variety of sizes, with heads ranging from one-quarter to three-quarters of an inch in diameter. Each nail was a single piece of brass with a domed head and square tapered shaft. Foundries cast these nails in sand molds, each mold containing hollows for many nails. The method remained commonplace until the third quarter of the nineteenth century when technological changes revolutionized the industry and new processes allowed nails to be made in two pieces—a wire shank and a stamped head. This technique is still in use today (fig. 48).

Iron tacks held each layer of upholstery in place. There were two basic types—the colonial equivalents of the modern upholstery tack and gimp tack (fig. 49)— and they came in several sizes. Upholsterers often stocked thousands in their shops. Theodore Wheelwright had "20m [thousand] Brass Nails" and "12m large Tax" among his shop goods at the time of his death in 1750.[27] The differences between eighteenth-century examples and their modern counterparts are quite marked (fig. 50). Until about 1790, nailmakers fashioned tacks of hand-forged shanks with hammered heads. Cut shanks were introduced during the 1780s, but heads continued to be hammered by hand. By the early-nineteenth century machine-stamped heads had replaced hammered ones. Iron tacks with cut shanks and stamped heads have stayed in common use up to the present.

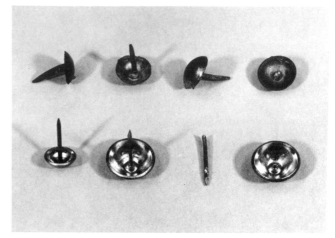

48. Brass upholstery nails. The upper row depicts four eighteenth-century cast nails. The one on the left was removed from the Boston leather chair illustrated in figure 56; the three on the right from a New York Federal chair made between 1790 and 1800. The lower row depicts modern brass nails made of wire shanks and stamped heads. Photograph by J. David Bohl.

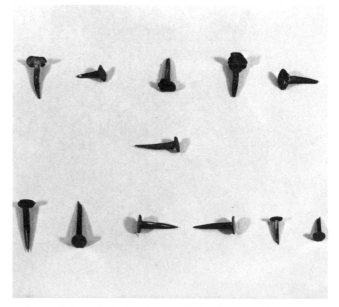

50. Iron upholstery tacks. The top row depicts five forged iron nails with hammered heads. The two on the left were removed from the English easy chair illustrated in figure 43; the one in the middle from the Boston leather chair illustrated in figure 56; and the two on the right from a Boston sofa made in 1808 or 1809. The one in the middle (with a cut shank and stamped head) was removed from a Norwich, Connecticut, chair made between 1795 and 1805. The bottom row depicts modern cut nails of several sizes. Photograph by J. David Bohl.

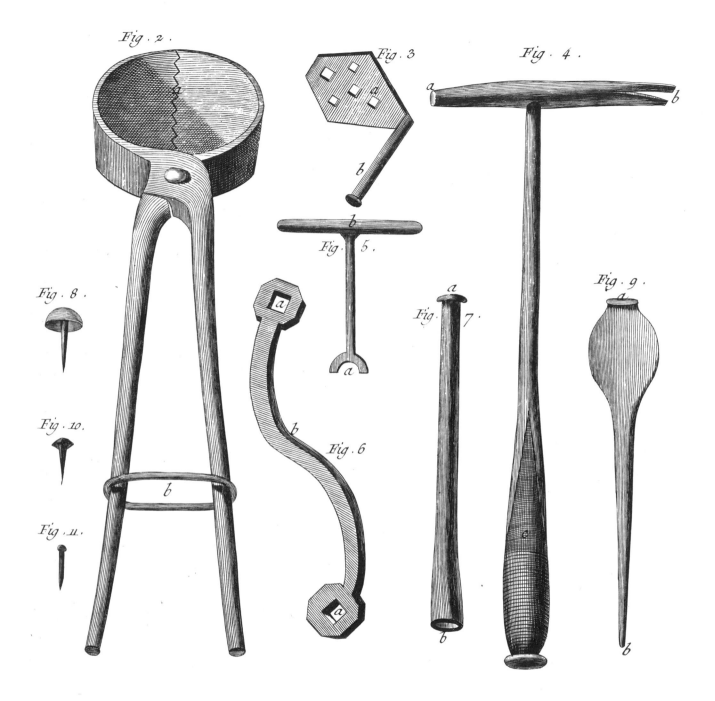

49. Upholsterer's tools and materials, including an iron upholstery tack (fig. 10) and a copper pin nail (fig. 11), which resembles the modern gimp tack, from Denis Diderot, ed., *Recueil Planches, sur les Sciences, les Arts Libéraux, et les Arts Méchaniques* (Paris, 1771), vol. 9, "Tapissier" section, pl. 4. The items are: fig. 2: upholsterer's pincers, called "strapping pliers" by Diderot, used to stretch webbing (compare to English pincers in figure 64); fig. 3: "turnscrew"; fig. 4: upholsterer's hammer; fig. 5: "turnscrew for screws with round heads"; fig. 6: large "screw-wrench"; fig. 7: "Driving-bolt serving to push in the gilt nail . . . in order that the hammer does not damage the gilting"; fig. 8: brass nail with gilt head; fig. 9: "Punch for making the hole in which to place the gilt nail"; fig. 10: iron tack; fig. 11: "copper pin nail." Courtesy, Society for the Preservation of New England Antiquities Library. Photograph by J. David Bohl.

51. Bedstead and tester, Boston area, 1755–1780. Mahogany, red oak,
maple, and white pine. Courtesy, Colonial Williamsburg Foundation.

In the mid-eighteenth century, pewter and brass curtain rings of various sizes were cast in molds or cut from pipe that had been brazed on a seam. Upholsterers used them to suspend bed and window curtains from iron rods.[28]

At the end of the trade card, Thayer included several items unrelated to upholstery: corks, wallpaper, writing paper, wool cards, and Lynn shoes (footwear made in the town of Lynn, north of Boston). Such merchandise was stocked by merchants, shopkeepers, and retailers, as well as upholsterers. For a Bostonian, mercantile activity offered the surest path to wealth, and Boston upholsterers pursued profit with the same entrepreneurial spirit that guided many other residents.

The primary function of the upholsterer, however, remained the construction of upholstered furniture. Unfortunately, although Thayer advertised beds, curtains, and upholstered seating furniture at the end of his card, we really know very little about his upholstery practice. On the other hand, the well-documented career of another Boston upholsterer, Samuel Grant, provides considerable detail about the actual operation of an upholstery shop in mid-eighteenth-century Boston. Born in Boston in 1705, Grant served an apprenticeship with Thomas Fitch. By 1728, he was working in his own shop, the Crown and Cushion, on Union Street. For the next fifty years, he continued his trade there and by the time of his death in 1784 had accumulated a substantial fortune.[29] Two surviving account books document his general activities between 1728 and 1760; two petty ledgers record his payments to workmen between 1755 and 1771.[30]

Grant's major craft activities were the fabrication of two items: bedding and seating furniture. The first constituted the largest portion of his business. He offered an array of items ranging from inexpensive bedrolls — made of bed ticking filled with wool or straw — to costly high-post bedsteads adorned with decorative hangings and feather ticks. The number of fully outfitted beds sold by Grant was small in comparison to the bedrolls. In 1755, for example, he made 371 straw or wool beds and only 21 feather ones. Yet the more elaborate examples provided significant income. For a single high-post bed with hangings, he could charge up to twenty-five times more than he got for a straw mattress.[31]

The production of ornate beds required the efforts of numerous specialists, both inside and outside Grant's shop. He first turned to a chairmaker for a bedstead and tester frame such as those depicted in figure 51. Between

1755 and 1771, he employed eight craftsmen for such work: George Bright, Abraham Howard, Clement Vincent, and five members of the Perkins family — Edmund, Sr., and his sons Edmund, Jr., Henry, John, and William.[32] If the patron desired carved details, Grant hired a carver. A bill from Simeon Skillin, one of three carvers Grant used, reveals that he specialized in carving headboards and cornices. In 1768 and 1769, Grant credited Skillin with the following:

By carvᵍ Cornishes mid[dl]ᵉ & End	1: 1:4
By carvᵍ best hᵈ. Board corner pieces	–:12:–
By carvᵍ cornish midle & End	1: 1:4
dᵒ a comon hᵈ board	–: 6:–
By 12 Sett corner Peices [for cornices]	1: 4:–
By carvᵍ. 1 Sett cornishes	1: 1:4
1 head Board	–:12:–
	£5:18:–[L.M.][33]

Skillin could have carved the cornices in a hardwood such as mahogany but more likely cut them in white pine. If made of the latter, they were probably covered with the same fabric used for the bed hangings, a technique recommended by Chippendale in the *Director* (fig. 52). Two American cloth-covered cornices — one with a New York provenance, the other from Connecticut — document this once popular practice.[34] Unfortunately, no carved headboards from the colonial period have survived, and we can only surmise their appearance from the illustrations in English pattern books.[35]

To complete the bedstead, Grant acquired a canvas or "sacking" bottom from a sailmaker.[36] A typical example consisted of a large rectangular panel of linen laced with cord to narrow linen strips that were nailed along the rails of the bedstead (fig. 53). Leather or linen tape often reinforced the strips to prevent their tearing around the nails. As an alternative, craftsmen sometimes inserted wooden pins into the rails and laced the linen panel to the pins.[37]

Grant oversaw the remaining production steps in his own shop. A journeyman, such as his nephew John Grant, made the mattress, bolster, and pillows.[38] For a particularly fine bed, he may have fabricated two mattresses, one of tufted wool topped by one of feathers.[39] The latter, filled with up to fifty pounds of feathers, had a thick, domed shape similar to that of a reproduction mattress at Colonial Williamsburg (fig. 54).[40] To create the bolster and pillows, the journeyman sewed bags of linen ticking into the desired size and filled them with feathers.

Pub.^d according to Act of Parliam.^t 1753.

52. Design of a bed from Thomas Chippendale, *The Gentleman and Cabinet-Maker's Director*, 3rd ed., (London, 1762), pl. 41. The bed is shown with an ornate carved cornice. A simpler cornice designated by the letter B is meant to be covered in cloth—"the same stuff as the curtains'," according to Chippendale (p. 5). The diagram in the lower right depicts the tester laths with pullies to draw up the curtains. Courtesy, Society for the Preservation of New England Antiquities. Photograph by J. David Bohl.

The hangings were the last and most elegant part of the bed. A complete set—tester cloth, inside and outside valances, headcloth, curtains, counterpane, and bases or skirts (fig. 55)—required a substantial amount of imported materials. When making a "Yellow bed" (without counterpane) for Samuel Ballard, a Boston bookkeeper, Grant used 43 yards of yellow cheney, 108 yards of binding, and 45 yards of braid, as well as an unspecified amount of buckram—a coarse, stiff linen—as a lining material.[41]

Upholsterers often employed women to cut out the cloth for the hangings, apply the braid and binding, and line the hangings.[42] For example, Grant's most produc-

tive worker from 1766 to 1768 was Elizabeth Kemble, a widow. She made up eighty-seven sets of hangings: fifty-three of cheney, eighteen of harateen, eight of printed fabrics, two of calico, and six of unspecified material for field beds.[43] Women like Kemble were important not only because of their sewing skills, but also because they provided inexpensive labor.[44] Elizabeth Kemble earned a daily wage of one shilling, four pence [L.M.] from Grant. For a set of hangings, which on average took just over a day to produce, she received between one shilling, seven pence and one shilling, nine pence. Grant's charge to customers ranged from two to nine pounds depending on the fabric.[45]

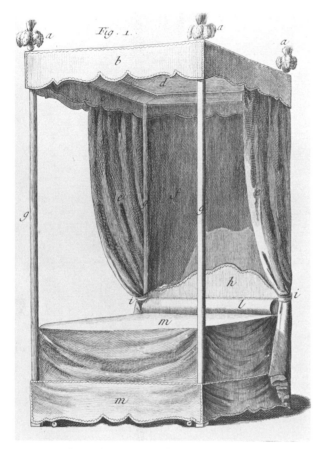

53. Detail of figure 51 with bottom and bases added. The bed bottom is secured with cord strung through hand-sewn grommets in the canvas panel and linen strips. The strips are nailed into rabbets in the side and foot rails of the bedstead. On this example, the strips are original; the panel and cord are reproductions.

54. Detail of figure 51 with bedding on it. The wool and feather mattresses are reproductions.

55. Design of a bed from Denis Diderot, ed., *Recueil de Planches, sur les Sciences, les Arts Libéraux, et les Arts Méchaniques* (Paris, 1771), vol. 9, "Tapissier" section, pl. 6, fig. 1. This view illustrates the major elements of a bed: (a) finial of ostrich feathers—often a wooden cornice was installed instead, (b) outside valance, (c) inside valance, (d) tester cloth, (e) curtain, (f) headcloth, (g) bedpost, (h) headboard, (i) tie back, (l) bolster, (m) counterpane, (n, incorrectly labeled as m) base. Courtesy, Society for the Preservation of New England Antiquities Library. Photograph by Richard Cheek.

Clearly, the cost of materials far exceeded that of labor as the essay by Heckscher in this volume also points out.

Grant offered three different types of hangings. The traditional and most common form consisted of curtains suspended from rods in the tester frame. (*See* figure 55). Usually this frame sat upon iron pins extending from the top of the posts. Occasionally the tester was hung from the ceiling with screws and line.[46] Grant termed the latter version a "raised" bed. Grant also made hangings for portable, compact bedsteads known as field beds. These required a second type of curtains in which the curtains were simply draped over the tester frame.[47] Grant had begun to make field beds by 1732 when he charged Henry Marshall, the local postmaster, for chintz, silk tape, thread, and "mak^g a field bed."[48]

During the second half of the eighteenth century, Boston upholsterers produced a third type of hangings, sometimes identified as "Draw-up Bed-Curtains."[49] For this variety, cord was strung through rings sewn to the back of each curtain, up over pullies in the laths of the tester, and down around brass pins in the bed post.[50] A tassel was fastened to the end of the line. By pulling the tassel, the curtain could be raised to form a swag or "drapery" as it was often called. (*See* figure 52.) Grant's account books do not refer specifically to draw-up bed curtains but do describe draw-up window curtains. In 1756, he billed Charles Apthorp for the following:

3 Tassells & Line 16/ leads &	
Silk ¼^d	−:17:4
Laths 2/8 rings 8^D 6 Brass heads 6/	−: 9:4
Alter^g./ & fixing curt^s. for 3 Wind^s	
to draw up	−:10:8[L.M.][51]

Grant must have also sold draw-up bed curtains, but their number and degree of elaboration cannot be determined from the general references to bed hangings.

To finish a bed, Grant needed a variety of small metal hardware. Boston braziers supplied imported brass pins, rings, and hooks. Blacksmiths in Boston and Lynn forged iron rods, and a number of dry goods merchants provided iron bed screws.[52] Today, stamped brass caps often cover the screw holes on early bedsteads. Yet Grant never mentioned caps in his accounts, and presumably they became popular later in the eighteenth century. He did refer to casters, beginning in the 1750s. William Bourn of Marblehead paid £5:7:4[L.M.] for a "mohogeny beds^t. cast^r Screws bott^m & c."[53] Made with brass or leather wheels, casters became a standard feature of stylish beds during the pre-Revolutionary era.

Once Grant had assembled all of the elements for a fully hung bed, they were carted to a customer's house and installed by one of Grant's workmen. For a patron living outside Boston, the parts were packed and shipped to the port nearest his home.

The cost of a complete high-post bed was considerable because of the great expense of the imported cloth, the feather mattress, and the specialized carved work. Grant sold a grand example for over £86 in 1739.[54] By comparison, the Boston cabinetmaker Job Coit charged only £50 in 1738 for a magnificent blockfront desk and bookcase.[55] Both Grant's bed and Coit's desk and bookcase are the finest of their type. The difference in price testifies to the importance of a fully hung bed. It was usually the most valuable item in one's home. The best bed provided comfort as well as elegance and, like silver, called attention to its owner's social status and economic wealth.

The upholstery of seating furniture provided a second major source of income for Grant. This type of work also required that Grant manage an intricate operation involving other craftsmen, both within and outside of his shop. Between 1755 and 1771, Grant obtained most of his chair frames from several of the same artisans who provided bedsteads—John and Henry Perkins, George Bright, and Clement Vincent. He bought curled hair for stuffing and leather for covering seats from Samuel Bass, Jr., a Boston tanner. Marsh grass and feathers, other useful stuffing materials, came from a farmer on Noddles Island in Boston harbor and several ship captains, respectively.[56] Grant undoubtedly upholstered some chairs himself but also employed two journeymen—Stephen Harris and Turrell Thayer—to do much of the work.

The subdivision of the various tasks involved in the manufacture of upholstered chairs enabled Grant to assemble in his shop large quantities of seating furniture, which he then marketed. His ledgers document the size of his operation. From 1729 through 1738, Grant sold 2,006 chairs, 138 stools, 49 couches, and 44 easy chairs and made 66 cushions and 182 chair seats—a total of almost 2,500 pieces of upholstered furniture. His output may well have been the highest in Boston during this period. Yet several other craftsmen ranked close behind. Thomas Baxter, William Downe, and David Mason maintained sizable establishments and cumulatively must have supervised the production of thousands of upholstered items.

The mainstay of Grant's business during the early years of his career was what we call the Boston chair

56. Side chair, Boston, 1725–1740. Maple and oak, with original leather upholstery. Courtesy, Wilton, a Property of the National Society of the Colonial Dames of America in the Commonwealth of Virginia. Photograph by Richard Cheek.

(fig. 56). Made of maple and covered with leather, this type of chair was sold in great numbers to merchants who exported them to towns along the coast and to the West Indies. A single entrepreneur bought 400 leather chairs, and Grant, himself, shipped more than 125 chairs to New York and Philadelphia. The form remained popular until about 1750. Its price escalated gradually because of inflation in the Boston economy during the second quarter of the eighteenth century. In 1729, Grant charged twenty-six shillings per chair. By 1737, the price had risen to thirty-two shillings and in 1743 to thirty-eight shillings. Although low in comparison with prices for bedsteads and easy chairs from Grant's shop, these charges far exceeded those for unupholstered examples. Slat-back chairs with rush seats sold for as little as five shillings each.[57]

In addition to leather chairs, Grant offered more elaborate and expensive seating furniture in the newest fashions. By 1732, he had begun to make chairs in the Queen Anne style, featuring round feet, "horsebones" (his term for cabriole legs), cushion seats (slip seats), and banister backs (solid splats).[58] In 1734, he first recorded the sale of chairs with compass seats (fig. 57) and in 1746 billed a customer for twelve chairs with "Marlborough" (straight) legs.[59] These references to particularly stylish details show that Grant, who catered to the wealthy of New England, worked in the vanguard of fashion.

Grant's level of production slackened during the second half of the eighteenth century. For the years 1755 through 1759, he sold only 347 chairs, 42 stools, 1 couch, and 17 easy chairs and made 80 cushions and 221 seats. These totals, while covering only a five-year period, still represent a major decline in production from his output of the 1730s. One form—the couch—had become obsolete, with production falling from twenty-nine to one, and other parlor furnishings, such as the settee and sofa, had not supplanted it. The Boston chair's fall from fashion and the lack of a suitable replacement also account in part for the decline in Grant's production. Growing competition from other upholsterers may have also reduced Grant's business. Only one area of his work increased: the "bottoming" of seating furniture. With greater frequency, patrons called upon Grant to cover chairs that they had acquired directly from chairmakers. As a result, his control over the entire process of construction seems to have declined.

Although his gross output decreased, Grant continued to supply many of Boston's elite with handsome furniture. His clients included Governor William Shir-

57. Side chair, Boston area, 1735–1750. Black walnut and maple with original leather upholstery except for the addition of a modern strip on the edge of the front and side seat rails. Courtesy, Marblehead Historical Society. Photograph by Richard Cheek.

ley, Lieutenant Governor Andrew Oliver, Frances Borland, James Bowdoin, and Charles Apthorp. Of all Grant's customers, Apthorp was the steadiest. He constantly ordered household items for himself and his sons. In 1755, for example, Apthorp acquired for his son James a cot, a crib, two fully outfitted beds with matching window curtains, a looking-glass, two sets of chairs, and a third set described as follows:

6 walnutt chairs carv'd tops knees
 & bares claw feet stuffd in Canv^s
1 Low ditto all cov^d wth Crim[so]^n &
 close naild   11:4:–[L.M.][60]

While splendid in appearance, Apthorp's chairs may not have been Grant's finest. His single most important commission was a "Crimson Velvet Chair for [the] Council Chamb^{er}" commissioned by the province of Massachusetts in 1757.[61] Unfortunately, the chair cannot be located today.

With the abundance of information available on the materials and shop activities of Boston upholsterers, it is disappointing to discover that few pieces of surviving Boston upholstered furniture can be definitely attributed to particular craftsmen. Only four documented examples are known, all in the collections of the Society for the Preservation of New England Antiquities.[62] The first two—a cradle and easy chair—were upholstered by Samuel Grant; the latter two—surviving examples from two sets of side chairs—were made by the cabinetmaker George Bright.

In 1731, Samuel Grant covered a cradle in leather for his infant son Samuel Grant, Jr. (fig. 58). The cradle, though now in poor condition, retains most of its original leather and brass nails. On the back of the cradle, a series of nails form young Samuel's initials and date of birth. Grant did not list the cradle in his ledgers because it was for family use. Yet the ledgers indicate that he did sell cradles, often at a high price. In 1743, a customer purchased a "Cradle Cov^d wth. leather & Matt[r]ess" for £7:4:0, a price equal to that for two leather-backed armchairs.[63] Few American cradles survive, and only three from Boston are known.[64]

The second documented example of Samuel Grant's work is an upholstered easy chair (fig. 59). In 1759, he sold the chair to Jonathan Sayward, a York, Maine, merchant. Despite the loss of its original outer covering, the chair remains an important document of Boston upholstery practices. On the back, widely spaced strips of linen girt web support a piece of coarsely woven linen, marsh grass stuffing covered with a thin skimmer of curled hair, and a cover layer of linen. On the wings,

58. Cradle, upholstered by Samuel Grant for his son, Samuel Grant, Jr., Boston, 1731. White pine with original leather upholstery. Courtesy, Society for the Preservation of New England Antiquities. Photograph by Richard Cheek.

rolls of marsh grass wrapped in linen outline the edges. Originally, each wing also had a piece of linen sackcloth nailed to its perimeter. This sackcloth was filled with grass and hair and then covered with another piece of linen nailed to the rear stile, pulled over the rolled edge, and nailed to the outside edge of the wing. The seat was upholstered much like the back but with the addition of a rolled edge along the top of the front seat rail. A thick feather-filled cushion completed the underupholstery. All of the elements—back, wings, seat, and cushion— were originally covered in a green worsted, probably a harateen with embossed decoration, and trimmed at the corners with green braid. The cost of the finished easy chair was £4:18:6 [L.M.].[65]

The other examples of documented Boston work are two pairs of chairs made in 1770 by the cabinetmaker George Bright in collaboration with an unknown upholsterer. Each chair still retains its original up- holstery. One pair—originally part of a set of twelve— has leather seats upholstered over the rails and embel- lished with brass nails (fig. 60). On each chair, a single row of nails runs along the lower edge of the seat rails. At the front corners, each line of nails turns upward, a common Boston convention. Bright charged £1:10:0 [L.M.] per chair for the set of twelve chairs. On the second pair, survivals from a set of six chairs with slip seats (fig. 61), the original underupholstery lies intact beneath the check covering. Bright sold the chairs

59. Easy chair, Boston, 1759. Frame by Clement Vincent or George
Bright, upholstery by Samuel Grant. Black walnut, maple, and white
pine, with original underupholstery on the back and original linen
rolls stuffed with marsh grass on the wings. Jonathan Sayward of
York, Maine, purchased the easy chair from Grant for £4:18:6 [L.M.].
Courtesy, Society for the Preservation of New England Antiquities.
Photograph by Richard Cheek.

60. Side chair, Boston, 1770. Frame by George Bright. Mahogany, birch, maple, and yellow pine, with original leather upholstery. This chair is one of a set of twelve purchased from Bright by Jonathan Bowman of Pownalborough, Maine. Courtesy, Society for the Preservation of New England Antiquities. Photograph by Richard Cheek.

61. Side chair, Boston, 1770. Frame by George Bright. Mahogany and maple, with original underupholstery. (The check cover is modern.) This chair is one of a set of six also purchased from Bright by the same Jonathan Bowman. Courtesy, Society for the Preservation of New England Antiquities. Photograph by Richard Cheek.

"Stufft in Canvis," suggesting that it was the owner's responsibility to obtain the finish material.[66] In this case, the owner probably bought either loose-fitting slip covers or a piece of worsted to upholster the seats permanently. Because he did not have to furnish the finish fabric, Bright's charge for this set of chairs was less than that for the first set. They cost approximately £1:5:8 [L.M.] per chair for the set of six chairs.[67]

Although these four examples are the only ones that can be ascribed to specific Boston craftsmen, many chairs from the Boston area retain much of their original upholstery. Over a dozen leather-backed chairs and almost as many splat-back chairs with cabriole or straight legs survive in excellent condition. Study of these examples reveals period upholstery materials, techniques, and contours.

The upholstery of a slip seat involved five steps (figs. 62 and 63). First, a strip of girt web was folded and tacked with large-headed upholstery tacks to one side of the seat frame. The upholsterer stretched the webbing across to the other side, pulled it tight with a device called a pincer (fig. 64; other tools are illustrated in figure 49), tacked it down, and cut off the excess. The flap was often folded over and tacked. Usually two strips of widely spaced webbing ran front to back, interwoven with one or two strips running side to side. Next, a coarse linen cloth was laid over the girt web and nailed to the top of the seat frame. Often this linen sackcloth was folded at the edges to protect it from tearing at the nails. (Sometimes, instead of folding the cloth, leather strips were nailed at the edges.) On top of the linen cover, the upholsterer placed a layer of stuffing, usually marsh grass. After 1750, curled hair was some-times added as a skimmer over the marsh grass or even replaced marsh grass altogether. Occasionally, raw wool and flax also served as stuffing materials in New England furniture. After placing the stuffing, the upholsterer tacked a second piece of linen, often more finely woven than the first, to the frame. He usually tacked it to the frame's edge or underside. Only rarely was it tacked to

62. Slip seat, Boston, 1755–1775. Cherry seat frame, original girt web and linen. On loan to the Society for the Preservation of New England Antiquities. Photograph by Richard Cheek.

63. Slip seat in figure 62 showing stuffing and outer layer of linen. On loan to the Society for the Preservation of New England Antiquities. Photograph by Richard Cheek.

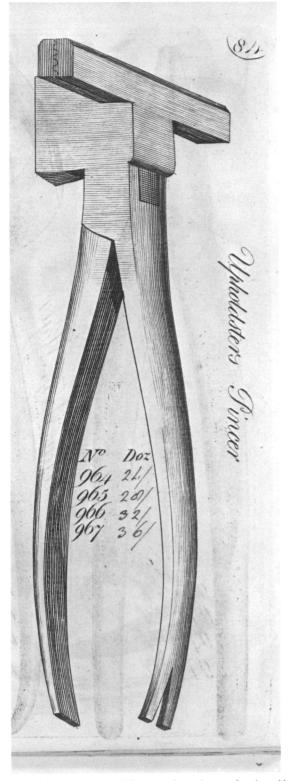

Upholdsters Pincer

Nᵒ	Doz
964	2 4/
965	2 8/
966	3 2/
967	3 6/

64. "Upholdsters Pincer," from a trade catalogue of tools and household utensils, Birmingham, 1798. The design of this pincer is typical of English examples; for a French version, *see* figure 49. Courtesy, Essex Institute.

the top of the frame. Finally, the covering material was pulled over the edges of the frame and nailed to the bottom.

Chairs upholstered over-the-rails involved the same basic sequence of steps with two differences: The upholsterer had the options of adding rolled or stitched edges and of decorating with brass nails. A roll of marsh grass was placed between the projecting ends of the front legs and tacked to the front seat rail (fig. 65). The roll enabled the upholsterer to build the seat above the rails and to keep the contours straight. After the Revolution, craftsmen began to use stitched edges to create the square, boxy contours popular at the time. (*See* the discussion of the Adam Haines' chairs in Richard Nylander's essay in this volume.) However, to date, no New England chairs in the Queen Anne or Chippendale styles have been found with stitched edges.

Brass nails were used throughout the colonial period. On Boston leather chairs from the 1720s and 1730s (*see* figure 56), two rows of nails often decorate the back and the front of the seat, with a single row of more widely spaced nails along the side seat rails. Leather chairs from the 1740s through the 1770s usually had more closely spaced nails either in a double row (*see* figure 57) or in a single row that extended vertically at each front corner (*see* figure 60).

The method for upholstering leather chairs also changed over time. On early eighteenth-century examples (*see* figure 56), a piece of leather was tacked to the rear seat rail, pulled over the top of the front and side rails, and tacked to the outside edges. A strip of leather, secured first with a few iron tacks and later with brass nails, was applied along the side and front rails. The strip covered the irregular edge of the leather panel. Often a square pattern of stitches was sewn through the seat to keep the stuffing from shifting. (*See* detailed discussion in Robert Trent's essay in this volume.) On chairs from the second half of the eighteenth century (fig. 66), the entire seat was made from a single piece of leather. While the cover was held in place by tacks, the upholsterer would trim off excess leather along the lower outside edge of the seat rails so that no leather extended below the rails (fig. 67). The craftsmen then completed the seat by adding brass nails along the seat rails.

During the eighteenth century, the contours of upholstery on Boston chairs became increasingly crisp and well-defined. Early leather chairs had slightly domed seats that reflected the interest in curves characteristic of the William and Mary and Queen Anne styles. Chippendale chairs display neat, precise contours

65. Side chair, Portsmouth, New Hampshire, 1790–1805. Cherry with original webbing, stuffing, and linen roll of marsh grass nailed to front seat rail. This chair originally belonged to Tobias Lear of Portsmouth, New Hampshire. Courtesy, Society for the Preservation of New England Antiquities. Photograph by Richard Cheek.

66. Side chair, Boston area, 1760–1780. Mahogany and maple with original leather upholstery. Courtesy, The Metropolitan Museum of Art. Photograph, courtesy, Israel Sack, Inc.

that emphasize the rectilinear qualities of that style. In both types of seats, the upholstery projects only 1½ to 2½ inches above the top of the seat rails. This contrasts markedly with the height and shape of the nineteenth-century spring seats described in the introduction of this article.

The study of colonial upholstery practices is just beginning. Information is needed on the upholstery trade in other American cities. Objects retaining any of their original upholstery need to be adequately catalogued, photographed, and published. The day may come, as Peter Thornton commented in a *Connoisseur* editorial, "when furniture-historians wax as enthusiastic about tufted fringes and shallow buttoning as they do today about patina of wood or the curve of a cabriole leg."[68]

NOTES

1. *The New Yorker*, June 13, 1977, p. 111.

2. Chippendale does not include sofas in either the first (1754) or second (1755) edition of *The Gentleman and Cabinet-Maker's Director*. Six sofas appear in the third edition: Thomas Chippendale, *The Gentleman and Cabinet-Maker's Director* (London, 1762; reprint ed., New York: Dover Publications, 1966), pls. 29–31 and 33.

3. Chippendale, *Cabinet-Maker's Director*, p. 4.

4. Robert Campbell, *The London Tradesman* (London, 1747; reprint ed., New York: Augustus M. Kelley, 1969), p. 170.

5. Campbell, *London Tradesman*, pp. 169–170.

6. Inventory of Thomas Fitch, Suffolk County Probate Court, Suffolk County Courthouse, Boston, Massachusetts, docket 6868. In this essay, all values are in Old Tenor unless specified otherwise. Although Massachusetts devalued its currency in 1750, setting an exchange rate of £1 Lawful Money [L.M.] for £7.10.0 Old Tenor, many people continued to use Old Tenor values.

7. Campbell, *London Tradesman*, p. 170.

8. The earliest working dates for Grant are April 15 and 26, 1728, when he purchased upholstery goods valued at £228:14:3 from his former master, Thomas Fitch. Account Book of Thomas Fitch, 1719–1732, Massachusetts Historical Society, Boston, Massachusetts, pp. 470–71. By November 25, Grant owed various individuals £654:16:2 for shop

67. Detail of bottom of figure 66.

goods. Account Book of Samuel Grant, 1728–1737, Massachusetts Historical Society, p. 2.

9. Five of Grant's business ledgers have survived: Account Book, 1728–1737, Massachusetts Historical Society; Receipt Book, 1731–1740, Bostonian Society, Boston, Massachusetts; Account Book, 1737–1760, American Antiquarian Society, Worcester, Massachusetts; Petty Ledger, 1755–1762, Boston Public Library, Boston, Massachusetts; Petty Ledger, 1762–1771, Boston Public Library.

10. The trade card, though undated, can be assigned a date of 1765. In that year, Thayer placed an advertisement in a Boston newspaper that repeated several phrases used on the trade card. *Boston Evening-Post* June 3, 1765, p. 2.

11. Only one English glass survives to document this common practice. On the backboard, it bears the name of the Boston upholsterer who sold it in the 1750s. Brock Jobe and Myrna Kaye, *New England Furniture: The Colonial Era* (Boston: Houghton Mifflin Company, 1984), pp. 452–53.

12. Abbott Lowell Cummings, ed., *Bed Hangings, A Treatise on Fabrics and Styles in the Curtaining of Beds 1650–1850* (Boston: Society for the Preservation of New England Antiquities, 1961), pp. 23–24, fig. 12.

13. Thayer's reference to moreen is one of the earliest in Boston. Samuel Grant does not use the term in his two account books, which span the years 1728–1760. According to Abbott Lowell Cummings, the first mention of moreen in a Boston newspaper occurred in 1770 when

an auction advertisement listed "1 Mohogony four Post Bedsted, with Crimson Moreen Furniture." Cummings, *Bed Hangings*, p. 31.

14. In 1710, Thomas Fitch, a Boston upholsterer, ordered "a very neat fashionable well made bed of good crimson in gr[ai]^n: Harratine well water'd" from London. Thomas Fitch to John Crouch and Samuel Arnold, November 15, 1710, Letterbook of Thomas Fitch, 1702–1711, American Antiquarian Society. For seventeenth-century Boston references to cheney, *see* Linda R. Baumgarten, "The Textile Trade in Boston, 1650–1700," in Ian M. G. Quimby, ed., *Winterthur Conference Report 1974: Arts of the Anglo-American Community in the Seventeenth Century.* (Charlottesville: University of Virginia, 1975), pp. 237, 250.

15. The similarity of moreen, harateen and cheney and the processes of watering and embossing are discussed in Florence M. Montgomery's essay in this volume; and, in more detail, in *Textiles in America 1650–1870* (New York: W. W. Norton & Company, 1984), pp. 199, 256–57, 300, 302–03, pls. D-27A, B, C, D and D-104, and figs. D-26, D-29, D-44, D-74.

16. Grant Account Book, 1737–1760, p. 814.

17. Grant Account Book, 1737–1760, p. 909.

18. *Boston Evening Post*, June 17, 1765, p. 3.

19. Brock Jobe, "The Boston Furniture Industry, 1720–1740," in Walter M. Whitehill et al., eds., *Boston Furniture of the Eighteenth Century* (Boston: Colonial Society of Massachusetts, 1974), p. 39;

Grant Petty Ledger, 1755–1762, pp. 11, 86; and Grant Petty Ledger, 1762–1771, pp. 74, 157. The two tanners were Joseph Calef and Samuel Bass, Jr. The majority of surviving colonial New England furniture with original leather upholstery is covered in undyed brown calfskin that has darkened with age and later waxing and varnishing. Nevertheless, documentation for dyed leather seats can often be found. On December 6, 1731, Samuel Grant billed one customer for "8 Leath Chairs [with] large black Seats doub[le] naild 28/[shillings per chair]." Grant Account Book, 1728–1737, p. 124. On August 30, 1737, Grant purchased from Joseph Calef "9 red Sile Skins [for] mak^g 25 Seats @ 5/6 [per seat]." Grant Account Book, 1728–1737, p. 601. Some leather seats were even dyed blue. *Boston Gazette*, November 13, 1758, p. 3.

20. Thomas Fitch to William and John Crouch and Company, March 19, 1705, Fitch Letterbook.

21. For eighteenth-century illustrations of line and tassels in use, *see* Montgomery, *Textiles in America*, pp. 20, 30, 53, 55; and Florence M. Montgomery, *Printed Textiles: English and American Cottons and Linens 1700–1850* (New York: Viking Press, 1970), pp. 49–63, 66–75.

22. Thomas Fitch to Eleazer Folger, April 15, 1706, Fitch Letterbook.

23. Thomas Fitch to Thomas Danforth, November 2, 1705, Fitch Letterbook.

24. *See* Grant Account Book, 1728–1737, pp. 32, 208.

25. Inventory of Thomas Baxter, Suffolk County Probate Court, docket 9695.

26. Grant Account Book, 1737–1760, p. 817.

27. Inventory of Theodore Wheelwright, Suffolk County Probate Court, vol. 44, p. 399.

28. For an excellent illustration of curtain rings in use, *see* William Hogarth's engraving, *After*, published in 1736 and depicted in Montgomery, *Textiles in America*, fig. 21.

29. Jobe, "The Boston Furniture Industry," pp. 26–27, 32–34.

30. *See* note 9.

31. In 1755, Grant usually charged £0:15:0 [L.M.] for a straw mattress; a fully outfitted bed could exceed £15:0:0. On October 7, 1756, he billed Epes Sargent of Gloucester, Massachusetts, for a "Green Harrateen shape bed" costing £17:15:4: Grant Account Book, 1737–1760, p. 833.

32. Numerous references to all eight individuals appear in Grant's Petty Ledgers. George Bright was the most productive of the group. For example, between October 13, 1756, and August 20, 1757, he made seven bedsteads: Grant Petty Ledger, 1755–1762, p. 55.

33. Grant Petty Ledger, 1762–1771, p. 37. The restricted areas for Skillin's carving implies that the chairmaker carved the feet and knees of the frame.

34. Montgomery, *Textiles in America*, figs. 23, 24.

35. Chippendale illustrates a variety of carved headboards and cornices in plates 37–48 of *The Gentleman and Cabinet-Maker's Director*.

36. Between 1755 and 1771, Grant purchased bed bottoms from Thomas Kemble. *See*, for example, Grant Petty Ledger, 1755–1762, p. 132.

37. Pins were usually mounted into the top edge of the rails. *See* Barry A. Greenlaw, *New England Furniture at Williamsburg* (Williamsburg: Colonial Williamsburg Foundation, 1974), pp. 22, 25. Occasionally, however, craftsmen chose another method for securing the pins. A slot was cut along the inside edge of each rail, pins were driven through the rail, and the cord to fasten the bottom was laced around the portion of the pins visible in the slot. *See* Jobe and Kaye, *New England Furniture*, pp. 445–47.

38. Between September 1758 and March 1759, John Grant made 886 "beds" and at least 227 bolsters for Samuel Grant. The vast majority of the beds were nothing more than straw mattresses. A few, however, must have been feather ticks for elegant high-post bedsteads. John Grant's charge for the work averaged about four pence [L.M.] per bed and one pence [L.M.] per bolster. Also making mattresses for Grant were Elizabeth Grant and Elizabeth Kemble. The latter seems to have specialized in fine bedding. In 1766, she billed Grant twelve shillings for "mak^g 6 Beds Bolsters & pillowes." Her average charge of two shillings for each set of bedding was over four times greater than John Grant's. Grant Petty Ledger, 1755–1762, p. 80; and Petty Ledger, 1762–1771, p. 86.

39. The use of two mattresses for an elegant bedstead is suggested by Thomas Hancock's purchase in 1757 of the following:

An Ozn^a[brig] Matt[res]^s	2:2:–
a feather Bed and Bedstead	8:1:4
	10:3:4[L.M.]

Grant Account Book, 1737–1760, p. 842. *See also*, pp. 877, 893. The use of two mattresses follows English custom of the period. Chippendale, for example, billed a patron in 1769 for:

A Featherbed & Bolster of very Good feathers	7: 7:–
2 fine down Pillows	1: 4:–
A White Flock Mattrass	1:13:–
	10: 4:–[sterling]

Quoted in Christopher Gilbert, *The Life and Work of Thomas Chippendale* (New York: Macmillan Publishing Company, 1978), vol. 1, p. 231.

40. The quantity and price of the feathers in a feather tick, bolster, and pillows is documented in Grant's bill to James Apthorp:

a Bedstead & Bottom	2:—:–
55 ^{lb}[pounds] feathers	5:10:–
th[rea]^d & mak^g bed bolster + pillows	: 4:8
	7:14:8[L.M.]

Grant Account Book, 1737–1760, p. 896.

41. Grant Account Book, 1728–1737, p. 190.

42. Diderot depicted four seamstresses sewing at a table in his view of a French establishment (this volume, fig. 41). Robert Campbell reported that in London such tasks as cutting out a valance or counterpane are all "part of the Work . . . performed by Women." Campbell, *London Tradesman*, p. 170.

43. Grant Petty Ledger, 1762–1771, pp. 86, 101. Kemble's output in 1767 is unspecified. In Grant's ledger, she is simply credited for "mak^g Curtains" valued at £5:5:10 [L.M.]. This total is larger than that for either 1766 (when she received £4:0:4 for forty-eight sets of curtains) or 1768 (when she received £3:10:7½ for thirty-nine sets of curtains) and probably represents the production of over sixty sets of curtains.

44. Campbell noted the meager wages of English seamstresses "a tradesman who is a good Hand in the Upholder's own Branch is paid Twelve or Fifteen Shillings a Week; and the Women, if good for any thing, get a Shilling a Day." Campbell, *London Tradesman*, pp. 170–71.

45. For the range in curtain prices, *see* Grant Account Book, 1737–1760, pp. 856, 881, 909–10.

46. Curtains suspended from rods are depicted in William Hogarth's 1736 engraving, *After*. (*See* fn. 28.) For a reference to Grant's use of ceiling screws, *see* Grant Account Book, 1728–1737, p. 119. For an illustration documenting their use, *see* William Hogarth's 1730 engraving, *The Harlot's Progress: Apprehension by a Magistrate*, depicted in R. B. Beckett, *Hogarth* (London: Routledge and Kegan Paul Ltd., 1949), pl. 47. Ceiling screws can still be found in several New England eighteenth-century houses such as the Golden Ball Tavern, now a museum in Weston, Massachusetts.

47. When describing his designs of four field beds, Chippendale commented that the "furniture [i.e. hangings] . . . is made to take off." Chippendale, *Cabinet-Maker's Director*, p. 7, description of plate 49.

48. Grant Account Book, 1728–1737, p. 159.

49. John Bright, a Boston upholsterer, used the term in an advertisement in the *Massachusetts Centinel and the Republican Journal*, September 25, 1784, p. 3.

50. Montgomery, *Textiles in America*, figs. 11A,B; 12A,B; 18. For the placement of pulleys in the laths, *see* Chippendale's plans for laths designed for a single swag and for a double swag. *Cabinet-Maker's Director*, pls. 44 and 41.

51. Grant Account Book, 1737–1760, p. 814.

52. The blacksmiths listed in Grant's petty ledgers were Elkanah Hawks of Lynn and Samuel Davis of Boston. Petty Ledger, 1755–1762, pp. 27, 44, 109; Petty Ledger, 1762–1771, pp. 4, 49, 67, 159. Each supplied Grant with sets of "fil[e]d" rods, bed screws, and pins as well as an occasional shovel or set of base hooks. Grant also obtained bed screws from Boston merchants Isaac Smith and Benjamin Dolbear. Grant Account Book, 1737–1760, pp. 781, 786, 853.

53. The complete bill to Bourn lists the following:

a mohogeny beds⁺ castʳ Scres bottᵐ + c	5: 7: 4
Materˡˢ + makᵍ a damask bed	10:14:9½
a box 8/ blank ⁺ 6/ to pack in	–:14: –
	16:16:1½[L.M.]

Grant Account Book, 1737–1760, p. 875.

54. Grant Account Book, 1737–1760, p. 97.

55. Nancy Goyne Evans, "The Genealogy of a Bookcase Desk," in Ian M. G. Quimby, ed., *Winterthur Portfolio 9* (Charlottesville: University of Virginia, 1974), p. 217.

56. The farmer was Henry Howell Williams; the ship captains included Silas Atkins, Samuel Paddock, Jonathan Freeman, Robert Gould, and Nathaniel Stone. Grant Petty Ledger, 1755–1762, pp. 49, 79, 140; Petty Ledger, 1762–1771, pp. 46, 53, 100.

57. Samuel Ridgeway, a Boston chairmaker, charged one pound in 1732 for "4 Chairs 3 Backs." The reference to "3 Backs" indicates that each chair had three slats. The price per chair was five shillings. Grant Account Book, 1728–1737, p. 173.

58. Jobe, "The Boston Furniture Industry," p. 42.

59. Grant Account Book, 1728–1737, p. 316; Account Book, 1737–1760, p. 507.

60. Grant Account Book, 1737–1760, p. 808.

61. Grant did not record a price for the finished chair. However, in his petty ledgers, he noted a payment of £1:4:0 [L.M.] to William Perkins for the chair frame. *See* Grant Account Book, 1737–1760, p. 842; and Petty Ledger, 1755–1762, p. 37.

62. For additional information on the four items, *see* Jobe and Kaye, *New England Furniture*, pp. 362–64, 389–91, 411–12, 437–39.

63. In the same year, Grant charged 3:10:0 for a leather armchair. Grant Account Book, 1737–1760, pp. 346, 363.

64. The three include the Grant cradle, one dated 1730 that descended in the family of Governor Joseph Dudley of Massachusetts and is now owned by the Massachusetts Historical Society, and one dated 1735 that descended in the family of William Heath of Roxbury and is now owned by the Society for the Preservation of New England Antiquities. *See* Jobe and Kaye, *New England Furniture*, pp. 438–39.

65. Jobe and Kaye, *New England Furniture*, pp. 362–63.

66. Bright's bill is illustrated in Jobe and Kaye, *New England Furniture*, p. 145.

67. The bill refers to two sets of chairs "Stufft in Canvis." The price per chair was £1:4:0 for one set, £1:6:8 for the other. Jobe and Kaye, *New England Furniture*, p. 145.

68. Peter Thornton, "Fringe Benefits," *The Connoisseur* 196 (September 1977): p. 2.

68. A view of the back stool before upholstering. All nails of modern
origin have been removed, but any period tacks or nail shanks that
remained are left as a document. Note that the triangular peak at the
top of each front leg projects above the rails. The height of the seat
upholstery is determined by the line struck between the top of the
peak and the bottom of the lower rail on the back frame. The peak is
usually ¼ inch to ½ inch higher than the bottom of the back's lower
rail, creating a slight backward slope in the seat. This photograph and
all the others in this essay courtesy, Colonial Williamsburg Foundation.

90

The Technique of 18th-Century Over-the-rail Upholstery

Wallace Gusler, Leroy Graves, and Mark Anderson

THE FOLLOWING pictorial essay documents the steps involved in doing over-the-rail upholstery according to methods of the mid-eighteenth century. The photographs are of three different chairs—two are old back stools, and one is a reproduction. Taken together, they illustrate the steps involved in the complete upholstering of a back stool.

Figure 68 shows the stripped frame of one English back stool from a set of fourteen owned by Colonial Williamsburg. Made in about 1770, this chair has a frame of mahogany and beech. Careful analysis of all the chairs provided evidence of the methods used for side webbing, French stitching, covering fabric, and looped tufting. The photographs in this essay, and others taken during the reupholstery process, and written conservation reports have become important sources of information on this set of back stools.

Figures 69 and 70 portray the early steps of foundation work in the reupholstering of a second set of eighteenth-century English chairs in the Colonial Williamsburg collections. Figures 71 through 80 show one of a set of reproduction back stools made by Mac Headley of Colonial Williamsburg for the entrance hall of the Governor's Palace at Colonial Williamsburg. The reproduction is based on the 1770 chair shown in figure 68. Reproductions were deemed necessary for reasons of both scholarly evidence and intended use. New upholstery of the old frames would cover up important evidence found on each of the frames. The placement of the back stools in a public area with extensive visitor traffic, where the potential for damage was great, also made the use of reproductions advisable.

69. The girt webbing bottom or support webbing of linen is nailed to the frame in the traditional English style; that is, the interwoven webbing does not completely cover the seat area but leaves space between adjacent bands of linen webbing. An exterior band of webbing, the "side webbing," is nailed along the face of the seat rails. This webbing extends above the rail; its height is determined by the corner peak of the front leg and bottom rail of the back. (The use of side webbing became obsolete during the second half of the nineteenth century; all we know about the process is derived from fragmentary surviving evidence.)

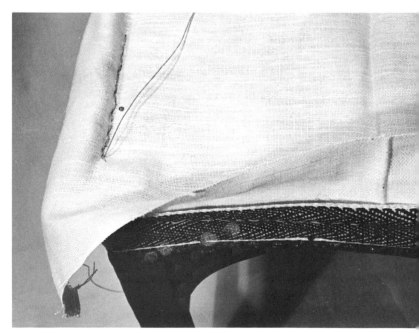

70. The "bottom linen," a coarsely woven heavy sackcloth, is tacked to the top of the seat rails over the bottom webbing and stitched to the side webbing. Several inches of the linen extend beyond the rails. The sackcloth thus forms a seat cavity defined by the side webbing and the interwoven bottom support webbing. The back is formed in a similar fashion.

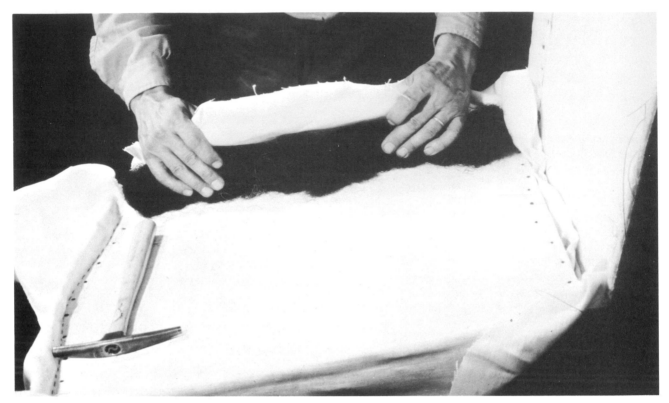

71. The remainder of the extra flap is pulled tightly around a roll of curled horse hair.

72. The flap is then nailed down to the top of the seat rails. The resulting tube of hair is called a "French roll," and when stitched to the side webbing, it forms the completed "French edge." On the chair's back, a French edge is constructed along the crest and the sides.

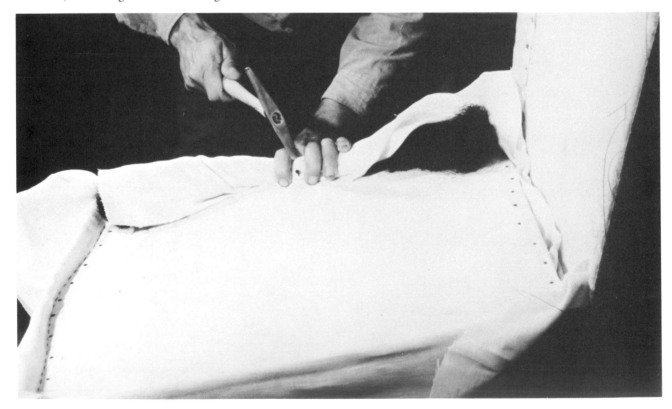

73. The French roll is tightly stitched into the side webbing using a saddle stitch in three rows along the length of the roll. In addition, a series of stepped-off saddle stitches, at right angles to the rows, add strength to the French edge and keep it from crumpling under weight. This photograph illustrates the saddle stitching in the upper left-hand corner of the back.

74. For the back, a stiffer bottom edge is desirable to define and hold the line where the covering of the chair back meets the covering of the seat. This is achieved by using a linen-covered roll of dry marsh grass (Juncus sp.) that is trimmed to fit between the French edge of the sides and is then tacked in place. Care is taken to make sure that the roll of marsh grass is exactly the same height as the French edge on the sides of the back frame. The seat and back cavities are now complete and ready to receive the curled hair stuffing. (Note the saddle stitches along the inside surface of the seat's French edge.)

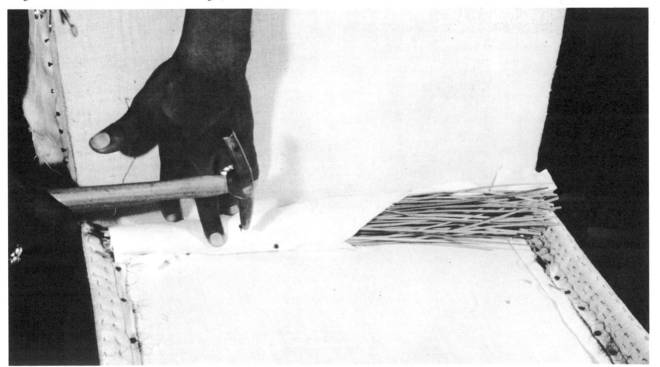

75. The seat is filled with curled hair and arranged to provide the proper loft and cushion. A network of quilting stitches holds the hair to the bottom linen and prevents it from shifting.

76. The "top linen," a tightly woven, medium-weight cloth, is stretched over the hair cushion and temporarily tacked, or baste tacked to the side rails.

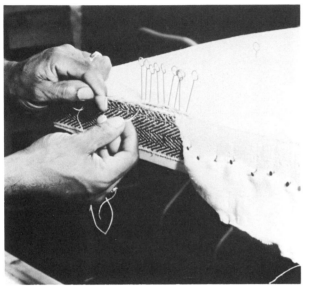

77. The line where the linen touches the top of the side webbing is marked by rubbing a pencil along this edge. This line indicates where the top linen will be stitched to the side webbing. (In Victorian and modern upholstery, the top linen is simply stretched over a French roll and nailed to the rails.) The union of the top linen and the French edge is accomplished a few inches at a time. The linen is trimmed back to ¼ inch from the lip of the French edge. It is then folded under and secured with upholstery pins where it meets the side webbing. The seam is then sewn using a tight, closely spaced whipstitch.

78. By trimming, pinning, and stitching, the top linen is gradually secured to the French edge on the front and sides of the seat. The flap of linen at the rear of the seat, which passes under the lower rail of the back frame, is freed from its temporary tacking. A small amount of additional hair may be added to the back of the seat to maintain the correct slope front to back and the clean line of the rear seat edge. Then the flap is pulled tight and nailed permanently to the back of the rear seat rail. (The adjusting and fastening of this rear edge is not illustrated.)

79. The back stool, stuffed and covered in linen, is ready for the final covering.

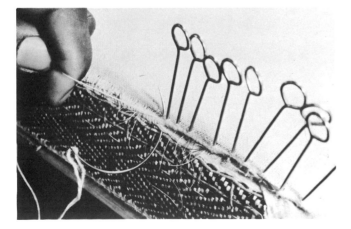

80. In the final procedure, silk damask covers the top of the seat and is lapped over the rails where it is tacked along the underside of the rails. A corded edge (piping) is blind-stitched to the French edge, and continuous rows of brass nails securely anchor the fabric at the top and bottom of the rails. The front surface of the chair back is covered in a similar manner: The fabric is pulled over the edges and tacked along the back side of the top, side, and bottom rails; and the corded edge is stitched in place. However, brass nails are not used at this point. The upholsterer first decorates the seat and back with looped tufting, which is anchored in the linen foundation. Next, the craftsman baste tacks silk damask on the backside of the chairback so that the fabric just turns the back edges. Finally he uses a single row of brass nails along the sides and crest rail.

The back of the chair is covered in a manner similar to that of the seat. Looped tufting completes the seat and back. (The looped tufting is derived from eighteenth-century paintings.)

Finished in crimson silk damask, the back stool exemplifies the upholstered approach illustrated in Chippendale's *The Gentleman and Cabinet-Maker's Director*. The elaborate and extremely tight stitching of the French edge resists compression and preserves the clean lines of the design. This finished upholstery technique firmly binds all layers of fabric, preventing them from shifting or moving out of shape. The aim of creating a finished product with a very low profile and crisp lines is well achieved through the use of the French edge.

81. Easy chair, Massachusetts, 1760–1790. Mahogany and maple. Shown as upholstered in modern wool damask, c. 1950. Height-45 inches, width-35¾ inches, depth-27 inches. Courtesy, The Metropolitan Museum of Art. Bequest of Flora M. Whiting. Photograph by Richard Cheek.

18th-Century American Upholstery Techniques: Easy Chairs, Sofas, and Settees

Morrison H. Heckscher

WHILE the basic facts about the outermost or finish fabrics of New England and Philadelphia upholstered seating furniture of the Queen Anne and Chippendale styles are well-known, similar information about the upholstery work itself is little understood.[1] There remain crucial questions about the foundation process. How did the upholsterer build up the form underneath the finish fabric? What materials did he use? What shapes and contours did he achieve? How did he treat the seams and edges once he had put on the finish fabric?

Written documents of the period are not much help to those who want to reupholster an antique easy chair or sofa and seek to recapture its original look. Written records only list the materials that upholsterers used. Contemporary illustrations are not very useful either. Portraits by John Singleton Copley and other painters reveal only the general outlines of furniture. The most dependable answers to these questions about upholstery foundations are obtained by examining furniture on which the original upholstery remains more or less intact.

Easy Chairs

The results of such an examination can be seen by comparing before and after photographs of a Massachusetts easy chair. Figure 81 shows the chair as it looked when acquired by The Metropolitan Museum of Art in 1971 as a bequest of the well-known collector, Flora E. Whiting. For use in the drawing room of her New York apartment, it was stripped to the bare frame, restuffed, and covered with an appropriate modern gold-colored wool damask by a master upholsterer. Figure 82 shows the same chair today, as displayed in the Almodington Room of the American Wing, a period room furnished as a Massachusetts Chippendale bedroom. In preparation for this new role, it was stripped again, restuffed, and recovered by Charles Anello, the museum upholsterer. Following eighteenth-century practice, he covered the chair with the same material as all the upholstery work in the room: in the winter, a raspberry red worsted with watered, waved, and figured designs pressed in (fig. 82), and in the summer, a green and white cotton check slipcover.

In material, color, and pattern, both new finish fabrics are painstaking reproductions of eighteenth-century fragments.[2] As such, they are somewhat more authentic than the reproduction damask available to Mrs. Whiting more than twenty years ago. But more fundamental, and indeed more controversial, is the difference in the

82. The same chair as in figure 81. Reupholstered in reproduction worsted, 1980.

shape of the chair now that the stuffing has been redone. The wings and the arms are much more heavily padded, and the seat cushion fuller. It can be argued that the chair now has lost some of its former trim elegance. This new shape, however, is based upon verifiable eighteenth-century practice and copies as closely as possible the treatment of a chair in the Brooklyn Museum that retains its original cover. (*See* figure 87.) In fact, there was a consistent, functionally based eighteenth-century style of stuffing and shaping easy chairs and sofas. That style differs substantially from generally accepted modern practice.

It may be well to begin by tracing the steps followed by eighteenth-century upholsterers in building up the stuffed foundations of easy chairs. A Massachusetts example at the Winterthur Museum, not unlike the one at the Metropolitan, had most of the original stuffing on the back, wings, and arms when the chair was acquired in 1970 (fig. 83). During the removal of the stuffing, a series of instructive photographs was taken (figs. 83–86). By studying these, in more or less the reverse order from which they were taken, we can follow the process of the upholsterer's art.

The upholsterer began by nailing webbing to the inside surfaces of the back (fig. 84), seat, and sometimes (although not here) the wings and arms. Narrow strips of webbing were interlaced to form an open lattice, in the English manner. (A rare exception to this rule is the chair illustrated in figure 96, with all-over broad strips of webbing tightly interwoven in the French manner.) The upholsterer then nailed a layer of coarse canvas over the webbing; this can also be seen in figure 84. Next, he built up the top edges of the wings and arms with tight rolls of marsh grass bound with canvas and nailed in place (fig. 85). At the same time, although it does not survive on this chair, the upholsterer applied a similar roll of straw to the front seat rail. The placement of these rolls inside the flat front edge of the wings and arms and on the top of the seat rail leaves the sharp outer edges unstuffed and clearly defined, as shown in figures 83 and 85.

The upholsterer then filled the cavities defined by the rolls of grasses with ample quantities of curled hair, laid a second layer of canvas on top, stretched it taut around the framing elements, and nailed it in place (fig. 86). He also stuffed the back, but because there was no defining roll at the top, he made the hair thicker at the center, tapering off toward the edges to follow the angle of the bevelled top of the crest rail. To ensure the stability of his work, the upholsterer tied the webbing, canvas, and stuffing together with large loops of heavy linen twine, bits of which are visible in figure 84. Dimples on the back of the chair at the left in figure 85 suggest that the twine may have also been used to tuft the chairback but that was not a common practice on American chairs.[3] Finally, as the last step in preparation for the finish fabric, he made a large and puffy seat cushion filled with down or what one contemporary called "live goose feathers."

We can be confident of the existence of this cushion and even get a reliable idea of what the whole chair must have originally looked like by studying two somewhat earlier but similar New England chairs that have survived virtually intact. One, at the Brooklyn Museum, retains its original watered, waved, and pressed red moreen cover (fig. 87). The other, at the Metropolitan Museum, is covered in its original Irish stitch needlework (fig. 88). Together these chairs provide the most important primary documentation of American easy chair upholstery work. On both pieces, the stuffing—

83. Easy chair, Massachusetts, 1760–1790. Mahogany and maple. Shown prior to the removal of the original padding and canvas on the back and wings. Height-45¼ inches, width-34 inches, depth-33 inches. Courtesy, The Henry Francis duPont Winterthur Museum.

84. Detail of easy chair in figure 83. An outside view of the back showing the original webbing and the layer of coarse canvas that was laid over the webbing and nailed to the frame.

85. Detail of easy chair in figure 83. The right wing with foundation canvas and rolled straw border.

86. Detail of easy chair in figure 83, showing the curled hair stuffing and canvas cover for the right wing.

87. Easy chair, New England, 1730–1790. Walnut and maple, with original worsted covering. Height-48 inches, width-35¼ inches, depth-34 inches. Courtesy, Brooklyn Museum. Henry Batterman Fund.

88. Easy chair, Newport, 1758. Walnut and maple, with the original Irish stitch needlework upholstery. Height-46¼ inches, width-32¼ inches, depth-26 inches. Courtesy, The Metropolitan Museum of Art. Gift of Mrs. J. Insley Blair.

firmly packed and tightly corseted by the covering canvas and finish fabric—has retained its original shape. (Because the original covering binds the upholstery so firmly, there is no way, as occasionally has been suggested, that the present shape could result from sagging.) On the inside, the profile is comfortably plump. The wings and arms bulge boldly beyond the tightly rolled straw edges, only to be drawn in tightly again at the juncture with the back, except at the top of the wing where the rolled straw edging prevents it. The cushion is very thick—its side panels are more than four inches high—and the top puffed up like a pillow (fig. 92).

On both chairs, the upholstery treatment of the outside is altogether different from that of the inside. The bulging padding on the inner surface of the arms tapers off to nothing as it comes around to the outer

surface of the conical arm supports. Similarly, the canvas and finish fabric covers of the seat deck (beneath the cushion) are pulled over the rolled grass on the top of the seat rail, drawn tightly across the bare wood of the front edge of the seat rail, and nailed underneath. The fabric panels on the back and sides are stretched taut over the wooden frame (figs. 89 and 90). The top edges of the back, wings, and armrests have virtually no padding at all, and there is very little on the front surface of the arms. Consequently, whether seen straight on (*see* figure 88) or at an angle (*see* figure 87) these chairs exhibit the graceful, sharp outlines of their wooden frames, despite being amply padded inside.

These two New England chairs are invaluable documents for another reason: Each has remnants of the ornamental finishing details originally employed over the outer fabric. From them we learn that it was customary to cover exposed seams with ornamental woven tape, usually about an inch wide. On the plump inside

89. The rear view of easy chair in figure 87 showing the back and side panels with remnants of the tape covering the seams.

90. The rear view of easy chair in figure 88 showing crewel work back panel and tape-covered seams of side panels.

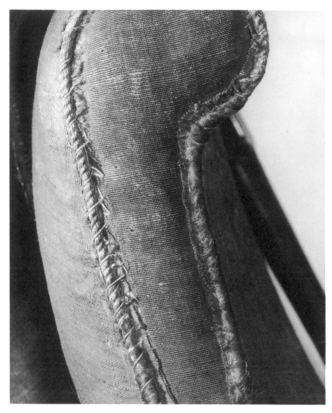

91. Detail of easy chair in figure 87. The welting and silk tape on the left armrest.

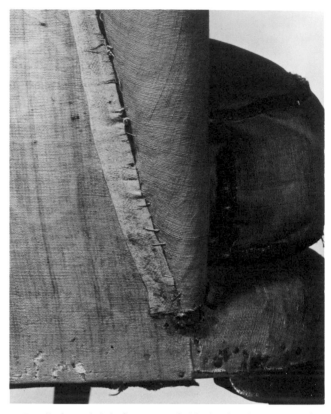

93. Detail of easy chair in figure 87. Left side showing the ornamental tape.

92. Detail of easy chair in figure 88. The seat cushion, in profile, with worsted side panels and raised seams.

surfaces of the chair in figure 87, tape sewn over welting or a thick cord (one-quarter inch in diameter) formed a raised border around the narrow strip of fabric that fronted the wing and armrest and was continued across the top of the crest rail. Figure 91 shows a well-preserved fragment of the red silk tape on the left armrest of the Brooklyn chair. On the Metropolitan chair, some of the welting but none of its covering tape remains. Tape was also employed on the seat cushion, but there the raised seams made cording unnecessary (fig. 92).

On the outside surfaces of the chairs, the tape was laid flat, either sewn or glued in place. Portions of tape survive on the back corners of the Brooklyn chair (*see* figure 89), at the backs of the conical armrests, and along the side seat rails of both chairs (figs. 93 and 94). Originally this tape was also carried around onto the front seat rails, but only as far as the legs and their knee brackets. (*See* figure 87). It served to cover the roseheaded nails used to secure the upholstery above the legs. (For a reconstruction of the original effect, *see* figure 82.) Because the tape on the side rails of the Metropolitan chair consists of two parts, it is worthy of special note (*see* figure 94). The primary strip of green silk, with geometric designs woven in yellow, was glued down first. Centered on top of this is a narrow secon-

dary tape, now black but originally probably silver. It was secured in place with round-headed iron nails, widely spaced.

In spite of their very different fabrics, these two chairs demonstrate remarkably similar upholstery techniques, both in shaping and finishing, strongly suggesting a consistent approach to upholstery work in eighteenth-century New England. Three additional examples corroborate this idea. The first is a Rhode Island chair that, prior to reupholstery, was photographed with its original blue wool moreen cover. (The seat and cushion had been recovered, but they still retained a correct period appearance.[4]) The second is a Massachusetts chair in the Bayou Bend Collection.[5] This chair is covered with needlework similar to that on the Metropolitan's Newport chair, and the profiles of its wings and back conform to our expectations; however, the lack of any welting and tape on the seams of the wings and on the raised seams on the cushion is uncharacteristic, and the cushion itself is flatter than expected. The fact that the cushion was disassembled and portions of the fabric were removed for cleaning and restoration some years ago may account for these differences.[6] The third chair, also with its original needlework covering, is at Winterthur. About 1930, it was stripped to the frame and restuffed, but not before a photograph had been taken showing its upholstery intact except for the missing cushion. At that time, the welting and tape on the arms and wings were well preserved.[7]

An additional fact gleaned from the study of all these New England chairs is that a different—usually less expensive—fabric was sometimes used on the back panel and other areas not readily seen from the front. The fronts and sides of the Metropolitan and Bayou Bend chairs are both covered with laboriously wrought Irish stitch, but the back of the former bears a landscape design worked in crewel, and that of the latter bears a faded red moreen with figured designs not unlike that used all over the Brooklyn chair. Similarly, figured moreens are employed for the side panels of the cushions of both chairs. (*See* figure 92.)[8]

Recently, two other New England Queen Anne easy chairs with original upholstery intact have been discovered.[9] In almost every respect, the upholstery on these chairs conforms to the methods heretofore described. The first, a Boston chair now at the Wadsworth Atheneum, retains the original dark green moreen covering on its back, wings, and arms. The second, a Newport chair presently owned by the Colonel Daniel

94. Detail of easy chair in figure 88. Left side showing the ornamental tape.

95. Easy chair, Philadelphia, 1765–1790. Mahogany, pine and poplar,
with original padding and canvas on the back, wings, and arms. The
damask covering the left half is of later date. Height-45½ inches,
width-36⅜ inches, depth-24½ inches. Courtesy, Collection of Peter
W. Eliot. Photograph by Richard Cheek.

Putnam Association in Brooklyn, Connecticut, was brought from Newport to Brooklyn in 1766 by Godfrey Malbone. Except for the missing back covering, its upholstery is virtually intact.

The red moreen covering and the binding tape of the Malbone chair are nearly identical to those on the Brooklyn Museum chair. The binding on the Malbone cushion is better preserved, and the welt on its crest forms a false crest like that of the Metropolitan chair in figure 88. The only significant difference is the shaping of the inside of its wings. Here the wings appear hollowed out behind the rolled edges, rather than plumply padded as in the chairs in figures 87 and 88; however, the wing stuffing looks to have lost its original shape, as did the chair's back, whose grass stuffing had subsided prior to restoration. Nevertheless, when compared to the straight and narrow profile of the wings in modern practice (*see* figure 81), there is nothing lean about this and other eighteenth-century chairs.

Thus far, we have confined our discussion to Queen Anne and Chippendale easy chairs of New England (1730–1790). Virtually all of them—whether made in Massachusetts or Rhode Island—are variations on one pattern or design: The legs are joined by turned stretchers and the arms terminate in vertical cone-like supports. The other great center for the manufacture of easy chairs was Philadelphia, where an equally distinctive local design held sway. On Philadelphia easy chairs, the legs are without stretchers, the front seat rails are curved to form a segment of a circle, and the arms terminate in bold *C*-scrolls.

No Philadelphia chair appears to have survived with its original fabric *in situ*, with its original cushion, or with any evidence of the original welting cords or ornamental tape used on seams.[10] On the other hand, over the years a number of easy chairs with the stuffing more or less intact have turned up, and at least three of these still have most of the original stuffing. They are in the collections of Peter Eliot (fig. 95); the dealer Joe Kindig, III; and the Colonial Williamsburg Foundation (fig. 96).[11] Photographs exist showing some other Philadelphia chairs, including one at The Metropolitan Museum (fig. 98), before the original upholstery was removed.

The shapes and profiles of the upholstery work on all these chairs are similar, not only to each other but also to the New England work already seen: The backs bow out slightly, and the wings bulge inward prominently; yet, the edges of the wings and the crest rails are bare but for the canvas cover. In addition, the method of upholstering some of these chairs is identical to that used on the New England examples. In figure 95, for example, the padding is contained within canvas covers that are stretched over the inner back and sides and nailed to the frame. No canvas covered the outer back and sides. Fragments of the original finish fabric, a red worsted, survive under the upholsterer's roseheaded nails.[12]

On some of the other examples, however, the canvas was applied in a different manner. Both inside and outside were encased in canvas, the different pieces of which were neatly sewn together. The result is a crisply defined and tightly fitted canvas cover. Figures 96 and 97 show such a padded inside surface; figure 98 shows an outside one. When a removable slipcover, instead of a nailed-down, permanent finish fabric, was intended, this treatment provided the necessary foundation.

Our knowledge of such slipcovers is scant. Although the accounts of Philadelphia upholsterers are full of references to them, it would seem that no surviving eighteenth-century American examples exist. In 1771, Plunket Fleeson billed John Cadwalader for "an Easy Chair - finishing in canvis & making Case £1-5-0."[13] Here the slipcover was called a "case," and the charge was for labor only. About half of the surviving examples of Philadelphia upholstered seating furniture were intended to have slipcovers, the other half permanent covers.

Slipcovers were also popular in New England. In addition to references to them in the accounts of the Boston upholsterer Samuel Grant, two New England Federal period easy chairs with the original canvas covering but without their slipcovers are known.[14] What these chairs looked like when covered can best be judged from contemporary paintings.[15]

It is well known that the woolen or silk fabrics that covered upholstered furniture in eighteenth-century America were costly imports. It is surprising, however, to learn from surviving accounts of New England and Pennsylvania upholsterers that the humble materials used to stuff an easy chair—the webbing, canvas, and hair—were also expensive, often costing more than the chair frame itself. For example, in 1731 Grant itemized his charges for an easy chair as follows: The wooden frame cost £1-17-6; the materials required to pad or stuff the frame (webbing, canvas, curled hair, and feathers) cost £2-5-8; the outer fabric and decorative braid cost £3-1-6; and the labor involved in the upholstery added an additional £1-16-0, for a total cost of £9-0–8.[16] Similarly, in Philadelphia in 1754, the cabinetmaker John

96. Easy chair, Philadelphia, 1750–1780. Mahogany, yellow pine, and poplar, with original padding and canvas on the back and wings. Height-46¾ inches, width-39 inches, depth-29½ inches. Courtesy, Colonial Williamsburg Foundation.

97. Detail of easy chair in figure 96, showing the profile of the padding of the right wing.

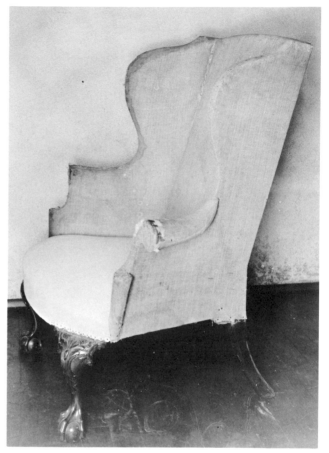

98. Easy chair, Philadelphia, 1760–1790. Mahogany, yellow pine and poplar. Prior to the removal of the original stuffing and fitted canvas case (except for the seat, which is new). Height-46 inches, width-37 inches, depth-28¼ inches. Courtesy, The Metropolitan Museum of Art. Gift of Mrs. C. F. Dickson.

Elliott charged a total of £8-6-11 for an easy chair with carved claws and knees. Of this, £1-16-0 was for the frame, £2-0–8 for stuffing materials, £3-4-3 for finish fabric, and £1-6-0 for labor.[17] In both instances, the upholstery accounted for more than seventy-five percent of the cost of the piece.

From our examination of New England and Pennsylvania easy chairs, we can reasonably conclude that easy chair frames were treated by all upholsterers in very much the same way: The inner surfaces were built up with padding, and the outsides and edges were left virtually bare, letting the shape of the wooden frame speak for itself. There must have been a compelling reason for such remarkable consistency, and the answer probably has to do with the original function of such furniture.

It is well known that in the eighteenth century easy chairs were, for the most part, bedroom furniture and designed for comfort.[18] They were big enough for one to move around in comfortably, with wings to deflect drafts and against which to rest one's head, and they often came equipped with casters for ready mobility or even with plumbing (a commode or "close stool" in the seat) so that, for example, elderly or sick people could sit in one all day. Perhaps the most perfect illustration of these functions is a newly discovered Federal-style Philadelphia easy chair (fig. 99). Its original slipcover and loose seat cushion are missing; otherwise, the

99. Easy chair, Philadelphia, 1790–1800. Mahogany and yellow pine, with the original padding and canvas. Height-45 inches, width-33 inches, depth-34½ inches. Courtesy, The Metropolitan Museum of Art. On loan from the Wunsch Americana Foundation.

canvas-covered upholstery foundation is intact, even to the padded commode opening. In a harsh world, easy chairs provided a haven of comfort. Consequently, the inner surfaces, where the sitter might rest, had to be thickly padded.

That harsh world, however, was also a world where beauty counted. The owners of New England and Philadelphia Queen Anne and Chippendale side chairs, forms so noteworthy for their simple elegance and grace, would have expected similar graceful lines in their upholstered chairs. Thus the outsides, which determine the profile and stance, had to be crisp, clean, and free of stuffing.

As time passed and fashions changed, so did the functions of upholstered furniture. By the middle of the

nineteenth century, the easy chair was relegated to the attic or, in more conservative households, updated with springs in the seat and modern fabrics added over the back and arms. Many of these chairs remained in this condition until, with the rise to respectability of antiques in this century, they were brought proudly into view in collectors' living rooms and parlors. For their new function as chairs for casual sitting, they have generally been stripped to the frame, with the casters and any earthy plumbing arrangements removed, and then reupholstered in a clean, spare style that appeals to modern taste. (*See* figure 81.) After all, as Albert Sack noted in his classic and pioneering book on American furniture, "No collector demands or desires the original upholstery on an antique wing chair or sofa, but he does require the original framework."[19]

That was written in 1950. Today, with examples of original upholstery growing more scarce every day, we might want to reconsider. At least we should remember that in the eighteenth century the upholstery materials and labor cost far more than the chair and that the upholsterer was as much a master craftsman as the chairmaker. Anyone fortunate enough today to find a chair with the stuffing intact should insist that the old material be left in place and new upholstery added around it as required.

Sofas and Settees

Eighteenth-century American sofas and settees, unlike easy chairs, were designed more for luxury and display than for utility. They were uncommon then, and they are even rarer today. In contemporary inventories, they normally appear only in the parlors of the finer houses, most often covered with costly silks. A portrait painted by Copley in New York in 1771 (*see* figure 39) depicts an elegant lady lounging languidly on a sofa that is upholstered in red silk damask and piled with plump pillows. While no other sitters pose so luxuriously as does Copley's lady, a number of other colonial portraits depict sofas, and all have one feature in common: The damask upholstery is always highlighted with brass-headed nails outlining the arms, seat rails, and crest rail. That this was not merely an artistic convention or fancy is attested by the newspaper account of what happened when lightning struck "Mr. Callows house in Wall Street," New York in June of 1762:

> It came down the Chimney, and run along the Brass Nails that was in a Settee near the Hearth, blackening the Heads of all of them; it then entered the Settee, shivered it to Pieces, and took its course thro' the Hearth into the Cellar.[20]

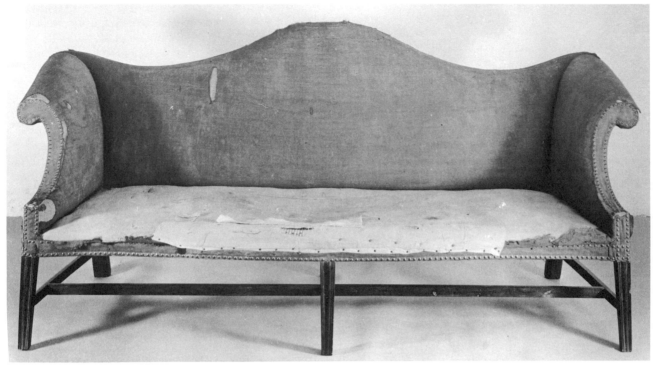

100. Sofa, probably Pennsylvania, 1785–1800. Mahogany, with
original padding and worsted cover. Dimensions unknown. Owner
unknown.

101. Detail of sofa in figure 100, showing the removable back panel.

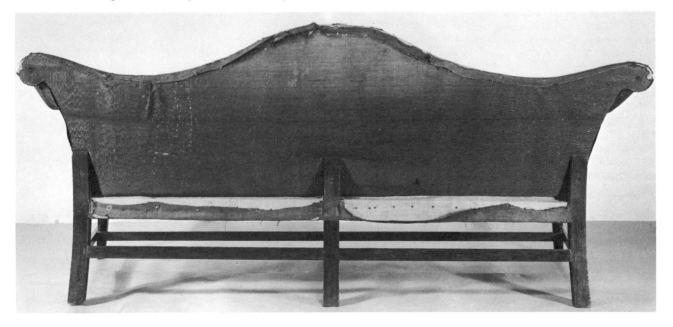

102. Detail of sofa in figure 100, showing the left side and the removable back panel.

Unfortunately, there appears to be no Queen Anne or Chippendale sofa on which either the original fabric or even the stuffing is still in place; however, a sofa that survived intact into this century was photographed some years ago (figs. 100–102). Although the tapered and molded legs indicate a date in the 1790s, the serpentine "camel" back and the splayed arms of the upholstered part are characteristic of the Chippendale style during the third quarter of the eighteenth century. Thus, these photographs can serve as prime evidence of how Chippendale sofas were upholstered.

Figure 100 illustrates the interior. The back is padded, with the stuffing tapering away gradually at the top of the crest rail. The arms are also gracefully padded out. Although broken down somewhat in the middle, the seat still retains a padded or dome-shaped appearance. In contrast, the fronts of the arms and seat rails are flat and hard. They are outlined with ornamental brass-headed nails, like those shown in period portraits. Moreover, the outside back and side panels, shown in figures 101 and 102, are simply covered with fabric pulled taut over the frame. There is no stuffing along

the outside. The method of padding this sofa is similar to that employed on easy chairs. Only the absence of a loose cushion on the seat is different, although the Copley portrait suggests that sofas had loose pillows in the corners.

Figures 101 and 102 illustrate an altogether remarkable feature that never appears on easy chairs: The back consists of a separate frame. Independently upholstered, the back simply slides into a slot between the armrests and the rear legs and is screwed into place. This seemingly extraordinary feature may not be that unusual. For example, when a straight-legged camel-back sofa at the Metropolitan Museum (60.114) was stripped of its modern upholstery, the back was found to have been made as a separate unit that was intended to be upholstered independently. Similar examples are in the Virginia Museum and a private collection. (*See* figures 103 and 104.) Just how many sofa frames of this type are concealed by modern upholstery remains to be seen.

What can we conclude from this survey of eighteenth-century upholstery techniques? First, that if we want to reupholster an eighteenth-century easy chair or sofa so that it looks the way it originally did, we must carefully study the surviving examples of original upholstery. Second, that owing to a longstanding lack of interest in historic upholstery techniques and the consequent destruction of most original examples, we must now strive to preserve what is left, even if it is only webbing, canvas, and hair. All of us—collectors and curators, dealers and upholsterers—must rethink our sometimes cavalier handling of upholstered eighteenth-century American seating furniture.

NOTES

In the research for this paper, I am particularly indebted to Brock Jobe, Charles Anello, Martin Wunsch, Wallace Gusler, and Nancy Richards.

1. One of the few articles that has dealt with the proper shaping of easy chair upholstery is "The Franklin Easy Chair and Other Goodies," by Robert F. Trent, Robert Walker, and Andrew Passeri, which appeared in *Maine Antique Digest* 7, no. 11 (December 1979): 26B–29B.

2. The worsted is from Brunschwig & Fils, no. 3869x.01. The embossed vermicelli pattern was a special order, as was the raspberry red color, based upon an antique fragment belonging to Florence M. Montgomery. The woven braid is from Scalamandre, no. V2-1, dyed to special order.

3. The tufting of chair backs was a common English practice. *See also* the tufted sofa in the Copley portrait illustrated in Brock Jobe's essay (fig. 39). In the Marblehead Historical Society, a Massachusetts bedrest with its original stuffing has a tufted back. *See* Trent, et al., "Franklin Easy Chair," fig. 8.

4. Albert Sack, *Fine Points of Furniture: Early American* (New York: Crown, 1950), p. 65; and *Antiques* 54, no. 1 (July 1948): 3.

5. David Warren, *Bayou Bend: American Furniture, Paintings and Silver from the Bayou Bend Collection* (Houston: Museum of Fine Arts, 1973), pp. 50–51.

6. According to the files at Bayou Bend, the cushion was taken apart, cleaned, and reconstructed, and modern red braid was added to the conical armrests and side seat rails. A comparison of photographs before and after restoration indicates that the needlework on the front rail and the front edges of the wings has also been removed. *See Antiques* 78, no. 1 (July 1960): 4; and Warren, *Bayou Bend*, p. 51.

7. For the chair today, *see* Joseph Downs, *American Furniture: Queen Anne and Chippendale Periods* (New York: Macmillan, 1952), no. 74. For the chair as originally upholstered, *see The Antiquarian* 15, no. 5 (November 1930): 15.

8. A slightly later, Federal-style, easy chair tells a similar story. *See* Israel Sack, *American Antiques from Israel Sack Collection*, vol. 2 (Washington, D.C.: Highland House, 1972), p. 381, no. 961. It was originally covered with a yellow silk damask in front and a yellow worsted in back.

9. These chairs were exhibited in the spring of 1983 in "The Regulator's Art: Early American Upholstery 1660–1830" at the Connecticut Historical Society. They are discussed in Andrew Passeri and Robert F. Trent, "Two New England Queen Anne Easy Chairs with Original Upholstery," *Maine Antique Digest* 11, no. 4 (April 1983): 26A–28A.

10. There are, however, two mid-eighteenth-century Pennsylvania easy chair cushion covers, their top surfaces embroidered, in the Chester County Historical Society.

11. The Kindig chair, which has never been restored, is similar to that illustrated in Downs, *American Furniture*, no. 86.

12. Another Philadelphia chair, presently on loan to the State Department from a private collection, retained its original padding and stuffing until recently. Fragments of the original blue worsted were found under the rosehead rails.

13. Nicholas B. Wainwright, *Colonial Grandeur in Philadelphia* (Philadelphia: Historical Society of Philadelphia, 1964), p. 41.

14. One is in the Duxbury (Massachusetts) Historical Society; the other is privately owned. For this information, I am indebted to Brock Jobe.

15. For a particularly good representation of an easy chair with its checked slipcover, *see* the painting *Love in a Village* in Victoria Manners and George C. Williamson, *Johann Zoffany* (London: John Lane, 1920), opp. p. 16.

16. Brock Jobe, "The Boston Furniture Industry, 1720–1740" in *Boston Furniture of the Eighteenth Century* (Boston: The Colonial Society of Massachusetts, 1974), p. 34.

17. The bill from which these figures were compiled was published in *Pennsylvania Museum Bulletin* 20 (January 1925): 71.

18. Morrison H. Heckscher, *In Quest of Comfort: The Easy Chair in America* (New York: The Metropolitan Museum of Art, 1971).

19. Sack, *Fine Points of Furniture*, p. 64.

20. From *The New York Gazette*, July 12, 1762, as quoted in Rita Susswein Gottesman, *The Arts and Crafts in New York, 1726–1776* (New York: New York Historical Society, 1938), pp. 123–24.

Evidence from the Frame of a Late 18th-Century Sofa

Edward S. Cooke, Jr. and Andrew Passeri

SMALL BITS of evidence from the frame and sackcloth of a Chippendale sofa (figs. 103 and 104) provide a good case history of how small bits of evidence can help one reconstruct the shape and appearance of an object's original upholstery. This type of sofa is among the most misunderstood upholstered forms. Few have survived with original cover fabric or underupholstery intact.

Late eighteenth-century Chippendale sofas—characterized by serpentine crest rails (often referred to as camel backs), scrolled armrests, and straight Marlboro legs—have been among the most prized forms of American seating furniture since the early national period. Their graceful lines, substantial seating area, considerable padded comfort, and lavish amount of finish fabric have made them particularly desirable and appropriate for use in formal entertaining spaces. In the 1920s and 1930s, many of the leading collectors of American decorative arts made such use of these old sofas. To coordinate their interior decoration, these collectors had their sofas reupholstered. In accordance with the usual practice of that period, upholsterers ripped out the old materials, put in spring seats, padded the inside

surfaces according to twentieth-century taste, and covered the frame with silk or damask. The pattern on the material was considered the major decorative feature of the final form. The tendency of these collectors to reupholster and recover also affected the appearance of those examples in museum collections because many of these early collectors provided the nucleus of major museum holdings in American arts. The presence of their sofas in leading cultural institutions influenced subsequent generations of upholstering. Thus most late eighteenth-century sofas that have survived present an incorrect appearance: the spring seats instead of tight seat decks—the foundation for the cushion that consists of webbing, sackcloth, a thin skimmer of marsh grass or hair, a cover sackcloth, and the finish fabric—and down cushions, silk and damask rather than worsted wools, plain surfaces rather than tufted decoration, and little decorative nailing.

Two key features of the appearance of the sofa illustrated in figures 103 and 104 are only known today through close study of the frame and surviving bits of evidence—the elaborate use of decorative brass nails

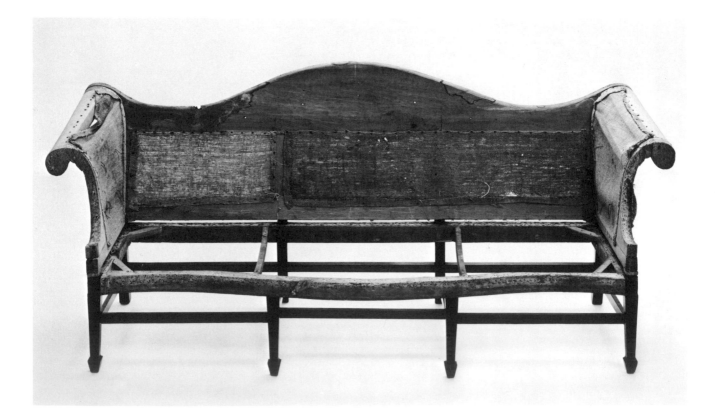

and the overall use of looped tufting in the covering fabric. Close examination of the seat rails reveals an elaborate nailing pattern that was so important to the overall design and ornate appearance of the sofa. The pattern consists of two straight lines of nails—one along the top edge of the seat rail and one along the bottom edge—that border a single swag line of nails. The surviving brass shanks in the wood indicate that the line of swags on the front rail and the side rails flowed right into a line of decorative nailing along the outside edges of the arm fronts (fig. 103). At the rear corners, the swags of the side rails continue along the side and top edges of the back (fig. 104). This nailing unified the front, side, and back surfaces of the sofa.

Although it has proved impossible to identify the original covering fabric, surviving evidence clearly demonstrates that the back and side panels of this sofa were finished with looped tufting, similar to the tufting that decorates the English back stool at Williamsburg. (*See* figure 80.) Evidence of tufting can often be found on the frame or the foundation, but such details were often covered over during past reupholstery jobs. Therefore, few reupholstered historic pieces have been tufted as they were originally.

The tufting on the back of figure 103 consists of three rows laid out to produce a diamond pattern. The upper line of tufting was secured through holes drilled in the back frame. The holes show that the five knotted tufts followed the serpentine line of the back (fig. 103). Below this serpentine line were two straight lines of tufting that paralleled the horizontal plane of the seat. Each of the six tufts in the uppermost of these two lines was anchored to the backside of the wooden frame with a small rose-headed nail. Below this line, the upholsterer placed another row of tufting, consisting of five tufts, in which the loops were simply secured to the sackcloth. Strands of the silk tufting thread can still be seen dangling from the coarse linen sackcloth of the sides. The tufting on the sides was secured on the sackcloth and formed a geometric pattern similar to that on the back. The upper rows slant slightly, following the lines of the arms; while the lower row is straight.

104. Detail of rear corner of sofa in figure 103. This close-up clearly shows the nailing pattern of the side rail. The line of brass nailing at the end of the swag continues up the side of the separately upholstered back.

103. Sofa, possibly Philadelphia, c. 1780. Mahogany, maple, yellow pine, beech, white pine, yellow poplar. Head-on view showing nailing pattern along front maple rail, holes drilled through yellow poplar back, and strands of tufting thread hanging from sackcloth on the sides. The line of brass nailing at each end continues up the inside edge of the arm front, around the perimeter of the armrest cylinder, and down the outside edge of the arm front, where it meets the swag line of the side rails. Private collection. Photograph courtesy, Museum of Fine Arts, Boston.

NOTE

1. Other sofas with evidence of tufting include one with its back foundation intact and one with holes drilled in the back frame: *Catalogue of Bernard & S. Dean Levy, Inc.* 5 (1986), p. 81; and a sofa owned by the Museum of Fine Arts, Boston (1985.810).

Richard Wevill, Upholsterer   *Patricia Chapin O'Donnell*

THE UNTIMELY death of Richard Wevill in 1803, at the height of his career, provides current scholars the opportunity to examine the business of a successful Philadelphia upholsterer at the beginning of the nineteenth century. His estate papers, including his will, shop inventories, debts received, and accounts paid, describe an upholstery business in its prime.[1] Indeed, the amount and kind of surviving information enable us not only to study a single craftsman but to compare his experiences with those of the artisans in late nineteenth-century Philadelphia.[2]

Wevill emigrated to Philadelphia from England shortly before 1799. He was already a skilled craftsman in his own right. When he first advertised his services to Philadelphians in October of 1799, he referred to his having had nearly twenty years experience in London, where he had supervised the work in two principal upholstery houses.[3] Upon arrival in Philadelphia, the craftsman set up his own business on Chestnut Street, taking over the house and stock-in-trade of the recently deceased upholsterer, Samuel Benge. It is likely that Philadelphia had the reputation then, as it certainly did seventy-five years later, as a city where a craftsman could successfully start his own business.[4] In fact, almost half of Philadelphia's upholsterers who advertised between 1760 and 1810 claimed to be recent immigrants or trained abroad.[5]

Richard Wevill carried on his trade in "all of its branches": making curtains, furniture coverings, and venetian blinds and selling carpeting and other imported textile goods. But Wevill was known for more than his artisanal expertise. Like his counterpart almost fifty years earlier, Plunket Fleeson, Wevill had entrepreneurial skills that enabled him to expand his business into related commercial ventures. His manufacturing and marketing flexibility is apparent in three different sources: contemporary advertisements, surviving correspondence, and his own estate documents.

Wevill's second advertisement in 1799 shows the scope of his furnishing business:

> . . . such as will please to favor him with their commands, who may depend on punctuality, dispatch, and a moderate charge, Bed and Window Cornices manufactured in the newest taste, gilt or painted, to suit the furniture, brass and iron rods and staples for stairs, carpeting, Venetian blinds, &c. Also, a large quantity of Prime New Feathers, which are properly seasoned, and which he warrants free from infection. Just imported in the Active, from London, and for sale at his house, No. 32, south Fifth Street, a quantity of Hair Seating, Gold Leaf, Composition, Glass Paper, Sattin Wood, and Mahogany Knife Cases, Portable Desks fitted

up complete, with Dressing Apparatus, and Mahogany Toilette Dressing Glasses, Also for sale, a quantity of Elegant Prints.[6]

Several letters and an accompanying receipt that date from this period document Wevill's relationship with one of his customers, Ann Ridgely of Dover, Delaware. She had originally requested that her niece, Williamina (Mrs. John) Cadwallader, find a second-hand bed for her at a shop in Philadelphia.[7] Due to the prevalence of yellow fever in the city, Mrs. Cadwallader suggested instead that Mrs. Ridgely contact Wevill, "a good Workman and an honest Man," directly, and enclosed a note from Wevill himself, in which he described new "canopy, Field, and Strait highpost bedsteds and their prices, according to the manner of finishing and size" (fig. 105).

Size and finish were important variables that enabled the upholsterer to produce a suitable product at an acceptable price. In regard to this custom work, Wevill wrote, "I have not set a specific price, as it is possible to make the same article for lesser or a greater price according to the manner of finishing it, and the quality." As a matter of additional information, Mrs. Cadwallader advised Mrs. Ridgely in her cover letter, "You will observe these prices are without curtains—should you be obliged to have new bedsteads I can purchase white muslin very low which will look neat at present and hereafter serve to line better." Apparently the older woman purchased goods from Wevill as an undetailed receipt for $141.50 signed by Wevill in 1803 was found among her papers.[8]

Richard Wevill died in the summer of 1803. The most important document among his estate papers is the inventory, appraised by John and Henry Connelly. (The entire inventory is transcribed in the appendix to this essay.) Goods in the "wareroom" were valued at $3,142.77, including stock, finished and unfinished upholstery work, other cabinetware in various stages of completion, tools, and personal goods. His tools were appraised at less than $30. Mahogany and other woods in the yard came to an additional $969.56.

The list of stock-on-hand includes quantities of chintz, dimity, and hair seating for final covers; hair, moss, and cattail for filling and edge rolls; tassels, line, lace, and fringe for finishing; window laths; brass hardware; veneers, stringing, and other wood supplies. Some of these items had been directly imported from London; others were purchased or exchanged locally. Cabinetmakers were one group with whom upholsterers conducted extensive exchange of goods, materials, and services. Not only did the two crafts perform piece work for one another, but the upholsterers' extensive importation of fine textiles allowed them the opportunity to bring over special woods that they could exchange for the services of their cabinetmaking colleagues. Wevill, for example, used his London connections to offer "fine Sattin-wood, tulip wood, and purple wood veneers, and an assortment of Stringing & c."[9]

The upholstered furniture in the inventory includes chairs (and frames), settees, easy chairs (and frames), as well as a "sopha." Also listed are a variety of bedsteads, including four post (mahogany or stained), field (mahogany or varnished), low post, French crib, and cot. Some of these had hangings; others were without curtains or bedding. At least one unmounted set of chintz furniture, already made, was listed, as well as a number of mattresses of various sizes and materials. The fact that there were so many finished and unfinished bedsteads implies that hangings were custom constructed, and, therefore, an appropriate vehicle for individual taste. In some cases, the customer may even have supplied the fabrics for the upholsterer, as the Ridgely-Cadwallader correspondence suggests.

When Wevill died, he had considerable quantities of chintz, dimity, and hair seating in stock. It is difficult to say whether these materials merely reflected the fact that it was summer or were more indicative of year-round taste.

In addition to marketing flexibility, Richard Wevill's career demonstrates mobility. By 1801, he maintained three locations: the original upholstery shop opposite Congress Hall at 193/195 Chestnut Street, a showroom at Fifth and Chestnut, and a mahogany yard on the corner of Seventh.[10] Maintaining three locations enabled Wevill to operate his business both in the older section of town and in the newly fashionable western section.[11] Having these multiple locations had other advantages. When the Congress Hall shop burned in 1802, Wevill was able to salvage some of the stock and to market it in his "Ware-Room."[12] The sale of the remaining goods for "ready money" apparently allowed him to meet immediate debts and to stay in business.

Although Wevill had three separate places of business, the evidence indicates that the number of his permanent employees was small. According to the U.S. Census of 1800, Richard Wevill's household—both family and employees—at that time consisted of one male between the ages of twenty-six and forty-five, one male between sixteen and twenty-six, one female between ten and sixteen, and four females between sixteen and twenty-

six.[13] Wevill reduced capital expenses by boarding apprentices and female employees. The older male was certainly the proprietor, and the younger one may have been one of his two sons—George or William—or a separate apprentice. Of the females, two were probably his wife, Ann, and daughter, Olivia. The others would have lived under his care and been employed at "women's work"—sewing curtains, drapery, and mattresses or making tassels.[14] In 1751, Denis Diderot, the French encyclopedist, described a similar workshop in which the master upholsterer, or *maitre tapissier*, dealt directly with his customers and presided over apprentices, journeymen, and female workers. (*See* figure 41.)

The production level of Wevill's establishment could have been expanded when needed by subcontracting with journeymen or other shops. The accounts of Wevill's estate record the disbursement of back wages to four workers who either boarded with Wevill or worked as independent piece workers: Mary and Rosanna Ourt, Lewis Nicholas, and John Ackland. The same document also lists payments to a carpenter, joiners, and other independent upholsterers. Many established upholsterers worked for others either in exchange for goods and services or for direct payment. The inventory of debts due and received shows that Wevill himself supplied or did work for other upholsterers, including Laforgue, Rea, Lawrence, Oliphant & Wilson, and Anthony. Other wholesale and retail customers included David Kennedy, Isaac Wharton, Henry Connelly, Dr. Shippen, and the Baptist Church.[15]

After Wevill died in 1803, his wife Ann continued to rent the property at Fifth and Chestnut for two years.[16] The new upholstery firm of Wevill & Nicholas (Wevill's son George and his former employee Lewis Nicholas) held it from 1806 to the expiration of the lease four years later in 1810.[17]

The existing documents that detail Richard Wevill's career indicate that his business operation was characterized by versatile business strategies. He ran a very cost-efficient household establishment, and he expanded the productive capacity of this shop when demand called for it by hiring pieceworkers, journeymen, and even other master upholsterers and cabinetmakers. The importance of part-time labor exceeded cost efficiency; it brought new, fresh ideas into Wevill's shop. His exchange of services with other shops exposed him to other fashions and customs and increased the variety of goods he sold. Wevill's system of production, in fact, resembled that which has been documented in Philadelphia later in the century. The textile mills of that later period were also distinguished by proprietary organization and flexible output within an interlocked set of "separate establishments." The separate establishments that characterized Philadelphia craft production as a whole in the late eighteenth and nineteenth centuries allowed the city to maintain a reputation as a style center.[18]

105. Letter from Richard Wevill to Ann Ridgely (through Williamina Cadwallader), July 17, 1802. Courtesy, Delaware Division of Historical and Cultural Affairs.

NOTES

1. Will, Inventory, and Estate Accounts of Richard Wevill, File No. 74, Will I, 133, 1803, Register of Wills for the County of Philadelphia, City Hall Annex, Philadelphia.

2. One of the finest studies of the textile industry in nineteenth-century Philadelphia is Philip B. Scranton, *Proprietary Capitalism: The Textile Manufacture of Philadelphia* (Cambridge: Cambridge University Press, 1983).

3. Advertisement of Richard Wevill, *Aurora*, October 28, 1799.

4. Scranton, *Proprietary Capitalism*, p. 42.

5. Patricia Chapin O'Donnell, "The Upholsterer in Philadelphia, 1760–1810" (M.A. Thesis, University of Delaware, 1980), p. 27.

6. Advertisement of Richard Wevill, *The Federal Gazette*, November 16, 1799.

7. Letter from Mrs. John Cadwallader to Ann Ridgely, July 18, 1802, Ridgely Collection, Delaware Division of Historical and Cultural Affairs, Dover, Delaware.

8. Receipt from Richard Wevill to Mrs. John Cadwallader, January 15, 1803, Ridgely Collection, Delaware Division of Historical and Cultural Affairs, Dover, Delaware.

9. Advertisement of Richard Wevill, *Aurora*, October 28, 1799.

10. Cornelius W. Stafford, *The Philadelphia Directory* (Philadelphia: W. Woodward, 1801).

11. The concentration of upholstery shops shifted to the areas of greatest urban expansion—the northern section of Philadelphia in the 1760s, the southern part in the 1780s, and the west in the early 1800s. O'Donnell, "Upholsterer in Philadelphia," p. 24.

12. Advertisement of Richard Wevill, *Pennsylvania Gazette and Daily Advertiser*, January 22, 1802.

13. Bureau of the Census, *Heads of Families, Pennsylvania*, 1800.

14. The advertisement of Ann King lists such women's work: *The Pennsylvania Journal*, May 17, 1775.

15. Estate Accounts of Richard Wevill.

16. Estate Accounts of Richard Wevill.

17. Estate Accounts of Richard Wevill; and James Robinson, *The Philadelphia Directory for 1810* (Philadelphia: J. Robinson, 1810).

18. Scranton, *Proprietory Capitalism*.

Appendix
Inventory of Richard Wevill's Upholstery Business

Inventory of Cabinet Ware & C° apprais'd by John and Henry Connelly. Part of the Estate of Richard Wevill September 20, 1803

Cabinet ware Room Corner of 5ᵗʰ & Chestnut

No.					
1	8	Cane color'd chairs	@ 1.25	10.	
2	12	Black & Yellow d°	1.	12.	
3	6	Fancy chairs	2.25	13.50	
4	2	Settees	10.	20.	
5	3	Fancy chairs	2.25	6.75	
6	6	Yellow d°	1.	6.	
7	12	Mahogany d°	6.	72.	
8	2	Stuff'd easy d°	16.	32.	
9	2	Mahogany Sideboards	46.	92.	
10	1	d° d°	36.	36.	
11	1	d° d°	46.	46.	
12	4	pair Sash corner'd Card tables	30.	120.	
13	4	oval Breakfast Tables	8.	32.	
14	3	pair circular Card tables	18.	54.	
15	6	Square Bureaus	15.	90.	
16	5	Circular d°	22.	110.	
17	8	Dining Tables	12.	96.	
18	7	Candle Stands	4.	28.	
19	1	Sopha	40.	40.	
20	2	pair Kidney Card Tables	24.	48.	
21	1	Secretary & Bookcase	70.	70.	
22	1	Secretary 35.	35.	35.	
23	1	Set of Dining tables	36.	36.	
24	2	Mahogany Cradles	6.	12.	
25	1	Round Tea Table	6.	6.	
26	1	Ladies Wardrobe	56.	56.	
27	1	Portable Desk	6.	6.	
28	3	Corner'd Wash stands	5.	15.	
29	3	Square d°	3.50	10.50	
30	1	Lobby Chest	24.	24.	
31	2	Toilet Tables	5.	10.	
32	3	Night Stools	4.	12.	
33	5	Knife Trays	1.	5.	
34	3	Butlers d°	2.75	8.25	
35	2	Clock Cases	22.	44.	
36	1	Mahogany Crib Bedstead	9.	9.	
37	1	d° 4 post d° compleat	26.	26.	
38	1	Staind d° d°	6.	6.	
39	3	easy chair frames	3.50	10.50	
40	1	small cattail Matrass	2.50	2.50	
41	1	d° moss	4.	4.	
42	1	large d°	5.	5.	
43	1	3/6 d°	4.50	4.50	
44	1	Hair Mattrass feather bed Bolster & Pillows	60.	60.	
45	12	Chairs black & yellow	1.	12.	
46	3	Cot Bedsteads	2.	6.	
47	1	d° Frame	1.	1.	
48	9	Glasses with drawers	6.	54.	
49	1	Mahogany Stool	.75	.75	
50	22	Swinging Glasses	3.75	82.50	
51	3	Small Gilt d°	14.	42.	
52	4	Large d°	36.	144.	
53	2	d° incompleat	14.	28.	
54	5	middling size d° compleat	28.	140.	
55	114	brass stair Rods ¾ yᵈ	.25	28.50	
56	40	d° d° ½ ell	.23	9.20	
57	3	Small square Glasses	.75	2.25	
58	2	Frames for d°	.25	.50	
59	20	ᵗᵇ of Hair	.25	5.	
60	20	ᵗᵇ of Moss	.03	.60	
61		A Lot of Cattail		1.	
62	1	Mahogany Field bedstead		25.	
63	1	large French d°		25.	
64	2	varnish'd field d°	5.25	10.50	
65	1	old Cornish		.10	
66	5	Window Laths a lot		.10	
67		A lot of Sattin wood Veneers		4.	
68		A lot of Mahogany d°		2.	
69		A lot of Federal wood d°		.5	
70	4	Mahogany turn'd vases	.05	.20	
71	5	Soap Cups	.02		
72	1	four post Chintz furniture		28.	
73	1	Field bedstead d°		15.	
74	2	pieces Chintz		30.	
75	27	yᵈˢ of d°		15.	
76		A Lot of twine		.50	
77	1	Field Bedstead with Mahogany posts		11.	
78	5	low post Bedsteads	3.	15.	
79	2	pair of Steelyards	1.	2.	
80	1	d° Scales & Weights		1.	
81	2	Mahogany posts fluted	2.	4.	
82	3	post & 1 rough board a lot		1.	
83	4	½ Logs of Sattin wood		66.	
85	1	Lot of Stringing		1.	
86	8	Cotton Tassels		.25	
87		A Lot of White Cotton line		2.50	
88		A large Mattrass tick		1.25	
89		A Sweeping Brush		.05	
90		A Wheelbarrow		.50	
91		A Mahogany Chair frame		2.50	
92		An old Buckett		.10	
93		A Lott of old Wool		.25	
94		A 4 post Mahogany bedstead		25.	
95	23	brass Astagals	.40	9.20	
	3	doz. wrought knobs & roses	.50	1.50	
	4	Setts small Castors	.20	.80	
		9000 brass nails	1.	9.	
		A Lot of Sand paper		3.	

1 m Clout nails		.20
8 Brass Locks & Keys	.20	1.60
5 doz. brass Key Holes	.09	.45
15 doz. Hinges	.80	12.
15 brass caps	.01	.15
3 do pulleys		.12
1 Hand vise & Bench 1.50		
11 Bed cords 1.10		2.60
A Lott of 2½ inch screws &		
3 Hammers		.50
95 Yards Hair Seating	1.40	133.
1 Oil Stone .25 1		
Hand brush .05		.30
1 Carpet Strainer and Stool		1.
2 Bags of Iron tacks		13.
7 Brass stair rods	.18	1.26
1 Lot of Iron wire		.05
9½ doz. bed screws	.50	4.75
1 Plane		.30
8 doz. Small Hinges	.25	2.
3 Gross Pulleys	.50	1.50
4 Bed Keys	.10	.40
1 set of dining table furniture		.50
7 brass Locks & Keys	.20	1.40
21 Table Handles	.05	1.05
6 Quadrant sets	.75	4.50
2 doz. Sideboard Handles	1.50	3.
3 Iron Locks & Keys	.06	.18
3 Setts of Castors	.50	1.50
22 doz. Commode Handles	1.50	33.
9 inch Pulleys	.04	.36
24 Hinges	.25	6.
4⅔ doz rack Pulleys	.30	1.40
6⅔ doz. Cloak Pins	.12	.80
10 m black tacks	.20	2.
3 old Candlesticks & Snuffers		.25
1 Mahogany Field Bedstead		20.
2 Cushions for easy Chairs		.80
Remnant of Tick lot		.10
1 Feather Bed Tick 5.		
Remnant of Check 80/100		5.80
5 Mattrass ticks 20. 11 White		
& Green Tassells 30/00		20.30
Remnant of Chintz Lace		
50/100 Do Bed Lace 50/100		1.
do of 2½ inch Fringe		.05
4 doz. White Cotton Tassels	.36	1.44
8 Gross Lace	1.50	12.
20 doz. Gimp & Plain head		
Cotton Fringe	1.50	30.
1¼ yds Dimity		.60
1 Cot Bedstead Bed Bolster		
& Pillow		3.50
1 Commode Bureau		22.
8 Moss Mattrass Ticks	.60	4.80
1 pair Sash corner'd		
Card Tables		24.
1 Breakfast Table		12.
3 remnants of Seating - Lot		4.
Lot of Iron wire		.25
Six plate Stove with pipes 10.		
1 Work Table 1.50		11.50
Remnant of Line 30/100 Lot		
Brass rings & Morocco		
50/100		.80
1 Bed Tick soild 2. Sundry		
paint pots & Brushes 50/100		2.50
2 Venetian blinds		2.
1 old Table & Chair 25/100		
1 Funnel Stove & pipe 1.		1.25
Sundries a Lot 5/100 1		
Secretary & Book case 65.		65.05
Sundry Books 43.80–8 Chairs		
@ 75/100		40.80
1 Chest drawers 20. 18 doz.		
White Cotton Tassels		
@ 36/100		26.48
2 ps Dutch ticking 12. 1		
Picture 1. 1 old Frame		
for bird 5/100		15.05
2 Cornishes 25/100 1 Pistol		
75/100 1 old Table 50/100		1.50
1 Cot Bedstead with Bedding		2.50
6 Mahogany Chairs	5.	30.
A Lot of small Screws 1.		
Sundry tools 12.		13.
Sundry Books 13.90		
1 Dining table 10.		23.90
1 Looking Glass 14.		
1 open Stove 16.		30.
1 Cradle 4. Carpet 9.		
1 Tea Tray 75/100		13.75
1 pair Andirons shovels		
and tongs		2.50
Lot Silver Tea spoons & c.		8.
A silver watch 18.		
Sundry Kitchen Furniture	35.55	53.55
Sundries in Wash House		5.30
6 Chairs 6. 1 small Glass 1.		
Bedstead Mattrass &		
blanket 12.		19.
Bedstead Bed & Bedding		30.
Crib 1.50 Chest 50/100 Stool		
stand & Tray 6.75		8.75
Chest of Drawers 8.		
Night Stool 2.		10.
Bed Bolster & Pillows 20.		
Sundries a lot 1.50		21.50
Go: Cart		.50

$3142.77

John Connelly
Henry Connelly

Philadelphia Sep[r] 15, 1803
Inventory of Mahogany boards, Plank & c. apprais'd by Jacob Mitchell & Sam[l] Williams Jun[r] being a part of the Estate of Rich[d] Wevill deceased

Lot No.					
	1	Six Pieces of inch Mahogany	:	15	:
	2	16 boards inch d° 180 feet ⅙	13	10	:
	3	20 ps boards d°	9	7	6
	4	2 Setts Mahogany Sides &			
		ends for Bedsteads	4	10	:
		2 Sett Short Poplar			
		Bed posts (turn'd)	:	6	:
		3 Sett poplar field Bedsteads			
		stuffs	1	2	6
		2 Setts Field Posts	:	5	:
	6	9 ps Mahogany	:	15	:
	7	11 ps d°	3	15	:
	8	A Lot small Pieces Mahogany	:	7	6
	9	A Lot Cuttings	2	5	:
	10	A Lot poplar & pine boards	1	13	9
		1535 feet inch Bay Mahogany			
		boards ⅙	110	12	6
		308″ ½ inch d° d° 9[d]	11	11	:
		389″ Bay Mahogany Plank ⅙	29	3	6
		307″ Inch Bay Mahogany ⅙	23	:	6
		80″ Bay plank ⅙	6	:	:
		321″ S[t] Domingo plank			
		@ 22/100	26	9	8
		1409″ Inch d° Boards	116	4	10
		46 Slabs Mahogany valued at	1	17	6
			£363	11	9

Jacob Mitchell
Samuel Williams J[r]

Source: Register of Wills, County of Philadelphia

106. *Canapé*, Paris, c. 1790. Painted wood with original silk upholstery.
Courtesy, Rijksmuseum, Amsterdam.

French Upholstery Practices of the 18th Century

Jeffrey Munger

THE IMPORTANCE of the correct reupholstery of eighteenth-century French seating furniture can be best appreciated when the value attached to upholstery by eighteenth-century patrons is understood. The owner of a piece of seating furniture would often pay as much or more for the silk covering as he would for the carved and gilt frames. Furthermore, the visual effect of a piece of seating furniture was usually more dependent upon the covering fabric than upon the frames that supported it. This impact would have been enhanced not only by the other pieces in the suite, all covered with the same fabric or variations thereof, but also by the wall hangings, bed hangings, curtains, and *portières*, or door curtains, that would have been of a similar, if not identical, color and design.

Indeed, in eighteenth-century France, enormous attention was given to all aspects of a room's furnishings. The art of interior design was highly developed in France by this time, as evidenced by the numerous classifications within each type of furniture. This concern for detail is also reflected in the many types of upholstery trimmings, known as *passementerie*, that were used. Braids, fringes, and tassels were important components of any piece of seating furniture. They were used not only to hide functional items, such as tacks, but also to provide a finished and more decorative appearance.

Today, if we are to ensure the accurate reupholstery of eighteenth-century French seating furniture, it is necessary to give this same careful attention to appropriate covering materials and to the proper shapes and proportions of upholstered areas. It is only when all the factors outlined in this essay are carefully considered that we may assume that a French chair or sofa's appearance reflects the intent of the original *tapissier* (upholsterer) and his patron.

The subject of upholstery is the least understood and least researched aspect of French furniture studies because very few examples of original upholstery survive, especially on royal furniture. For one thing, few of the various fabrics used to cover furniture of high quality were sufficiently durable to withstand either constant use or the passage of time. For another, those coverings that did not deteriorate were rendered obsolete by changes in fashion and therefore discarded. The resulting lack of period examples has led to the state of affairs where much of what we see today is incorrect both in the choice of covering material and in the manner in which the upholstered form has been built up and defined.

One widespread misconception regarding French covering materials holds that tapestry was widely used on seating furniture. The furniture historian Francis Watson has, however, argued persuasively that tapestry coverings were not commonly found on furniture produced for the court or the nobility and that most French eighteenth-century furniture that is now covered in tapestry was reupholstered in the nineteenth century to accommodate the taste of the later period.[1] This view is substantiated by various inventories and the records of the Garde Meuble, the department within the French government that commissioned and supervised the furnishings of the various royal chateaux.

Watson points out that in fact many of the tapestry coverings woven in the eighteenth century were actually intended for export or as gifts from the Crown to foreign sovereigns or their ambassadors. As evidence, he cites the study of the Gobelins factory done by French textile scholar, Maurice Fenaille: Of thirty-five sets of furniture tapestry woven between 1750 and the beginning of the French Revolution, approximately one-third were made for export.[2] The Beauvais factory produced tapestry furniture coverings in greater quantity but still only received 197 orders between 1723 and 1789, a small number in relation to the large number of seating furniture frames produced annually by the approximately 130 Parisian workshops.[3] The tapestries of two other factories, the Aubusson and Felletin firms, were considered inferior in quality to those of Gobelins and Beauvais and thus were rarely used on furniture of high quality. (Savonnerie carpeting was used more commonly than tapestry coverings for seating furniture, but it was employed primarily for stools and benches.)

In actual fact, silk was the most widely used covering fabric for eighteenth-century royal seating furniture, according to contemporary documents—in particular the *Journal du Garde-Meuble*. The silks were used in various weaves: lampas,[4] silk damasks, plain or cut velvets, satins, and brocades. Other fabrics were also employed, such as embroidery *au point* (*gros* or *petit*), leather, linen, and, in the latter part of the century, printed cottons. Leather was used primarily to cover the seats of *fauteuils de cabinet* (desk chairs), the backs of which were often caned.

The more expensive seating furniture of the period often had two different types of covering fabrics. They were designed so that the upholstery fabric could be changed seasonally or twice a year. The fabrics used for summer coverings were usually light in color and less formal in design than the silk damask coverings preferred for winter; cottons, printed with chinoiserie designs, were especially popular. This changing was accomplished by the use of slip seats, loose back cushions, and arm pads that were commonly attached to the frames with screws or turn buttons. Seating furniture with these features is referred to as *à chassis*.

We can also find evidence for the use of silk in the important contemporary source for eighteenth-century French upholstery practices—the manual *Principes de l'art Tapissier* written in 1770 by Jean-Francois Bimont, a Parisian *maître-marchand tapissier*. In this book, Bimont discusses different upholstery materials for a wide variety of seating furniture. He also lists prices and appropriate quantities for various components. Bimont's text indicates that silk damask, which he simply calls damask, is the primary covering fabric. In the first chapter he writes:

> . . . the material which is most used for all sorts of furniture is damask. It has a brilliance that other materials do not have—the colors are good and in consequence, permanent . . . When it is strong, it has two advantages: the first is that it is better suited for use on seats, the second is that the flowers show up better.[5]

In his conclusion, Bimont defends his choice of damask as the only fabric that he discusses extensively:

> It is true that I speak only of Damask, which is used universally, because it would take too long to speak of other materials, but it is sufficient to speak of damask and it can serve as a rule for the others.[6]

Another mistaken notion about eighteenth-century upholstery that still persists today is the belief that only pale or pastel colors were used for silks in the eighteenth century. However, although the records of the Garde-Meuble and contemporary inventories customarily list the color or colors of the covering material without specifying their intensity, there is other evidence that rich, strong colors were indeed used. A gold and enamel snuffbox owned by the Duc de Choiseul, made in 1770 and decorated with painted miniatures by Louis-Nicolas van Blarenberghe, depicts the interiors of the Duc's Parisian house with seating furniture as well as walls and bed hangings in colors of deep magenta, deep green, and bright royal blue.[7]

Other sources also corroborate the use of strong colors in the eighteenth century. References to the color "crimson," for instance, appear frequently in contemporary records and inventories of seating furniture.[8] Another corroboration is the actual original silk covering found on an unsigned *canapé*, or sofa, of about 1790

in the Rijksmuseum, Amsterdam (fig. 106). This rare surviving example is extraordinarily well preserved, and is a vivid blue with a design woven in shades of green, yellow, pink, and white. Similarly, a deep green ground color is found in the silk upholstered armchair in the portrait, painted in the 1780s, of the Marquis d'Ossun, presently in the National Gallery of Art, Washington, D.C. The surviving fragments of the silk that originally covered the seating furniture of Marc-Antoine Thierry discussed below have a dark steel-blue ground. Moreover, several recent studies of eighteenth-century silks—especially Peter Thornton's *Baroque and Rococo Silks* and a publication by the Musée Historique des Tissus in Lyon—illustrate examples of furnishing silks with ground colors of various highly saturated hues.[9]

Bimont's *Principes de l'art du Tapissier* provides much invaluable information not only about finish fabrics, but also about eighteenth-century upholstery materials and techniques. In the back of his manual, Bimont lists the items necessary to upholster various types of furniture. In his entry for *fauteuil à la Reine* (the precise classification for Thierry's pair of armchairs), Bimont lists *damas* (silk damask); *polisot* (an unidentified material);[10] *toile à damier* (checked linen or cotton); *grosse toile* (sackcloth or linen); *galon d'or* (gold braid); *clous dorés* (gilt nails or tacks); *crin* (horsehair); and *sangle* (webbing).

In discussing the actual upholstery process, Bimont states that the webbing on the seat bottom should be applied closely together so that "there is no point at which daylight can enter."[11] In contrast to the English upholsterer who placed the webs quite far apart and then laid a piece of rough cloth on top to receive the horsehair, the French *tapissier* positioned the webs so close to one another that the horsehair could be placed directly on top of the webbing (fig. 107).

When washed and treated, horsehair provided substantial resiliency. A greater quantity of horsehair was placed in the front and the middle of the seat to offset the greater wear on these areas. The horsehair was covered by linen, and then this linen covering and hair were stitched together so that the hair would not shift with use. Bimont stresses several times the importance of arranging the horsehair evenly to eliminate any bumps or depressions and notes that this arranging would "contribute greatly to the good appearance of the seat."[12] At this stage, the seat was ready to be covered with the desired fabric, which would be secured with tacks in roughly the same manner as the linen beneath it. Bimont notes the necessity of stretching the fabric to

107. Detail of the underside of an armchair, Paris, c. 1755. Made by Nicholas Heurtaut. This illustrates the tightly interwoven webbing characteristic of French upholstery techniques. The dark threads are the original geometric quilting stitches; the lighter threads are newer quilting stitches, added when the chair was recently covered with new linen. Courtesy, Museum of Fine Arts, Boston. Gift of Robert Treat Paine II.

eliminate creases and to align the flowers.

The back of an upholstered French chair had two different covering materials. The inner side of the back, or the inback, would be covered in the same fabric as that used for the seat. But the outer side of the back, or the outback, was often covered with a less expensive checked cloth, usually cotton or linen, as Bimont notes in his list of necessary items. A fabric of the same color as the inback fabric but less elaborately woven could also be used. The plain fabric was usually of a lesser quality. The use of a different material for the outback was common for both a *siege meublant* (a decorative

chair that was placed against a wall) and a *siege courant* (a chair that stood out from the wall and could be moved). Prints of the period illustrate this custom (fig. 108).

In upholstering the back of a chair, the fabric for the outback was applied first. According to Bimont, the upholsterer would tack this in place and then start to build the foundation for the back. On the inside of this outback, he then placed a layer of linen and webbing. The horsehair was applied next, thinly in the middle and more densely at the top than at the bottom. The hair was then stitched in place, a layer of linen applied,

108. *Qu'en dit l'Mobé?* by Nicolas Delaunay (1739–1792), after Nicolas Lavreince. French engraving. Courtesy, the Metropolitan Museum of Art. Harris Brisbane Dick Fund.

and lastly the inback material was added, which Bimont recommended be affixed with gilt nails.

Although Bimont is not very specific about the shapes of the upholstered areas—how flat or rounded the seat and back should be or what is the desired fullness of the armrests—he does describe several kinds of upholstered edges. In his discussion of the back of an armchair, for example, he seems to suggest that one can have either a rounded or a squared form. The reference to a squared form may mean the deep, box form, now referred to as *à tableau*. Used only on square-backed chairs or sofas to echo the lines of the frame, it was created by a stitched edge. On the upholstery of a *canapé*, Bimont mentions a type of stitching that he calls *la piqure à l'Angloise* (English stitching). He defines the stitch as that made "with a thread interlaced from the border to the edges from above and below."[13] (Ironically, Bimont may be referring to what is now known as a French edge.) A stitched or square edge is created by repeated diagonal stitching that draws the horsehair upward, creating an edge that projects from the surface of the inback. By pulling and compacting the horsehair to create such an edge, the upholsterer forms a cavity in the center. To make the crown of the seat level with or higher than the edges, more hair must be added. This second layer of hair is then covered with a linen lining before the covering is applied.

There is some uncertainty as to the country in which the stitched edge originated and when it was first used in France. It would not have been necessary before the neoclassical style of chair evolved, as a square edge was clearly unsuited to the earlier curvilinear rococo chair. The first chairs in the neoclassical style appeared in France in 1768–1769, but it was not until 1770 or 1771 that they became at all common. Thus, if Bimont were referring to the stitched edge in his 1770 manual, he was at the very forefront of neoclassical furniture upholstery techniques.

The vast majority of eighteenth-century French seating furniture has been reupholstered with new materials, and thus most of these pieces have acquired a shape and an overall line quite different from that which they originally possessed. This is particularly true of square-backed chairs and sofas in the neoclassical style that, when reupholstered, are rarely given the deep boxed padding created by a stitched edge. This, despite the fact that numerous contemporary prints and paintings in which neoclassical furniture appear illustrate such a boxed edge (fig. 109). This edge is also visible in a photograph of the previously mentioned Rijksmuseum

canapé that retains its original silk covering (*see* figure 106).

Another frequent error in the reupholstery of eighteenth-century seating furniture is that the padding and cushioning is not given sufficient thickness. Comfort was a major consideration in the design of a chair or sofa, and thus most seat cushions were quite full, often rising almost to the height of the arms (fig. 110). A typically generous cushion can be seen in one of the few *bergéres* (an armchair in which the area between the arm and the seat is upholstered) that survives with its original covering cushion (fig. 111).

Similarly, armchairs designed without cushions had more fully padded seats than most of those that have been reupholstered. In fact, contemporary prints show that armchairs without separate cushions, such as side chairs, often had markedly dome-shaped seats. Armrests were also amply upholstered. Those of square-backed armchairs and sofas usually featured square edges.

Several good examples of how misunderstandings regarding shaping and finish fabric have distorted the proper appearance of French eighteenth-century furniture today can be found in the collection of the Museum of Fine Arts, Boston. These include a suite of upholstered bedroom furniture made in 1787 for Marc-Antoine Thierry de Ville d'Avray, general administrator of the King of France's furniture,[14] and a pair of *voyeuses* (chairs especially designed for watching card games) that were part of a large set of furniture ordered for the *salon des jeux* at the royal chateau at St. Cloud.[15]

None of these pieces retain their original upholstery, but because there is extensive documentation as to their origins, it is possible to reconstruct their original appearance with a good deal of certainty. It is highly instructive to compare this with their present appearance.

As pieces of furniture produced for the French court, both sets were recorded in the registers of the Garde-Meuble, the government department that commissioned and supervised the furnishings of the various royal chateaux. Four of the ten pieces of furniture built for Thierry de Ville d'Avray and the two *voyeuses* bear labels that have made their precise identification possible.[16] The corresponding entries in the royal registers list the date of the commission, the number and types of pieces ordered, the various craftsmen involved in their production, and the original upholstery materials.

The suite of furniture that Thierry ordered for his bedroom comprised a bed, two armchairs (one is illustrated in figure 112), a *bergére*, four side chairs, a *voyeuse*

109. *L'assemble au concert*, by François-Nicolas-Barthélemy Dequevauviller (1745–1807), after Nicolas Lavreince. French engraving.
Courtesy, Fogg Art Museum, Harvard University.

(fig. 113), and a firescreen,[17] all of which have come to
the Museum through the descendants of James Swan, a
Bostonian who acquired the suite in Paris in the 1790s
after the French Revolution.[18] The bed and firescreen
from Thierry's suite of furniture were upholstered with
the original material when they entered the museum in
1927; however, these have been recovered, probably
because, as old photographs of these objects indicate,
they were both very poorly preserved.[19] For example,
the material on the firescreen had been cut and crudely
resewn with little regard for the overall design, thus
destroying the original pattern and effect of the upholstery. Although the fabric that was used to cover the
bed was in significantly better condition, it too had
apparently been resewn (fig. 114).[20]

The original fabric covering of Thierry's furniture is
described as *damas lampas* in the registers of the Garde-
Meuble. The same sort of *lampas* had been used to
cover the seating furniture of a suite made in the previous year for the king's *salon des jeux* at Fontainebleau
and at that time had been described at greater length in
the registers as "lampas bleu, gris et blanc, d'un grand
dessin arabesque."[21]

110. *La consolation de l'absence*, by Nicolas Delaunay (1739–1792), after
Nicolas Lavreince. French engraving. Courtesy, Museum of Fine
Arts, Boston. Gift of the Visiting Committee.

111. *Bergère*, Paris, 1788. Made by Jean-Baptiste Boulard. Painted wood with original needlework upholstery. Courtesy, Musée du Louvre.

112. *Fauteuil*, Paris, 1787. Made by Jean-Baptiste-Claude Sené. Beech with gilt finish. Courtesy, Museum of Fine Arts, Boston. Gift of Mrs. Helen Howard Hudson Whipple and Mrs. Alice Wayland Hudson White.

113. *Voyeuse*, Paris, 1787. Made by Jean-Baptiste-Claude Sené. Beech with gilt finish. Courtesy, Museum of Fine Arts, Boston. Gift of Mrs. Helen Hudson Whipple and Mrs. Alice Wayland Hudson White.

The *lampas* was woven of silk in a gray and white design on a slate-blue colored ground. Its design was in the prevailing neoclassical style composed of blacksmiths in antique costume, grottoes, sea horses, arbors, lion masks, and a border of rinceau scrolls. The silk was supplied by the Lyons firm of Louis Reboul, Fontebrune et Cie, and was applied to the frames of Thierry's suite by Capin, the royal *tapissier* from 1764 to 1788.

As supervisor, Thierry had access to the craftsmen working for the Crown and naturally turned to them to produce, at court expense, furniture for his own apartment in the Hôtel du Garde Meuble. Capin was only one of the many highly skilled craftsmen who worked on his furniture. The *menuisier*, or joiner (whose job was to provide the basic frames), was Jean-Baptiste-Claude Sené, a member of one of the established family dynasties of Parisian chairmakers. The decorative carving on the frames was executed by Vallois, and the gilding was applied by Chartard, the primary gilder to the Crown from 1786 to 1789. Chartard's label remains on four of the frames.

114. Wall hanging or bed cover, Lyon, France, 1786. Reboul et Fonte-brune. Courtesy, Museum of Fine Arts, Boston. Gift of Mrs. Helen Howard Hudson Whipple and Mrs. Alice Wayland Hudson White.

115. *Voyeuse*, Paris, 1787. Made by Georges Jacob. Beech with gilt finish. Courtesy, Museum of Fine Arts, Boston. Bequest of Forsyth Wickes.

The two *voyeuses* (one is illustrated in figure 115) made for St. Cloud are of equally high quality. They are the work of Georges Jacob, the leading *menuisier* of the Louis XVI period. Jacob not only supplied the frames for the suite, but it is probable that he carved their decoration and gilded the frames.[22] (The *voyeuses* appear to retain their original gilding in addition to their Garde-Meuble labels.)

Several documents provide us with detailed descriptions of the upholstery fabric for the *salon des jeux* suite. Capin served as the *tapissier* and his account, dated 31 October 1788, lists the covering as "fabric from Lyons with a checked grey-green ground and a raised design of rose vines."[23] The silk fabric was supplied by the Lyons firm of Pernon, with which the famous textile designer Philippe de Lasalle was affiliated. An entry from a 1789 inventory of St. Cloud identifies the silk as

"gros de Tours of shaded silk with a design of rose vines on a grey-blue ground."[24] The inventory further notes that the silk used for the *voyeuses*, having "a small design of scattered bouquets of roses,"[25] was slightly different from that used for some of the other pieces of furniture in the suite. Occasionally, variations of a textile pattern were used when a large suite of seating furniture needed to be covered. Intended to complement one another, the different fabrics were commonly of the same ground color.

The present upholstery of both sets of furniture, and of Thierry's armchairs in particular, reflects the general lack of awareness of eighteenth-century French upholstery practices that has prevailed until recently. It is probable that the inbacks of the Thierry armchairs were upholstered originally with a deep boxed edge that would have echoed the rectangular shape of the frame. The boxed edge gives further definition to the form of a chair and creates an effect that is both more weighty and severe.

In contrast, the present upholstery of the backs of the armchairs lacks sufficient padding and, more importantly, a defined shape. The armrests are also too meager in their proportions and most likely would have originally had square edges—the equivalent of the boxed edge of the inback—in keeping with the rectilinear design of the chair. The seat cushions would have been much fuller, approximately double their present height; the down filling of the cushions would have compressed when sat upon, allowing the user to sit at a normal height in the chair. (Inexplicably, the present seat cushions were notched at each corner to accommodate arm supports and stiles although these vertical members in fact do not interfere with the profile of the cushion.)

The outbacks of the Thierry chairs are covered with the same fabric as the other upholstered areas of the chair, rather than with a less expensive plain or checked fabric that would have been used for the outback in the eighteenth century. The fabric that was chosen for the reupholstery was a readily available silk *lampas* in the Louis XVI style, and the scale of the woven design approximates that of the original upholstery fabric. However, while reasons of cost may have prohibited the reweaving of the original fabric, it is regrettable that a fabric with a ground color close to the original was not chosen.

The mistakes in the reupholstery of the Thierry armchairs done in the early 1970s point to the obvious necessity of thoroughly researching both contemporary written documents and visual documents such as prints and paintings in order to understand more fully eighteenth-century upholstery practices. Furthermore, careful examination of the evidence on the seating furniture itself—such as tacking holes; original webbing, if extant; and remaining threads of original covering fabric—often provides crucial evidence for reupholstery. The Museum of Fine Arts is extremely fortunate in possessing numerous pieces of the original covering fabric for Thierry's suite. In spite of the fact that four of the pieces of the suite were reupholstered so recently, the importance and quality of the suite demands a more historically accurate upholstery of all its components. It is hoped that funds can be raised for the reweaving of the original fabric and for the reshaping of the upholstered forms. Then, one of the finest and most complete sets of French late-eighteenth century seating furniture will more closely approximate its original appearance.

NOTES

The writer would like to thank Christina Corsiglia, Anne Poulet, and Robert Trent for their many helpful contributions.

1. Francis Watson, "French Tapestry Chair Coverings: A Popular Fallacy Re-examined," *Connoisseur* 148, no. 596 (October 1961): 166–69. The numerous publications of Francis Watson and Pierre Verlet, in particular, provide much of the basis for eighteenth-century French furniture studies.

2. Watson, "French Tapestry Chair Coverings," p. 166. Maurice Fenaille, *Etat general des tapisseries de la Manufacture des Gobelins depuis son origine jusqu'a nos jours, 1600–1900* (Paris: Hachette, 1903–1923).

3. Watson, "French Tapestry Chair Coverings," p. 167.

4. *Lampas* is a compound satin weave that has the appearance of a two-color damask but is not reversible.

5. Jean-Francois Bimont, *Principes de l'art Tapissier* (Paris: Lottin l'aine, 1770), p. 5.

6. Bimont, *Principes de l'art Tapissier*, p. 209.

7. Francis Watson, *The Choiseul Box* (London: Oxford University Press, 1963).

8. For the inventory of the Palais de Bourbon of 1779, *see* Pierre Verlet, *The Eighteenth Century in France: Society, Decoration, Furniture* (Rutland, VT: Charles E. Tuttle, 1967).

9. Peter Thornton, *Baroque and Rococo Silks* (New York: Taplinger, 1965); *Etoffes Merveilleuses de Musée Historique des Tissus, Lyon, tome 1, Soieries françaises du XVIII siècle* (Japan: Editions Gakken, 1976).

10. Although numerous eighteenth- and nineteeth-century French dictionaries were consulted, a definition for *polisot* was not found.

11. Bimont, *Principes de l'art Tapissier*, p. 55.

12. Bimont, *Principes de l'art Tapissier*, p. 58.

13. Bimont, *Principes de l'art Tapissier*, p. 66.

14. Thierry's official title, which he held from 1784 until his death in the September Massacres of 1792, was *Commissaire général de la maison du Roi au département des meubles de la couronne.*

15. From this set, two side chairs are in the University Museum, Pittsburgh, and one armchair is in The Metropolitan Museum of Art, New York. A person would sit astride the low seat of a *voyeuse*, facing the back and resting his arms on the upholstered crest rail.

16. The labels on the *voyeuses* are handwritten and read: *Garde-Meuble de la Couronne; Ordre No. 3, du 31 8 bre 1787; Voyeuse, pour le Salon de Jeux du Roi à St. Cloud.* The most complete label on the furniture belonging to Thierry is printed and reads: *Année 1787 Garde-Meuble du Roi; CHATARD, Peintre & Doreur, Faubourg Montmartre, à Paris, Pour M. Thierry, chambre à coucher, Suivant l'ordre du 17 Juillet, No. 181, à Paris.* The furniture made for Thierry was first identified by Howard C. Rice, Jr., in "Notes on the 'Swan Furniture,'" *Bulletin of the Museum of Fine Arts, Boston* 38, no. 227 (June 1940): 43–48. The pieces were subsequently described in detail by Pierre Verlet, *French Royal Furniture* (London: Barrie and Rockliff, 1963), pp. 179–80, no. 37; and Eleanor P. Delorme, "James Swan's French Furniture," *Antiques* 107, no. 3 (March 1975): 452–61. Three pieces from the suite were discussed by Francis Watson in *The Eye of Jefferson*, William Howard Adams, ed. (Washington: National Gallery of Art, 1976), p. 218, nos. 380, 381. The pair of *voyeuses* was also described by Verlet pp. 181–82, no. 38.

17. There is a discrepancy, as noted by Verlet in *French Royal Furniture*, p. 180, between the rectangular shape of the present firescreen and its description as *à chapeau cintré* (with an arched top) in the account of Jean Hauré, principal *fournisseur de la Cour*, who supplied the suite to Thierry.

18. For an account of James Swan and his acquisitions, *see* F. J. B. Watson, *The Wrightsman Collection* (Greenwich: New York Graphic Society, 1966), vol. I, pp. xxii-xxv; and Delorme, "Swan's French Furniture," pp. 452–61.

19. Rice, "Swan Furniture," pp. 46–47.

20. It is likely that this large piece of *lampas* was probably either a counterpane or a wall hanging from Thierry's bedroom.

21. Quoted in Verlet, *French Royal Furniture*, p. 173.

22. Pierre Verlet, *Le Mobilier Royal Français* (Paris: Libraire Plon, 1955), vol. 2, p. 153.

23. Quoted in Verlet, *Le Mobilier Royal Français*, p. 153.

24. Quoted in Verlet, *Le Mobilier Royal Français*. In the glossary to Verlet's *French Royal Furniture* (p. 193), Francis Watson defines *gros de Tours* as "a textile of woven silk somewhat similar to taffeta but thicker and of rather coarser weave."

25. Quoted in Verlet, *Le Mobilier Royal Français*, p. 154.

26. The two armchairs, the *voyeuse*, and the firescreen from Thierry's suite were reupholstered in 1976 with Scalamandre's "Louis XVI lampas," a one-hundred-percent silk *lampas*.

Beyond the Fringe: Ornamental Upholstery Trimmings in the 17th, 18th and Early 19th Centuries

Linda Wesselman Jackson

TRIMMINGS—cord, braids, tapes, fringes, piping— were extremely important to the appearance of furniture and hangings during the seventeenth, eighteenth, and early nineteenth centuries. Trimmings were often the most expensive component of an upholstery job; yet, studies of historical upholstery have been remarkably lacking in their coverage of these decorative elements. Period information on the subject of trim is scarce. For example, while the early pattern and design books such as those of Chippendale, Hepplewhite, and Sheraton do illustrate fringes, tassels, and other forms of trim, they give neither detailed descriptions nor instructions for their application. Undoubtedly, this paucity of information has made the study of trimmings very difficult. More is known about the trimming of clothing, and it is tempting to correlate the two in an effort to date and identify upholstery trimmings. The scale and character of costume trimmings, however, are so very different from those used on furnishings that such a correlation would not produce any reliable conclusions.

This essay presents a brief survey of what is known about fiber upholstery trimmings from the early seventeenth century, when upholstered furniture began to be developed, through the eighteenth and early-nineteenth centuries when upholstered pieces were created by master craftsmen with ever more sophisticated and refined techniques, to the mid-nineteenth century, when the manufacture of furniture became highly mechanized and adapted to mass production.[1]

During the period under discussion, trimmings of various sophistication and cost were made by professional artisans in England and America. In Boston, for example, between the years 1704 and 1755, several makers or importers of "fancy goods" and "narrow goods" (as trimmings were variously called) were in business.[2] In addition, there is ample evidence that housewives in both countries made trimmings for their homes.

Master trimmings makers (*passamentiers* to the French) of the seventeenth, eighteenth, and early nineteenth centuries drew on a common technology involving intricate looms designed especially for different types of trim and complex arrangements of wheels and bobbins as well as a wide variety of specialized implements. These are illustrated in detail in Volume II of Diderot's *Encyclopedie* (figs. 116–119). Some work, of course, had to be done by hand and this—usually the tedious work such as finishing fringe—was generally done by women working at low wages as piece workers. (*See* figure 119.)[3]

As we have learned from the many trade cards that survive, upholsterers sold trimmings along with all of their other wares, such as bed and window curtains, upholstered furniture, mattresses, tapestries, and wallpaper. (*See*, for example, the trade card of the Boston upholsterer, Ziphion Thayer, shown in figure 42. Thayer lists "nonsoprettys, Bed laces, Fringe, Line and Tassels.") Indeed, it seems that as a general rule the upholsterer both determined *and* provided the correct trimmings for finishing his handiwork. This may be the reason for the silence of Chippendale, Hepplewhite, and Sheraton on the subject, as noted above. After all, their books were intended not for the practicing craftsman but for gentlemen who sought to cultivate their taste for the latest decorative fashions. Further evidence for this view of the upholsterer's role can be found in the way that the subject is treated in the French upholstery guide written in 1770 by Jean-Francois Bimont, *Principes de l'art du Tapissier*. The only mention of trimmings Bimont includes is a price list of different trimmings.[4]

Before we examine the historical use of trimmings in detail it will be useful to clarify the often confusing terminology used for different trims in different periods. There are five major groups of trim: cord, gimp, woven tape, fringe, and piping.

Cord or line is one of the simplest of trimmings. It was often used together with tassels for hangings. Wrapping a cord with silk, cotton, or worsted resulted in an open-work braided trimming known as gimp, a word derived from the French work *guiper* meaning to wrap. Gimp was used primarily for the edge decoration of hangings. In the last half of the nineteenth century, the edges of furniture covers also featured gimp (*see* figure 257). (Today, gimp has taken on a different meaning. It chiefly refers to a narrow woven trim nailed or glued to the fabric edges of upholstered furniture.)

Of the more complex trimmings that are correctly known as gimp, the most common are "shell" and "embassy." While both are identical in construction, they differ in configuration. Embassy gimp is symmetrical and stiff. Shell gimp is more asymmetrical and flexible; therefore, it can be applied easily to curves or shaped edges (fig. 120).

Woven tape, which includes what period documents called galloon and braid, is a flat trim that has been used on occasion by upholsterers both to cover and to decorate edges and seams. Galloon, or in French, *galon*, is a narrow, closely woven ribbon-like tape made of gold, silver, silk, or a combination of these materials. Galloon

116. View of *passementier*'s shop (trimmings-maker's shop) from
Denis Diderot, *L'Encyclopédie, ou Dictionaire Raisonné des Sciences, des
Arts et des Metiers* (Neufchastel: Samuel Faulche, 1764), vol. II,
Planches, pl. 3. The wheel for twisting cords was used for making
gimps and other trimmings. Courtesy, Society for the Preservation of
New England Antiquities Library. Photograph by J. David Bohl.

117. A galloon-making loom from Diderot, *L'Encyclopedie*, vol. II,
Planches, pl. 5. Courtesy, Society for the Preservation of New England
Antiquities Library. Photograph by J. David Bohl.

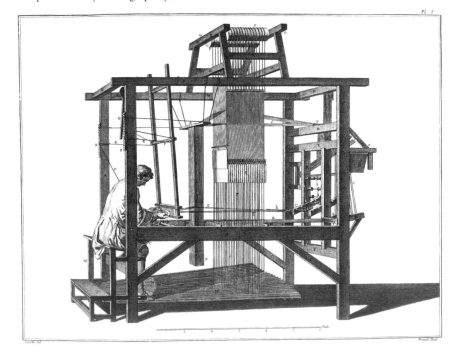

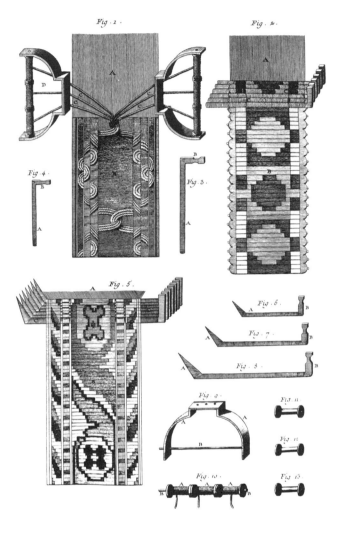

118. Print showing galloon weaving from Diderot, *L'Encyclopedie*, vol. II, *Planches*, pl. II. Fig. I shows the design of galloon used on the livery of the King of France. Implements in the lower right are the mechanism for carrying bobbins. Courtesy, Society for the Preservation of New England Antiquities Library. Photograph by J. David Bohl.

was originally used in the early seventeenth century for trimming clothing.[5] In England, however, it came to be used on furniture: A great deal of seventeenth-century English furniture that survives with original upholstery retains some form of this trim. In America, it seems to have been rarely used, if at all, for upholstery, judging from the few examples of seventeenth-century American upholstered furniture that survive. Rather, American period advertisements for fancy goods indicate that galloon was used as hat and bonnet trimming.

Braid, which is now such a generic and confusing term, was originally a narrow woven tape of wool that was often used as binding or as a component part of more complicated woven trims.[6] In seventeenth- and eighteenth-century inventories, the term *lace* was also frequently used for braid. This usage can be traced to the beginning of the sixteenth century when lace was defined as an "ornament of braid."

There has been less confusion surrounding the word *fringe*. Fringe has virtually always been used to describe a decorative border of hanging threads or cords. The stylistic development of fringe can be more easily followed than can that of other kinds of trim, particularly gimp and galloon. An assortment of basic fringe types is described in Randle Holme's *Academy of Armory*, published in 1688. Probably arranged in increasing order of richness, they are listed as "inch fring, caul fring, tufted fring, snailing fring, gimp fring with tufts and buttons, vellum fring, etc."[7] To these types should be added campaign fringe, thread fringe, and bullion fringe. Campaign fringe is often made from silk and composed of small, bell-like tassels (hence the French name campane; while thread fringe is always made of linen and composed of unspun warps (fig. 121). Bullion fringe was used for epaulets; it consisted of heavy cords that often included gold or silver threads. The term derived from bullion hose, a man's trunk hose of the seventeenth century that had puffs at the top that corresponded to the twists in the strands of epaulet fringe. Only bullion fringe had heavily twisted cords. Other early fringes were composed of unspun rather than spun or twisted elements.

The last major group of trimming—piping—was, like woven tape, originally used for costume trimming in the mid-seventeenth century. Toward the end of the century, piping began to be used to accent the edges of cushions and other upholstery components. An early representation of piping on a tufted cushion can be seen in a 1685 French engraving that depicts a young woman washing her feet.[8] Later, piping was also used to accent

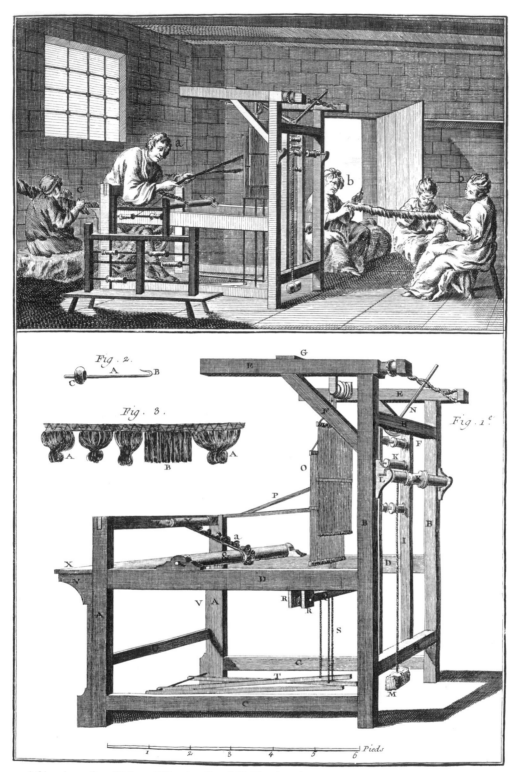

119. A fringe loom from Diderot, *L'Encyclopedie*, vol. II, *Planches*, pl. 15. The women (b and c) are doing the hand finishing of the fringes as described by Robert Campbell in *The London Tradesman*, published in 1747. Courtesy, Society for the Preservation of New England Antiquities Library. Photograph by J. David Bohl.

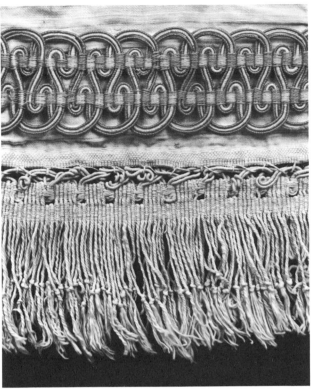

120. Gimp trimmings, nineteenth century. The upper trimming, with yellow and red wool wrapped over vellum, is "embassy" gimp. It was probably made in the mid-nineteenth century. Below this symmetrical trimming, note the asymmetrical "shell" gimp that serves as a heading of the fringe from a fragment of some early nineteenth-century white dimity bed hangings. The asymmetry made it possible to apply "shell" trim to curved edges. Note also the fringe with its hand-tied knots on each strand, designed to make small tassels. This is characteristic of late eighteenth- and early nineteenth-century fringes. Courtesy, Society for the Preservation of New England Antiquities. Photograph by J. David Bohl.

the seams of upholstered forms. In the hall at Osterley Park, England leather benches made about 1767 had linen tufting and narrow piping of leather.[9] *The Work-woman's Guide*, published in 1838, alludes to the making of decorative slipcover cases "with or without piping."[10]

There are several techniques for creating piping on upholstered furniture. When each first became widely used is not known. Conventional piping is made by stitching a strip of fabric—cut on the bias—so as to encase a cord with a "pipe" of fabric. Other types of piping include braid or tape folded and stitched over piping cord and braid applied over a French seam, formed when two raw edges are folded underneath and then stitched on the outside through all layers of the fabric. The appearance of piping could also be achieved with the technique of French cord, or applied cord edging. Popular in the seventeenth century, this involved hand-stitching a cord—often twisted—over a seam. (*See* figure 17.)

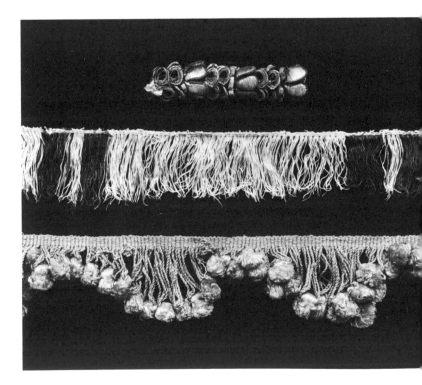

121. A tassel ornament and fringes, eighteenth century. The small trimming at the top is a portion of an eighteenth-century tassel. Several embellishments like this one (made by wrapping silk floss over vellum, as the exposed loops at the far right show) overlaid the skirt of the tassel. The middle trimming is thread fringe, a homemade blue and white linen fringe that finished the edge of linen bed curtains. Note the "whiskery" quality of the unspun warps. This thread fringe probably dates from about 1760 to 1790. The lower trimming is "campaign" fringe with small bell-shaped tassels at the end of the wefts. The uneven warps produce a scalloped configuration. This gold silk fringe was made in Europe in the eighteenth century. Courtesy, a private collection and the Society for the Preservation of New England Antiquities. Photograph by J. David Bohl.

17th-Century Trimmings

As Peter Thornton has suggested in *Seventeenth-Century Interior Decoration in England, France and Holland*, seventeenth-century upholstery work was probably far cruder than we might expect.[11] It is hard to reconcile such crude craftsmanship with the fact that upholstery fabrics and trimmings were so rich and elaborate. Nevertheless, trimmings such as galloons or lace were used both to finish seams and to obscure the frequent joins necessitated by the narrow fabrics produced on seventeenth-century looms.

The outlining of narrow widths of fabric with galloon or lace gave upholstered furniture and curtains of the period a paneled effect characterized by a boldness of handling and scale. Such an effect was further enhanced by the use of fringes and other trimming techniques and the combination of different types of fabrics. These features are found on surviving English and European upholstery. An English sofa at Knole in Kent, dating from the second quarter of the seventeenth century and retaining nearly all of its original upholstery, yields many clues to the rough workmanship and costly materials of seventeenth-century upholstery. The couch is completely covered with fabric. Vertical strips of gold galloon conceal joins in the narrow-width fabric on the back. A horizontal accent is provided by a strip of gilt netted fringe across the middle of the back. It also displays a short, elaborate gilt fringe under the seat rail.[12]

The paucity of surviving seventeenth-century American upholstered seating and the lack of any hangings from that period make conclusions about American practices more difficult, but period documents offer some hints about paneled fabrics and the bold use of fringe. For example, a deposition made in 1656 by Sarah Buckman listing the household furnishings of the Widow Glover of Cambridge, Massachusetts, provides this information:

> Eleven featherbeds of downe all well furnisht and fitten for use . . . one of them haveing philop and Cheny curtaines in graine [green] with a *deep silke fringe* on the vallance, and a smaller one on ye Curtaines, and a coverlett sutable to it, made of red kersie & *laced with a green lace, round ye midle* . . . [italics supplied][13]

Elaborate fringes were very popular in the seventeenth century as can be seen on the typical seventeenth-century English bed depicted in an English painting, *The Saltonstall Family*, a work from about 1638 attributed to David Des Granges.[14] The deep fringe of the bed hangings has a netted top band or heading called "cre-

pine" and is partially made of gilt thread. For fringes such as this, various materials including silk, silk and worsted, linen, cotton, and gilt or silver thread were used in combination. An illusion of depth was created either by using more than one color or by overlaying a plain fringe with a netted fringe. These elaborate fringes with complex headings were called "trellis" fringes (fig. 122). Toward the end of the century, a simpler style of fringe with flat headings woven in a chevron, checkered, or plain pattern became popular. (*See* figure 21.)

The trellis fringe illustrated in figure 122, now owned by the Society for the Preservation of New England Antiquities (SPNEA), edged a popular type of embroidered or "worked" hanging that was available in kit form. A housewife would embroider these hangings at home by following a design stamped or "drawn" on the fabric and then assemble the set. Whether or not the fringes to edge the curtains were included in finished form in the kit or were to be made by the housewife remains a mystery. The consistent configuration of the SPNEA fringe and the fact that the fringe is made from the same worsted linen as the hangings suggests the work of a professional.

These particular bed hangings and fringes were found in a house in Devonshire, England. They were made of worsted linen with crewel embroidery in two shades of green; they have the initials *AP* and the date *1674* in one corner. The fabric and the yarns are English, and the design is typical of those that were drawn on fabrics. The curtains were most likely assembled from the kind of "mail order kit" that many colonists ordered from English merchants.[15] For example, Samuel Sewall of Boston ordered a set of hangings for his wife in 1687. He wrote to England for "white Fustian drawn, enough for curtains, wallen, counterpaine for a bed, and half a duz. [doz.] chairs, with four threaded green worsted [crewel thread] to work it."[16] Another example is found in the inventory of the estate of Dr. Leonard Hoar of Boston, dated January 14, 1767, which lists "fustian drawn for a shute [suit] and woosted [worsted] to work it."[17]

The embellishment of seventeenth-century back stools in both Europe and America often included some form of fringe. The headings of these fringes were simpler than those of trellis fringes, although more than one color was used to provide a patterned heading. These short, less elaborate fringes were called "mollet."

The Turkey-work back stool was a production item in seventeenth-century English furniture shops and was considered a more bourgeois version of silk and velvet back stools. Nevertheless, fringe may have been used on these chairs, and it would most likely have been similar to that used on a silk English back stool in the Victoria and Albert Museum. This particular back stool retains its original silk needlework upholstery and checkered-headed fringe tacked in swags under the rails.[18] Evidence of fringe on Turkey-work chairs is seen in the Worcester Art Museum portrait *Mrs. Freake and Baby Mary* painted in the early 1670s by an unknown artist. Mrs. Freake, the wife of a wealthy seventeenth-century Massachusetts merchant, is seated on a Turkey-work chair that has polychrome fringe, probably of slackly-twisted crewels, on the lower back rail.[19]

The well-known Turkey-work couch in the Essex Institute exhibits another sort of decorative trimming, a deep crewel fringe. (*See* figure 35.) Fragments of the original fringe heading also survive. Fastened to the rail with brass nails, these small scraps include red, blue, and yellow wools, characteristic of seventeenth-century polychrome campaign fringe. (For similar evidence, *see* figure 33.) Campaign fringes were often tacked in swags to chair rails.

A chair in the Museum of Fine Arts, Boston, has been accurately reupholstered in seventeenth-century fashion with green wool upholstery and silk trimmings. (*See* figure 21.) Made in Salem in the last quarter of the seventeenth century, this serge chair is a less expensive version of a Turkey-work chair and displays more wood than its Turkey-work counterpart. Although worsted fringes were often employed for these chairs, silk was used just as often. Here the heading of the silk fringe has been augmented with a matching silk braid tacked to the chair with brass nails, to give the impression of the coarse headings of seventeenth-century fringes.

Seventeenth-century tassels were uncomplicated in their construction compared to those of later centuries. Those reproduced for the cushion of the Endicott chair in the Museum of Fine Arts, Boston (*see* figure 17), have the characteristic pear-shaped body or mold and netted covering. Eighteenth-century tassels often have chevron-patterned tops.

It should be noted that many of the smallish, white tassels that appear on furniture and cushions in museums appear to have been crocheted, knitted, or knotless netted. Undoubtedly, these were not intended for upholstery but rather were used to finish the band strings of seventeenth-century lace and linen collars. The portrait of Mr. John Freake in the Worcester Art Museum shows a pair of these tassels pinched in his left hand.[20]

122. Detail of bed hangings, England, 1674. These hangings have a heavy "trellis" fringe applied to the continuous valance. (A more diminutive version of the fringe appears along the upper edge of the valance.) Note that the fringe is made of the same material as the hangings. The heading features linen bobbles. Courtesy, Society for the Preservation of New England Antiquities. Photograph by J. David Bohl.

18th-Century Trimmings

In contrast to the rich upholstery trimmings favored in the seventeenth century, eighteenth-century trimmings appear remarkably restrained. New tastes in fashion called for large, textile-surfaced forms. The upholstery fabrics became more important and a large variety of fabrics, including worsteds, silk damask, and velvets, were used. Narrow braid or piping were more appropriate sorts of trim than elaborate fringes or galloons.

In the early eighteenth century, English styles continued to exert great influence on American taste in bed and window curtains. Indeed the colonists imported such large quantities of English upholstery fabrics and materials, including woolen fabrics, fringes, tapes, tassels, and drapery hardware, that it would seem that most materials used to create bed curtains and valances were of English manufacture and style.[21] Correspondence from the period provides further evidence. In 1720, the same Samuel Sewall of Boston who had imported white fustian "drawn" bed hangings for his wife some thirty years earlier, again ordered fabric from London, this time for his daughter Judith. He requested yellow worsted fabric "with Trimming, well made, and Bases, if it be the fashion" for a set of bed hangings.[22] Sewall, by now a wealthy Massachusetts justice, wanted to be sure that he followed the latest furnishing fashion. In December 1725, the Boston upholsterer Thomas Fitch wrote to Silas Hooper, a London merchant, concerning materials for a set of bed hangings:

> ". . . Let the whole be of a good Air of fancy for a room 10 feet high, and trim'd with the same lace of the Inclosed pattern packing up for me full enough of the Same binding and breed suitable to finish ye Curtains bases and base moldings here."[23]

American upholsterers of the period, using imported materials, constructed elaborate valances, the majority of which were made from woolen fabrics — by far the most popular "stuff" for home furnishings prior to the Revolution. For example, an English-style valance, in the Essex Institute, was probably made between 1720 and 1735 in Salem or Boston from imported English materials (fig. 123).[24] The worsted material consists of linen warp threads striped in green, red, and yellow, and weft threads made of green wool. The fabric has been calendered (pressed or glazed between revolving cylinders) in a wavy motif and is lined with buckram. A pattern of volutes is formed by three types of applied woven wool braids and tapes. The small puckers and pleats, formed by hand-stitching the braids in curved patterns, create a decorative texture. These braids and tapes may be what the author Alice Morse Earle calls "inkle" in her book *Costume of Colonial Times* published at the end of the nineteenth century. She describes "inkle" as "a woolen tape or braid formerly used as trimming (sewed on in patterns), sometimes striped."[25] Inkle may be the period name for the kind of trimmings found on the Essex valance, but this cannot be positively proven.

Another English-style valance, similar to although less elaborate than the Essex one, is found in the Society for the Preservation of New England Antiquities (SPNEA) collection. Made of blue harateen — a worsted fabric — with wavy calendered patterns created by hot rollers, the hanging has three types of braids applied to it in patterns. Originally owned by the Robbins family

123. Detail of bed valance, English materials, 1720–1735. Calendered cheney with wool tape, lined with buckram. Courtesy, Essex Institute.

of Arlington and Lexington, Massachusetts, the valance can be dated between 1730 and 1760.[26] (A possible English prototype for the scrolled patterns of braid found on the Essex and SPNEA valances may be found in the headcloth from a bed at Ham House, Richmond, Surrey. Made in the second quarter of the eighteenth century, it consists of embossed red harateen with green braid embellishments.[27])

Another example of English-inspired bed-furnishings and valances from the mid-eighteenth century with related decoration and a history of American ownership is now in the collection at the Winterthur Museum. (*See* figure 152.)[28] This set, once owned by Thomas Hancock of Boston, has a coverlet that combines similarly applied braids with crewel embroidery on white linen. The stitched braids form a trellis for the embroidered vines, floral motifs, and strapwork reminiscent of English-inspired bed furnishings.

An alternative to the high-style wool, silk, or professionally embroidered hangings, curtains, and slipcovers made by upholsterers were bed and window hangings that were embroidered at home. Numerous examples of this domestic needlework have survived for they were often preserved by family descendants for sentimental reasons. One white fustian bed valance, without a provenance, features fanciful crewel embroidery, predominantly stitched in blue yarns (fig. 124). Stylistic elements date the valance to the 1720s, but it may have been made later. Its lower edge is bound with a linen or cotton tape of a "honeycomb" weave, while the upper edge is bound with a different tape, probably not contemporary with the date of manufacture of the valance. The white bobble fringe affixed to the honeycomb tape

124. Embroidered bedstead valance, America, 1720–1750. The white bobble fringe consists of a linen cord with wool tufts. The tufts are made in continuous loops, and the cord is braided and affixed to the edge of folded tape that encases the perimeter of the valance. Courtesy, The Brooklyn Museum.

is a remarkable piece of handiwork and consists of braided linen cord with wool tufts in continuous loops.

In the eighteenth century, tape, whether printed or woven, handmade or factory produced, provided important delineation to emphasize the various configurations not only in hangings but also in upholstered furniture. Inventories of several eighteenth-century Boston upholsterers list extensive quantities of "binding and braid." For example, the entries in upholsterer Samuel Grant's account books, dating from 1728 through 1737, list large yardages of tape, referred to as binding, often in silk.[29]

Plain tapes, essential components of much clothing and many household textile articles, provided ties and binding for pockets, bags, needlework wallets, as well as upholstery. This wide demand for tapes was met by both factory-woven plain tape and by homemade tape created on a tape loom, an important piece of equipment in American colonial households (fig. 125). Usually of linen but also of cotton or wool, homemade tape was woven while holding the tape loom between the knees. Children often performed this duty. The weave of these plain tapes did not vary from the seventeenth to the nineteenth centuries.

A more elaborate "honeycomb" weave tape executed in cotton, linen, wool, or silk and produced on sophisticated factory looms finished many eighteenth- and early nineteenth-century textiles. Multicolored honeycomb tapes were a particularly popular finish for bed hangings and curtains of printed fabrics. For example, the hangings in figure 123 feature this tape. A similar linen tape of red, brown, blue, and yellow edges a boxed cushion cover of brilliant block-printed glazed cotton (figs. 126

and 127). Such tapes could also be monochromatic.

Decorative edges were crucial to the design of eighteenth-century easy chairs. Two New England easy chairs that retain their original upholstery and two slipcovers provide valuable clues for dating seam finishes. Both chairs have French edges and seams that are covered with a flat braid or French cord, as was customary in New England upholstery practice. One of these easy chairs, now owned by the Brooklyn Museum (*see* figure 87), has cord applied over the seams of the chair itself, while a flat tape was used over the seat cushion seams. The other easy chair, now owned by The Metropolitan Museum of Art (*see* figure 88), is trimmed with two types of tape. On most seams, tape of green wool warp with a pattern of yellow silk floats and yellow weft has been applied. Along the side rails, different tape—once silver but now appearing black—is secured with brass nails over the first tape. This wool and silk jacquard tape is virtually identical to one on the edges of an Irish-stitched bench cover in the Museum of Fine Arts, Boston. The edges of the needlework on the Boston bench cover consist of a braid applied over a French seam, a decorative technique that gives the appearance of piping. The braid features an olive-green warp with a bronze silk float and a bronze wool weft. The resulting geometric pattern (apparent only on the reverse side, as its exterior is worn) resembles that exhibited on the Metropolitan easy chair.

Also in the Museum of Fine Arts, Boston, is a crewel-embroidered slipcover for a New England easy chair dating from the third quarter of the eighteenth century.[30] (Unfortunately, the easy chair itself has not survived.) This fustian cover is patterned all over with

125. Tape loom, probably American, mid-eighteenth century. Found in the attic of the Arnold House, Lincoln, Rhode Island. Courtesy, Society for the Preservation of New England Antiquities. Photograph by J. David Bohl.

126. Cushion cover, fabric printed by Richard Ovey, London, c. 1818. Probably from 39 Beacon Street, Boston. This blue, red, and yellow printed chintz cover was owned by the Appleton family. For the same fabric with a different border, *see* figure 253. Courtesy, Society for the Preservation of New England Antiquities. Photograph by J. David Bohl.

delicate vine and small flower designs, and sections of the cover are joined by French seams with folded braid stitched over them. Again, this technique imparts the appearance of piping to the piece. The braid has a white linen and blue wool warp with blue wool floats, in a weave that forms a pattern of scrolls with an edge, perhaps in imitation of hand-stitching. The delicate design of the braid is harmonious with the handworked embroidery and the scale of the slipcover's motifs. This blue and white braid poses an interesting problem for scholars interested in upholstery trimmings, however. While this braid is a common one, appearing on many eighteenth-century curtains and valances of printed cotton and linen, its origin is uncertain.

Evidence from the last quarter of the eighteenth century documents the popularity of a certain type of tape. Beginning about 1765, Boston newspapers began to advertise "None-so-Pretty Tapes," which may be a period term for the small-figured braids that embellish so much surviving eighteenth-century upholstery (*see* figure 42). A clue to the meaning of none-so-pretty is found in a 1772 advertisement of the Boston Evening Post. The advertisement noted the availability of "Blue & white, Red & white, Green & white Furniture checks

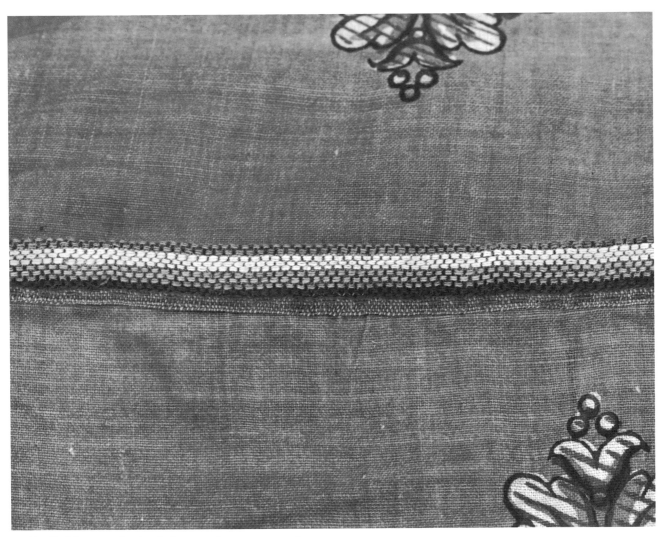

127. Detail of figure 126 showing the honeycomb woven tape on the edges of the boxed cushion cover. Tape is red, blue, brown, and yellow linen.

with None-so-Prettys to match."[31] Alice Morse Earl provides additional information about none-so-pretties. In her 1886 investigation of the relics in an old brick store in Wickford, Rhode Island, she found a box labeled "None-so-Prettys." It contained linen braid, about three-quarters of an inch wide, "with little woven figures, white, red, or black dots or diamonds." Earle felt confident that, due to their faded appearance, these braids remained from the original stock of the store, acquired in 1771.[32]

Two types of braid were used on slipcovers. One type had the design woven into the fabric, while the other, less expensive type had a printed design. As a rule, the type used varied according to the cost of the fabric. Woven braid, however, is found both on expensive imported woolens and home-worked crewel coverings, as well as on some less expensive printed cottons. More commonly, the cheaper printed trims are found on printed cottons.

Cotton slipcovers and bed hangings printed by a copperplate process were extremely popular from the time of the American Revolution to the beginning of the nineteenth century.[33] Such printed textiles emulated the more expensive wool and silk fabrics. A fragment of red and white none-so-pretty tape that formed the binding for a set of copperplate bed hangings was given to SPNEA by the late Miss Gertrude Townsend, former curator of the Textile Department at the Museum of Fine Arts, Boston. The red and white curtains were purported to have belonged to the Boston merchant Isaac Smith, and according to family tradition, they survived the 1775 siege of Boston. This places their manufacture sometime prior to 1775. The tape from the curtains, woven from wool and linen, is identical to that found on the Museum of Fine Arts crewelwork slipcover that can definitely be dated to the third quarter of the eighteenth century. This slipcover provides additional proof that none-so-pretties became fashionable at that time.

In the Essex Institute, a similar woven braid is folded and stitched over the edges of a blue and white cotton panel block-printed with chinoiserie, dated between 1750 and 1760. Pagodas, water buffalo, and Chinese figures comprise the printed design on the panel. The edges of a set of bed hangings with a similar blue and white copperplate pattern, owned by the Winterthur Museum, are finished off by a printed border. A similar printed trimming also appears in a sequence of "callicoe" swatches attached to the letter of James Alexander of New York to David Barclay & Son of London, dated October 2, 1749.[34] Such printed borders obviously were imported, but at present we can only speculate on their place of manufacture.

Another inexpensive tape was made by a process called "resist dying," usually with one or two shades of indigo on cotton fabric. Several surviving "blue resist" valances, made in England or in parts of the Hudson Valley and Long Island, feature resist borders that imitate woven or printed tape.[35] The bold floral pattern of the valances, in two shades of blue, contrasts with the small-scale border.

Fringe was another popular trim for bed and window furnishings throughout the eighteenth century, as evidenced in upholsterers' advertisements. In addition, the home production of fringe by women of all social classes was quite common. Mrs. Delany, the English diarist and accomplished needlewoman of the mid-eighteenth century, who commented profusely on the interior decoration of English homes that she visited in her travels, reported that a Miss Hamilton "made up with two netting needles" a very pretty fringe for Mrs. Delany. Also, Mrs. Delany recorded that when she and the Duchess of Portland were received by Queen Charlotte at Windsor Castle, the queen showed them a frame for fringe making.[36] In America, such a loom can be seen in John Singleton Copley's double portrait of Mr. and Mrs. Thomas Mifflin, painted in 1773.[37] The portrait shows Sarah Morris Mifflin working at a small tabletop loom. Below her left hand is a simple white looped fringe, ready to be clipped after the length of the fringe is finished.

Plain white cotton or linen fringe, like that which Mrs. Mifflin produced, is common to many simple eighteenth-century bed hangings and curtains. The thread fringe in figure 121 is such a handmade trim. Its alternating blue and white wefts would have accented the large blue and white checks of the linen curtains that the fringe edged.

Imported factory-made fringes of the late eighteenth and early nineteenth centuries often have complex headings known as gimp headings. A set of bed hangings belonging to Dorothy Quincy Hancock Scott of Boston was edged with such a fringe—made of linen and wool—in green, brown, beige, and light blue colors. (*See* figure 156.) The edges are bound with an olive-green silk tape—called "quality"—to which the fringe has been applied by hand stitching. Like other late eighteenth-century examples, the weft threads of this fringe are knotted at the mid-point, perhaps to prevent tangling, and then unplied below the knot to achieve the effect of small tassels.

A set of SPNEA bed hangings, made of printed cotton, displays a similar fringe with a shell heading. This set, composed of a counterpane, four curtains, and two pieces of valance were found in the attic of the Lewis house in Gorham, Maine. They are an example of the "drab style," popular in London about 1800.[38] Drab style fabrics feature yellow, tan, and black colors, and the rich fringe of this set is made of brown and gold wool and cotton. (The brown is possibly a faded black, which would have made the fringe colors more compatible with the black and gold print.) The wefts looped into the heading are wrapped cord. Those wefts forming the fringe are also knotted to achieve the effect of small tassels.

In contrast to these high-style hangings are simpler sets of white-fringed dimity, a type advocated by George Hepplewhite in *The Cabinet-Maker and Upholsterer's Guide*. A set owned by SPNEA has edges bound with honeycomb weave tape, with a cotton fringe applied to the bound edges. (*See* figure 157.) This fringe is identical in construction to the colored wool fringe on printed cotton sets; however, the cotton fringe proves less sumptuous in appearance and does not fall as well.

Valances made in the late eighteenth century characteristically have cord and tassels in combination with fringed edges—a decorative treatment often referred to as "line and tassel." The inclusion of a swagged drapery edged with tassels is a common artistic device in eighteenth-century American paintings (fig. 128).

An example of a valance from this period is one that was owned by the Burnham family of Newburyport, Massachusetts. (*See* figure 146.) Dated before 1789, this valance has a plain fringe along the top edge and a fringe with a shell heading along the scalloped lower edge. (This scalloping simulates festooning.)[39] The fringe along the lower edge consists of a plain fringe overlaid by small dangles or "hangers" that consist of silk loops and silk-covered vellum loops. Such a treat-

128. *Mary and Elizabeth Royall*, oil painting by John Singleton Copley,
Boston, 1758. Courtesy, Museum of Fine Arts, Boston.

ment was called "block fringe." The petals of the hangers were hand-made by wrapping silk floss around a vellum or copper core. (Brass cores were used to form the loops at a later point, and in some cases, even cardboard cores were used. This last is a sign of cheap, inferior craftsmanship because the paper tended to deteriorate rapidly.)

The trimmings of the Burnham valance also demonstrate that eighteenth-century upholstery tassels are somewhat different in form than those of the seventeenth century. For example, the shape of the later tassels had a definite "waistline," and it was common for the main fringe or skirt of the tassel to be overlaid with smaller tassels or ornaments. Also typical of eighteenth-century tassels were ruffs, chevron patterns in the fibers wrapping the mold, at the base of the mold.[40] A portion of one tassel, formerly part of the line and tassel treatment of some brocade draperies, features the silk-covered hangers that are also found on eighteenth-century block fringes. (*See* figure 121.)

Early 19th-Century Trimmings

At the beginning of the nineteenth century, changes in upholstery forms began to reflect the rising influence of the neoclassical style. Metal trim, both cast and chased, brass nails, and wide braids or borders were used extensively on seating furniture. The choice of such trimmings was a response to the shift from large fabric-covered surfaces with a variety of edging treatments, to more complex upholstery treatments involving separate cushions, tufting or buttoning, and large tassels. Well-circulated publications such as Rudolph Ackermann's *The Repository of Arts, Literature, Commerce, Manufacture, Fashions and Politics*, published in London from 1809 to 1828, popularized this changing taste in trimmings.

A Boston Empire sofa is virtually the same design as a "dress sofa" in the 1821 issue of Ackermann's *Repository* (*see* figure 223) and is today embellished with a reproduction woven silk and cotton trimming. The braid closely resembles a printed French cotton border in the Cooper Hewitt Museum, New York.

Less expensive printed trimmings for washable slipcovers and curtains were heartily endorsed by the English interior designer J. C. Loudon in his 1833 *Encyclopedia*. Loudon extolled the virtues of hygienic, glazed calico slipcovers "with a narrow piece of different coloured calico or shawl bordering laid on about a couple of inches from the edge."[41] Shawl bordering was available in many different fashions, including the Greek and

Indian taste, and often came in pairs, a wider one for the bottom border and a narrower one for the top. Figure 129 illustrates matching borders in the Indian fashion, with a Greek shawl border in between.

Shawl bordering was also popular for accenting window curtains. For example, a set of white net window curtains, one of two pairs owned by SPNEA, displays a printed red and black Greek key border (fig. 130). Williamina Ridgely described such trimmings on heavier draperies in a letter to her mother in 1803:

> Her house [possibly that of Fanny Erskine] is completely, neatly elegant but not extra-vagantly furnished—the window curtains in the parlour are scarlet worsted with black Grecian trimmings laid on, not fringes as I wrote before.[42]

As in the eighteenth century, these trimmings printed in imitation of woven ones were quite popular with those who could not afford fancier trimmings such as fringes with dangling wooden pendants wrapped by hand with wool or silk. (*See* figure 173.)

The Mid-19th Century and After

As the nineteenth century progressed, public taste in upholstery favored the use of heavily patterned fabrics, deep buttoning and tufting, and opulently encrusted trims. The heavily upholstered, spring-seated furniture of the mid-nineteenth century required trimmings of equally substantial proportions. Drapery of the Victorian period was also lavished with plentiful trimmings.

Very little is currently known about the factory production of trimmings in America during the mid- to late-nineteenth century but the amount of trimmings used for upholstery and drapery suggests that it was a very prosperous business. Unfortunately, this period of vitality did not last long. By the late nineteenth century, the manufacture of upholstered furniture and trim became increasingly mechanized, reducing the crafts of upholstery and trimmings makers to minor trades. At the same time, trimmings began to be less important than the fabric in upholstery so that by the end of the nineteenth century trimmings were no longer the most expensive component of the upholsterer's bill. Early in the twentieth century, the interest in decorative trimmings had declined to the point where their use could be described as "taboo" as an interior decorator of the day complained:

> To some pretentious and conscientious Americans, trimmings are taboo. They do not regard them as sufficiently "structural." They maintain that whilst self-fringes are

129. Shawl bordering, mid-nineteenth century. The upper border at
the top of the illustration matches the wider one at the bottom. The
unrelated printed border with the Greek key pattern is a cheap version
of a popular woven trimming. Courtesy, Society for the Preservation
of New England Antiquities. Photograph by J. David Bohl.

130. Net curtain with printed cotton shawl bordering, c. 1840. The Greek key pattern is printed in red and black. Courtesy, Society for the Preservation of New England Antiquities. Photograph by J. David Bohl.

legitimate, a sewed on fringe is insincere and dishonest. In other words, they think in phrases instead of facts and trust to memory instead of taste for their decorative decisions.[43]

From the seventeenth through the nineteenth century, upholsterers integrated fabric and trimmings in the production of upholstered furniture, bed hangings, and window curtains. They achieved a complementary relationship between covering material and decorative finish that has been emphasized considerably less in the twentieth century. Indeed, today's "decorative decisions" nearly always eliminate trimmings in upholstery. As a result, the production of galloon, braid, fringe, and other trimmings has declined drastically. If we are to provide accurate reproduction upholstery, we must try to revive this industry.

NOTES

1. Metal trims (such as chased borders), decorative brass nails, papier mâché ornaments and borders, feathers and plumes, tufting devices, and modern gimp will be excluded from this survey.

2. George Francis Dow, *The Arts and Crafts of New England, 1704–1775* (Topsfield, Massachusetts: The Wayside Press, 1927), pp. 154–72.

3. John Cornforth, "The Art of the Trimmings Maker," *Country Life* 148, no. 3836 (December 1970): 110; and A. C. Edwards, "Sir John Petre and Some Elizabethan London Tradesmen," *London Topographical Record* 23, no. 115 (1972): 80. I am indebted to Robert St. George for drawing my attention to this reference.

4. Jean-Francois Bimont, *Principes de l'art du Tapissier* (Paris: Lottin l'aine, 1770).

5. James A. H. Murray, *A New English Dictionary on Historical Principles* (New York: Macmillan, 1888), vol. IV, p. 29.

6. Murray, *Dictionary on Historical Principles*, vol. II, p. 1048.

7. Book III, chap. XIV, p. 16. Quoted in Peter Thornton, *Seventeenth-Century Interior Decoration in England, France & Holland* (New Haven: Yale University Press, 1978), p. 127. Snailing fringe is evident on the drapery in the portrait of Mrs. Samuel Hill by John Singleton Copley (1764). Jules David Prown, *John Singleton Copley* (Cambridge: Harvard University Press, 1966), vol. 1, fig. 148.

8. Illustrated in Thornton, *Seventeenth Century*, p. 316.

9. Personal conversation with Peter Thornton, London, October 1978.

10. *The Workwoman's Guide* (London: Simpkin, Marshall, and Co., 1838), p. 206.

11. Thornton, *Seventeenth-Century*, p. 127.

12. Illustrated in Thornton, *Seventeenth-Century*, p. 174.

13. Abbott Lowell Cummings, ed., *Bed Hangings: A Treatise on Fabrics and Styles in the Curtaining of Beds, 1650–1850* (Boston: Society for the Preservation of New England Antiquities, 1961), p. 21.

14. Illustrated in Thornton, *Seventeenth Century*, plate II.

15. Anne Pollard Rowe, "Crewel Embroidered Bed Hangings in Old and New England," *Museum of Fine Arts Bulletin* 71 (1973): 106.

16. Cummings, *Bed Hangings*, p. 23.

17. Rowe, "Crewel Embroidered Bed Hangings," p. 106.

18. Peter Thornton pointed out the chairs in the Victoria and Albert Museum to the author in the fall of 1978.

19. Mrs. Freake's chair is somewhat difficult to make out in the painting. For the best reproduction of the painting, *see* Jonathan Fairbanks and Robert Trent, eds., *New England Begins: The Seventeenth Century* (Boston: Museum of Fine Arts, 1982), vol. 3, p. 434. In some cases, the Turkey-work covers were woven with integral borders at the lower edge, eliminating the need for a chevron or checkered heading in the crewel fringe. For an illustration, *see* Thornton, *Seventeenth Century*, p. 111.

20. Alice Morse Earle, *Costume of Colonial Times* (New York: Charles Scribner & Sons, 1894), p. 50. Fairbanks and Trent, *New England Begins*, vol. 3, p. 462. Similar band strings with tassels can be seen on the portraits of Governors Edward Winslow (1645) and John Endicott (1660s).

21. Florence Montgomery, *Printed Textiles: English and American Cottons and Linens, 1700–1850* (New York: Viking Press, 1970), p. 47.

22. Cummings, *Bed Hangings*, p. 19.

23. Brock Jobe, "The Boston Furniture Industry, 1720–1740," in Walter Whitehill et al., eds., *Boston Furniture of the Eighteenth Century* (Boston: The Colonial Society of Massachusetts, 1974), p. 30.

24. Jobe, "Furniture Industry," p. 28.

25. Earle, *Costume*, p. 142.

26. Jobe, "Furniture Industry," p. 30.

27. *Furniture History* 16 (1980): fig. 62.

28. Robert Bishop and Carlton L. Safford, *American Quilts and Coverlets* (New York: Weathervane, 1974), p. 58.

29. The Account Book of Samuel Grant, Boston, Massachusetts, 1728–1737, Massachusetts Historical Society, Boston. The original accounts have been transcribed by Brock Jobe. I thank him for the opportunity to examine them for Grant's utilization of trimmings.

30. Rowe, "Crewel Embroidered Bed Hangings," p. 148.

31. Earle, *Costume*, p. 174.

32. Earle, *Costume*, p. 175.

33. Cummings, *Bed Hangings*, p. 23.

34. Montgomery, *Printed Textiles*, pp. 195, 197.

35. Montgomery, *Printed Textiles*, pp. 197–206.

36. Cornforth, "The Trimmings Maker," p. 112.

37. Prown, *Copley*, vol. 1, fig. 331.

38. Montgomery, *Printed Textiles*, p. 152.

39. Cummings, *Bed Hangings*, fig. 63.

40. For the only completely illustrated chronology of tassels and other upholstery trimmings, *see Des Dorelotiers aux Passementiers* (Paris: Musee des Arts Decoratifs, 1973), an exhibition catalogue sponsored by Chambre Syndicale de la Passementerie.

41. Charles Montgomery, *American Furniture: The Federal Period* (New York: The Viking Press, 1966), p. 44.

42. Letter of Williamina Ridgely to her mother, February 15, 1803, Philadelphia, Ridgely Family Papers, Delaware Division of Historical and Cultural Affairs, Dover, Delaware.

43. George Leland Hunter, *Decorative Textiles: An Illustrated Book on Coverings for Furniture, Walls, Floors* (Philadelphia: J. B. Lippincott Company, 1918), p. 394.

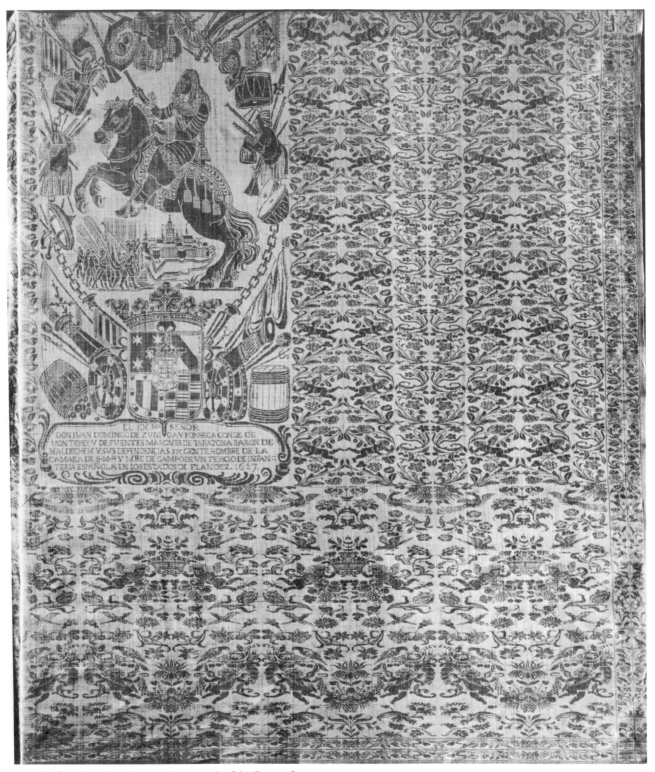

131. Detail of a tablecloth with equestrian portrait of the Count of
Monterey, surrounded by flowers, Flanders, 1667. Linen damask:
Length-4 Dutch ells, width-4 Dutch ells (approximately 280 cm
square). Author's collection.

Some Notes on Western European Table Linen from the 16th through the 18th Centuries

C. A. Burgers

DETAILED descriptions of linens in European household inventories of the sixteenth, seventeenth, and eighteenth centuries reveal not only the important role that linen played in everyday domestic life but also its importance as an indicator of the social status of the owners.[1] Analysis of such inventories and the corroborative evidence of paintings and prints often afford insight into the surprising esteem given to a cupboard well-filled with linen.[2] Only in the nineteenth century can one speak of linen as a cultural object in decline.

Although table linens are often grouped together with bed linens in these inventories, this essay will only consider table linen. (A comparison of table and bed linens should, however, be the subject of further research.) The work here is intended as a general introduction to the subject of table linen used by the middle and upper classes and will focus on measurements, uses, and finishes. Footnotes that refer to surviving pieces of table linen will, however, include descriptions of patterns and a discussion of provenance.

At the beginning of the sixteenth century, damask table linen, characterized by its elaborate reversible patterns achieved by complex looms, was still reserved for royalty, the church, high nobility, and the very rich among the bourgeoisie.[3] As the century progressed, however, linen damask weaving developed into an important branch of the textile industry, with its main centers in Flanders in the Southern Netherlands and Haarlem in Holland, and the use of table linen by merchants, trades people, and others belonging to the middle and upper classes grew. By 1600, most of these households had at least one complete set of table linen, consisting of one or more tablecloths, one or more hand towels, a number of napkins, and one or more banquet napkins.

Tablecloths

According to the sixteenth-century municipal guild statutes in Courtray and Haarlem, tablecloths were woven in six different widths, measured in quarter ells, an old measure equal to approximately 17.5 centimeters. The broadest width was sixteen quarter ells or, as it was commonly expressed, 16/4 ells. This was the equal of 4 Dutch ells or 280 cm (fig. 131). The other widths in descending order were 14/4 (245 cm), 12/4 (210 cm), 10/4 (175 cm), 8/4 (140 cm) and the narrowest 7/4 (approximately 122 cm).[4] These have remained the standard widths for damask linen tablecloths up to our own time.

To judge from surviving linen of the seventeenth and eighteenth centuries, the most common width for tablecloths was 12/4 ells (210 cm).[5] This is seldom apparent from inventories, however, where the length of tablecloths seems to be more important, and the width is often omitted.

Tablecloths were either woven to size, with borders all around, or else made as piece goods with borders at the sides only.[6] In the first case, a line was usually woven between two cloths, where they could be cut apart.[7] In the second, a piece of any required length was cut off the bolt. Tablecloths woven as piece goods could be made in any length because the pattern presented no problem and simply could be broken off abruptly.

A set of table linen included tablecloths of different lengths and widths.[8] Occasionally, an inventory refers to the varying sizes. In 1758, the following are listed: "Two tablecloths of the feather [this was the pattern], 4¾ ells (332.5 cm) long. One ditto narrower, 4¼ ells (297.5 cm) long."[9]

A 1604 Haarlem guild statute prohibited damask linen weavers and manufacturers from sewing narrow pieces of table linen together to make a wide piece or, conversely, from making narrower pieces from a wide piece.[10] Thus, old examples of such made-up damask linen are rare. Of those few that do survive, there is no certainty as to where they were made and when or by whom they were sewn together.[11]

Some tablecloths woven in a simple diamond or diaper-pattern, however, were made up of two lengths sewn together. In the Rijksmuseum, Amsterdam, there is a pieced-together diapered tablecloth, measuring approximately 203 cm wide, that consists of two strips, each of which is 101.5 cm wide; the cloth is 227 cm long.[12] The reason is that diapered linen could be woven on looms far less complicated than those used for making damask; thus, there was substantial cottage production of diapered linens. This unregulated domestic production led to a considerable variety in sizes.[13] Even in sets of sewn-together tablecloths and napkins, the widths of the component strips in the tablecloth often did not correspond to the widths of the napkins.[14]

Laying the Table

When a table was laid, the cloth was allowed to hang well over the edge. Such conventions even applied to tables set for parties out-of-doors.[15] In M. Rumpolt's *New Cookbook*, first published in Frankfurt in 1587 and reprinted as late as 1666, there are directions for laying a perfectly prepared table. First, the dining table should

132. *A Party*, panel by Isaac Elyas, 1620. Rijksmuseum, Amsterdam.

be covered with a fine carpet that hangs down almost to the ground on all four sides. Over this is laid a large tablecloth that has been folded into a square or rectangle and pressed. This tablecloth must cover the carpet down to a handspan above the ground (fig. 132).[16] Over this is laid yet another tablecloth that has been folded and pressed in different ways. This second tablecloth should be a hands-breadth shorter than the previous one all the way around. In seventeenth-century paintings, this layering of tablecovers is seen repeatedly, although usually they are not as elaborate as M. Rumpolts's but have only a single tablecloth or one cloth and a lace-edged runner over it.[17] (The carpet remained on the table virtually all the time, particularly in the Netherlands.[18]) By degrees, however, this way of layering

tablecloths fell into disuse, and by the end of the seventeenth century, the practice was no longer popular.[19]

A most remarkable method of laying tables is described in another German book of the seventeenth century.[20] Here, the folded tablecloth is rolled up, twisted, and then wrung until it is crinkled all over. When the cloth is unfolded and laid over the table, the "waves" are easily pressed in by the placing of the plates and dishes. Such an extraordinary method of laying the table was exceptional and certainly the tablecloths suffered, as the author notes. In daily life, table linen was generally treated in a more straightforward way.[21]

Napkins

In making napkins, weavers were also subject to statutes that specified certain widths. Before the seventeenth century, the two official widths were 4/4 and 3/4 ells (70 cm and 51 cm). The second of these widths was probably not very popular, judging from the fact that few have survived.[22]

Napkins, like tablecloths, were either woven with borders all around or made from piece goods with borders at the side only, in which case they were cut off to the required length through the pattern.[23] Sometimes there were no borders at all. This was often the case with diapered patterns.[24]

In contrast to tablecloth sizes that generally remained constant, the dimensions of napkins appear to have been subject to changes in fashion. At the beginning of the seventeenth century, the customary dimensions of napkins were slightly less than 1½ ells long (approximately 98 cms) by one ell wide (72 cm).[25] Before the second quarter of the century, napkins were somewhat longer and wider; the length was close to 1½ ells (104 cm) and the width slightly more than one ell (about 76 cm).[26] In the third quarter of the century, the trend towards wider and longer napkins continued, although many napkins were still woven to the old measurements. Some napkins of that period are even exceptionally long—as much as 134 cm.[27] From 1660 onwards, napkins were quite wide—80 to 82 cm (fig. 133) and, at least, initially, quite long—approximately 115 cm. Around the beginning of the eighteenth century, however, they became slightly shorter—about 100 cm—while the width remained more or less the same.[28] During the eighteenth century, napkins became square rather than rectangular. Their dimensions were usually one ell square (70 cm), a size still in style today. (It is possible that such square napkins were already in use at the end of the seventeenth century.[29])

During the seventeenth century there was a fairly demonstrable line of development in the size of napkins, but this was not true in the eighteenth century when many more sizes of napkins were used. One reason for the proliferation of sizes may be that new centers of weaving had developed in Germany, Sweden, Scotland, and Ireland, among other places, and each area wove to different measures. Another reason may be that linen damasks were now used by many more people from a much broader segment of the population.

At the beginning of the century, both large and small napkins were made in the same pattern.[30] Nevertheless, throughout the century people generally seem to have preferred larger sizes.[31] At the end of the eighteenth century, the dimensions of napkins underwent another big change when very wide napkins were in fashion for a short time.[32]

Napkins were usually folded in the same way throughout the sixteenth, seventeenth, and eighteenth centuries: They were first folded lengthways four times, then the ends were folded into the center, and, finally, the napkins were folded over double. In this way, the hems remained hidden inside the napkin or else were placed on the outside.[33] In the seventeenth and eighteenth centuries, folded napkins were placed flat beside or on top of the plates when the table was laid.[34] Sometimes a dinner roll was placed inside the folded napkin, just as it is today.[35] During use, the napkin—either wholly or partly opened out—was laid over the knees.[36]

At certain courts, much attention was devoted to folding napkins. For example, at a banquet in 1672 given by the Prince of Orange (later King William III of England) for the members of the States General of the United Netherlands (a legislative body consisting of representatives from the various provinces), "the napkins were very nicely folded in the forms of doves, rabbits, peacocks, dolphins and all sorts of fowl."[37] Seventeenth-century manuals depict numerous examples of napkins made in the shape of fans, fishes, birds, animals, and fortresses.[38] In fact, one could make napkins in any form one liked (fig. 134). These unusual figures served only for show at great feasts and banquets. They were cleared away just before eating began or were used as decorations once the food was served.

Hand Towels

Along with the tablecloths and napkins listed in inventories, one or more matching hand towels are regularly included. Mentioned in a 1664 inventory are "a tablecloth with 24 napkins and a hand towel of damask with animals" and "139 napkins, 6 tablecloths, 9 hand towels, the Hague knot" (the latter probably a diaper pattern).[39] Hand towels usually bear the same woven pattern as the napkins in a set, as the inventory discussed above shows; they can be distinguished from napkins by their length.

Hand towels were used for the important ritual of washing one's hands at a meal. They were carried around by a servant with a ewer and basin to the individual diners and certainly predate the use of napkins. By the seventeenth century, the functions of hand towels were more or less overshadowed by the individual use of napkins. Even then, however, the servant making rounds with ewer, basin, and hand towel over

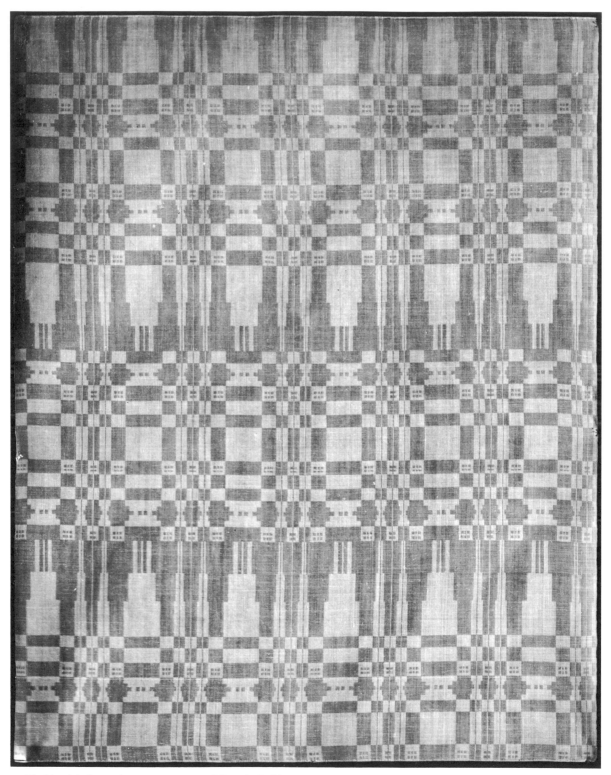

133. Napkin with diapered pattern "Tower Work," marked with a
crown and *WG/44/1742*, probably Netherlands. Linen damask:
Length-107.5 cm, width-82 cm. Rijksmuseum, Amsterdam. Gift of the
Stichting Twickel, 1980, inv. Twickel A 7.

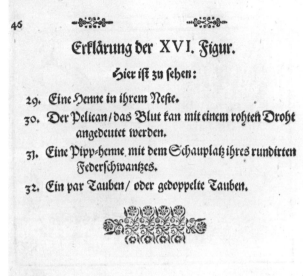

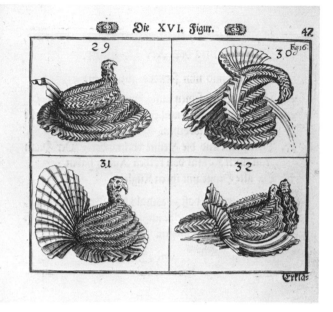

134. Patterns for how to fold napkins. Plates 29–32 in George Philipp Hartssdörfer's *Vollstandig und Von Neuem Vermehrtes Trineir Buch* (Nurnberg, 1665). Copies of this book are at the Cooper-Hewitt Museum of Design in New York and the Germanisches National-museum in Nürnberg.

his shoulder or arm was a familiar sight in well-to-do homes.[40] In middle-class households, hands were washed at a side table or a lavabo and dried on a hand towel that either hung neatly on a rack or upon a hook on the wall.[41]

At court it was a great honor, reserved for dignitaries, to present a hand towel to the king or prince at table. Middle-class households also appear to have paid close attention to the status of guests during the handwashing ritual as the following directions from a 1735 account suggests:

> If it happens that someone of rank invites us to eat, one must never wash one's hands at the same time as the same and if any Lady or Gentleman of much higher rank than we are and there is no Servant to do so, then we must ourselves hold the hand towel and offer it to the same for drying, thus we must at least not suffer that anyone should do this who is superior.[42]

Hand towels also were used traditionally for serving food (fig. 135).[43] At banquets for royal personages, for example, hand towels were worn over the shoulder by high officials who performed services at the royal table. This custom continued to be observed at the French court until the middle of the eighteenth century.

The dimensions of hand towels followed the same general development as those of napkins. At the beginning of the seventeenth century, both hand towels and napkins in the same set of table linen were approximately an ell (72 cm) wide.[44] During mid-century, both became somewhat wider—hand towels being around 77–78 cms. From the third quarter on, hand towels became even wider, as wide as 86–87 cms (fig. 136).[45]

The use of the hand towel probably began to decline in the last quarter of the seventeenth century, although they were still being made until the end of the eighteenth century.[46] These later hand towels, however, are now very rare suggesting that not many were produced.

As with tablecloths, household inventories usually specify only the lengths of hand towels. Varying considerably in their measurements (probably related to their uses), some hand towels are scarcely as big as napkins,[47] while others are as long as two to three ells (140 cm to 210 cm), and even longer. In the inventory of Hardwick Hall in England, for example, a large number of hand towels are mentioned, varying in length from two to nine yards (184 cm to 828 cm).[48] The hand towels in the 1650 estate of a Haarlem linen manufacturer are from

135. *The Parable of Lazarus and the Rich Man* (detail), canvas attributed to Cornelius van Rijck (1598–1628), early seventeenth century. Height-198 cm, width-272 cm. Rijksmuseum, Amsterdam.

136. Hand towel with scattered flowers and the added arms of Dr. Nicolaes Pietersz Croeser and his wife Magteld van Senten, probably Netherlands, 1670s. Linen damask: Length-237.5 cm, width-86.5 cm. Dutch private collection.

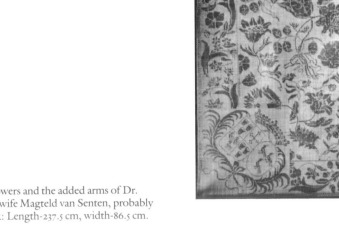

two to twelve ells long (140 cm to 840 cm) and come in various patterns.[49] A surviving linen damask of 1640 may be regarded as an example of a long hand towel of this kind.[50] Perhaps such long hand towels are the "buffet cloths" listed in some household inventories.[51]

Banquet Napkins

A fourth type of linen damask was of a size midway between tablecloths and napkins. These linen damasks are called "banquet napkins or cradle sheets" (fig. 137) in a 1605 weaver's bill for table linen that the States General of the United Netherlands wished to present to the Prince of Wales.[52] This type was made from the sixteenth century into the early eighteenth century. The width of these damasks measures approximately 1½ (approximately 105 cm), a width that also occurs in the weavers' statute of 1592 mentioned earlier. Their length is approximately 2 ells (140 cm). Only a small number of these have survived, and it is still not clear how they were used. A remarkable late example dates from 1756.[53]

Hems

New tablecloths and napkins were first cut off the bolt and then hemmed with either rolled (narrow) or flat (wide) hems. Narrow hems were more customary. When flat hems were used, they generally measured less than half a centimeter wide. Sometimes hems were done in fine openwork with hem-stitching worked in a chevron pattern or overcast bars.[54] The selvages were usually left as is, although very occasionally they were finished off with openwork.[55] This practice, however, seems to have gone out of fashion around the middle of the seventeenth century.

Another way in which hems were finished off was with a row of little points of thread made with the needle.[56] This treatment gave the long straight hems a livelier appearance. Table linen was also finished off with fringe, although few examples have survived.[57]

A very refined finish was achieved by edging table linen with lace.[58] Occasionally this is mentioned in inventories: "one damaske square cloth, laced about."[59] Cloths finished with lace were sometimes depicted in early Haarlem still life paintings, the so-called "breakfast pieces," and in other paintings and prints.[60]

It should be noted that in numerous pictures of the seventeenth and eighteenth centuries, women can be seen bent over their sewing, testifying to the care that housewives gave to the finishing off or repair of their linen.[61]

Marks

A completely different kind of finish for linen was the application of marks of ownership. This was a frequent practice, and such marks are often mentioned in inventories, such as this one of 1633: "In this cupboard is to be found (the) linen, it is not all marked, but the finest and most important is marked. . . ." A 1758 inventory of the Stadtholder of Holland, the Prince of Orange, lists: "Bought in the year 1758 6 dozen fine Haarlem napkins for the princely persons, not yet hemmed, 1¾ ells long[122.5 cms], which will be marked P.V.O. 72 1758 F."[62] Here we find a specific indication of one method used for marking: first came the initials, *P.V.O.* for Prince or Princess Van Orange; then *72*, reference to the number of napkins in the set; then *1758* for the year of purchase; and finally an *F* for *Furstelijk* (princely). Other linen in the same list was marked in the same way but with different last letters, according to the purpose. Some were marked with an *H* for Hofmeester (House-steward), others with a *K* for kitchen, and still others with an *L* for lackeys or servants. Napkins in the same set usually bear the same number; only rarely can they be found numbered in succession.

Inventories seldom specify the colors or techniques used in marking linens, although several early references do attest to the use of blue and red thread. A document from 1597 included "1 pair of sheets, made anno 1596 the 19th of July . . . marked with blue thread GVL 96."[63] In the household books of Lord William Howard of Naworth Castle, 1621, we find an entry for "Coventry blue to mark napkins etc."[64] Unfortunately, very few blue marks have survived on table linen.[65]

Red thread is noted in the inventory of a 1597 estate that included "3 pillow covers made the 20th of June anno 1596, marked with red silk GVL 96." A later inventory from 1661 noted the use of black thread, listing "three dozen new damask napkins with a black crown."[66]

Due to frequent washings and wear, colors used for embroidered marks have often faded to an indeterminate color, sometimes turning completely white. Marks made on table linen in cross or stem stitch were more susceptible to wear and tear than the linen itself. In a 1633 inventory, the appraisers described two tablecloths: "the one of the year 15 and on the other the date is washed out," and two dozen napkins "where the letters are worn away."[67] Undoubtedly, a great deal of the seventeenth- and eighteenth-century linen that is now without markings was originally marked.

Marked napkins are occasionally depicted in paint-

137. Banquet napkin with the English royal arms and the initials of the
weaver Paschier Lammertijn, Haarlem. Linen damask: Length-134
cm, Width-107 cm. M.A.O.C. Gravin van Bylandt Stichting,
's-Gravenhage.

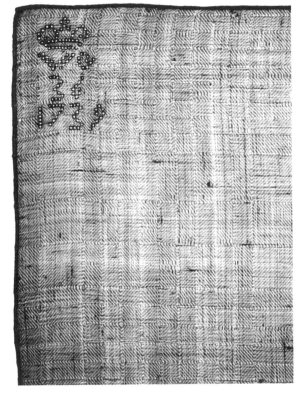

138. Detail of a napkin with diapered pattern, marked with a crown and *WG/36/1739*, probably Netherlands. Linen: Length-110.25 cm, width-85 cm. Rijksmuseum, Amsterdam. Gift of the Stichting Twickel, 1980, inv. Twickel B8.

139. Detail of a napkin with a floral design, marked *E V A* (eyelet hole letters) and dated *1642* (white embroidery), probably Netherlands. Linen damask: Length-106 cm, width-75 cm. Author's collection.

ings, such as a still life painted in 1646 by the Amsterdam artist J. J. Treck.[68] A napkin with a similar escutcheon mark may have been worked originally in colored thread (*see* fig. 140).

Whitework marks or "cutwork letters in white thread"[69] have been found on diapered linens that could have been used either as hand towels or as napkins, depending on how their measurements are interpreted.[70]

Several examples of linen damasks with marks made of woven arms have already been mentioned. Embroidered arms were also used; these are found mainly in Scandinavia. The earliest known example probably dates from 1553, but for the most part, linens with arms embroidered on damask in this way date from the seventeenth century.[71]

Marks were also worked in eyelet stitch, a more durable method than surface embroidery (fig. 138). Sometimes the two methods are combined, with initials worked in eyelet hole letters and the date or the number of the napkin stitched in white embroidery (fig. 139). In some cases, both kinds of marks are applied separately in different corners.

140. Detail of a napkin with geometrical pattern in broken twill weave, marked *AKD* with an escutcheon and dated 1618 below, Denmark (?). Linen: Length-90.5 cm, width-76.5 cm. One or more of these marks may have been worked originally in colored thread. Rijksmuseum, Amsterdam.

In conclusion, a brief word should be said about dating table linen. The illustrations and references in this essay represent the best documented and dated damasks. They include a relatively large proportion with embroidered arms (fig. 140) or flower patterns because it is necessary to begin with these dated pieces so one can then attempt to place the undated linen damasks in their correct period. This last process, however, must be done with caution because there were many different types of patterns, some of which remained in favor for long periods.[72] The use of dimensions in dating linens presents similar problems. Comparisons between eighteenth-century linen damask patterns and similar patterns used by the silk industry may prove helpful.[73] In addition, it should be remembered that embroidered initials are rarely useful. It is the exceptional case where the provenance can be traced back to the original owner. The marks on damasks may, however, represent later owners.[74]

NOTES

The following essay has been edited to fit within the format of the collected essays. The original essay as submitted by the author underwent significant reworking.

1. References given to linen damasks, paintings, drawings, and prints in the notes are closely related to the slides shown by the author at the Conference on Historic Upholstery and Drapery (1979), with the limited photographic material then available. For problems involved in photographing white linen damask, *see* Marta Clareus, "Fotografering av vit damast," in *Fataburen* (Nordiska Museet och Skansens Aarsbok, 1967), p. 239 ff. Photographers at the Rijksmuseum, Amsterdam, have also conducted successful experiments in this field.

2. *Interior with Women Beside a Linen Chest*, oil on canvas, by Pieter de Hooch, 1663, Rijksmuseum, Amsterdam.

3. Fragments of a tablecloth with apocryphal story of Susanna bathing and the added arms of Maximilian van Egmond-Buren and Françoise de Lannoy, second quarter of the sixteenth century, Rijksmuseum, Amsterdam (lent by H.M. Queen Juliana).

4. State Archives (Municipal Archives), Courtray, Politieke Ordonnanties, Reg. #I, pp. 188–189vo (1545), p. 195vo (23 November 1577). Municipal Archives, Haarlem, coll. MS 100, pp. 135vo (1592) on the model of the Courtray statute. An example of the widest sort is a tablecloth with the arms of Haarlem and the arms of the Princess Royal, 1660–1663, 4 by 9 ells (280 cm by 630 cm), H. M. Queen Juliana; C. A. Burgers, *Damast* ('s-Hertogenbosch, 1959), fig. 40.

5. Tablecloth with a "banquet on the table" (a laid table) in the center, borders with agricultural scenes and ships, and the arms of France and Navarre, Haarlem, 1604, 12/4 by 6 ells (210 cm by 420 cm), Rijksmuseum, Amsterdam (loan). For a similar pattern, *see* G. T. van Ijsselsteyn, *White Figurated Linen Damask: From the 15th to the Beginning of the 19th Century* (The Hague: Van Goor Zonen, 1962), no. 198, fig. 74; and J. Six, "Het Einde van Passchier Lammertijn," *Oud-Holland* 33 (1915): 43, fig. II.

6. An example with borders all around is a tablecloth with allegorical representation of Caritas, first quarter of the seventeenth century, 12/4 by 3 ells (210 cm by 210 cm), author's collection. For the design, *see De Vork in de Steel* (Zeist, 1962), no. 232. Side borders decorate a tablecloth with a biblical story of Joseph and his brothers, second quarter of the seventeenth century, Nordiska Museet, Stockholm.

7. Linen damask with flower pattern, mid-seventeenth century, Skokloster Castle, Sweden.

8. A surviving set of diapered table linen, marked *AVS 1648* comprises: 2 tablecloths, approximately 152 cm by 228 cm; 1 tablecloth, approximately 220 cm by 230 cm; 53 napkins, approximately 72 cm by 96 cm (slightly shortened in the eighteenth century), Dutch private collection. Also, in the Rijksmuseum, table linen with a wreath and flower pattern: 1 tablecloth, 272 cm by 344 cm; 1 tablecloth, 204 cm by 276 cm; napkins 86.75 cm by 120.5 cm, inv. R.B.K. #1977, inv. Ruurlo.

9. S. W. A. Drossaers and Th. H. Lunsingh Scheurleer, *Inventarissen van de inboedels in de verblijven van de Oranjes* (The Hague: Rijks Geschiedkundige, 1974), vol. 2, inv. Stadtholders' Palace 1757–1759, p. 673.

10. Municipal Archives, Haarlem, coll. MS 100, 1604, p. 140.

11. Two hand towels with the "Creation of Man" sewn together, 176 by 220 cms, first half of the seventeenth century, Swedish private collection. In the Rijksmuseum, Amsterdam, the Nordiska Museet, Stockholm, and the Nationalmuseum, Copenhagen, there are examples of two hand towels (some with different patterns) sewn together to make a tablecloth.

12. The diapered tablecloth of two lengths sewn together is marked *WG 3 1737*. The matching napkins, marked *WG 36 1737* are 92 cm by 112 cm. There are no borders. Rijksmuseum, Amsterdam, inv. Twickel D 26.

13. The bleaching of diapered linen in Haarlem, however, did fall under the jurisdiction of the Haarlem authorities.

14. Napkin with diapered pattern, "The Orange Tree," marked *GS 60 1726*, 78.5 cm by 115.75 cm, and matching tablecloth marked *GS 5*, two lengths, each approximately 104 cm wide and 241 cm long, Rijksmuseum, Amsterdam, inv. Twickel D 27. In the near future, I hope to publish photographs of a large collection of white diapered table linen of the seventeenth and eighteenth centuries. Comparisons among these and the patterns of American colored coverlets of the nineteenth century is particularly interesting.

15. *La Benediction de la Table*, engraving by A. Bosse (1602–1676), Rijksprentenkabinet, Rijksmuseum, Amsterdam. *An Outdoor Party*, panel attributed to Dirck Hals (1591–1656), Rijksmuseum, Amsterdam.

16. *Le Goust*, engraving by A. Bosse, Rijksprentenkabinet, Rijksmuseum, Amsterdam. *A Garden Party*, panel by Esaias van de Velde, 1615, Rijksmuseum, Amsterdam.

17. The comments in the 1619 inventory of the castle of Buren are probably connected with this: ". . . because double tablecloths are laid" and "because people want to have them, the tablecloths, double." *See* Drossaers and Lunsingh Scheurleer, *Inventarissen van de inboedels*, p. 178. *An Outdoor Party*, panel by Dirck Hals, Frans Hals Museum, Haarlem.

18. *Man and Woman Sharing a Meal*, canvas on panel by Gabriel Metsu (1629–1667), Rijksmuseum, Amsterdam.

19. *Rumor erat in casa*, canvas by Cornelis Troost, 1739, Mauritshuis, The Hague.

20. *Vollständig Vermehrtes TRINCIR BUCH Von Tafeldecken, Trinciren, Reitigung der Mundkoste, Schauessen und Schaugerichten, benebens*

XXV Gast-oder Tischfragen (Nürnberg: Paulus Fürsten Kunsthändlern, 1665). A copy is at the Cooper Hewitt Museum of Design, New York. A similar edition is in the Germanisches Nationalmuseum, Nürnberg. *See also Höfliches und Vermehrtes Komplementier Büchlein* (1650), British Library, London.

21. *The family of Joos Lambrechtse and Susanna Langenes at Table*, unknown artist, 1654, Atlas van Stok, Rotterdam. *Outdoor Party*, Gesina ter Borch, c. 1660, Rijksprentenkabinet, Rijksmuseum, Amsterdam.

22. Napkin with the "Sacrifice of Isaac" embroidered in the center with the initials *GL AK* and with the arms of Gunde Lange and Anne Krabe, 1627, approximately 53.5 cm by 70 cm, National Museum, Copenhagen.

23. Napkin with exotic flowers and added monogram and arms of David Rutgers and Margaretha Block, 1680s, 82 cm by 119 cm, Rijksmuseum, Amsterdam. *See Bulletin van het Rijksmuseum* 21 (1973): 134, 141, fig. 16. Napkin with a bizarre pattern, c. 1707–1708, 79 cm by 100 cm, author's collection. C. A. Burgers, "Bizarre patronen in linnen damast," in *Nederlands Kunsthistorisch Jaarboek* (1980), fig. 6. There is a tablecloth with a closely related pattern in the Daughters of the American Revolution Museum, Washington, D.C.

24. Napkin with diaper pattern "The English Wardrobe," marked *WG 36 1739*, 85 cm by 110.2 cm, Rijksmuseum, Amsterdam, inv. Twickel B 8. For the design, *see Nederlandse Rijksmusea 1977*, 99 (1979): 41, fig. 38.

25. Napkin with arms and monogram of Christian IV of Denmark, 1604, 71, by 98 cm, author's collection. C. A. Burgers, "Dutch Damasks for Denmark," *Documenta Textilia: Festschrift Für Sigrid Müller-Christensen* (München: Deutscher Junstverlag, 1981), fig. 1. For a napkin with an identical pattern, but dated 1602, *see* van Ijsselsteyn, *Linen Damask*, no. 20, fig. 10.

26. Napkin with scattered flowers and added arms of Adriaen Van Veen and Helena Van Foreest, 1645, 76 cm by 104 cm, author's collection. For the same flower pattern, but with different arms woven in and dated 1658, *see* Peter Thornton, *Baroque and Rococo Silks* (London: Faber and Faber, 1965), pl. 14A.

27. Napkin with the arms of the Princess Royal, widow of Stadtholder William II, woven between 1660 and 1663, 90 cm by 117 cm, H. M. Queen Juliana. *See* Burgers, *Damast*, fig. 41. Napkin with equestrian portrait and arms of the Count of Monterey, 1667, 90 cm by 134 cm, author's collection. For an identical napkin, *see* A. C. Weibel, *Two Thousand Years of Textiles: The Figured Textiles of Europe and the Near East* (New York: Pantheon Books, 1952), fig. 282.

28. Napkin with vines and the added arms of Van Essen quartering Van Varick, c. 1680, 82 cm by 115 cm, author's collection. *See* C. A. Burgers, "Tafelgoed in vroeger tijd," *Voedingsnieuws* 60 (1969): 939, fig. 6. For a napkin with the same design but different arms, dated 1682, and measuring approximately 86 cm by 116.5 cm, *see* van Ijsselsteyn, *Linen Damask*, no. 251, fig. 85. Napkin with the capture of Meenen by General Salisch, 1706, 80 cm by 109 cm, author's collection. Napkin with a bizarre pattern, c. 1711, 79 cm by 100 cm, *see* C. A. Burgers, "Bizarre Patronen in Linen Damast," in *Nederlands Kunsthistorisch Jaarboek* (1980), fig. 12. A similar pattern may perhaps be the one meant by the reference in the 1765 inventory of the estate of Marie Louise of Hessen Cassel: "damask, pillars with vases." *See* Drossaers and Lunsingh Scheurleer, *Inventarissen van de inboedels* vol. 3, p. 136.

29. Napkin with "lace pattern," 71.5 cm by 66.5 cm, first quarter of the eighteenth century, author's collection (cf. note 66).

30. Napkin commemorating the marriage of Philip V of Spain to Marie Louise of Savoy, 1701, 88.5 cm by 110.5 cm. *See Gebilddamast, Krefelder Gewebesammlung* (Bestandskatalog I, 1968), fig. VI. The same pattern is seen on a napkin 78.5 cm by 106 cm, author's collection. Napkins with a view of Turin, 1707, one 77.5 cm by 115 cm and the other 89.5 cm by 113 cm, both in author's collection. *See* van Ijsselsteyn, *Linen Damask*, no. 330, fig. 109.

31. Napkin with "lace pattern" and added arms of Hendrik van Ysselmuden, 1731, 85 cm by 115 cm, Rijksmuseum, Amsterdam. *See Nederlandse Rijksmusea 1976*, 98 (1978): 33, fig. 29. The "lace pattern" itself was copied and rewoven in the nineteenth century. Witness a surviving pattern drawing on millimeter squared paper, 106.75 cm by 257.5 cm, for jacquard cards, author's collection. The latter pattern was probably drawn at Gustav Berndt's, Crefeld (Germany), for a Dutch factory, Gebroeders Rath, Veghel N. Br. Napkin with a late "lace pattern" and added arms and initials of Pieter De Wolff Pieters and Ursula van Mekeren, 1730s, 88 cm by 118 cm, Rijksmuseum, Amsterdam. *See* C. A. Burgers, "Een achttiende eeuws servet met bloemmotieven," *Bulletin van het Rijksmuseum* 23, no. 1 (May 1975): 76–78.

32. Napkin with diaper pattern, marked *SW 34 1785*, 108.5 cm by 117.5 cm, Rijksmuseum, Amsterdam, inv. Twickel A 10.

33. This method of folding can be studied, for example, in numerous still life paintings such as *Breakfast Piece*, Clara Peeters (1589–after 1657). *See* the catalogue *Nederlandse Stillevens uit de 17de eeuw* (Dordrecht: Dordrechts Museum, 1962), no. 73, fig. 16. *See also* the painting mentioned in note 35, following.

34. *Les Quatres Saisons*, engraving by A. Bosse, Rijksprentenkabinet, Rijksmuseum, Amsterdam. *A Meal in Friesland*, unknown artist, Netherlands, eighteenth century, private collection (formerly on loan to the Fries Museum, Leeuwarden). *See De Vork in de Steel*, no. 285.

35. *The Crossbowmen's Civic Guard*, Bartholomeus van der Helst, 1648, Rijksmuseum, Amsterdam.

36. *Crossbowmen's Civic Guard*, Van der Helst. *Pesach-meal at a Portuguese-Jewish Family in Amsterdam*, B. Picart, 1725, Joods Historisch Museum, Amsterdam.

37. *Banquet presented by the Prince of Orange on 1 March 1672*, Gerard de Lairesse (1640–1711), Rijksprentenkabinet, Rijksmuseum, Amsterdam. *Banquet presented by the Prince of Orange on 1 March 1672*, Romeyn de Hooghe (1645–1708), Rijksprentenkabinet, Rijksmuseum, Amsterdam. K. van Alkemade, *Nederlandsche Dischplechtigheden* (1732), vol. 1, p. 504.

38. *See* note 20, above. *See also L'ecole parfaite des officier de la Bouche: Instruction pour bien plier la linge, serviette frisée pliée par bandes, pliée en forme de melon simple etc.* (Paris, 1666). To make a sculpturally folded napkin, one first strengthened it with a dressing. Then the complicated folds were sewn firmly in place. Where necessary, the napkins were cut. Eyes were inset in figures of birds and animals.

39. National Archives of Friesland, Leeuwarden, collection of Frisian Society, Sminiaarchief 599. National Archives of Gelderland, Arnhem, Archief Rozendaal 805.

40. *A House of Pleasure*, Eglon van der Neer, 1675, Mauritschuis, The Hague. *Woman at her Toilet*, Gerard ter Borch, 1660s, Detroit Institute of Arts, Detroit, Michigan.

41. *Merry Company*, Willem Buytewech (1591–1624), Boymans-van Beuningen Museum, Rotterdam. *Domestic Interior*, Gesina ter Borch (1631–1690), Rijksprentenkabinet, Rijksmuseum, Amsterdam.

42. C. van Laer, quoted in *Het groot ceremonieboek de beschafde zeeden* (Amsterdam, 1735), p. 474. The quotation was probably borrowed

from a book like *Traité de la civilité que se pratique en France parmi les honnestes gens* (1673).

43. D. Philippe after J. Toornvliet, *Banquet given by the States General for Charles II of England in the Mauritshuis in The Hague on 30 May 1660* Rijksprentenkabinet, Rijksmuseum, Amsterdam. *See also* K. van Alkemade, *Nederlandsche Dischplechtigheden*, p. 434.

44. Hand towel with hunting pattern, first quarter of the seventeenth century, 72 cm by 203 cm, author's collection. *See* C. A. Burgers, "Tafelgoed in vroeger tijd," p. 942. For the same pattern, but with added arms, *see* van Ijsselsteyn, *Linen Damask*, no. 181, fig. 67.

45. Hand towel with small scattered flowers, marked *E V E 1660*, 77.5 cm by 210 cm, author's collection. The Rijksmuseum possesses a hand towel similar to that in fig. 136, but without any arms (inv. R.B.K. 1977 inv. Ruurlo), 87 cm by 238 cm. A slightly narrower napkin with the same pattern, c. 1670, 78 cm by 112 cm, author's collection. For the design, *see* J. Six, "Oud Tafellinnen," *Het Huis Oud en Nieuw* 6 (1908): pl. III. A napkin with the arms of Dirck Tulp and Catharina Resteau, between 1676 and 1686, 86 cm by 115 cm, Dutch private collection.

46. Hand towel with a typical late eighteenth-century pattern, marked *WS 2*, approximately 88 cm by 177 cm, last quarter of the eighteenth century, Rijksmuseum, Amsterdam, inv. Twickel C 27.

47. Hand towel with diaper pattern "Tower work," marked *WG 6 1742*, approximately 82 cm by 114 cm, Rijksmuseum, Amsterdam, inv. Twickel A 7. This table linen is listed in the 1812 inventory of the estate of H. U. W. Graaf van Wassenaar: ". . . 6 hand towels marked *WG*."

48. Lindsay Boynton and Peter Thornton, "The Hardwick Hall Inventories of 1601," *Furniture History* 7 (1971): 37–40.

49. J. Six, "De Boedel van Quirijn Jansz Damast," *Oud-Holland* 28 (1910): 29–33.

50. Hand towel with the biblical story of Ahab and Naboth, 1640, 70.5 cm by 410 cm, author's collection.

51. Drossaers and Lunsingh Scheurleer, *Inventarissen van de inboedels* vol. 2, p. 63, inv. Leeuwarden 1633: "2 buffet cloths of the year 30"; and vol. 1, p. 618, inv. Dieren 1699: "Two dozen napkins, two tablecloths, two buffet cloths." Boynton and Thornton, "Hardwick Hall Inventories," pp. 37–40: "A cubbard Cloth of damask a yard and a half brode and too yardes long" (138 cm by 184 cm long) and "A Cubberd cloth of damask to Cover the same lynnen," and so forth.

52. C. A. Burgers, "Nogmaals Passchier Lammertijn," *Oud-Holland* 80 (1965): 48–49. Napkins with the same subject, but slightly narrower borders are also known. *Nederlandse Rijksmusea* 92 (1972): 66–67, fig. 42; and van Ijsselsteyn, *Linen Damask*, no. 22.

53. *Elisabeth van der Mersche*, Michiel van Musscher, 1669; and *Two women Busying over their Needlework*, Geertruydt Roghman, 1647, Rijksmuseum, Amsterdam.

54. Napkin with representation of Caritas, first quarter of the seventeenth century (*see* note 6), author's collection. Hand towel with a geometrical pattern in broken twill weave and with whitework marks *MP* approximately 71 cm by 94 cm, possibly first half of the seventeenth century, Rijksmuseum, Amsterdam. *Still Life*, Floris van Schoten (15?-after 1655), Dienst verspreide Rijkscollecties, 's-Gravenhage.

55. Fragment of a tablecloth with a geometrical pattern in broken twill weave, first quarter of the seventeenth century, approximately 88.5 by 129 cms, author's collection.

56. Napkin with the "Instruments of the Passion," sixteenth century or first quarter of the seventeenth century, 68 cm by 101 cm,

Rijksmuseum, Amsterdam. *See* C. A. Burgers, *Antiek Damast Modern Gedekt* (Enschede, 1964), fig. 2.

57. Napkin with diaper pattern, c. 1700, 88 cm by 108 cm (with fringe, 88 cm by 111 cm), author's collection.

58. Napkin with pattern known as "Plus Oultre," first quarter of the seventeenth century, approximately 98 cm by 108 cm (with lace, 106.5 cm by 116 cm), Rijksmuseum, Amsterdam. A hand towel with diaper pattern, mid-seventeenth century, 74 cm by 170 cm, Dutch private collection.

59. Inventories made for Sir William and Sir Thomas Fairfax, *Archeologia* 48 (1884): 133. I am most grateful to my colleague Santina Levey of the Victoria and Albert Museum for allowing me to look at her notes on these and other English inventories.

60. *Breakfast Piece*, Florisz Claezs van Dijck, 1613, Frans Hals Museum, Haarlem. *Le Mauvais riche et le Lazare*, engraving by A. Bosse, Rijksprentenkabinet, Rijksmuseum, Amsterdam.

61. Banquet napkin with diaper pattern marked *G 2 1756*, approximately 107.5 cm by 141.5 cm, Rijksmuseum, Amsterdam, inv. Twickel A 4.

62. Drossaers and Lunsingh Scheurleer, *Inventarissen van de inboedels*, vol. 2, p. 44, inv. Leeuwarden, 1633; and vol. 2, p. 677, inv. Stadtholder's Palace, 1757–1759.

63. Drossaers and Lunsing Scheurleer, *Inventarissen van de inboedels* vol. 2, p. 20, inv. Leeuwarden, 1597.

64. *The Surtees Society* 68 (1877): 136.

65. Linen sheet (two lengths sewn together), 106.5 cm and 106.5 cm by 284 cm, marked *EB* (blue cross stitch); *BM* (blue cross stitch); *1632* (blue cross stitch); and, in addition, *BH 1* (faded?), Victoria and Albert Museum, London. (It is questionable whether the letters *BH* were marked at the same time as the date.) Napkin and hand towel with diaper pattern, possibly mid-seventeenth century, marked *CH 42* and *CH 3* respectively (both blue cross stitch), approximately 76 cm by 107 cm and 76 cm by 102 cm, respectively, Rijksmuseum, Amsterdam.

66. Napkin with "lace pattern," marked *VS 8* (red cross stitch, eighteenth or nineteenth century?), first quarter of the eighteenth century, approximately 71.5 cm by 66.5 cm, author's collection. Napkin with flower pattern and the added arms of Adriaen Nocolaesz Boogaert and Anne Briel, marked with a crowned monogram obliquely in the corner, third quarter of the seventeenth century, 82.25 cm by 116.5 cm, Dutch private collection. Drossaers and Lunsingh Scheurleer, *Inventarissen van de inboedels*, vol. 2, p. 119, inv. Leeuwarden, 1681; vol. 2, p. 20, inv. Leeuwarden, 1597.

67. Drossaers and Lunsingh Scheurleer, *Inventarissen van de inboedels* vol. 2, p. 63, inv. Leeuwarden, 1633.

68. *Still Life with Fish*, Anne Vallayer-Coster, signed on the napkin *VC 6, 1787* (red cross stitch), Dutch private collection. *See France in the Eighteenth Century* (London: Royal Academy of Arts, 1968), no. 290, fig. 120. Natalie Rothstein of the Victoria and Albert Museum kindly drew my attention to a still life by J. M. Hambach signed with a monogram *IMH* (cross stitch). *Still Life*, J. J. Treck, signed and dated 1646, National Gallery, London.

69. Drossaers and Lunsingh Scheurleer, *Inventarissen van de inboedels* vol. 2, p. 20, inv. Leeuwarden, 1597.

70. Hand towel or napkin with a diaper pattern, marked *H E* and *1651* 69.5 by 87 cms, Rijksmuseum, Amsterdam, inv. Twickel B 18. For another example, *see* note 54, above.

71. Fragment of a tablecloth with a geometric pattern in broken twill weave, marked *GG KFD* beneath the arms of Gabriel Gyldenstjerne

and Kirsten Friis Datter and the date *1553*, 54 by 107 cms, National
Museum, Copenhagen. Tablecloth with the apocryphal story of
Daniel, and with the embroidered initials and coats of arms of Oluf
Rosensparre and Lisbeth Guldenstierne, dated 1615, Swedish private
collection. For another example, see note 22.

72. Napkin with the same flower pattern as the one in note 74,
following, dated 1642 and napkin with identical flower pattern with
the added arms of Douwe van Aylva and Lucia van Meckema and the
woven date 1662, Dutch private collection. The pattern of the Sacrifice
of Isaac of 1627 (*see* note 22, above) was still woven in exactly the same
way in 1663, albeit with borders that were completely redesigned
about 1660. For an example, *see* napkins with the "Sacrifice of Isaac"
and with the added arms and names of Duco Martna van Burmania
and Lucia van Iuckema, 1663, also embroidered *evb 1664*, 76 by 105 cms,
Fries Museum, Leeuwarden. (*See* van Ijsselsteyn, *Linen Damask*, Cat.
no. 71, fig. 24.)

73. Napkin with a large branch of flowers and leaves, c. 1732–35,
approximately 86.5 by 118 cms, Rijksmuseum, Amsterdam. *See* the
design for a woven silk by Anna Maria Garthwaite, c. 1734, Victoria
and Albert Museum, London.

74. Napkin with diaper pattern, seventeenth century, 72.5 by 102 cms,
marked *HVA* with eyelet hole letters in one corner and *IEVB 30 1763* in
another, author's collection. The dimensions of the napkin point to a
seventeenth-century origin, and the pattern certainly fits in there, too.
If one compares the initials, then the *HVA* is worked entirely in the
seventeenth-century tradition. The cautious conclusion of someone
through whose hands countless linen damasks have passed is that
notwithstanding the embroidered date 1763, we have a seventeenth-
century napkin.

141. Plate from *Werken van D. Marot* (Amsterdam, 1707[?]), p. 81.
Four window curtains in the Venetian style, by Daniel Marot, designer
to the courts of France, Holland, and England. The designs date from
about 1700. Curtains covering the window opening are raised vertically by means of tapes and rings stitched to the back through which
cords were run. The cords were wound around pairs of cloak pins
fastened to the window frame at a convenient height. In this way the
curtains could be raised to any desired level. Courtesy, The Henry
Francis du Pont Winterthur Museum Library.

18th-Century American Bed and Window Hangings

Florence M. Montgomery

BED AND WINDOW HANGINGS, like clothes, have in times past bestowed status upon their owners. This was particularly true in America in the eighteenth century, when textiles were the primary forms of decoration in the home. Indeed, the quality and richness of the fabrics used in bed and window hangings distinguished the homes of the rich from those of the middle class.

Although window and bed hangings are the subject of this essay, the reader should be aware at the outset that neither bed hangings nor curtains were used in every home in colonial America. For example, a comprehensive study of estate inventories in Philadelphia County from 1700 to 1775 has shown that while many estates listed bedding, only half mentioned bedsteads, and only about a third of these included hangings.[1] Window curtains were found even less frequently: Only one of every ten inventories referred to some sort of window coverings.

Undoubtedly, the reason that bed and window hangings were not widely used was their great expense. For example, the same study shows that when a householder did own bedding and bed hangings, these were among the most valuable possessions in the estate. In fact, during the colonial period in Philadelphia, the valuations of bed furnishings exceeded those of silver plate. Like silver, hangings and bedding were symbols of prosperity.

The style of bed and window hangings in eighteenth-century America closely followed that of England, as did all colonial upholstery and furnishing practices. The colonists who were mainly from England, had a natural preference for English fashions, and this continued to be so even after the American Revolution.

American colonists learned about the latest in English fashion from many sources. They could see the rich furniture, curtains, and bed hangings brought to the colonies by English royal governors or ordered from London to the specifications of wealthy colonists. Colonists received advice on "the newest fashion" and "the most approved manner now in Vogue" from upholsterers "lately arrived from London," as those craftsmen proudly described themselves in newspaper advertisements.[2]

Colonists could also study English pattern books, like Thomas Chippendale's *The Gentleman & Cabinet-Maker's Director*, for clues to cosmopolitan taste. These pattern books outlined in detail the look of fashionable rooms in detail, including the materials best suited to a drawing room, dining room, or bed chamber, and their

fashion dictates were often followed quite precisely. For example, Chippendale advocated that furnishing materials match in color, if not always in fabric. Colonists tried to match, or at least harmonize, the upholstery fabrics and curtain materials when possible. Furnishings chosen for the new State House in Hartford, Connecticut, in 1796, included red silk velvet for two armchairs for the speakers of the House, red moreen for the window stools, and red morocco for other chairs.[3]

No doubt because of this intense interest in all things English, great quantities of English furnishing fabrics were imported during the eighteenth century, along with hardware and a great variety of trimmings. (*See* Linda Wesselman Jackson's essay in this volume for a detailed discussion of trimmings.) Regarding the particular subject of this essay—American window and bed hangings in the eighteenth century—newspaper advertisements and merchants' orders clearly show that, for the most part, these hangings were made from English materials.

Window Curtains

During the eighteenth century, three distinct treatments of window curtains, or variations thereof, were used: straight hanging, Venetian, and festoon. After the American Revolution, French rod curtains suspended from rings connected to pulley cords also came into vogue.

For straight hanging curtains, pieces of cloth were tacked to the window frame and held back by tiebacks. The curtains hung to the sill and sometimes were finished off with a straight, fringed valance. Examples of these simple curtains are found in American paintings such as the portraits of Mr. and Mrs. James Eldredge, painted by an anonymous artist in about 1790 and presently on loan to the Wadsworth Atheneum, Hartford.

Venetian curtains (fig. 141) were raised like Venetian blinds and resembled modern Austrian shades. Tapes and rings were sewn vertically on the back of a single width of material that covered the window completely and hung to the sill. *The Workwoman's Guide*, first published in London in 1838, describes a Venetian curtain as an "old fashioned simple curtain still in use in churches, small houses and for housekeepers' rooms." The *Guide* continues:

> The curtain is in as many breadths as is required for the width of the window, and of the proper length. The top is nailed to the cornice, and small loops or rings are put down the seams of the breadths, at equal distances. . . . Through

142. *The Sargent Family*, an oil painting by an anonymous American painter, c. 1800. A simple festoon curtain hangs at the window. The material was drawn up in two festoons with points hanging down at either side of the window frame. Courtesy, National Gallery of Art, Washington, D. C. Gift of Edgar William and Bernice Chrysler Garbisch.

these rings are passed cords which unite in one long cord, and on pulling this cord, the whole curtain draws up, forming as many festoons as there are breadths, or rather lengths. This cord must be wound round and round two pins or hooks placed at the side of the window.[4]

Festoon curtains (fig. 142) were made of two straight pieces of cloth hanging to the sill, with the tapes and rings sewn diagonally on the back from the bottom center to the outer top. When the cords were pulled, the cloth was gathered up from the center of the window in festoons with tails or points hanging down at each side of the window frame. A copperplate-printed festoon curtain with tapes and rings stitched to the back in this manner survives in the collection of the Litchfield Historical Society, Litchfield, Connecticut.

French rod curtains were a major innovation of the late eighteenth century. The rods, using a mechanism similar to the modern traverse rod, allowed the curtains to be opened by drawing them from the center to each side of the window. By making it possible to open curtains without their being raised from the floor, the rods eliminated the awkward bunches of material that were so often a problem with raised-up curtains.[5]

Among the fabrics used for curtains (as well as for other furnishings), a kind of hierarchy can be observed, ranging from plain woven linens and cottons, to checks, to printed linens and cottons, to wools with handsome stamped finishes, and, most important, to patterned silks and damasks. Materials of wool are most frequently listed in the late seventeenth and first half of the eighteenth century. By the time of the American Revolution, cotton materials such as dimity (fig. 143) and a great variety of printed textiles were in vogue. Silk fabrics were used infrequently for furnishings in America. They were costly and far less durable than worsteds.

Nevertheless, some wealthy individuals did upholster their rooms lavishly with silk. In 1773, John Apthorp, a wealthy Bostonian, who had "A very rich Silk Damask Bed, with Window Curtains, Chairs, and an easy Chair, all in the newest Taste," together with "A large Sopha and ten Chairs covered with the best crimson Silk-Damask and four large Window Curtains of the same." "A small Sopha and five Chairs of the same Damask, in the Chinese Taste" completed the list.[6]

In 1771, John Cadwalader of Philadelphia ordered deep blue silk damask from London mercers for curtains in his front parlor. The curtains were fashioned by John Webster, a London-trained upholsterer who emigrated to Philadelphia in 1767. The same damask covered three

143. Swatch of flowered dimity, made in the area of Manchester, England, c. 1750. Cotton and linen. This sample is from the John Holker manuscript. Flowered dimity was used for clothing as well as furnishing. Courtesy, Musée des Arts Decoratifs, Paris.

sofas and twenty chair seats in the room. In Cadwalader's back parlor, yellow silk damask (also from London) was used for curtains lined with yellow sarcenet, a thinner silk.[7]

The painter John Mare, in his 1767 portrait of New York merchant Jeremiah Platt, now in the Metropolitan Museum of Art, posed his subject against a red silk damask curtain edged with fringe and trimmed with a large tassel. This curtain would ordinarily be considered an artist's prop, but an inventory of Platts' possessions lists seven red window curtains, red cord, and tassels.[8]

Unlike patterns for silk dress fabrics that were woven in small yardages with new designs introduced as often as once or twice a year, the production of silk upholstery patterns was more conservative. For example, stylized leafy patterns, some featuring large pomegranates had first been woven in Italy in the late seventeenth century, but continued to be produced. Similar designs were woven at Spitalfields, London, nearly a hundred years later.

During the first half of the eighteenth century, woolen fabrics were by far the most commonly used. Of woolens, the scholar Herbert Heaton has said, "Both in colonial days and for at least half a century thereafter, America was the best single external market for British woolen and worsted fabrics."[9] These were finished in a variety of ways to produce a wide range of handsome, practical materials. It is difficult today to differentiate among many of these fabrics: mohair, cheney, camlet, calimanco, moreen, or harateen. Few examples of these woolens survive. Sunlight caused them to fade and rot, and moths and vermin have taken their toll, leaving us little to go on. The chief means of identifying and distinguishing many of these woolen textiles is through merchants' sample books. On their pages, hundreds of tiny pieces of cloth are neatly mounted and numbered for convenience in ordering.

Especially well-documented are worsted cloths woven from long woolen fibers that were combed rather than carded. These fibers were laid parallel to one another and, when lightly twisted together, formed hard, silky, shiny yarns similar to those used for crewel work. Many of these worsteds were then pressed under great weights with the aim of making them resemble glossy silks. Often, this finishing involved the creation of a watered or moiré effect. Depending on the finishing treatment, worsteds were called harateens, moreens, or cheneys.

Harateen had a wavy pattern achieved by pressure. The sample book of the Englishman John Holker, dating from about 1750 (and now in the Musée des Arts Decoratifs in Paris), contains four examples of harateens. Of these two were given a waved finish by pressure, and two were given an additional pattern that resembles a foliate silk damask, an effect achieved by applying an engraved, hot copper cylinder to the fabric.[10] Another example of harateen on which a second pattern was imposed is in the Essex Institute, Salem. The second pattern of scattered carnations and butterflies was impressed by rollers to make it resemble a floral silk damask.[11]

Watered moreens in a wide range of handsome, bright colors are found on a folding pattern card in the London Public Record Office and on a trade card privately owned in Yorkshire.[12] The yarns of moreens seem to be coarser than those of harateen (figs. 144–145).

Cheney was a worsted furnishing fabric dyed red, green, blue, yellow, or purple and was sometimes watered. We know that it was related to harateen and moreen, but because no documented example of the material has been found, it is not now clearly distinguishable from these.

In several pattern books, worsted fabrics are particularly designated as bed satins and bed damasks; these were woven in one or two colors and in several different grades. Another name for these furnishing textiles was "russels." These can be identified from scraps in the papers of the New York merchant, James Alexander, in the collections of The New York Historical Society. Neatly pasted to the copy of Alexander's order to Lon-

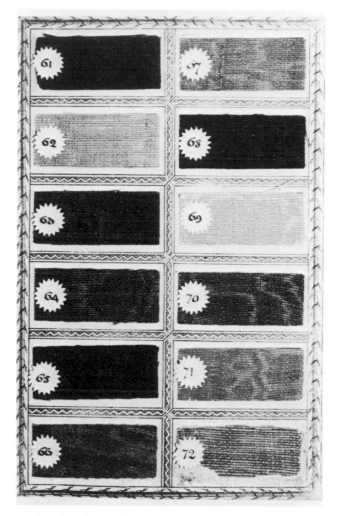

144. Samples of worsted moreens from an eighteenth-century folding pattern card. Courtesy, Public Record Office, London. C217/70.

don, dated 1738, for "Rushells" are two small slivers of worsted damask, one in light blue and the other in light green.

References to the use of worsted for furnishing are found in Samuel Sewall's Boston letter book dated 1719:

To be Bought. Curtains and Vallens for a bed, with Counter-pane, Head-Cloth and Tester, of good yellow waterd worsted camlet, with Trimming, well made, and Bases, if it be the fashion. Send also of the same Camlet and Trimming, as may be enough to make Cushions for the Chamber Chairs.[14]

In eighteenth-century advertisements, we find mention of "a fashionable yellow Camblet Bed lin'd wih

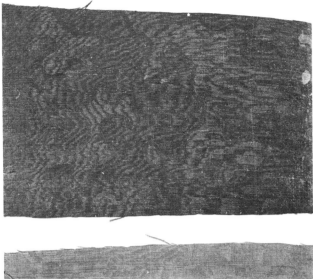

145. Swatches of worsted harateen, Norwich, England, c. 1750. These samples are from the John Holker manuscript. Courtesy, Museé des Arts Decoratifs, Paris.

146. Panel with a shaped valance, eighteenth century. Gold silk and worsted damask; valance edged with silk and worsted fringe. These were owned by the Burnham family of Newburyport, Massachusetts. Courtesy, The Henry Francis du Pont Winterthur Museum.

Satten . . . a Field Bedstead and Bed, the covering a Blew Harrateen," or "Five crimson moreen drapery window curtains, with laths, cornices, and three yellow ditto."[15]

Less common are references to mixed silk and wool materials such as "rich yellow silk and worsted damask" (fig. 146) and "a sofa, twelve chairs, and three window curtains of sky-blue silk and worsted damask, stuffs garnished and fringed."[16] In 1739, the letter book of the Rhode Island merchant John Bannister lists "2 ps Crimson Silk and Worsted Bed Damask 80 yds."[17] William Franklin, son of Benjamin, wrote from Burlington, New Jersey, in 1765 to William Strahan about curtains that Franklin wished to have made up by Timothy Golding, a London upholsterer. Franklin determined to have Golding make "Three curtains of Yellow Silk and Worsted Damask . . . to be hung festoon fashion" with yellow fringe for binding.[18] These curtains were to match his dining room chairs covered in yellow damask.

Bed Hangings

The bed was the most important object in the house in Europe and in the colonies. The quality of its hangings made it a symbol of station and wealth. George Hepplewhite, in his *The Cabinet-Maker and Upholsterer's Guide*, was quite specific about the value of beds. "Beds are an article of much importance, as well on account of the great expense attending them, as the variety of shapes, and the high degree of elegance which may be shewn in them." He went on to detail the proper materials to be used for bed hangings:

> They may be executed of almost every stuff which the loom produces. White dimity, plain or corded, is peculiarly applicable for the furniture, which, with a fringe with a gymp head, produces an effect of elegance and neatness truly agreeable. The Manchester stuffs [cotton velvets] have been wrought into Bed-furniture with good success. Printed cottons and linens are also very suitable; the elegance and variety of patterns of which, afford as much

scope for taste, elegance, and simplicity, as the most lively fancy can wish . . .

In state-rooms, where a high degree of elegance and grandeur are wanted, beds are frequently made of silk or satin, figured or plain, also of velvet, with gold fringe, etc.[19]

Early bed hangings were fashioned without any of the bedstead showing. The bed posts and the wooden frame supporting the mattress and bedding were concealed by valances, long curtains, a bedspread, and base valances. Bed curtains might also be hung from a continuous iron rod fastened to the wall at the head of the bed and suspended from hooks in the ceiling above the foot. Half-tester beds, similar to more recent Murphy beds, could be turned up during the day and concealed beneath a headcloth and long curtains. The tester and side curtains of such half-headed beds were sometimes suspended from a hook in the ceiling, or long curtains were hung from a narrow wooden tester frame supported by diagonal braces that were attached to the two head posts.

Following English upholsterers, urban colonial upholsterers advertised a wide array of beds, including canopy or tester beds, dome beds (in which the tester had a domed shape), field or camp beds (a portable kind of bed), and four-post beds. All types have survived except the dome bed, which was probably too expensive to construct in any quantity.

Eighteenth-century American upholsterers showed elaborate drapery on their trade cards but whether or not this drapery was ever created is open to conjecture. The elegant 1771 advertisement of Richard Kip, a New York upholsterer, shows two designs for bed pillars as well as short drapery in the Chinese Chippendale taste (fig. 147).

By this time, furniture carvers excelled at their craft, and their skill affected the way bed hangings were hung. The curtains got shorter probably because owners who commissioned elaborate beds wished the fine carving to show. Some of these curtains may not have been cut shorter, but were actually long curtains that were drawn up by means of cords. That this was the case is suggested by two examples from the same period. One, a bed illustrated in plate XXXIV of *A Compleat Treatise on Perspective* by Thomas Malton, published in 1778, shows a bed furnished with a pair of cloak pins on which cords to raise the hangings are wound.[20] The other example is an American mahogany bedstead that has foot posts equipped with pairs of transfer-printed knobs also to hold cords that raise or lower the curtains.

After the middle of the eighteenth century, cotton

147. Advertisement of Richard Kip, upholsterer, c. 1771. Courtesy, Rare Books and Manuscripts Division, the New York Public Library. Astor, Lenox and Tilden Foundations.

148. Polychrome block-printed chintz, England, c. 1750. Courtesy, The Henry Francis du Pont Winterthur Museum.

149. Bed curtain and valances, England, c. 1785. These were printed in
England from copperplates. Pattern known as *Apotheosis of George
Washington and Benjamin Franklin*. Courtesy, The Henry Francis du
Pont Winterthur Museum.

materials were listed with increasing frequency among upholsterers' goods. Advertisements noted, for example, "Elegant printed Cottons for Bed Furniture [and] a Variety of printed Cottons and Linnens . . . just imported." A Philadelphia advertisement mentioned "A few pieces of the most elegant chintz, both for fineness and richness of patterns, that has been imported into this country." More specific was a 1775 Philadelphia offer for sale of "a genteel four post Bed, with very fine flowered cotton furniture, fringes and ornamented with a cornice."[21] These cottons were polychrome materials, block printed in vertical repeating patterns suitable for window curtains, bed hangings, and matching slipcovers (fig. 148).[22]

The John Holker manuscript mentioned above also contains thirteen large pieces of English block print in the full chintz style, which included several shades of red, purple, brown, blue, yellow, and the latter two overprinted to make green.[23] Handsome arborescent patterns with long-tailed birds were popular in both France and England from about 1775 to 1790, and many fragments of such patterned bed hangings are known in American collections. Chintzes patterned after Chinese wallpapers were also fashionable as were a great variety of floral designs.

Indigo blue resist prints with large-scale exotic floral patterns were apparently popular in the area around New York. They have been found in homes along the Hudson River, on Long Island, and in the areas of Connecticut served by New York City, suggesting that they were imported mainly into that port.

Equally favored for hangings were textiles printed in single colors of red, blue, or purple from engraved copper plates that sometimes measured as much as a yard square. This technique, characterized by fine detail and shading (fig. 149), was equal to the brilliance of engravings printed on paper and was also used for the well known *toiles-de-Jouy* of France, as well as for others from English print works. Soon after the discovery of the copperplate printing technique in Ireland and its establishment in England about 1756, Benjamin Franklin ordered "56 Yards of Cotton, printed curiously from Copper Plates, a new Invention, to make Bed & Window Curtains; and 7 Yards Chair Bottoms, printed in the same Way, very neat."[24]

Plunket Fleeson, the eighteenth-century Philadelphia upholsterer, made bed curtains for General John Cadwalader in the 1760s. In surviving bills, we have Fleeson's description of a "phestoon bed full trimd with Plumes, bases [foot valances] and head board, fringed."

150. Bed curtain, eighteenth century. Blue-and-white checked linen. The reverse of the panel (shown here) has tapes and rings stitched in parallel, curved lines. Currently on display at Stenton Mansion, Germantown, Pennsylvania. Courtesy, the National Society of the Colonial Dames of America in the State of Pennsylvania.

151. Curtain in figure 150 raised in a double festoon or "double drapery."

For this bed, "56 yards fine red & white Copper plate Cotton" were ordered that cost the princely sum of £19.12.0. In addition, Cadwalader ordered a "Sett of Cutt open Cornices" and "2 Window ditto" from the Philadelphia cabinetmaker Thomas Affleck.[25]

Bed cornices upholstered with copperplate-printed cottons are found in the collections of Colonial Williamsburg and The Metropolitan Museum of Art, New York. The latter institution possesses a set of painted and shaped cornices upholstered in cotton with monochrome decoration reminiscent of a farmyard scene, a common subject in copperplate printed cottons.

Surviving bed drapery shows how beds were hung. For example, a set of blue-and-white checked linen curtains at Stenton (figs. 150 and 151), the Germantown, Pennsylvania, home of James Logan, has tapes and rings stitched to the backs in two curved, parallel lines. When drawn up on cords, the curtain becomes a kind of double festoon or "double drapery." Also at Stenton is a headcloth for a bed fashioned from an English chinoiserie copperplate print. A slit along the edge of each side, finished with tape, permitted the ends of a slotted headboard to fit into the posts. Along the top edge, a narrow tape was stitched in scallops, and presumably the bed valances were also scalloped.

Among the glories of surviving American bed furnishings are those ornamented with crewel embroidery. The most complete set known, wrought circa 1745 by Mary Bulman, is owned by the Old York Gaol, York, Maine. The set consists of four curtains that enclose the bed completely, a spread to which the base valances were later stitched, a headcloth, and top valances.[26]

Another beautiful example of crewel work, more sophisticated in its overall pattern than the York Gaol spread and reminiscent of Queen Anne scrollwork, is one now at Winterthur. This spread was made in about 1730 and inherited by John Hancock from his uncle. Blue-green woolen tape, a replacement of the original, forms a scrolled trellis for the floral needlework and is very similar to that on a headcloth (fig. 152), also at Winterthur, that once may have belonged with the spread.[27] Colorful bed hangings and bedspreads such as these, stitched with imported crewel yarns, are certainly among the most beautiful American textile survivals.

152. Headcloth, American, eighteenth century. Linen with blue-green
worsted tape forming a trellis for crewel work. Courtesy, The Henry
Francis du Pont Winterthur Museum.

NOTES

1. Susan Prendergast Schoelwer, "Form, Function, and Meaning in the Use of Fabric Furnishings: A Philadelphia Case Study, 1700–1775," *Winterthur Portfolio* 14, no. 1 (Spring 1979): 25–40.

2. For examples of contemporary claims to London training and new fashion, *see* the newspaper advertisements transcribed in Alfred Coxe Prime, *The Arts and Crafts in Philadelphia, Maryland, and South Carolina 1721–1785* (Topsfield, Massachusetts: The Walpole Society, 1929); and Rita Gottesman, *The Arts and Crafts in New York, 1726–1776* (New York: The New York Historical Society, 1938).

3. Jonathan Bright's bill for upholstery work at the New State House, Connecticut State Library, Hartford, Connecticut. Quoted in Charles F. Montgomery, *American Furniture: The Federal Period* (New York: Viking Press, 1966), p. 47, fn. 3.

4. *The Workwoman's Guide* (London, 1838; reprint, Owston Ferry, Doncaster, England: Bloomfield Books, 1975), p. 205.

5. Florence M. Montgomery, *Textiles in America, 1650–1870* (New York: W. W. Norton & Company, 1984), p. 60, figure 10.

6. George Francis Dow, *The Arts and Crafts in New England, 1704–1775* (Topsfield, Massachusetts: Wayside Press, 1927), p. 126.

7. Nicholas B. Wainwright, *Colonial Grandeur in Philadelphia: The House and Furniture of General John Cadwalader* (Philadelphia: The Historical Society of Pennsylvania, 1964), pp. 51–52.

8. Helen Burr Smith, "A Portrait by John Mare Identified: 'Uncle Jeremiah,'" *Antiques* 103, no. 6 (June 1973): 1185–87.

9. Herbert Heaton, "Yorkshire Cloth Traders in the United States," *Thoresby Society Publications* 37 (1945): 226. For a more complete discussion of these woolen fabrics, *see* Montgomery, *Textiles in America*, pp. 143–377.

10. For further information on this manuscript, *see* Florence M. Montgomery, "John Holker's Mid-Eighteenth-Century *Livre d'Echantillons*" in Veronika Gervers, ed., *Studies in Textile History* (Toronto: Royal Ontario Museum, 1977), pp. 214–31. The swatches are illustrated in color in Montgomery, *Textiles in America*, pl. D27.

11. Abbott Lowell Cummings, ed., *Bed Hangings: A Treatise on Fabrics and Styles in the Curtaining of Beds, 1650–1850* (Boston: Society for the Preservation of New England Antiquities, 1961), fig. 15.

12. The Yorkshire samples are illustrated in color in Montgomery, *Textiles in America*, pl. D–104.

13. *See* Montgomery, *Textiles in America*, pl. D–8.

14. *Massachusetts Historical Society Collections* vol. 2, 6th series (Boston: 1886–1888), Letter Book II, p. 105.

15. Advertisement from 1735 in *Boston News-Letter*, as transcribed in Dow, *Arts and Crafts in New England*, p. 110; and advertisement from 1779 in *Pennsylvania Journal*, as transcribed in Prime, *Arts and Crafts in Philadelphia*, p. 213.

16. Advertisement from 1784 in *New York Packet, and The American Advertiser*, as transcribed in Gottesman, *Arts and Crafts in New York* vol. 2, p. 147.

17. The original is at the Newport Historical Society. A microfilm copy is in the Joseph Downs Manuscript Collection, The Henry Francis du Pont Winterthur Museum.

18. "Letters from William Franklin to William Strahan," ed. Charles Henry Hart, *The Pennsylvania Magazine of History and Biography* 35 (1911): 440–41.

19. George Hepplewhite, *The Cabinet-Maker and Upholsterer's Guide* (London: I. & J. Taylor, 1789), pp. 17–18.

20. The Malton plate is illustrated in Montgomery, *Textiles in America*, p. 29.

21. Advertisement from 1763 in *Boston Gazette*, as transcribed in Dow, *Arts and Crafts in New England*, p. 171; advertisement from 1779 in *Pennsylvania Packet*, as transcribed in Prime, *Arts and Crafts in Philadelphia*, p. 213; advertisement from 1775 in *Pennsylvania Journal*, as transcribed in Prime, *Arts and Crafts in Philadelphia*, p. 212.

22. For examples of changing styles as seen in English pattern books, *see* Peter Floud and Barbara Morris, "English Printed Textiles," *Antiques* 71, nos. 3–6 (March-June 1957); and *Antiques* 72, no. 3 (September 1957). For examples surviving in American collections, *see* Florence M. Montgomery, *Printed Textiles: English and American Cottons and Linens, 1700–1850* (New York: Viking Press, 1970).

23. Montgomery, *Printed Textiles*, figs. 9–18.

24. Letter from Benjamin Franklin to Deborah Franklin, The American Philosophical Society, Philadelphia.

25. Wainwright, *Colonial Grandeur*, pp. 40, 44.

26. Charles F. Montgomery and Patricia E. Kane, eds., *American Art: 1750–1800, Towards Independence* (Boston: New York Graphic Society, 1976), fig. 235.

27. Anne Pollard Rowe, "Crewel Embroidered Bed Hangings in Old and New England," *Museum of Fine Arts Bulletin* 71 (1972): fig. 29.

153. Sitting Room Chamber, Salem Towne House, Old Sturbridge
Village (OSV). Festoon window curtain and bed hangings, Salem,
Massachusetts, style of c. 1810. Block-printed reproduction cotton of a
1798 English cotton in the OSV Collections. The style of the bed
hangings is that of the Curwen family set from the early nineteenth
century, owned by the Essex Institute, as shown in a c. 1895 photograph and illustrated in Alvan Crocker Nye's *Scale Drawings of Colonial
Furniture*. (*See* figure 154.) There are forty-one pieces in the Curwen
set of hangings, one of the most elaborate to remain intact. Courtesy,
Old Sturbridge Village. Photograph by Donald F. Eaton.

Bed and Window Hangings in New England, 1790–1870

Jane C. Nylander

Bed Hangings

AT THE BEGINNING of the nineteenth century, the traditional means of furnishing a best bed, for those who could afford it, involved the use of fully enclosing curtains, a headcloth, a tester or canopy cloth, valances, bases (bedskirts or flounces), and a counterpane. Window curtains and upholstery in the bed chamber were usually made of matching fabrics (fig. 153).[1] Although we tend to think of bed hangings as an eighteenth-century fashion, they were, in fact, used well into the nineteenth century. For example, in the 1856 edition of the *Treatise on Domestic Economy*, Catherine Beecher stressed that "it is in good taste to have the curtains, bed quilt, valance, and window curtains of similar materials."[2] This suggests a departure from the strict eighteenth-century practice of having everything match, but a general similarity seems still to have been desirable.

Beginning about 1800, and continuing through the early part of the nineteenth century, bed hangings were the subject of considerable controversy among authors of medical publications and household advice books. They pointed out that bed hangings harbored dust and vermin, prevented free circulation of air, and invited danger from fire, especially if one used candles in order to maintain a night light for children or to indulge in the "absurd and reprehensible practice of reading in bed."[3] As late as 1839, the writer Sarah Josepha Hale, in a book called *The Good Housekeeper*, still felt it was necessary to explain that "Bed Curtains are unhealthy. They confine the air about us while we sleep."[4]

Nevertheless, there is plentiful documentary and material evidence to show that, despite the controversy, the use of bed hangings actually increased for a time in the nineteenth century. The hangings even became somewhat more elaborate as textiles and upholstery materials became more affordable. Indeed, the abundance of inexpensive fabrics encouraged the use of elaborate hangings based on English and French styles of the late eighteenth and early nineteenth centuries. This fashion continued through the first half of the nineteenth century.

Many fabrics used for bed hangings were not easily laundered, so it should not surprise us that the stationary parts of bed furnishings—the tester cloth, headcloth, valances, and sometimes the bases—were attached to the frame of the bed with iron tacks. Many surviving sets of bed furnishings testify to this with their rusty holes; wooden bed cornices and tester frames also give evidence of the same practice.

During the first half of the nineteenth century, the tester cloth on flat tester beds might be shirred, or made with a radiating central star, or occasionally stretched taut. The headcloth continued to be a straight hanging piece extending from the canopy to just below the bottom of the headboard. The valances were usually deeper than earlier ones, reaching a length of as much as twenty or twenty-two inches. They were fuller as well, being either gathered on a string or tape drawn through a casing on the valance or sewn directly onto the tester cloth itself. Some sets of valances consisted of fabric cut in simple repeating scallops, but others were composed of many complex shapes sewn and folded together to give the appearance of festoons and cascades. While in the eighteenth century bases were straight pieces that usually repeated the shape of the valances, in the early nineteenth century bases were usually gathered quite fully and supported either with nails or, more commonly, with a drawstring pulled through a narrow casing at the top of the skirt and tied to each bedpost. Sometimes, for additional support, pairs of tapes were sewn at intervals along the length of the skirt and then tied to the bed rails.[5]

In the last half of the eighteenth century and the early years of the nineteenth, some bed curtains (fig. 154) were fitted with a series of cords threaded through rings and over pulleys that permitted the curtains to be drawn up in single or double drapery both to admit air and to expose the carving on the bedposts. This technique was sometimes called "festooning." (*See* figures 150 and 151.)[6] By 1838, however, judging from a treatise on domestic economy entitled *The Workwoman's Guide*,[7] the term "festoon" seems to have come to mean a purely decorative piece of fabric that was "carried over a pole" and gave the appearance of being all one piece. Festoon bedstead trimming could be used with or without the full curtains, according to the dictates of function or fashion.

During most of the period under consideration, two additional forms of beds that required hangings were used. One kind was called variously a "camp," "field," or "tent" bed; the other was the so-called "French" or sofa bed.

The term *tent* bed had become so common by the 1830s that when J. C. Loudon wrote his *Encyclopedia* in 1835, he stated that "Tent beds are in universal use and scarcely require description."[8] Tent beds had arched tester frames and were hung with complete sets of bed hangings, as the very name suggests. Numerous period illustrations show this form of bedstead fully enclosed by curtains (fig. 155). The custom of hanging such beds

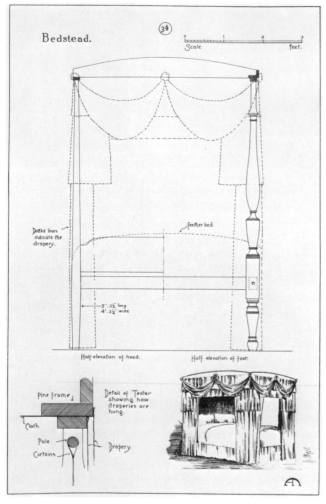

154. Plate 34 from Alvan Crocker Nye, *Scale Drawings of Colonial Furniture* (New York: W. Helburn, 1895). Drawing of the Curwen family hangings.

155. "Getting Up," from *Rhymes for the Nursery* (New York, 1831). A fully enclosed tent bed with valance resembling those on military tents in the eighteenth and early nineteenth centuries. Festoon window curtains. Courtesy, Old Sturbridge Village.

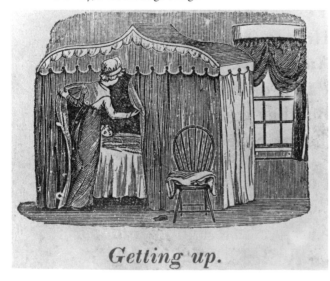

with netted canopies seems to date from the latter years of the nineteenth century when the fashion for fully enclosed beds had passed. Netted canopies were an attractive way to decorate the old tester frames, while providing increased ventilation.

"French" or sofa beds with one long side against the wall were, according to Thomas Sheraton, "so named not from having ever seen any of theirs [Frenchmen's] shaped in this manner, but on account of its being after their style of dress."[9] According to Sheraton, canopies are "generally used as a covering or tester, for French or sofa beds; and are often of a spherical figure, or otherwise of a bell shape. They are certainly a handsome ornament to a bed, when they are executed in a tastey manner."[10]

Inventory references make it clear that French beds were considered a great luxury in New England in the early nineteenth century. They were expensive and were frequently hung with silk. The 1811 inventory of James Bowdoin lists together "4 silk window curtains with tassels $32.–, 1 French mahogany bedstead, 1 bed, 1 mattress, yellow silk counterpane, silk curtains, canopy," the latter valued at $360.[11] The Boston residence of David Hinckley, the "handsomest house in the city,"[12] contained three rooms with French beds, each with silk hangings. One of the rooms was called the "red French room." Among its furnishings were "1 French bedstead with curtains . . . $150 . . . set of crimson silk curtains with cornices and blinds . . . $120 . . . 1 red lamp globe . . . $15 . . . " and a "group in marble of Cupid and Psyche and wooden pedestal . . . $40."[13]

Although silk became the height of fashion for bed or window hangings in the early part of the nineteenth century, there is very little documentation of its use for household furnishings in New England prior to the American Revolution.[14] However, inventory references to damask do not always indicate clearly whether the fabric described is silk or wool. For example, the will of Abigail Gray of Boston, recorded in 1815, contains a bequest to her niece Nabby Rogers of the following:

> . . . my red damask bed curtains, window curtains and counterpane, the seven red damask bottom chairs and easy chair with the covering belonging to the same, the best feather bed, the mahogany bedstead with the bolster, and one pair of pillows and all that belongs to the red damask bed.

That this damask was silk, not wool, is confirmed by the appraisers of Widow Gray's personal property. They carefully listed "1 suit of red damask silk curtains and 4 window curtains and 1 counterpane valued at $75.[15]

156. Valance matching the curtain in figure 158, c. 1790–1795. Said to have belonged to Dorothy Quincy Hancock Scott, c. 1795–1800. Block-printed cotton with polychrome cotton fringe, tape heading, and cotton-covered gimp. Late eighteenth-century fringes are typically found with knots tied at the center of each thread, perhaps to prevent tangling. Courtesy, Society for the Preservation of New England Antiquities.

Silk was expensive and lacked durability. In addition, sets of bed and window curtains involved immense yardages. No wonder frugal New Englanders viewed silk curtains as a great luxury. This attitude colored Sarah Anna Emery's description of the home near Bowdoin Square in Boston that was furnished by Nathaniel Parsons early in the nineteenth century.

> . . . resplendent with French luxury and novel elegance . . . The furniture had been imported expressly for the house, it was both rich and stylish . . . The silken canopy to the bed in the guest chamber, was gathered around an oval mirror set in the center of the arched top.[16]

To correlate expensive luxury and French taste was typical of New England thought at that time. Silks were an essential part of this linking.

Imported British woolens were the most commonly used fabrics for bed hangings before the American Revolution and continued to be used for decades afterwards, despite their expense and susceptibility to destruction by moths and infestation by vermin. Even in the second quarter of the nineteenth century, the worsted fabric moreen was still described as "very serviceable" for bed hangings, being "well suited to cold situations; it requires no lining, and therefore, is less expensive than chintz, though not so pretty."[17]

Cottons were selected for bed hangings in the late eighteenth and early nineteenth centuries because they were increasingly available, less expensive, and easily cleaned. However, because laundering destroyed the glaze on chintz and re-glazing was a difficult and expensive process, chintz bed hangings were not laundered as frequently as one might think. In fact, one author cautioned that "every time . . . a chintz bed has to be washed, the expense [of French calendaring and relining] is equal to that of buying a new one."[18]

Many cotton bed furnishings were nailed in semipermanent fashion to the wooden bed frame. They might be ornamented with elaborate silk or woolen fringes (fig. 156), as described in a Boston auction notice of 1826 that listed "part of the furniture of a gentleman giving up housekeeping" including "1 mahogany high post bedstead and cornice, with two suits of elegant chintz curtains, trimmed with silk ball fringe, nearly new. . . ."[19]

The bright colors and gay designs of printed chintzes made them quite fashionable, and they were used for hangings on high style beds. Printed cottons may have been considered especially suitable for painted bedsteads, as there are many inventory descriptions of this practice. For example, the Bostonian Elizabeth

157. Festoon curtains, Bristol, Rhode Island, early nineteenth century.
Dimity short curtains over fully enclosing long curtains that have
been wrapped around the bed posts to permit a view of the painted
decoration. The bedroom furniture is attributed to the Boston
cabinetmaker, Samuel Gragg, c. 1807–1815. Courtesy, Society for the
Preservation of New England Antiquities.

Bowdoin, Lady Temple, used hangings of "strip'd chintz" on beds having pine "cornishes."[20] Some of the cornices were covered with fabric; others were painted in imitation of the printed cotton.

White cotton dimity was the easiest furnishing fabric to care for, which is one reason for its long standing popularity for both bed and window hangings (fig. 157). It became available in the late eighteenth century and continued to be used for over one hundred years.

Another fabric used for bed and window hangings was checked linen. Well into the 1830s, some New Englanders still spun yarn and wove checked linens for their own use; however, many similar fabrics were imported, and it is not always possible to distinguish the home-made from the commercially made. The origins of trim for checked linens can often be equally difficult to identify. Some surviving examples of checked valances are trimmed with homemade fringes,[21] while others are decorated with imported tapes that have woven patterns. Blue and white checks are the most common survivals, but other colors were made as well. In her memoir of life in Lancaster, New Hampshire, Persis F. Chase recalled that about the year 1800 her "mother put up some green and white checked bed curtains, home made, out of flax and wool and trimmed with yellow fringe."[22]

Window Curtains

In 1790, few New England homes had window curtains. Those that did were apt to be the residences of relatively wealthy people who lived in cities or in town centers. The curtains were usually hung in the best bedchamber where they matched the fabric and style of the bed hangings and upholstered seat furniture. In some homes, the best parlor might also have had window curtains. These were the only two rooms with such elaboration. The styles of window curtains in 1790 were limited to straight hanging, festoon (*see* figure 142), and Venetian curtains (*see* figure 141).[23]

The years between 1790 and 1850 saw a dramatic increase in the number of houses in which window curtains were used, as well as the distinct evolution of new styles. The simple, earlier styles, however, continued to be used in secondary rooms and by the less wealthy.

In New England documents of this period, there are many references to French curtains or French drapery. These references are to the neoclassical style of swagged drapery, arranged in layers, that originated in France during the late eighteenth century (fig. 158), rather than

to the French rod mechanism by which the curtains were opened or closed that Florence Montgomery described in the previous essay in this volume. Indeed, there is little evidence that French rods were actually used in New England.

The success of French drapery, and of layered window curtains generally, depended on the skill with which the folds were arranged. Because curtains were opened and closed on a daily basis, their appearance probably varied from day to day, and their conformity to the original design depended on the care with which they were handled. For example, the authors of *An Encyclopedia of Domestic Economy*, T. Webster and Mrs. William Parkes, warned that "some housemaids excel others in this part of their duty."[24]

A mid-nineteenth century publication gives a good description of the basic elements of French drapery (fig. 159).

> Besides the rod on which the curtain slides, there is generally a piece of the same material with the curtain, called a valance, suspended before it, to conceal the rod. . . . This valance gives great richness and finish to the window; but when the rooms are low, they should not be deep, as they hide much of the light; on the contrary, when the windows are very lofty, they are often useful in moderating the too great glare of light.
>
> Valances are sometimes made in the form of festoons, and are then, by upholsterers, termed *draperies*; the festoon itself is called the swag, and the end that hangs down is termed the *tail*. . . . These are frequently ornamented with fringes, tassels, and cords in various ways. This, which is the former French style, was introduced some years ago, as being richer and more elegant than ours; at present it is less used.[25]

In early nineteenth-century interiors, as noted above, the fashion for matching all textile furnishings in a room continued. The residence of David Hinckley had a "First Drawing Room" embellished with "one blue silk sofa and linen cover 60–; ten blue silk chairs and linen covers 60–; two blue silk arm chairs & do. 16–; one set blue silk curtains and cornices, hooks &c. 150–; one set muslin and linen curtains & blinds." The "Second Drawing Room" was furnished with similar pieces in yellow silk instead of blue.[26]

The use of silk was, of course, still confined to the wealthy few. On May 11, 1834, Christopher Columbus Baldwin visited the home of George A. Tufts in Dudley, Massachusetts, where he noted that "The house is well furnished having silk damask window curtains and other furniture to correspond, which is quite unusual in the country."[27]

158. Festoon curtain for the head of a bed, c. 1790–1795. Block-printed cotton, blue threads in selvage; with cotton gimp and fringes. Back view showing narrow hems, brass rings sewn up the center pleat for festooning, narrow linen tape, and short tape loops at the upper edge. Courtesy, Society for the Preservation of New England Antiquities.

159. Figure 164 from T. Webster and Mrs. Williams Parkes, *An Encyclopedia of Domestic Economy* (New York: Harper & Brothers, 1848).

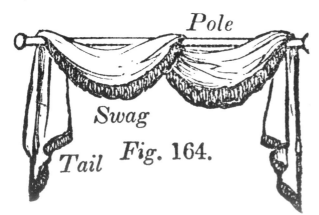

French curtains were enhanced by the use of contrasting colored linings and decorative borders and trimmings to emphasize the folds (fig. 160). An excellent description of the use of such drapery in Boston is afforded by the 1825 notice of the sale of the contents of the "house recently occupied by Marshall B. Spring, Esqr. in Summer St." The furnishings included the following:

DRAWING ROOM CURTAINS AND DRAPERY, of blue French Damask, lined with yellow silk, laced and fringed, with muslin curtains, draperies supported with rich ornaments; one Curtain and Drapery, same as preceeding, for side Room; 12 Rosewood Chairs and Couch, covered with blue damask to match the above, Brussels Carpets and Rugs, same color as the Curtains.[28]

Muslin undercurtains contributed importantly to the total layered effect sought in French drapery. It is not known when they were first adopted; however, we do know that as early as 1812, muslin curtains were listed in the inventory of the estate of Esther Ellery: They hung in the windows of the double parlors of her house on Franklin Place in Boston.[29]

A variation on the French drapery was the use of one cornice or rod or a single panel of drapery for two or more windows on a wall, thus creating a unified effect. This style was illustrated by George Smith in *A Collection of Designs for Household Furniture and Interior Decoration*, published in London in 1808. It was popularized by Rudolph Ackermann in his style-setting magazine *The Repository of Arts, Literature, Commerce, Manufacture, Fashions and Politics*, which was also published in London and widely read on both sides of the Atlantic. There is some evidence that this unifying treatment was used in New England—particularly in newspaper advertisements for household auctions.

In 1825, the contents of Marshall B. Spring's house on Summer Street, mentioned previously, also included a "suit of Chintz Curtains and Draperies, lined and fringed for 2 Windows and Pier."[30] In the parlor of the Rundlett-May House in Portsmouth, New Hampshire, there is a long painted and gilded wooden pelmet (a javelin-like rod) indicating a unified treatment of two windows.[31] (The other fixtures that supported the curtains and drapery survive in the attic of the house, although unfortunately there is no evidence of the original textiles.)

Hand-colored illustrations of many other variations of French drapery appear in Ackermann's *Repository* between the years 1809 and 1828 (figs. 160 and 161). The accompanying descriptions imply that the skills of a professional upholsterer were required for successful implementation of the designs. This complexity was noted by Webster and Parkes in their book of domestic advice:

One inconvenience in the elegant French draperies was the great skill and taste required to put them up well, and it is said the cutting out of this part of the upholsterer's work was kept as much as possible a secret, and seldom taught, even to their apprentices.[32]

Despite the complicated appearance of French drapery and the desire of professional upholsterers to keep the cutting process mysterious, these valances and cornices in fact depend on very simple geometric shapes for their effects. James Arrowsmith's *Analysis of Drapery*, published in London in 1819, not only illustrates a proportional system for scaling curtain and drapery designs to windows of various sizes, but he also illustrates, perhaps for the first time anywhere, the simple cutting diagrams on which they are based. That he codified common practice is evident when one compares his designs to surviving examples of antique curtains.[33] The rough sketches drawn by Thomas Jefferson when ordering curtains for Monticello from a Philadelphia supplier also provide important proof of the simple cuts required for French drapery.[34]

It is important to recognize that few of these curtains from the early nineteenth century were lined or interlined, that the pieces were usually sewn together without attention to matching the printed or woven designs in the fabric, and that the sizes often depended on the width of the available fabric. Many curtains and valances were nailed to a window frame or to a wooden lath attached to the frame. Some curtains were pleated irregularly, and nails were put through each pleat. In other cases, the curtain was gathered into a tape at the upper edge, or irregular broad flat pleats were casually arranged and then bound down with tape. Small brass curtain rings or hooks were used to hold the curtains and pieces of drapery to thin rods or wires.

As early as 1819, valances with vertical pleats extending the entire depth of the valance were introduced as an alternative to the swags and festoons of French drapery (fig. 162).[35] They were hailed as being much easier to clean because they were less likely to harbor dust.[36]

In the 1820s, another alternative to elaborate French drapery was introduced. It made use of massive exposed rods with decorative finials and large (two or three inches in diameter) rings to support the curtains. The rods were supported by simple brackets at each end, usually outside the frame of the window itself. The

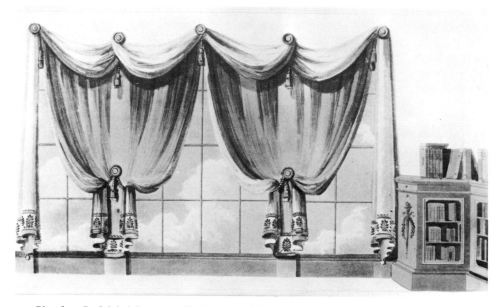

160. Plate from Rudolph Ackermann, *The Repository of Arts, Literature, Commerce, Manufacture, Fashions and Politics* 8 (July 1812): pl. 3, showing French drapery "suitable for a library or morning room in the cottage style." The drapes are layered and fastened with brass rosettes or cloak pins. Contrasting linings were often employed to emphasize the folds and swags of this type of drapery.

161. "A Sett of Continued French Drapery Window Curtains." Ackermann's *Repository* 6 (July 1811): pl. 27.

fabric completely concealed the architectural molding of the window. Fabric valances in any of a variety of nineteenth-century styles—Grecian, Gothic, Elizabethan, Louis XIV, or Moorish—could be hung in front of the curtains. By the 1840s, stamped brass or richly gilded wooden cornices were sometimes placed over the tops of these fabric valances.

Loudon's *Encyclopedia*, published in 1835, illustrates "Plain," "Grecian," and "Gothic" valances either suspended by large rings from poles or nailed to the window frame. Each of these techniques has vertical pleats and was used with long curtains of matching fabric, and in some cases, muslin undercurtains. The function of the muslin curtain was "to exclude insects, and in some degree to soften the direct light of the sun."[37] These same valance designs were published again and again over the next twenty-five years until 1860 in Godey's *Ladys Book* and other magazines. The only apparent changes were the use of different fabrics, greater amounts of trimming, and new colors.

Another simple curtain style involved the use of flat valances or lambrequins. Designs for these are first seen in *The Workwoman's Guide* in 1838, where they are praised as being "very simple and may be cut to any shape."[38] Lambrequins are seen in published American and European design sources until the revival of French drapery in the last quarter of the nineteenth century. Even then, they continued to be used by some—principally those who wished to embellish their rooms at very little expense in new colors or with more trimming.

The shapes of lambrequins varied with the styles currently in vogue, but the construction was the same: a decoratively-shaped piece of fabric—usually stiffened with buckram, paper, or even wood—and lined with glazed brown chintz or holland that was nailed to the window frame. Underneath, a rod supported sheer white cotton curtains or, after about 1845, curtains of machine-made lace (fig. 163).

Harriet Beecher Stowe and Catherine Beecher in *The American Woman's Home* (1869) suggested that "the patterns of these [lambrequins] can be varied according to fancy, but simple designs are usually the prettiest. A tassel at the lowest point improves the appearance." The Beecher sisters went on to say:

> The influence of white muslin curtains in giving an air of grace and elegance to a room is astonishing. White curtains really create a room out of nothing. No matter how coarse the muslin, so it be white and hang in graceful folds, there is a charm in it that supplies the want of other things. Very pretty curtain muslin can be bought at thirty-seven cents a yard. It requires six yards of a window.[39]

162. Window curtain, France, c. 1830. Roller-printed cotton. Irregular flat pleats typical of the upper heading on early and mid-nineteenth-century window curtains; applied strips cut from striped fabric as decorative borders. Courtesy, Old Sturbridge Village. Photograph by Donald F. Eaton.

Thirty-seven cents a yard is a long way from the state of affairs some eighty years earlier in 1790 when bed and window hangings were both costly and rare. By the mid-nineteenth century, almost everybody could afford these textile furnishings. Most importantly, as is so clear in the Beechers' writings, the symbolic value of bed and window hangings had changed from a representation of wealth to an expression of domesticity.

163. *Grandmother's Bedroom*, c. 1860, by M. J. Kilbourne. This view of
a Brookfield, Massachusetts, interior shows a common kind of
window treatment found in rural homes in nineteenth-century New
England. A single panel of white cotton is swagged back over a
curtain pin that is fastened directly to the window frame. Curtains of
this type were used in parlors, sitting rooms, and chambers; sometimes they were bordered with bands of fringed cotton netting about
three inches wide. Courtesy, Old Sturbridge Village.

NOTES

1. Abbott Lowell Cummings, ed., *Bed Hangings: A Treatise on Fabrics and Styles in the Curtaining of Beds, 1650–1850* (Boston: Society for the Preservation of New England Antiquities, 1961), pp. 10–11.

2. Catherine Beecher, *Treatise on Domestic Economy* (New York: Harper & Brothers, 1856), p. 313.

3. A. F. M. Willich, *The Domestic Encyclopedia* (Philadelphia: Abraham Small, 1802), vol. 1, p. 299.

4. Sarah Josepha Hale, *The Good Housekeeper* (Boston: Weeks, Jordan, 1839), p. 121.

5. Cummings, *Bed Hangings*, pp. 49–58.

6. For an American example, *see* Florence Montgomery, "Eighteenth-Century English and American Furnishing Fashions," *Antiques* 97, no. 2 (February 1970): 269.

7. *The Workwoman's Guide* (London: Simpkin, Marshall, 1838), p. 194.

8. John Claudius Loudon, *An Encyclopedia of Cottage, Farm and Villa Architecture and Furniture* (London: Longman, Rees, Orme, Brown, et al., 1835), p. 334.

9. Thomas Sheraton, *The Cabinet Dictionary* (London: 1803; reprint, New York: Praeger, 1970), vol. 2, p. 213.

10. Sheraton, *The Cabinet Dictionary*, vol. 1, p. 127.

11. Inventory of James Bowdoin, 1811, Suffolk County Probate Court, case no. 23856. Suffolk County Courthouse, Boston, Massachusetts.

12. *Columbian Centinel*, April 4, 1827.

13. Inventory of David Hinckley, 1826, Suffolk County Probate Court, Case no. 27827.

14. Nathalie Rothstein, "Silks Imported into America in the Eighteenth Century: An Historical Survey," in *Proceedings of the 1975 Irene Emery Roundtable on Museum Textiles: Imported and Domestic Textiles in Eighteenth-Century America* (Washington, D.C.: The Textile Museum, 1976), p. 21.

15. Will and Inventory of Abigail Gray, 1815, Suffolk County Probate Court, Case no. 24591.

16. Sarah Anna Emery, *Reminiscences of a Nonagenarian* (Newburyport: William H. Huse, 1879), p. 243.

17. Mrs. William Parkes, *Domestic Duties: or Instructions to Young Married Ladies* (New York: J & J Harper, 1829), pp. 182–83.

18. Parkes, *Domestic Duties*, pp. 182–83.

19. *Columbian Centinel*, March 18, 1826.

20. Inventory of Lady Temple, 1809, Suffolk County Probate Court, Case no. 23436.

21. Cummings, *Bed Hangings*, fig. 8.

22. Persis Chase, *The Lancaster Sketch Book* (Lancaster, N.H., 1887), p. 106.

23. Montgomery, "Eighteenth-Century English and American Furnishing Fashions," pp. 267–71; Florence Montgomery, *Textiles in America 1650–1870* (New York: W. W. Norton & Company, 1984), pp. 49–61; and her article in this volume.

24. T. Webster and Mrs. Williams Parkes, *An Encyclopedia of Domestic Economy* (New York: Harper & Brothers, 1848), p. 251.

25. Webster and Parkes, *Domestic Economy*, p. 251.

26. Inventory of David Hinckley.

27. Christopher Columbus Baldwin, *Diary* (Worcester, Massachusetts: The American Antiquarian Society, 1901), p. 301.

28. *Columbian Centinel*, May 18, 1825.

29. Inventory of Esther Ellery, 1812, Suffolk County Probate Records, Case no. 23901.

30. *Columbian Centinel*, June 18, 1825.

31. Collections of the Society for the Preservation of New England Antiquities.

32. Webster and Parkes, *Domestic Economy*, p. 251.

33. *See* article by Elisabet Stavenow-Hidemark in this volume and figures 164 through 176.

34. Fiske and Marie Kimball, "Jefferson's Curtains at Monticello," *Antiques* 52, no. 4 (October 1947): 266–68.

35. Rudolph Ackermann, *The Repository of Arts, Literature, Commerce, Manufacturing, Fashions, and Politics* 8, no. 46 (July 1, 1819): 244–45, pl. 22.

36. Webster and Parkes, *Domestic Economy*, p. 251.

37. Loudon, *Architecture and Furniture* p. 1075.

38. *The Workwoman's Guide*, p. 204.

39. Harriet Beecher Stowe and Catherine Beecher, *The American Woman's Home* (New York: J. B. Ford, 1869), p. 88.

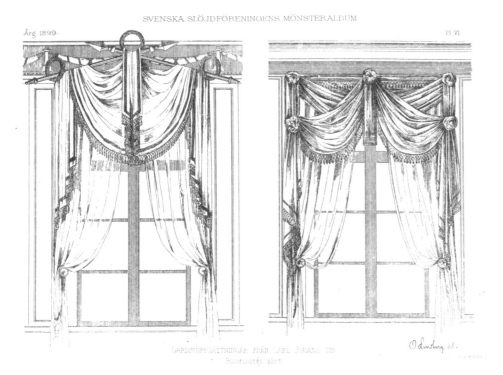

Pl VI

CARDINUPPSÄTTNINGAR FRÅN CARL JOHANS TID
Rosersbergs slott

O Lindberg del.

164. Drawing of draperies in the queen's bedroom (on the left) and
the queen's blue antechamber (on the right) from *Svenska
Slöjdföreningens Mönsteralbum* (1899). We know that the curtains in
this drawing and the curtains in the similar two drawings were in use
in 1823, although some of them might have been there as early as 1813.
The queen's bedroom had light blue silk taffeta curtains with brown
trimmings. The curtains for the antechamber have not survived.
Courtesy, Nordiska Museet.

165. Photograph of the queen's bedroom, c. 1900. Note the apparently
incorrect hanging of the side tails. Courtesy, Nordiska Museet.

Swedish Royal Curtains from the Early 19th Century

Elisabet Stavenow-Hidemark

STUDENTS of historical upholstery are very fortunate that in Sweden five sets of fine early nineteenth-century curtains from the main floor of the royal Summer Palace at Rosersberg have survived in good condition. We are even more fortunate that all are documented in photographs and/or drawings showing how they looked *in situ*.[1] In addition, we have written documentation, in the form of detailed inventories of the rooms, that describe the curtains over a period of years. Taken together, all this provides invaluable information about drapery practices in the early nineteenth century and, in particular, about the techniques of cutting and hanging curtains in use at that time.

Some of these curtains were originally installed in the Summer Palace between 1810 and 1813 when the palace was extensively renovated for King Carl XIII and his queen. Several others date from 1823 when Carl XIII's successor, King Carl Johan XIV, refurbished the palace.

All the curtains from Rosersberg are consistent with the highest fashion of the early nineteenth century. Both the fine quality of the materials used and the complex, elaborate styles of their hangings reflect the fact that Sweden, though distant from the European centers of fashion, was not entirely provincial.

This essay will focus on three sets of these curtains and will discuss their fabric, their cutting out, and their draping. The first to be examined is the light blue silk taffeta set that hung in the writing room (later, the bedroom for the new queen); the second is the set of yellow taffeta curtains used in what was an antechamber; and the third, the set of green and white taffeta curtains made for the queen's "green antechamber." All three sets belong to the Royal Collections.

When the Rosersberg Palace was renovated between 1810 and 1813, it was done according to the fashion of the Empire period. Each of the rooms on the main floor was redecorated *en suite* in its own clear and intense color scheme. Silk damask was used to cover all the walls and to upholster the furniture. Most rooms had plain taffeta curtains, but the royal bedrooms featured silk damask curtains, and in one—the blue antechamber—no curtains are mentioned in the inventories.

After the death of Carl XIII in 1818, his successor, Carl Johan XIV, took over Rosersberg. Before he began to bring his family there for part of the summer, he commissioned some redecoration, which was apparently completed in 1823. The accounts for this work have disappeared, but there are detailed inventories from 1818 and 1825[2] showing that the alterations were not exten-

sive. In all the rooms, the costly silk damasks on the walls and on the furniture were left untouched, thereby preserving the color scheme of Carl XIII. Most of the curtains also seem to have been retained.

For example, the original writing room was transformed into a bedroom for the new queen, but the light blue silk damask wall coverings and blue taffeta curtains were kept. The yellow antechamber also seems to have had the same taffeta curtains during both the reign of Carl XIII and of Carl Johan XIV. However, when the original queen's state bedroom was transformed into the green antechamber, the old green silk damask bed and window curtains were replaced with new curtains made in green and white taffeta.

Fortunately, these three sets of curtains (and two others not discussed here) were taken down and stored in the Royal Collections before they got badly damaged. It has, therefore, been possible for me to examine and measure them. By supplementing this first-hand observation with the detailed drawings of the curtains made while they were still in place around 1900 and with the good photographs that show the curtains in exactly the same position as the drawings, we know how the curtains were draped, how they were cut out and sewn, and what the quality and width of the fabrics were.

Such insights into the process of cutting out, sewing, and hanging of drapes are important. While there are many designs for richly draped, early nineteenth-century curtains in style books such as George Smith's *A Collection of Designs for Household Furniture and Interior Decoration*,[3] actual patterns and practical advice on cutting out and draping these curtains is rare. Indeed, the only pattern for a curtain of this early date is in James Arrowsmith's *An Analysis of Drapery*, published in London in 1819.

When the 1818 writing room was transformed into the queen's bedroom in 1823, as noted above the blue taffeta curtains were retained (figs. 164–165). A bed was added with hangings of a similar silk. These bed hangings and the window draperies featured a border of patterned brown silk tape and a fringe of wooden pendants encased in silk.

The window curtains were draped over javelins supported by laurel wreaths. The swag and tails were no doubt intended to look like a single piece of material that had been thrown over the javelins and drawn through the central wreath as was the fashion of the day. There are, however, four separate pieces: two side tails, the central swag, and the center tail (fig. 166). Each of these pieces was hung separately. In the photograph

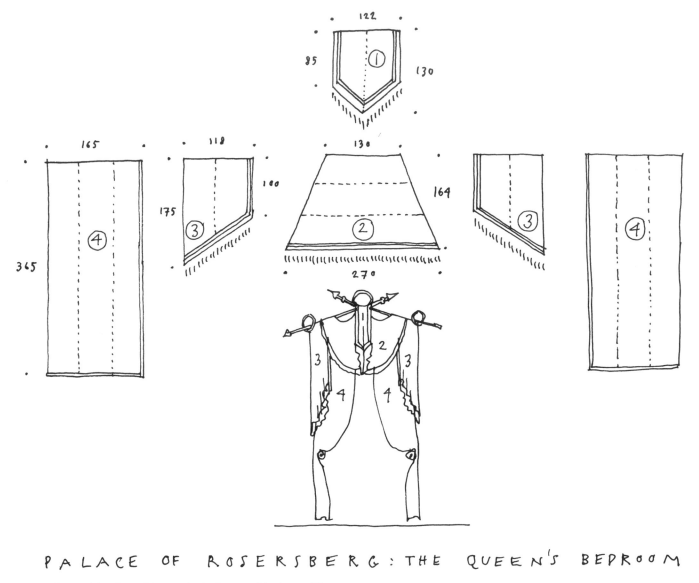

PALACE OF ROSERSBERG: THE QUEEN'S BEDROOM

166. Measured drawings of the curtains in the queen's bedroom. The drawings illustrate the several parts of the curtains: (1) central tail, (2) central swag, (3) side tails. Drawing by Ove Hidemark.

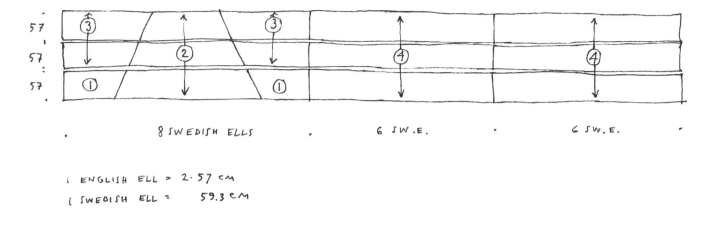

1 ENGLISH ELL = 2·57 CM
1 SWEDISH ELL = 59.3 CM

· P A L A C E O F R O S E R S B E R G : T H E Q U E E N'S B E D R O O M ·

167. Reconstruction of the cutting out of the curtains from the
queen's bedroom. The parts are numbered as in figure 166. Drawing
by Ove Hidemark.

shown in figure 165, taken some eighty years after the
curtains were first installed, the side tails seem to be
incorrectly arranged. Logically, they should have come
from back to front in order to give the impression that
they were part of the same piece as the swag. Instead,
they go from front to back.

Like all the curtains at Rosersberg, the blue taffeta
curtains were draped in complex and elaborate ways;
yet, they were cut from extremely simple patterns. In
the case of the blue taffeta curtains, all four pieces of
each curtain were cut with straight edges but with sharp
angles; the upholsterer made no use of curved outlines
to facilitate draping.

If one lays out the pieces in order to try to reconstruct
how they were cut out, one can see that all angles have
been so carefully thought out that not one inch of the
material has been wasted (fig. 167). The upholsterer
used the width of the material as a standard measure:
Every piece is either two or three widths wide. The
material was narrow—only 22¼ inches (57 cm) wide.
The central swag is made from three widths sewn together. The center tail, like the side tails, was made from
two widths. When calculating the length, the up-

holsterer used the Swedish ell measurement, 59.38 cm.
The swag and tails were cut from three pieces of fabric,
each eight ells long.

The second set of curtains—those of the yellow
antechamber—are made of yellow taffeta, and trimmed
with brown and yellow patterned silk tape and fringe
made of wooden ball pendants encased in silk (figs.
168–169). These draperies are more complicated—they
have more swags and tails—than those of the queen's
bedroom. The two shield-shaped swags were tightly
gathered in their upper parts and have no hem what-
soever on three sides, which made them less bulky. Only
the lower edge was finished with the fringe sewn onto
the selvage. The large tails cascading down at the sides
of the draperies were meant to look as if they were of
the same piece as the two swags. The middle tail was
intended to unite the two swags. The smaller tails to the
right and left appear to belong to another swag behind
the curtain, but we cannot be certain of this because no
such swag survives.

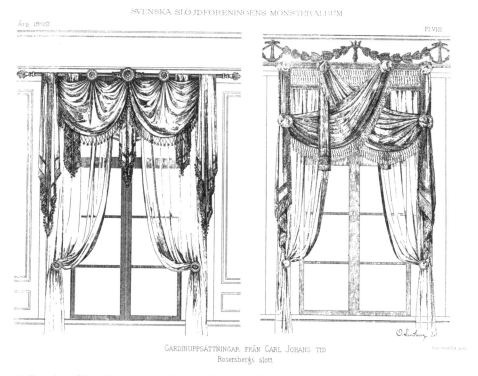

168. Drawing of the yellow antechamber (on the left) and the council room (on the right) from *Svenska Slöjdföreningens Mönsteralbum*. The yellow antechamber curtains are of yellow taffeta with brown trimming. The council room hangings, not discussed in this essay, are of green taffeta with white and green trimmings. Courtesy, Nordiska Museet.

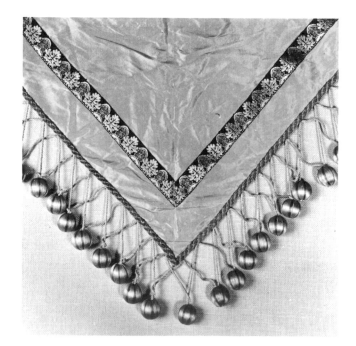

169. Detail of the curtain from the yellow antechamber. Courtesy, Nordiska Museet.

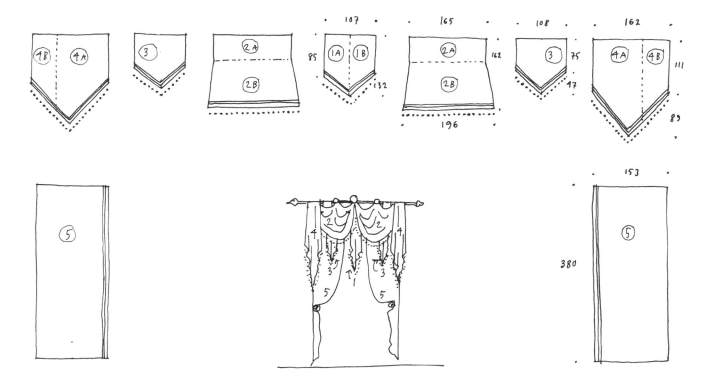

· P A L A C E   O F   R O S E R S B E R G :   T H E   Y E L L O W   A N T E C H A M B E R

170. Measured drawings of the curtains in the yellow antechamber. The drawings illustrate the several parts of the curtains: (1) middle tail, (2) shield-shaped swags, (3) smaller tails, (4) large side tails, (5) curtains. Drawing by Ove Hidemark.

171. Reconstruction of the cutting out of the curtains from the yellow antechamber. The parts are numbered as in figure 170. Drawing by Ove Hidemark.

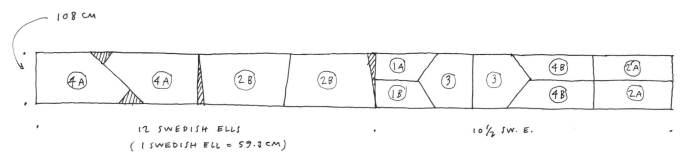

108 CM

12 SWEDISH ELLS
(1 SWEDISH ELL = 59.3 CM)

10½ SW. E.

FABRIC: YELLOW TAFFETA

P A L A C E   O F   R O S E R S B E R G :   T H E   Y E L L O W   A N T E C H A M B E R

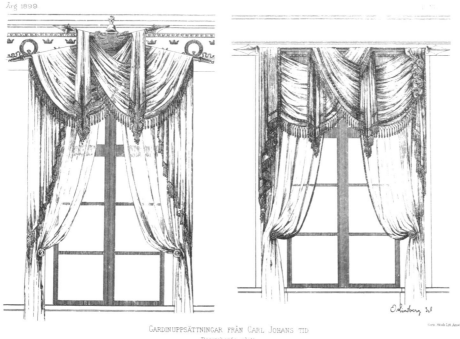

GARDINUPPSÄTTNINGAR FRÅN CARL JOHANS TID
Rosersbergs slott

172. Drawing of the blue cabinet (on the left) and the green antechamber (on the right). The blue taffeta curtains of the cabinet no
longer exist. The green and white taffeta curtains with green and
white trimmings were hung in 1823. Courtesy, Nordiska Museet.

173. Detail of a green taffeta curtain from the green antechamber.
Courtesy, Nordiska Museet.

174. Detail of a white taffeta curtain from the green antechamber.
Courtesy, Nordiska Museet.

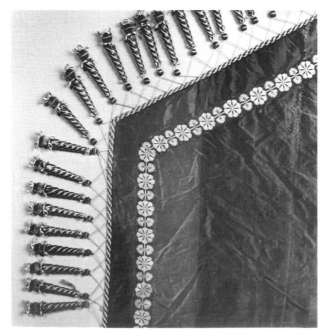

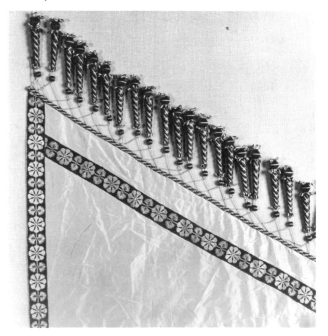

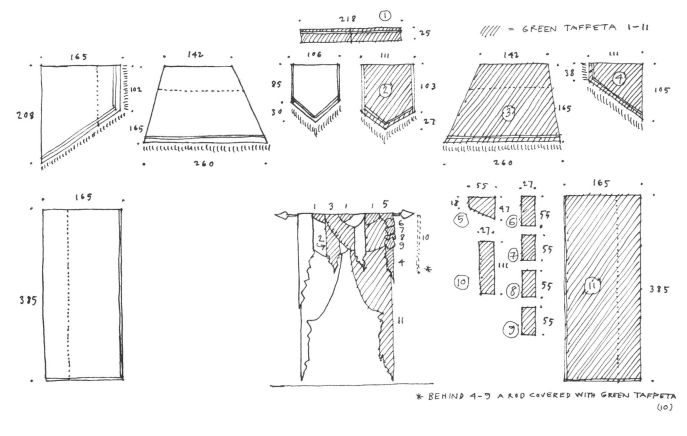

· PALACE OF ROSERSBERG ; THE GREEN ANTECHAMBER ·

175. Measured drawings of the curtains in the green antechamber.
Drawing by Ove Hidemark.

Faded areas and traces of folding provide important information on the hanging techniques used (fig. 170). For example, the middle tail was folded toward the back; the two small tails were folded forward.

The width of the fabric is 42½ inches, much wider than the curtain in the queen's room. Here, we see again how decisive the width of the fabric has been in the creation of the curtain: Every part of this set is either one width or one and one-half widths. However, if we try to recreate the pattern used to cut out the curtains (fig. 171), it cannot be done quite as economically as was the pattern for the curtains in the queen's bedroom. Nevertheless, because the angles were arranged to correspond, very little fabric was wasted. Selvage was sewn to selvage. This tight cutting out was possible because the taffeta is reversible; in addition,

there is no design or obvious structure that gives only one possible direction to the fabric, a factor that would have required much more material.

The third set of curtains is from the green antechamber and is dated 1823. This room featured two windows with a big mirror in between. The curtains can be seen on the right in figure 172. The set is actually composed of two pairs of draperies, one white and one green. Each curtain was asymmetrically draped but their positioning around the window resulted in a symmetrical composition. Details of the white and green curtains are illustrated in figures 173 and 174. The white draperies are a bit larger and formed the outer parts. They look as if they were formed of one piece but were actually made in three parts (fig. 175). A green swag was then fastened to the side against a vertical rod

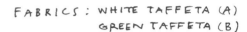

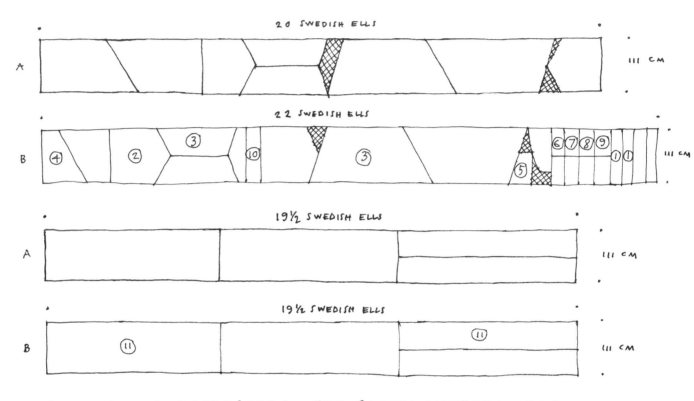

176. Reconstruction of the cutting out of the two sets of curtains for the green antechamber. Drawing by Ove Hidemark.

with five decorative bronze discs. The rod itself was covered with green taffeta, and the pinning of the swag was hidden by four green rosettes. The green side tail below this arrangement was consequently very small. Braids with white flowers on a green ground embellished the curtains. The braids look green against the white taffeta and white against the green fabric, thereby adding to the interlacing effect. The fringe, of wooden pendants and parchment flowers encased in silk, is hung in a lattice work. The weight of all the elaborate fringes was essential for the proper hang of the draperies.

The pattern used for cutting out the curtains for two windows is shown in figure 176. Once again the width of the fabric, 43½ inches (111 cm), was decisive for all the measurements. Every piece is one width or one and one-half widths. Only a few inches could be added by a braid. The big swags, comprised of one and one-half widths, were sewn selvage to selvage. The lower edge is bordered with a fringe. The three other sides were not hemmed, just cut so that they would fold and drape easily. The lack of lining and the use of fringe only along the lower edge further facilitated the hanging of these curtains.

The long curtains behind all the draperies in 1818 were apparently made of the same material as the draperies. Later, however, long curtains of cotton were substituted in a few rooms. The braids of the original curtains were moved to the new cotton ones to create a unified appearance.

The curtains at Rosersberg were hung on a variety of different poles and accessory supports, such as spires, laurel wreaths, fasces, javelins, and other martial devices. Some of these were placed just at the top of the windows; others were fastened above the windows. The different heights of the poles and the elaborate arrangements of the accessories, like javelins and wreaths, made the windows of each room appear different, even though they are of uniform size.

The analysis of these draped curtains from Rosersberg reveals the existence of several consistent principles of craftsmanship. First, a skilled upholsterer cut out his patterns with straight outlines. Secondly, the composition was always built up with the width of the fabric as a standard measure, although the width varied from fabric to fabric. Third, the weight of the fringes selected for the curtains was critical for an attractive hang.

It was certainly more difficult to drape these straight-cut pieces in a natural and graceful manner than to drape the oddly shaped swags and cascades cut with bold curves that were based on plates from late

eighteenth-century upholsterers' guidebooks. It would be of interest to find additional documents that demonstrate how other draped curtains of the early nineteenth century were cut. It is possible that most, like those at Rosersberg, were made from very simple patterns.

Finally, the fact that three pairs of surviving Rosersberg curtains are still in good enough condition not only to have been shown in recent exhibitions, but also to have been shown draped in their old folds, attests to the fine quality of their fabric and workmanship.

NOTES

I wish to thank Lis Granlund and Bo Vahlne of the Royal Collections for their help and interesting discussions and Kent Edström, Nordiska Museet, for helping me to measure the curtains. My husband, Ove Hidemark, architect, helped me reconstruct the cutting schemes and made the drawings. Jane Nylander, when she was at Old Sturbridge Village, kindly showed me James Arrowsmith's *Analysis of Drapery.*

1. Two more sets of curtains that apparently have not survived are also documented in photographs and drawings. The drawings of all the curtains under discussion appeared in the book *Svenska Slöjdföreningens Mönsteralbum* published in Stockholm in 1899. Both the photographs and book are in the Nordiska Museet, Stockholm.

2. The inventories of Rosersberg used in this analysis are from the years 1818 and 1825. They are in the Slottsarkivet, Stockholm.

3. George Smith's style book was published in London by J. Taylor in 1807.

No. 6. — OLD-FASHIONED DRAPERY.

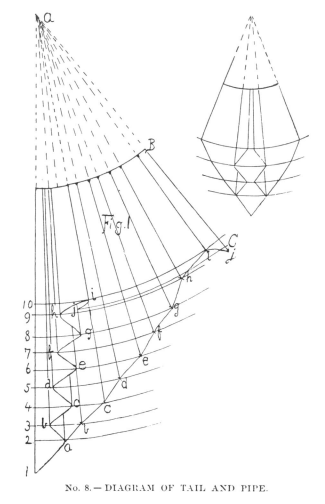

No. 8. — DIAGRAM OF TAIL AND PIPE.

177. Plate 6, "Old-Fashioned Drapery," from *The Curtain-Maker's Handbook, A Reprint of F. A. Moreland's Practical Decorative Upholstery* (New York: E. P. Dutton, 1979).

178. Plate 8, "Diagram of Tail and Pipe," from *The Curtain-Maker's Handbook.* Moreland's "pipe" is a central cascade.

F. A. Moreland's *Practical Decorative Upholstery*

Martha Gandy Fales

WHEN The Brick Store Museum in Kennebunk, Maine, was preparing its Taylor-Barry House for exhibition in 1977, the staff was looking for an appropriate design for the window hangings in one of the upstairs rooms. Although the house had been built in 1803, this particular room had been refurbished during the Victorian period, and it was decided that a later nineteenth-century interpretation would be desirable for it. By coincidence, the volunteer who was asked to help with this project, Jean Harriman, owned a book published in 1890 that proved to be an important and useful discovery. The book was a second edition of *Practical Decorative Upholstery* by F. A. Moreland. I had never heard of it, and in asking others more knowledgeable than I in the field of textiles and window treatments, I discovered that others were unaware of both the book and the man who wrote it.

With the publication of a new reprint edition in 1979, Moreland's book has become an important source on nineteenth-century upholstery practices, particularly draperies. Some of the book's valuable contributions in this area will be summarized and discussed in detail later in this essay. (Also, *see* Anne Farnam's essay in this volume for a discussion of both Moreland's book as it reflects the social and economic trends of his day and for a history of one of his employers, the firm of Ezra Brabrook.)

We have also learned a great deal about the author. He was born Francis Alfred Moreland in Danvers, Massachusetts, on November 16, 1836, the son of John Moreland of Salem, New Hampshire, and Hannah Larrabee of Lynnfield, Massachusetts. From about 1847 to about 1853, he and his family lived at Stage Point in Salem, Massachusetts. On several occasions during the early years of adulthood he worked on ships in the China trade.[1]

In 1872, when he was thirty-six, Moreland's name first appeared in the city directories of Boston, where he was working as an upholsterer on Washington Street. He apparently maintained his residence in Everett, however, as indicated in the 1874 directory. At the age of thirty-nine, he married for the first time. It was the first marriage, too, for his 32-year-old bride Sarah, the daughter of Ebenezer and Rebecca Pitman of Marblehead.[2]

Although Moreland worked for several different firms at various times, including a short stint in 1878–1879 as foreman for the firm of Ezra H. Brabrook, one of the leading upholstery firms of its day, by 1886 he had settled down at Shepard, Norwell and Company where he stayed for nearly forty years. Shepard, Norwell was a large wholesale and retail dry goods store on Winter Street in Boston that claimed in their advertising to have one of the most complete drapery and upholstery departments in the country. Moreland served there as foreman, superintendent of upholstery, and finally, as interior decorator.[3] It was during his tenure there that his book was published. The first edition appeared around 1889, followed by a second edition in 1890, and a third edition in 1899.[4] He retired when he reached his late eighties, around 1924, after a career of more than fifty years in the upholstery/interior design business.

Moreland's wife Sarah had died in 1908.[5] He continued to live in his house at 170 Bradford Street in Everett with his son Benjamin P. Moreland until about 1930 when, at around the age of 94, he moved with his son to Hamilton, Massachusetts.[6]

After his retirement, Moreland continued to work with his hands. For example, in his ninetieth year, he made a handsome model of the Frigate *Essex*, which he presented to the Peabody Museum in Salem.[7] He also contributed a sketch and his reminiscences of Salem's Stage Point to an article in the 1930 *Essex Institute Historical Collections*, explaining that he was certain his drawing of the area was very correct. Although his hand had become quite unsteady, he prided himself on a very retentive memory, especially for matters of long ago. He also made several donations to the Essex Institute, of which he was a member, including a 1922 book, *Period Furnishings*, and some miniature furniture that he had made.[8] Frank Moreland died on July 28, 1936, three and a half months before his one hundredth birthday.[9]

Moreland's book, *Practical Decorative Upholstery*, which he wrote, illustrated, and first published himself contains much information for the student of decorative arts of that period, not the least of which is that contained in the advertisements of Boston firms that appear in the back of each edition of the book. The most prominent ad is that of the drapery and upholstery department of Shepard, Norland and Company, Moreland's employer. The firm advertised the following:

> We shall be pleased to visit houses, and advise with owners in regard to the proper combinations of colors tending to produce harmony with carpets and wallpapers, furnishing estimates and drawings when desired. Many interiors can be arranged charmingly at a moderate cost, if the proper thought is given to it, hence the value of consultation with men of taste and experience.

Moreland was undoubtedly one of these men.

T. F. Swan on Cornhill advertised a large stock of new

designs in wallpapers at "10% lower than any other store in Boston." Burr, Brown & Company on Devonshire and Arch Streets advertised all kinds of upholstery trimmings. Joel Goldthwait & Company, a carpet warehouse on Washington Street, offered Scotch Axminster, English Wilton, and Brussels carpetings, as well as "some very Rare and Choice" orientals. T. F. McGann, the Boston Brass Monger on Portland Street, provided furniture trimmings and "household art goods," either furnishing the designs themselves or working from designs provided by the customer. Two other advertisements were for McFarlin's China Parlor and Nelson H. Brown's clock shop, both on Franklin Street.

Practical Decorative Upholstery contains trade secrets regarding cutting, making, and hanging all kinds of interior curtains and upholstery decorations as well as advice on such diverse subjects as decorating different rooms, mending curtains, moth-proofing mattresses, and installing awnings. Above all, however, it is a book on drapery. It does not, for instance, tell how to upholster furniture. In his preface, Moreland himself outlined the purpose of the book:

> to describe the methods of cutting and making drapery and other necessary accessories of the house . . . not intended as a book of design, and the sketches given, with a few exceptions have been introduced simply to assist the explanations or to approximate the expense of the average drapery.[10]

Presented in a clear manner, Moreland's treatise was intended for "the uninitiated, the housekeeper as well as the amateur draper." Moreland felt that the drapery room of the commercial upholsterer was too exclusive and that it was time to share his own professional experience with the owners of homes for whom drapery "contributes so much to the elegance, or to the feeling of cosiness and comfort . . ." (pp. 8–10).

Here is a summary of some of the most interesting points in the book. Moreland begins with general remarks about trends in furnishings, color, what is appropriate for each room, and suitable types and colors of fabric. He notes that the present tendency is toward light furnishing, particularly the styles of the First Empire and Louis XIV and XV, with woodwork of white or old ivory "relieved by gold" and walls and ceilings in delicate tints. The drapery is usually in festoons and of an airy tone. Tapestry materials with floral designs in natural colors and silks or brocatelles with subdued colors are especially appropriate. "The variety of color and design," he says, "is almost endless; for thanks to a growing taste, the draper is not now, as

thirty years ago, confined to a few crude colors, and something can be found suitable for every occasion" (pp. 10–12).

He recommends repeating the architectural frieze design in the hangings to create a good effect. The current fashion is for the French style of drapery— loosely hanging festoons and folds. The style had fallen briefly into disfavor in the 1870s at the time of the Eastlake reform but then "recovered its prestige to such an extent that in some cases it descends to actual slovenliness by overcrowding with material; whereas the object should be to decorate and not encumber the spaces" (p. 12).

Of all the rooms in a house or suite, parlors represent the height of excellence and give the keynote to the rest of the furnishings. Long curtains are most appropriate for parlor windows. If these are not sufficiently elaborate, an over-valance can be added or the curtains can be carried into festoons at the top. Lace curtains are added underneath, and short laces or glass curtains are hung on rods next to the glass.

Because, in the typical city parlor, all the light comes in at one end through three or four windows close together in a row, it is best here to use a full, long curtain at each side, covering a little more than half of each outside window, and to connect the curtains with a valance in festoons, or in a plainer style. This preserves as much light as possible while still decorating the windows. Bay windows are treated in the same way. It is desirable to make the hangings look as though they were all "in one piece." This effect is increased by using the same trim on the long curtains as on the valance.

"Cosey corners" and alcoves are usually found in the modern house of 1890. Their drapery can be seen from both sides, so either the lining has to be nearly equal in quality to the drapery material, or else a double-faced material has to be used. Moreland goes on to deliver a mild diatribe against inside shutters or blinds that swing into the room, saying they are one of the most intrusive features. Instead, he suggests folding the shutters and installing "an inside shade of dark, agreeable color, running next the glass" (pp. 15–16, 19).

Because the dining room ordinarily exhibits greater simplicity in its furnishings, the general effect is more restrained than that of the parlor or drawing room. A plainer method of draping is desirable. Moreland recommends that the valances and curtains be made up in plush or plain velours with appliqué or embroidery. Another suggestion is to substitute a treatment similar to the fabric valance but with the sort of grillwork just coming into fashion. This grillwork was made of the same kind of wood as the rest of the finish in the room. It could be an open lattice with the light showing through and the curtain drawing behind it, or it could be backed with the same material as the curtain (pp. 19–20).

Stronger colors are used for dining room curtains because a natural-colored wood such as oak, ash, or butternut is customarily used in this room. Shades of blue, brown, or dull red harmonize well with such wood. With ebonized woodwork shades of gold, olive, or orange-red are compatible. Black walnut needs more intense coloring in the choice of fabric or else "its deep, strong color will cause soft tints to appear insipid." Tapestries with dull grounds are especially suitable for the dining room. For plain inexpensive materials, nothing is as effective as the different grades of velours. If lighter goods are used, some of the ready-made curtains in cross stripes or colorful figured madras are nice. Long laces are not often used in dining rooms because they contrast too sharply with the general tone of the room (pp. 20–23).

After this general introduction, Moreland focuses upon the measuring, cutting, and hanging of seven different drapery types. The proper way to measure a house for drapery, he says, is to make a good-sized floor plan of each story or suite of rooms and to make drawings of the doors and windows to be hung. Even a single room should be treated in this way. Simple outline sketches suffice if they are well-defined and correctly done. One inch to a foot is a good scale for a working plan. Moreland cautions that a tape should always be used in measuring any distance over two feet, unless measuring windows for shades. For this, a ruler could be used. He recommends that the tape used for measuring also be used for cutting. If not, it is important to use one that agrees exactly with the tape used previously (p. 24).

Moreland uses sketches of old-fashioned drapery to explain first how to cut a regular festoon or swag, admitting that it is a little out-dated (fig. 177). "It contains," he said, "the principle of all festoon-cutting, and the sketch as it is shown will be of assistance to the beginner in establishing proportions, and is the basis, as it were, from which to project other ideas" (p. 39). The proportions for this and similar designs require the side wings or tails to fall about half-way down the side of the window. The festoon should fall between one-quarter and one-third, and the "pipe" or central cascade should be a little over half the depth of the festoon.

Moreland explains how to measure a festoon to determine first the width at the bottom, then the distance between pleats, and finally the width at the top. He next explains how to figure for the pleats and how to cut the pattern. His plate 8 (fig. 178) shows how to plan and cut the wings or tails and the pipes or center pieces, which he says are cut in the same way, but, he warns, "Do not attempt to make too many folds in such small spaces" (pp. 39–47).

The second type was the French drapery festoon (pp. 50–54). In the old-fashioned festoon described above, there is no attempt to make the whole drapery look as if it is all of one piece. In the newer style, the festoon is intended to look like one piece simply thrown over the pole, and thus has to be cut in a different way. Because the festoon was to droop below the pole in the middle of the window, the pleats also have to be executed in a different manner. Instead of being gathered together in a small compass, the pleats are spread along the pole to correspond to the width of the wing or long curtain to which the festoon is attached.

Figure 179 shows the well-draped room of 1890, with long curtains, valances, lace curtains, portières, mantel drapery, scarves on tables and pianos, and rugs on rugs. The window treatment is suggested as an easy lesson in French drapery festoon for the beginner and is also suitable as an over-drapery for portières. A modified version could be made in silk as a light drapery over

179. Plate II, "Design of French Drapery Valance," from *The Curtain-Maker's Handbook.*

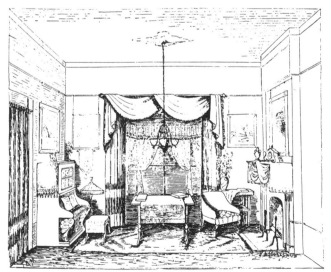

NO. 11. — DESIGN OF FRENCH DRAPERY VALANCE

laces or as a festoon on the front of a mantel. This drawing was signed on the right, *F. A. Moreland* and on the left *F. A. M.* (Most of the illustrations in the book are signed with one or both of these two autographs.)

The third type of drapery illustrated is irregular drapery (fig. 180), in which the festoons are spread more on one side than the other, and the festoon or swag appears to be a continuation of the curtain. The diagram of irregular drapery shows how to drop a plumb line through the deepest and heaviest part of the festoon and from this how to determine the side lines of the pattern (pp. 57–69).

Raised drapery (fig. 181), the fourth type, is recommended for treating a wide space like the middle section of a bay window or for uniting several windows under one drapery. Raised drapery relieves a monotonous level line and makes a room look higher. A diagram shows how the spaces for each part could be laid out on a draper's pole according to the scale drawing of the design and how the plumb line is dropped through the heaviest part of the festoon. In cutting this type of design, the perpendicular line does not come in the middle of the festoon (pp. 69–77).

Moreland also explains how to cut drapery so that the festoons, pipes, and tails are all joined together instead of being made up in separate pieces. Some claim this is the better way and less stiff in appearance, especially on a bed canopy or flounce, where it is hung under a cornice so that the head is concealed. The drapery is best made up of a light material requiring no lining. If a cornice is not used, rosettes could be put over the shirring of the sides of the festoons. Moreland calls this "transient decoration," made by gathering up the material in one's hand and tying it with a string, and then forming the bunch into a rosette (pp. 79–83).

The fifth type of drapery, narrow festoons, is not in "general favor just at the present time," but he gives the methods of cutting anyway (pp. 84–92). Moreland shows an inexpensive type of drapery similar in effect to a full festoon but requiring only half the material. This type can be used in any space that is four feet or less in width.

The sixth type, looped-up drapery (fig. 182), can be made in several different ways. In the design shown, the curtain is made to appear as though it were drawn up with a rope. Looped-up drapery was suitable for a hall or archway, with a lattice or grillwork above it, but the curtain requires sufficient height to allow a proper depth and also to permit a person to pass under it. Looped drapery was especially adaptable to light mate-

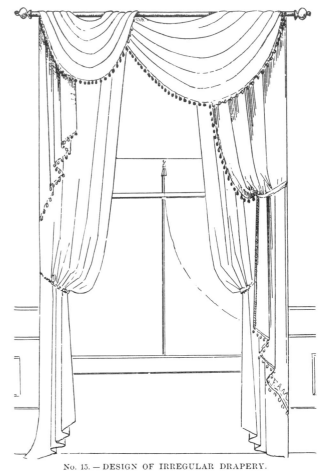

No. 15. — DESIGN OF IRREGULAR DRAPERY.

180. Plate 15, "Design of Irregular Drapery," from *The Curtain-Maker's Handbook*.

rials requiring no linings, such as silks and madras. More elaborate versions are used over lace curtains (pp. 92–106).

The last type of drapery is the flat valance (fig. 183). Plain or figured materials like cretonnes are used; striped or flowing designs are not appropriate. Moreland tells how to make a ruffled edge for trimming this design; he admits "ruffle trimming is a little out of date, but many still prefer it to fringe, and we are not suggesting aesthetic ideas but teaching practical work. . . . Flat valances are things of the past except when used in connection with festoon work to heighten its effect." Flat valances are usually made over buckram to help preserve the flat surface. The diagram shows how to transfer the scale drawing to the paper pattern in full size. Another design

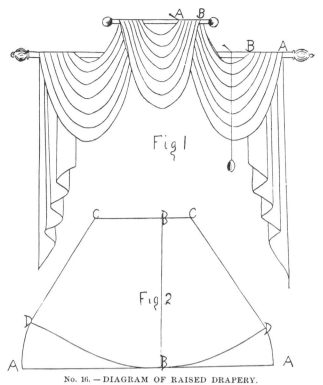

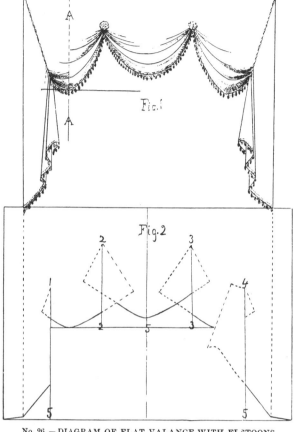

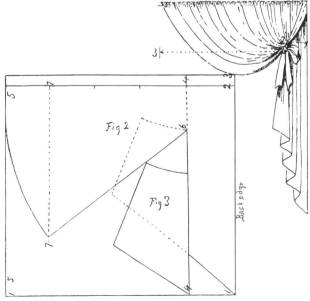

No. 16.—DIAGRAM OF RAISED DRAPERY.

181. Plate 16, "Diagram of Raised Drapery," from *The Curtain-Maker's Handbook*.

182. Plate 24, "Diagram and Design of Looped Drapery," from *The Curtain-Maker's Handbook*.

No. 26.—DIAGRAM OF FLAT VALANCE WITH FESTOONS.

183. Plate 26, "Diagram of Flat Valance with Festoons," from *The Curtain-Maker's Handbook*.

No. 24.—DIAGRAM AND DESIGN OF LOOPED DRAPERY.

shows the modern way of using flat valances, which could be made of plush with silk over-drapery.

As to the proper length for curtains, Moreland says it was a matter of taste, "but the fashion for the last fifteen years has been to have them just reach the floor. Many have preferred quite recently, however, to have them two or three inches longer" (pp. 106–24, 146).

Flat valances could be combined with looped drapery. In addition to such decorative drapery conventions as the pleated wing, appliqué work, and fringe, there could be a large puff or rosette at one side of the curtains. For the finishing touch, Moreland suggests that a heavy cord and two tassels be put around the rosette to look as though the cord were holding it all in place. Another form of flat valances — box-pleated connecting valances—always looks attractive, especially in a bay window, dining room, or library. These box-pleated valances also use less material, can be employed anywhere except in rooms decorated in the French style, and are well adapted to either a pole or cornice.

Next, Moreland takes up alcove and archway drapery, which could be made of silk or a double-faced material and looped over a pole. Portières at entrances are indispensable. He suggests a pair for each side of the casing of large double sliding-doors so that the doors, when closed, can be concealed by the curtains. Portières are not only used to cover openings that never had doors.

> The idea of decorating the doorways is coming more into general favor, many discarding their doors as useless incumbrances. Of course, the outside doors and others separating rooms requiring special seclusion must be retained. All other doors might as well be removed, and their places filled with curtains.

Removal of doors allows a freer circulation of air and more consistent temperature. For a boudoir, Moreland recommends a very dainty portière made of silk plush that can be painted with flowers (pp. 127–35, 179–89).

In addition to portières, Moreland also discusses lace and glass curtains. "Laces are now sold so low," Moreland points out, "that some kinds are within the means of almost everybody, and nothing freshens up the room so, or suggests to an outsider the refinement within, so much as a bit of lace in the window." Lace curtains are hung on their own pole and not attached to the same rings that support the long curtains or valances. As a result, they can be easily removed without taking down the other work. To launder laces, he says, it is best to send them to a professional cleaner, but he also provides instructions, taken from *The Decorator and Furnisher*, on how to wash laces. Moreland tells how to mend lace curtains as well (pp. 158–60).

Glass curtains are the short curtains inside the window casing. Made of a light material such as silk, muslin, or madras, and trimmed with soft fringes, they are usually hung on a small rod with sockets on the stop beads of the casing. "A dainty way of trimming glass curtains is to use a lace 2 or 2½ inches wide." They also can be purchased in pairs in regular lace patterns, such as Brussels, Swiss, Irish point, or Nottingham. These are finished to reach the sill or, as many prefer, a few inches below it, and are tied back with ribbon or small loops made of silk (pp. 161–62).

After his discussion of types, materials, techniques for cutting, and proper care, Moreland describes the appropriate drapery fashions for specific spaces or uses.

For cottage curtains, he prefers a shirred top, with small rings on the back, instead of the hemmed top. The rings allow the curtain to be moved back and forth easily. The rods are placed with the brackets on the inside member of the casing so that the ornamented ends of the rods show. Curtains made of thin silk have the bottoms weighted with a little shot to keep them from flying around when the window is open (pp. 162–65).

Silk was also used for the most complex sort of shade, an "Austrian curtain," as Moreland calls festoon shades when he describes how to make and hang them. No other thin fabric combines so much weight with flexibility. (Interestingly, only in reference to this type of work does he use the word *upholsteress* instead of *upholsterer*, saying "the excellence of the whole depends chiefly on the skill of the upholsteress" [pp. 170–77]).

Mantel drapery generally conforms to the style of the window curtains but in simpler form. "Much of the mantel woodwork is now so elaborate," Moreland notes, "that it requires no draping beyond a tasteful arrangement of scarfs of silk. Dark colors give a better ground to show off the usual mantel ornaments." For a more elaborate treatment, he recommends the use of a large rectangular false shelf, larger than the actual mantle. Upon this is laid a plain plush scarf lined with flannel and then festoons of silk hung over a rod are added along the edge of the board. Figure 184 shows a Moreland design for the mantel in a "den." A scarf is thrown over the false shelf and slashed up the middle to allow the under-drapery to be drawn through. On the right side, the scarf is raised and fitted to a rod at the front of a separate small raised shelf, "which affords a position of especial prominence for the trophy of the regatta and a nice tuck-away place underneath." The long curtains at each side below are hung on a rod so that they can be pulled back when the fire is burning. Plush or velours are most appropriate; silk would be too combustible (pp. 270–79).

Dressing tables are also objects for special-purpose drapery. "The dressing-table can be made a very convenient and attractive addition to the furnishing of a chamber especially for a summer house, as its usual light and airy dressing is in keeping with the general treatment of the room for the season." For materials, Moreland suggests plain or figured silks, cretonnes, chintz, some of the cheap printed sateens, cream and ecru madras trimmed with colored ribbons, or muslin with box-pleated silk ribbon or soft ball fringe. "Pretty goods suitable for the purpose can be purchased for ten cents per yard and upwards, and the work after the can be achieved by using cretonnes and chintz. They give a fresh, charming, and homey feeling to the room. "Very pretty chamber draperies are made with cream madras or muslins, with light silk over-drapery; or the entire draping may be of muslin or cream madras over colored silesia [a thin twilled linen]" (pp. 225–38).

Bed hangings repeat the general design of the window draperies but are not necessarily the same material or color. Harmony is important. "The full canopy covering the entire bed is seldom used, though this could easily be done in imitation of the four-poster if one desired, by making a light frame and attaching it to the ceiling. . . ." Usually just a half-canopy, with drapery at the head only, is used. Because most wooden bedsteads of the late nineteenth century are built with-

185. Plate 49, "Dressing-Table," from *The Curtain-Maker's Handbook*.

No. 65.—MANTEL DRAPERY IN "THE DEN."

184. Plate 65, "Mantel Drapery in 'The Den,'" from *The Curtain-Maker's Handbook*.

frame is made can be done by any lady of taste." It would be, Moreland imagined, "a sort of grown-up doll dressing."

Some dressing tables, he admits, have been made from old packing boxes or discarded tables and bureaus. "To have a frame made by a carpenter, however, would not be very costly, and would, no doubt, be more satisfactory." He includes a diagram for a frame seven feet from floor to canopy, about four feet wide, with shelves added below. He recommended that this frame be mounted on casters so that when sweeping the floor the whole thing could be moved without dragging it by the curtains or upsetting and breaking things. A design (fig. 185) suitable for figured silk or dotted muslin with box-pleated ribbon edge trimming shows five well-defined pleats in the skirt as well as shirring between the pleats (pp. 201–25).

Moreland says that the chamber or sleeping-apartment, no matter how luxuriously furnished, should be quiet and restful. The best effects for the least expense

No. 49.—DRESSING-TABLE.

No. 57. — BED WITH BOX-PLEATED CANOPY.

186. Plate 57, "Bed with Box-Pleated Canopy," from *The Curtain-Maker's Handbook*.

out canopies, if bed hangings are desired a false canopy could be made and attached to the wall. This arrangement makes it easy when the drapery is taken down or rehung, as is usually done in the spring and fall. A pretty way of treating a canopied bed in a low-studded room that has a deep architectural frieze is to carry the frame right up to the ceiling and to use a valance, the same height as the frieze, all around the canopy. The valance then looks like a continuation of the frieze. If ruffled trim has been used elsewhere, ruffled bands are more appropriate for holding the curtains back than cord loops. Bands made in crescent forms sit better than those cut straight.

"Brass bedsteads are much in favor and are tasteful pieces of furniture when curtained," Moreland explains in reference to a design (fig. 186) in pleated work that is simple, easily made, and a favorite with those who do not like fancy festoon work. He suggests treating it in

China silk, with the back and canopy lining in silk of a different color. He also tells how to measure for bedspread and bolster, for mattress and tick, for pillows, cushions, and window seats, and how to make them all up. The bed curtains are finished in a length that reaches to the top of the caster so that the curtains will not get under the wheels and be torn when the bed is moved (pp. 239–53).

In draping old four-post beds without canopies (fig. 187), a light wooden frame could be made to fit between the poles so that the center of the canopy is raised "more or less, according to fancy." A simpler method is to dispense with the poles and bring the canopy frame out to their places. In this method, the festoons and curtains are tacked to the frame and finished with a four-inch ruffle all around the canopy. "Cretonnes seem specially adapted to these old fashioned bedsteads, using ruffled trimming instead of fringe" (pp. 252–56).

Moreland also tells how to moth-proof mattresses with naphtha and, quoting the *London Furniture Gazette* (which he recommends as a valuable monthly for everyone engaged in the furnishing business), gives instructions for cleaning and preserving the feathers in feather bedding (pp. 259–69).

Regarding slipcovers, Moreland says they are indispensable for protecting furniture during the "dusty season." They are to cover the entire piece of furniture, woodwork and all, as nicely-finished frames or intricate carving suffer as much from dust as the covering material. Slipcovers should be made in as few pieces as possible and loose enough to allow for shrinkage in washing (fig. 188). "The better way is to have the required quantity shrunk before cutting, but in this age of haste few will wait to have it done." The best materials are plain brown linen (either striped or figured), dimity, French cottons, or cretonnes. He cautions against the old-fashioned way of binding seams because the binding shrinks more than the linen and is apt to pull off in washing. Instead he recommends joining the pieces with a folded stitched seam known as a French fell seam. He gives yardage estimates for covers of typical furniture as well (pp. 280–91).

Moreland also discusses the covering of walls. The use of upholstery material rather than paint or wallpaper produces a better effect even if it is often more expensive. This is especially true for "picture galleries or other rooms where many paintings are to be displayed, as a softness and depth of tone is obtained by the use of velours or similar goods in suitable colors that would be impossible by other means" (pp. 194–200).

No. 60. — OLD FOUR-POST BED

187. Plate 60, "Old Four-Post Bed," from *The Curtain-Maker's Handbook.*

188. Plate 66, "Chairs, Showing Working Plan for Slip Covers," from *The Curtain-Maker's Handbook.*

No. 66. — CHAIRS, SHOWING WORKING PLAN FOR SLIP COVERS.

Even though carpets—which had once been included with general upholstery furnishing—formed a separate business by the late nineteenth century, Moreland tells how to identify orientals and various types of manufactured carpets and discusses Chinese and Japanese mattings. Mattings are nice for summer wear on floors, dadoes, or even walls. He also mentions painted carpets or oilcloths, linoleum, and lignums, the latter being a wood flooring ground with oil. For all these materials, he gives instructions for measuring and installing, for borders, and for cleaning. In measuring front halls, he suggests planning the position of the chandelier so that the figures of the carpet can be arranged in relation to it. Moreland also provides helpful information on measuring and installing outdoor Italian awnings, even though this business too had "drifted into the hands of specialists" and was no longer part of the upholsterer's trade (pp. 292–316).

Moreland's book is filled with practical information. There is a section on choosing poles and cornices, including advice on what the poles should be made of and how they should be finished. The rings and the end finials, for instance, should be of the same material as the pole because combinations of brass and wood look "tawdry." Moreland suggests covering the poles of cretonne curtains with the same material. Likewise, plush-covered poles look attractive with plush curtains. Using poles for hanging drapery is most fashionable at this time and is well suited to the period's style of festoon draping. But, predicts Moreland, "the cornice will come again." Moreland also includes helpful hints on how to tell if a window is not square and how to adjust the springs on the two main types of roller shades.

One of the most valuable sections in the book is the information on where and how to hang poles, cornices, traverse rods, and shades (pp. 33–36, 190–93, 167–70). This sort of information is an enormous help to someone who is trying to determine the date and purpose of the accumulated hardware and holes found on windows of old houses, making it possible to piece together much of the history of what has actually hung at those windows over the years.

Practical Decorative Upholstery is a most significant book for the student of decorative arts and practices prior to the twentieth century. Not only does the book describe what was fashionable in the late nineteenth century, but it also covers what was by then old fashioned and out-of-date, thus also giving us important information about earlier periods.

NOTES

1. Danvers, Massachusetts, *Vital Records*, Certificate of Death, vol. 5, p. 206, Massachusetts Division of Vital Statistics. J. Foster Smith, "Stage Point and Thereabouts," *Essex Institute Historical Collections* 66, no. 1 (January 1930): 1–20. *Salem Evening News*, July 30, 1936, obituary. Letter to author from John H. Merrow, Curator, Marblehead Historical Society, Marblehead, Massachusetts, Feb. 1, 1979.

2. Boston City Directories, 1860–1928. Everett City Directories, 1889–1928. Certificate of Death, vol. 5, p. 206. Marriage Records, vol. 281, p. 76 and vol. 280, p. 235, Massachusetts Division of Vital Statistics. The November 1935 issue of *Upholstering* contains an article, written by Moreland when he was ninety-nine years of age, that describes his early years and his experience in the drapery business. The magazine's editor calls him "the first man in America to publish an illustrated book on the subject of drapery cutting."

3. Boston City Directories. Ezra H. Brabrook was in the furniture and upholstery business with various partners until his death in 1880 when the firm was bought by A. H. Davenport. Shepard, Norwell and Company continued in business until 1936. In 1872, Moreland was located at 164 Washington Street; in 1874, at 183½ Washington; from 1875–1877, at 116 Tremont Street; in 1879, at 96 Washington; from 1880–1881, at 350 Washington; from 1882– 1885, at 26 Charles Street; from 1886–1887, at 30 Winter Street. After 1887 until 1904, Moreland's name does not appear in Boston directories but is listed in Everett directories. While the Everett directories indicate that he worked in Boston, his place of work is cited only from 1904–1908 as being 26 Winter Street, a part of the Shepard, Norwell and Company complex of buildings. According to an article which appeared in an unidentified newspaper clipping on November 15, 1935, Moreland started his own business after working for Shepard, Norwell and Company and served clients in the Boston area as well as in New York, Chicago, St. Louis, Washington, D.C., and Maine. This clipping was given to the Library of the Essex Institute by Moreland's great-niece, Miss Helen F. Moreland.

4. The first edition of the book was published by Moreland himself. A second edition was published by Lee and Shepard in Boston in 1890 and C. T. Dillingham in New York. Both editions are the same size (about seven by nine inches), have 320 pages, and seventy drawings and diagrams. A third edition, published by Clifford and Lawton in New York in 1899, was slightly smaller in size but had the same number of pages and illustrations. Copies of the original editions are difficult to obtain now, but a paperback reprint of the second edition was published by E. P. Dutton in 1979. The reprint is entitled *The Curtain-Maker's Handbook*. Copies of the first edition can be found in the libraries at Yale University and the University of Michigan and at the Library Company of Philadelphia. Copies of the second edition are located at the Essex Institute, the Library of Congress, the Boston Public Library, and the John Crear Library in Chicago.

5. Certificate of Death, vol. 9, p. 109 and vol. 34, p. 312, Middlesex County Probate Court Records.

6. Everett City Directories, 1889– 1928. Beverly City Directories, 1929–1933. Letter to author from Susanna M. Austin, Reference Librarian, Parlin Memorial Library, Everett, Massachusetts, January 24, 1979.

7. Letter to author from Mrs. G. M. Ayers, Staff Secretary, Peabody Museum, Salem, Massachusetts, March 16, 1978.

8. Smith, "Stage Point." Letter to author from Mrs. Arthur R. Norton, Reference Librarian, and Anne Farnam, Curator, Essex Institute, Salem, Massachusetts, January 19, 1979.

9. Certificate of Death, vol. 34, p. 312. *Annual Report of the Essex Institute* for the year ending May 1, 1937. Obituaries appeared in the *Salem Evening News* on July 29 and July 30, 1936.

10. F. A. Moreland, *Practical Decorative Upholstery* (Boston: Lee and Shepard, 1890), Preface. Subsequent references to this book will be by page number in the text.

Drapery Documents in the Study Exhibition

Jane C. Nylander

DURING the Conference on Historic Drapery and Upholstery in 1979, a study exhibition of drapery documents was held at Old Sturbridge Village (figs. 189 and 190). Forty-five objects were shown from the collections of the Essex Institute; the Genesee Country Museum, Mumford, New York; the National Society of the Colonial Dames of America in the State of New Hampshire; Old Sturbridge Village; the Rhode Island Historical Society; the Society for the Preservation of New England Antiquities; and the Valentine Museum. In addition, several pieces were provided by private lenders. The documents were chosen to show a variety of styles and fabrics, from a mid-eighteenth-century bed valance to a complete stamped wool window hanging in the neoclassical style to a common dimity curtain of the nineteenth century to a window cornice of the late-nineteenth century in the aesthetic taste. While it is hard to recapture the impact of the original exhibition where the viewer could analyze closely the individual hangings and make comparisons, the examples illustrated here do provide some sense of the breadth of the fabrics and drapery treatments used in America from the mid-eighteenth century to the end of the nineteenth century.

189. View of Exhibition of Drapery Documents, Old Sturbridge Village, Sturbridge, Massachusetts, March 1979. Photograph by Henry E. Peach.

190. View of Exhibition of Drapery Documents, Old Sturbridge Village, Sturbridge, Massachusetts, March 1979. Photograph by Henry E. Peach.

191. Foot valance for a bed, c. 1730–1760. Light blue stamped worsted with blue and white tape. From the John Brown family of Providence. *See Antiques* 101, no. 3 (March 1972): 496. Valance: Width-65 inches, height-12 inches, width of fabric-28½ inches. Courtesy, Rhode Island Historical Society.

193. Bed valances (side and foot), c. 1770. Blue-and-white checked linen, possibly the "piece of check" mentioned by Jonathan Sayward in his diary as being purchased in Kittery in 1771. From the Jonathan Sayward House, York, Maine. In the Sayward House collection, there also survive the remaining side valance, two foot curtains, and one additional set of bed valances that are sewn together at the foot corners, all of the same check. *See Antiques* 116, no. 3 (September 1979): 574. Side valance: Width-75 inches, height-13½ inches; foot valance: width-55 inches, height-13½ inches. Courtesy, Society for the Preservation of New England Antiquities. Photograph by Henry E. Peach.

192. Side valance for a bed, c. 1775–1785. Copperplate-printed cotton in blue. The pattern is called "Tyger" in the Bromley Hall pattern book. (Bromley Hall was England's largest eighteenth-century textile printing firm.) This pattern is illustrated in *Catalogue of a Loan Exhibition of English Chintz* (London: Her Majesty's Stationery Office, 1960), no. 106. *See Antiques* 101, no. 3 (March 1972): 500. Width-88 inches, height-11 inches. Courtesy, Rhode Island Historical Society.

194. Bed valance (side), probably third quarter of eighteenth century. Crewel-embroidered linen, with later fringed border. The border, with its fine mesh, swags, and tiny tassels, may be dated as late as the 1790s. Width-79 inches, height-10 inches, length of fringe-7 inches. Courtesy, Society for the Preservation of New England Antiquities. Photograph by Henry E. Peach.

195. Valance, England, c. 1795–1800. Block-printed cotton, blue threads in selvage, cotton gimp and fringes. This belongs to the same set as the curtain in figure 158. Width-58 inches, height-12¾ inches. Courtesy, Society for the Preservation of New England Antiquities. Photograph by Henry E. Peach.

196. Complete set of drapery for one window, early nineteenth century. Stamped blue wool with floral designs, blue and yellow wool braid and fringe, tan cotton linings. From the Moffatt-Ladd House, Portsmouth, New Hampshire. Three full sets survive, each of which is made with one pair of long panels, one pair of short panels, one simple swag, and one long swag that is looped around a large brass cloak pin installed above a painted wooden rod with brass finials. Matching cloak pins were used at each side of the window to loop back the curtains during the daytime. The curtains may date from a refurbishing of the house that took place in 1807 at the time of the marriage of Maria Tufton Haven and Alexander Ladd. Curtain panels: Width-42 inches, height-100 inches. Courtesy, National Society of the Colonial Dames of America in the State of New Hampshire. Photograph by Henry E. Peach.

197. Window drapery, England, c. 1810. Block-printed glazed yellow, red, and brown cotton, with blue selvages; the decayed tan chintz lining has been removed. The fabric is similar to designs in *Duddings' Furniture*, a sample book dated 1800–1814 at the Victoria and Albert Museum. Two pairs of these curtains survive—this pair at Old Sturbridge Village and a pair at the Victoria and Albert Museum. Additional pieces of fabric in this design exist, one of which (after being washed) served as the document for the Brunschwig & Fils reproduction "Osterly." It is thought that these curtains originally hung at Boscobel in New York State, and reproductions based on this pair have recently been installed there. Overall width at top-56¼ inches, overall height-151 inches. Courtesy, Old Sturbridge Village. Photograph by Henry E. Peach.

198. Figure 197 with center panel lowered.

199. Detail of the reverse side of the draperies shown in figures 197 and 198 showing printed border and hanging rings.

200. "Head" belonging to French bed, Boston, 1838. Wooden rod covered with red silk, two red and yellow cords, and tassels; four original brass hooks and finials. Affixed to the rod is a paper label, written in the nineteenth century. It provides the proper term for this rod with tassels. Length of rod-40 inches. Courtesy, Society for the Preservation of New England Antiquities. Photograph by Henry E. Peach.

201. A swag and a tail or cascade, England, c. 1825–1830. Roller-printed glazed cotton in a chinoiserie design, with red, green, and yellow wool tapes and spool fringes covered with yellow silk. Lined with tan chintz. The swag shows evidence of having had rings at the side. Tack holes along the upper edges of all pieces indicate that they were pleated somewhat irregularly when originally hung. A partial set of bed hangings with the same fabric and trimming survives. Swag: width-34½ inches, height-55 inches; cascade cut: width-48 inches, height-47 inches. Courtesy, Old Sturbridge Village. Photograph by Henry E. Peach.

202. White cotton dimity curtain, nineteenth century. In every collection surveyed for this exhibition, there were quantities of white dimity bed hangings, counterpanes, and some window curtains. This simple panel is included here to remind us of the long-time popularity of this fabric for furnishing uses in both complex and simple styles. Width-23 inches, height-51 inches. Courtesy, Old Sturbridge Village. Photograph by Henry E. Peach.

204. Detail of window curtain, c. 1835–1845. Roller-printed glazed cotton in the Gothic style, with wool tapes and fringes and wool covered spools. The tape loops at the top of this curtain appear to be later additions. Some other pieces, including a stool cover, survive with this curtain, indicating its probable original use as a set of bedroom furnishings. Width-41 inches, height-87 inches. Courtesy, Essex Institute. Photograph by Richard Merrill.

205. Section of *trompe l'oeil* valance fabric, attributed to James Burd, Mt. Zion Works, Radcliff, near Manchester, England, c. 1850. Roller-printed. Fabric width-25 inches, vertical pattern repeat-16 inches. *See* Florence Montgomery, *Printed Textiles: English and American Cottons and Linens, 1700–1850* (New York: The Viking Press, 1970), pp. 333–34. Courtesy, Old Sturbridge Village.

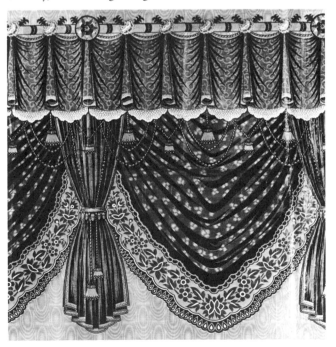

203. Tails or cascades from a set of bed hangings, second quarter of the nineteenth century. Roller-printed chintz, with striped cotton tapes. On the left is a tail for one of the foot posts of the bed; the other is for the head post. A foot curtain survives with this set. Cascade for the head post (as hung): width-8 inches, height (of both)-50¾ inches. Courtesy, Essex Institute. Photograph by Henry E. Peach.

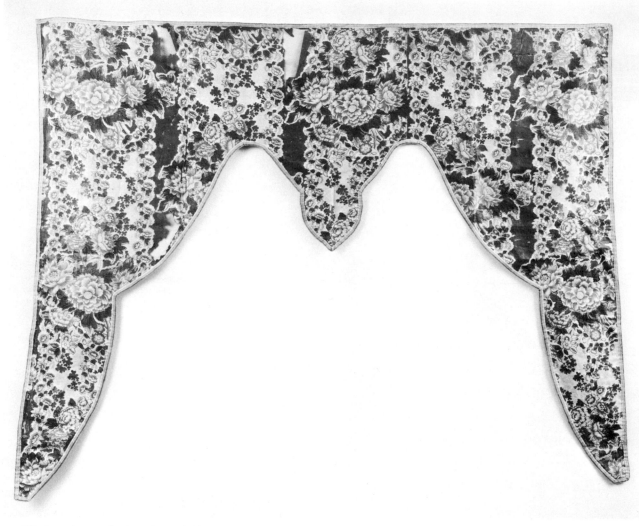

206. Window valance or lambrequin, probably England, c. 1850–1860.
Roller-printed cotton, lined with tan chintz and bound with striped
cotton tape. Flat valances with scalloped edges flowing down the sides
were referred to as lambrequins. Width-38 inches, height-31 inches.
Courtesy, Old Sturbridge Village. Photograph by Donald F. Eaton.

207. Drapery panel, Boston area, c. 1850. Block-printed chintz in a striped pattern of lilac and roses. Original gimp and 3-inches diameter brass rings. Width-35 inches, height-115½ inches. Courtesy, Society for the Preservation of New England Antiquities. Photograph by Henry E. Peach.

208. Lambrequin, c. 1850–1860. Red silk brocatelle with tassels. Brocatelle was a popular nineteenth-century upholstery and drapery fabric. It consisted of a cotton or linen filling with a silk relief surface. Width-62 inches, height-60 inches. Courtesy, Society for the Preservation of New England Antiquities. Photograph by Henry E. Peach.

209. Drapery panel, Boston, c. 1865. Green and cream silk lampas with pink flowers, lined with white china silk. Original silk cords and tassels. Width-63 inches, height-12 feet. Courtesy, Society for the Preservation of New England Antiquities. Photograph by Henry E. Peach.

210. Detail of the top back of figure 209.

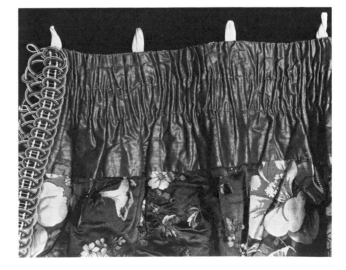

211. Lambrequin, c. 1855–1865. Glazed cotton with pink fringes. Width-160 inches, height-37 inches. Courtesy, Society for the Preservation of New England Antiquities. Photograph by Henry E. Peach.

212. Window valance, c. 1860. Printed glazed cotton with silk braid. Width-104 inches, height-52 inches. Courtesy, Society for the Preservation of New England Antiquities. Photograph by Henry E. Peach.

213. Window valance, c. 1860–1880. Style of Louis XVI. Green and cream silk lampas with wool fringe. Rings appear to be original. Three valances and two curtain panels survive. Width-83 inches, height (including fringe)-57½ inches. Courtesy, Society for the Preservation of New England Antiquities. Photograph by Henry E. Peach.

214. Window valance, c. 1868–1880. Green and gold damask with wool fringe. Two straight panels and another valance that has been cut down in size also survive. Width-113 inches, height-49 inches. Courtesy, Essex Institute. Photograph by Henry E. Peach.

215. Straight valance with original cords and tassels, late-nineteenth century. Pink, green, and yellow silk with patterned white chintz lining. From the Paine and Emery families of Boston. Width-78 inches, height-23 inches. Courtesy, Society for the Preservation of New England Antiquities. Photograph by Henry E. Peach.

216. Tieback and two curtain pins from same set as figure 215.

217. Window valance, c. 1860–1870. Red silk damask, matching gimp sewn across the top. Width-62 inches, height (including fringe)-33¾ inches. Courtesy, Society for the Preservation of New England Antiquities. Photograph by Henry E. Peach.

218. Drapery panel, New England, c. 1870–1880. Mulberry and green wool with silk gimp. Width-39 inches, height-10 feet. Courtesy, Society for the Preservation of New England Antiquities. Photograph by Henry E. Peach.

219. Window valance in the aesthetic taste, c. 1878–1885. Green velvet and white linen embroidered in green and rust, some painted areas. Width-101 inches, height-31 inches. Courtesy, Society for the Preservation of New England Antiquities. Photograph by Henry E. Peach.

220. Portière, c. 1880–1890. Block-printed gold velvet with couched metallic threads and gilt spangles. From a house at 249 Commonwealth Avenue, Boston. Width 33¼ inches, height-101 inches. Courtesy, Essex Institute. Photograph by Henry E. Peach.

221. Lambrequin in the aesthetic taste, late-nineteenth century.
Cretonne (printed cotton) with heavy knotted wool fringe. One of a
set. Width-53 inches, height-40 inches. Courtesy, Genesee Country
Museum, Mumford, New York. Photograph by Henry E. Peach.

222. Swag and tails, made by Irving & Casson—A. H. Davenport,
Boston, for the Pingree House, 1935. Red silk damask with old spool
fringe, lined with cotton satin. This piece was made to go over a
boxed cornice. Width-66½ inches, height (including fringe)-44
inches. Courtesy, Essex Institute. Photograph by Henry E. Peach.

223. Empire sofa, Boston, c. 1825–1835. Mahogany, birch, yellow poplar, oak. Height-33¾ inches, length-88 inches, depth-23½ inches. Courtesy, Museum of Fine Arts, Boston. Gift of Colonel and Mrs. Thomas R. West.

Fig. 138.

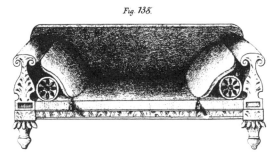

224. Plate 25, fig. 138, in John Hall, *The Cabinetmakers' Assistant* (Baltimore: John Murphy, 1840).

The Re-dressing of a Boston Empire Sofa

Jan Seidler Ramirez

AN IMPOSING Empire dress sofa, dating from between 1820 and 1840, now in the Museum of Fine Arts, Boston (fig. 223), provides an illuminating case study of the difficulties and pitfalls faced by museum curators and others who wish to achieve period accuracy in restoring antique upholstered furniture. The story of the reupholstering of this sofa also demonstrates how overeager curators may rush their research and analysis and thereby make mistakes that could prove costly. And finally, the sofa's reupholstery affords an important opportunity to document and analyze the step by step recreation of early-nineteenth-century upholstery methods.

At the time the sofa was given to the museum in 1966, American Empire furniture had received little attention from curators, scholars, or connoisseurs of American decorative arts. Staff members at the museum, largely unacquainted with the stylistic idiom of this period in American furniture, were uncertain of the maker and provenance of the new acquisition. They noted, however, that the sofa resembled a design reproduced in the Baltimore furnituremaker John Hall's book *The Cabinetmakers' Assistant* (fig. 224), published in Baltimore in 1840,[1] the first such design book published in the United States. The museum staff, therefore, assumed that the sofa represented the work of an American craftsman conversant with this widely-circulated "grammar" of furniture patterns.

This American attribution was soon reinforced when other sofas of similar design were discovered in New England. The use of native woods in their construction confirmed the American attribution. Further, because many of these seats had been found in Boston and its environs, the conclusion—that the sofa represented a distinctive furniture form favored by Bostonians and manufactured by Boston cabinetmakers—seemed warranted. That this was a popular sofa in Boston may well account for the fact that when the Swiss-born portrait painter Edward L. Custer settled in Boston in the mid-nineteenth century, he featured a similar seat as a prop in an oil study that he produced of a curly-haired Boston child (fig. 225).[2]

Indeed, the similarities among the dozen or so sofas in this Boston cluster are striking. The seats exhibit nearly identical structural features and are composed of the same woods, with mahogany employed for the exterior framework, and birch, yellow poplar, and oak used as secondary woods in the interior bracing. The frame designs appear to have been drawn from a shared repertoire of standard decorative motifs, including arm

225. *Anonymous Boston Child*, by Edward Custer, Swiss, 1872. Oil. Private collection. Photograph by Richard Cheek.

supports shaped in the form of ionic-capped urns ornamented with carved acanthus leaves; supporting plinths carved with stylized rosettes; heavy baluster-shaped legs accented with gadrooning or ribbing; and a subtly bowed back rail often decorated with carved waterleaves or volutes. Even the character of the carving on the sofas is consistent from piece to piece, projecting a sense of depth, crisp cutting, and a somewhat conservative respect for confining ornament within the borders of the basic structural elements. This congruity in carving technique suggests that the frames were made by craftsmen who were both well-versed in the archeologically-based Empire style and attuned to the preferences of a local clientele.

Based on the collective, though admittedly circumstantial, evidence outlined above, the curators in 1977 decided that the sofa warranted refurbishing so that it could be displayed as an instructive example of Boston taste during the second quarter of the nineteenth century. They retrieved the sofa from storage and planned to have it upholstered in sleek black horsehair, which, at that time, research indicated the most appropriate historic fabric for Empire furniture.

Fortunately, just before the sofa was to be recovered, the curators noticed a plate in an English publication showing a very similar sofa. Not only was the plate of English origin, having been found in Rudolph Ackermann's popular London monthly, *The Repository of Arts, Literature, Commerce, Manufacture, Fashions, and Politics* — a source that had not been much consulted in decorative arts studies prior to that time — but it was dated 1821, some nineteen years before Hall's publication. The plate depicted a "dress sofa" that was so much closer to the design of the Museum's sofa in every detail than the one illustrated in Hall's that it seemed likely the craftsman who made the sofa might well have been directly following the Ackermann prototype (fig. 226).[3]

The appearance of such an unusually applicable document of taste contemporary with the date of the sofa's construction could not be ignored. In the interest of historical accuracy and with the hope that new information about the little-studied craft of upholstery in the early nineteenth century might be gathered in the process, the decision was made in 1979 to reupholster the sofa with green satin, in the Ackermann mode.

The curators also had to revise their theories of the sofa's design origins. Ackermann's *Repository* credits the design for the dress sofa to a "Mr. J. Taylor, who has obtained considerable experience in furniture in the house of Oakley of Bond Street [the upholstery firm of Oakley and Evans]."[4] Although it is difficult to measure the popularity of this design among Ackermann's English readers, that sofas of this pattern were in fact produced by Mr. J. Taylor, or Oakley and Evans, or other English cabinetmakers is suggested by the appearance of an English example in a 1927 advertisement of a British antiques dealer.[5] Thus the sofa could no longer be regarded as an indigenous American form.

In retrospect, it is clear that the curators should have been more cautious about claiming the form as exclusively American, and as indigenous to the Boston area, even though most scholars at the time took this attribution for granted. The appearance of the sofa in Hall's book simply verifies that American craftsmen were familiar with a similar design at the time of the book's publication. In fact, we know that Hall borrowed freely from preexisting furniture design sources, such as Thomas Sheraton's pattern books, published earlier in the century in England. Hall, himself, acknowledged

his adaptation of designs already in currency in his preface: "Novelty, simplicity and practicability are blended with the present designs, in which originality mostly prevails."[6] Further, the appearance of so many closely related sofas in the Boston area does not necessarily mean that only Boston craftsmen made such forms. Such patterns may suggest only that a particular Boston shop or network of related shops made sofas in this style. The cluster of Boston sofas does not preclude the possibility that other craftsmen elsewhere could also have produced similar types of seats.

From the outset, the Museum's effort to restore the sofa to resemble the 1821 Ackermann plate was aided by a number of factors. Ackermann's *Repository* itself proved helpful in some respects (though not in others, as we will see). The text accompanying plate 9 in Ackermann's *Repository* provides important information regarding its decorative finish. The text describes the sofa as "an elegant essential to the drawing room," the framework of which could be left unadorned in rosewood or embellished with burnished gilt and matte gold. Appropriate upholstery could further enrich the sofa. Satin damask, adorned with woven gold lace and tassels, was recommended as fabric suitable for "decorations of the higher class." For a drawing room of less splendor, a fabric of a simpler, more subtle material such as patterned velvet was advised. For decorators aspiring to the grander upholstery scheme, Ackermann suggested purchasing English-woven silk damask, as "the loom of our country is now in that state of advanced perfection, the damasks of the most magnificent kind, in point of intensity of colour and richness of pattern, are manufactured at prices that permit their free use in well-furnished apartments."[7] In a way, the plate itself was a less effective guide: It is difficult to tell, for instance, whether the upholstery fabric is a plain damask or has a figured pattern. What is clear is that the artist who illustrated the sofa depicted it with an attractive, apple-green covering, accented with golden yellow tassels and decorative banding.

Two other factors were of immeasurable help to the Museum in restoring the sofa: the existence of a second sofa in the pattern and the talents of a master upholsterer.

In 1979, the Museum acquired for the collection another Boston sofa of the same design and approximate date as that depicted in Ackermann's *Repository*. When divested of its late Victorian covering and separated into component parts, this analogous example served as a useful guide to the period upholstery treat-

J Taylor Del 16 Bedford Court Cov.t Gard.n

Duvall Sc

226. Plate 9 in Rudolph Ackermann's *The Repository of Arts, Literature, Commerce, Manufacture, Fashions, and Politics* 2, no. 61 (January 1821). "Dress sofa," designed by J. Taylor. Photograph by Daniel Farber.

ment, because construction features and original tacking holes were evident through the muslin undercovering, details that were obscured or not detectable on the museum's first example. Happily, the museum also was able to secure the services of Andrew Passeri of Revere, Massachusetts, an accomplished modern practitioner of the art of upholstery. Passeri's experience proved essential because the Ackermann plate posed many problems for the twentieth-century upholsterer endeavoring to imitate its impressive but inconveniently undetailed appearance. The sofa's handsome appearance today is largely due to Passeri's skillful solutions (and occasional, unavoidable compromises) in response to the puzzling questions about materials and working methods that the dress sofa presented.

A careful record of the steps followed by Passeri as he attempted to reconstruct the procedures employed by his early nineteenth-century counterparts was kept and is recounted here for historical interest as well as for

practical guidance for those intending to reupholster a similar sofa.

To prepare the sofa for reupholstery, the sofa frame is initially separated into its main structural parts, consisting of a seat, a back panel, and two arm supports. These are the units that receive special attention from the upholsterer as he methodically shapes, stretches, and stitches the various layers of stuffing and covering required to fashion a comfortable seat that also retains an attractive silhouette of lines. After stripping these parts of modern fabrics and worn stuffing, cleaning them of old tacks, and repairing any damage to the wooden tacking surfaces, the upholsterer is ready to proceed with his work.

By tradition, the sofa seat is the first component selected for attention. To produce the foundation required to support the weight of an average adult, the upholsterer begins by bracing the seat frame with wide, durable strips of linen webbing, pulled and tacked across the frame in an interlaced pattern. He then sheathes this with coarse linen sackcloth tacked to the soft wooden frame. This strong undercovering will serve as the major support for the twelve or so pounds of horsehair stuffing required to form the 2½-inch cake or stitched seat foundation.

Once the sackcloth has been tacked over the webbing, the upholsterer pierces the cloth with twine stitches—inserted approximately two inches from the frame's edge—pulling each stitch across the surface of the linen at approximately 4-inch intervals before reinserting the needle. (Such stitches can be seen in figure 241.) The upholsterer then pushes the horsehair stuffing into the loops until he has the whole foundation evenly covered. The loops hold the horsehair and prevent it from shifting about once it is covered.

After completing this important preliminary procedure, the craftsman distributes stuffing (Passeri used washed horsehair, the usual stuffing for the best furniture in the second quarter of the nineteenth century) across the linen foundation, tucking some under the twine and carefully molding it to the proper height. He then covers it with another protective layer of linen. To prevent the stuffing from slipping out of shape, the upholsterer next relies on one of the major skills of his craft, the art of quilting (or stitching) the layers of linen-covered stuffing with twine so that the hair is locked in place without disfiguring the desired surface profile of the upholstered seat. (It is important to note that the finished appearance of an upholstered chair or sofa disguises the intricate, mathematical stitching patterns that the craftsman has woven through the interior layers of stuffing. Much of the time and skill involved in upholstering furniture is consumed in the formation of such strong interior bracing, a painstaking aspect of the craft that is so often overlooked in the presence of the sleek, shimmering surface textiles that camouflage the object's internal structure.) Employing a double-ended needle, the upholsterer secures the stuffing between the linen by piercing the cake with twine at 2½-inch or 3-inch intervals in a grid-like pattern. These long stitches compress the hair into place and prevent the sagging that might otherwise occur when pressure is exerted on the seat.

Another procedure undertaken at this stage is the shaping of the front seat edge, the critical visual line in the sofa's overall design and one that is subjected to considerable stress in daily use. Initially, the craftsman baste-tacks the linen cover to the sofa frame to keep it taut during the quilting process. Once the hair or other

stuffing is secured with stitches, however, the upholsterer is free to remove some of these tacks so that the seat edge can be formed. With nimble fingers, he pushes or pockets hair into a linen crease that he has created to form an edge of predetermined height and contour. (*See* figure 240.)

For the Museum's Boston Empire sofa, a subtly defined, softly curved edge was created, instead of a more assertive and squared "French" edge. Employing a bowed needle, the upholsterer then "sets" the edge by locking the hair into place with double rows of stitches. It is difficult to standardize the individualized system of stitching pattern employed by craftsmen in this process. Most upholsterers calculate their own mathematical formulas for inserting and knotting stitches according to uniform measurement based on the distance from the seat edge itself. For the Museum's sofa, Passeri formed the first row of stitches by inserting his needle approximately one-fourth of an inch underneath the calculated edge and drawing it out approximately one-half of an inch in front of the first row of quilting stitches previously set into the cake. He then locked the twine with a double loop stitch, and reinserted the needle into the linen, approximately an inch in front of the edge line. This stitching pattern, repeated across the seat edge at 1¼-inch intervals in a bottom-to-top direction, effectively nudges the hair into the calculated shape. A second row of stitches is usually introduced across the edge in identical fashion, the twine being inserted slightly higher than the original row and at even intervals between the original needle entry points of the first row. This supplementary row of twine stitches imparts additional strength to the edge, preserving its shape under the constant pressure of sitters who lower and raise themselves to and from the sofa seat.

After the edge has been shaped and stitched and the first layer of hair firmly secured between linen, a second layer of stuffing is required to give softness to the seat. The upholsterer again creates a grid of twine across the linen to hold the second layer of hair in place. When this additional, thinner layer of stuffing has been pushed under the twine loops, a thin cotton batting is applied to the top of the hair, followed by a protective muslin covering that is tacked to the seat of the frame.

The seat is then ready to receive its exterior textile covering, which, in the case of the Museum's sofa, was an unfigured green satin obtained through the fabric and decorating house of Brunschwig & Fils. A total of eleven yards of satin (stock no. 34520.00, color 6040) were ordered for the sofa; the material closely matched the upholstery color featured in Ackermann's *Repository*.

After gently but snugly arranging the satin over the padded seat, the upholsterer secures the material to the wooden frame with very slender tacks. Once tacked, the entire seat is finished, with the important exception of the ornamental trim. For the Museum's sofa, an appropriate decorative woven border of gold and green was obtained—also from Brunschwig & Fils (stock no. 90066/9). An order of 2½ yards was sufficient for the sofa. Although the pattern of the detail does not precisely match that indicated in the Ackermann banding, the gold color is the same and proves a sympathetic complement for the green silk. The stylized neoclassical motifs woven in the trim's pattern recall the decorative carving found elsewhere on the sofa's frame. This trim was attached to the satin with a delicate running stitch applied with thin thread and a small, delicately curved needle.

After the sofa's seat has been upholstered, the craftsman directs his attention to the back panel. Because the sofa's back does not receive as much stress as the seat, the padding and stitching procedures involved are less complicated. Like the seat, the back panel is webbed and covered with sackcloth tacked into the soft wood of the frame. Once again, twine is stitched into the sackcloth to form loops (inserted approximately twelve inches apart, a more dispersed pattern than on the seat) that serve to secure the hair stuffing. The back panel does not require the additional quilt-stitching to stabilize the hair.

Once the hair has been laid carefully across the linen, a thin sheet of cotton batting is superimposed, followed by a protective covering of muslin. The panel now is properly prepared to receive the outer upholstery fabric, which is stretched across the back and neatly tacked to the frame. The process of tacking demands great patience on the upholsterer's part, as well as sensitivity to the nature of the fabric selected for use. Tacks must be hammered into the frame steadily and in a manner assuring that the shafts pierce the wood at a right angle. In the case of silk or satin, the craftsman must use as small a tack as possible to avoid creating unsightly wrinkles or draws (called "cat's paws" in the trade), often formed when a large tack shaft penetrates delicate fabric, or the creases that occur when the tack enters at an improper angle. The upholsterer also should be aware of the fabric's tension as he stretches it across the frame. Pulling silk too tightly invariably produces ridges that interrupt the smooth contour of the upholstered surface. (This situation can occasionally be

remedied by making a small incision with a tiny knife in the silk underneath the tack head, thereby relieving some of the strain on the fabric.)

A concluding, decorative step in upholstering the sofa's back panel is the gluing of the braid to the upper edge of the upholstered frame. (The braid selected for the museum's sofa was also ordered through Brunschwig & Fils: eleven yards of stock no. 90109, color 05/1069, dyed to match the green satin.) Customarily, craftsmen initially affix braid to the frame with small (no. 3 or no. 4) tacks, inserted into the border at six-inch intervals. Then the upholsterer gingerly glues the braid along the curved wooden silhouette, systematically removing the tacks as each six-inch section is attached securely to the frame.

One of the most challenging tasks confronting the craftsman reupholstering a sofa of this particular form involves the padding and covering of the arms so as to preserve and emphasize the pronounced, pleasing curves of the urn-shaped supports and their overhanging capitals. Each arm-support unit is composed of eleven pieces of solid wood: the front or exterior mahogany vertical piece, a similarly-shaped piece of birch behind it, another identically-shaped piece of birch at the rear of the arm, and eight shaped pieces of yellow poplar running front to back. To provide cushioned padding across the upper curve of the arm unit, the upholsterer first tacks about six twine loops, running side to side, across the top of the arm supports. These loops are tacked into the wood without an intervening piece of burlap. Once they are fastened, the upholsterer pushes horsehair under and around these loops as he did with the seat. The loops serve to anchor the shallow cake of hair (about one-half of an inch to three-quarters of an inch in depth) to the unit.

The hair is subsequently arranged to provide adequate comfort for a sitter's arm. It is next covered with sackcloth that is then tacked to the wooden frame underneath the overhanging capital. To maintain the crisp arc of the design, the craftsman must be careful to pull the cover over the projecting edges of the upper arm surface, securing the cover underneath these edges so that the tack heads will not rip the satin cover fabric at this dramatic, sweeping point in the curve. To form the crescent-shaped profile that is visible across the front silhouette of the padded arm, the upholsterer uses two rows of twine stitches to draw the linen (left untacked along this facade) into an edge similar to that on the front seat edge but smaller. To further protect the armrest from daily wear and tear, the upholsterer may choose to overlay a supplementary stratum of padding or stuffing across the unit. He then covers the unit with consecutive layers of thin cotton batting, muslin, and finally green satin, tacked underneath the overhanging capital.

The two undulating side panels of the arm supports demand a different method of upholstery (figs. 227–228). Because padding is not essential to these surfaces, the upholsterer covers the curved wooden panels with a single layer of linen overlaid with a thin cushion of cotton batting and protective muslin to prevent the satin outer-covering from catching splinters. To maintain a neat appearance, the upholsterer attaches these coverings to the wooden panels with a method known as "blind tacking." This technique involves precutting the three layers of material—linen, muslin, and satin—to conform to the shape of the wood panel and then arranging them in an overlapping stack, in order of their application to the panel. The top border of the fabrics is placed, finish fabric on the inside, along the edge of the arm panel just underneath the overhanging arm support edge. The craftsman lays a folded starched strip of muslin across this border and then tacks the fabrics into the frame through the muslin stiffener. The fabrics are then flipped down over the cardboard strip a layer at a time, with the linen first, followed by the thin batting and muslin, and the satin last. A tidy, clean border edge is created at the intersection of the side with the central panel, concealing any unsightly tacks. (It is important to note that the upholsterer uses saw horses to prop up each unit of the sofa as he works, thus enabling him to move freely around and under each piece before it is rebolted to the frame.)

Having attached the fabrics to the side panels at the upper end only, the upholsterer must now secure the remaining loose ends to the unit, taking care to insure that these materials will snugly drape the curves of each panel. At this critical point, the craftsman gently pulls the fabrics to conform to the fixed urn shape of the wooden arm support. Although this may sound simple, it is a complex job requiring considerable skill, for if too little or too much tension is exerted in pulling the fabric or if it is pulled in the wrong direction, the resulting upholstered silhouette will not complement the sinuous shape of the urn support. Before tacking the materials to the end of the panel, the upholsterer must pull them in a horizontal direction, stretching the fabrics across the wooden shape rather than down. (If he pulled the fabrics down over the curved indentation of the urn support, he could create an air pocket.) Once the desired

227. Detail of arm support from the second Empire sofa owned by the Museum of Fine Arts, Boston (1979.48). This shows the original muslin covering. Photograph by Jock Gill.

tension and shape have been obtained, the fabrics are attached to the wooden support, the tacking line ultimately being disguised along the front edge by braid, along the lower edge by the upholstered seat, and along the back edge by the back panel that will nestle against the rear of the sofa's arm.

When these covered side panels have been secured, the upholsterer starts to work on the front of the armrests (fig. 228). He applies the satin front panels to the unfinished, linen-covered frontispieces of the curved armrests. These satin panels, cut to conform to the curve of the design, are then carefully hand-stitched in place. To allow for the decorative fabric rosettes balancing each overhanging end of the armrests, the upholsterer must incorporate extra fabric into the panel pattern, which will permit him to bunch the satin into folds resembling flower petals. A gold silk tassel (obtained by the Museum from Scalamandre Silks) is inserted into the center of each fabric rosette and secured to the wooden frame with a tack (to prevent its easy loss from any tugs on the part of an overly-curious passerby). The satin rosette is then pinched in and stitched at the neck and carefully pulled into peaks to achieve an attractive, full-blossom effect. As a finishing effect, decorative braid is glued along the borders of the arm support to accentuate the urn-shaped contours of the arms.

228. Detail of newly upholstered arm support from the sofa shown in figure 223. Photograph by Jock Gill.

Having upholstered the sofa's arm supports, the craftsman now adds the satin lining to the rear side of the back panel. Because this area is purely decorative rather than functional, he simply tacks a cover of muslin across the panel and covers it with the green satin outer-covering. Some upholsterers may decide to separate these materials with a thin layer of wadding or cotton batting to produce a softer, fuller appearance at the back. Once he has tacked the satin to the frame and has glued the ornamental braid along the appropriate borders, the craftsman reassembles the upholstered parts to form the whole seating unit.

One final task to be performed after the reassembly is the fashioning of decorative pillows for the sofa seat. These plump pillows with rosette corners proved difficult to reproduce in the manner suggested by the Ackermann plate. The artist employed by the nineteenth-century periodical indicated that each pillow corner should be drawn into a tight, stylized rosette, but he failed to provide enough details in the sketch to demonstrate how these rosettes were tied or attached to the pillows. Repeated modern attempts to create separate satin rosettes that could be sewn onto the pillows, while still retaining the puffy, knotted effect, produced consistently disappointing results. Passeri persisted, however, eventually devising an acceptable and accurate pillow. His solution was based on his conclusion that

the rosettes in the Ackermann's plate were accounted for originally in the cutting pattern for the pillow, rather than fashioned separately and attached with thread. The pattern that he developed (fig. 229) consisted of two identical oblong pieces and two ovoid side panel pieces. The oblong pieces, designed to conform to the curving shape of the pillow when seamed, had extra fabric at each of the four corners to permit the easy bunching of material for the rosette.[8] Before the pieces were sewn together inside-out and reversed to form an envelope or casing for the pillow stuffing, Passeri fastened a 5- or 6-inch length of sturdy thread to each of the four corners of the main pattern piece. Later, after the pieces had been sewn together and the pillow stuffed, these threads would be pulled from the inside, thus fashioning an indentation in the swollen, stuffed corners to form the center of the decorative rosette.

229. Patterns for sofa pillows. Courtesy of Andrew Passeri. Photograph by Museum of Fine Arts, Boston.

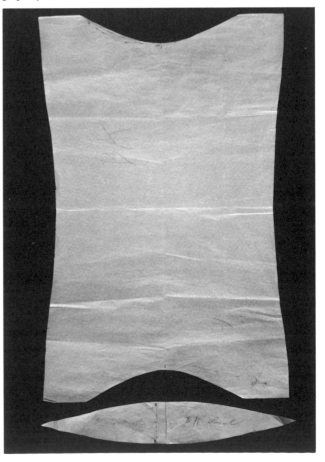

Once cut, the pattern pieces are stitched together: First the upholsterer attaches the side panels to the back piece. He next stitches the front and back panels along the upper edge, and then hand-stitches the pillows along the two front edges of the sides. An opening is left along the bottom seam just large enough to permit the craftsman to stuff the pillow and to pull the attached corner threads. Hair or down was probably used to stuff the pillows in Ackermann's day; however, today Dacron (a modern synthetic), was substituted for the Museum's sofa, as it costs less than down and maintains a pleasing, "full" effect as long as the pillows are not subjected to great pressure from use, as they would not be in a museum setting.

After the pillows are stuffed and the rosette corners "dimpled" with the help of the interior draw strings, the upholsterer finishes these corners by creating a flower-like effect. He loops a durable thread (a no. 24 green thread was employed here) around the satin approximately 3½ inches from the corner edge, thereby defining the corner with a bunched, blossom-like effect. The pillows are then sealed, puffed, and distributed across the sofa seat.

In all probability, Rudolph Ackermann himself would have been impressed with the end product of Andrew Passeri's meticulous workmanship. Although modern reproduction fabrics, materials, and tools were used, the sofa's resulting appearance seems sympathetic to, and congruous with, the smart, stately upholstery effects reflected in the original document plate from Ackermann's *Repository*.

A final postscript should be added to this exploration of the steps involved in "correctly" reupholstering a dress sofa in the Empire taste. While the sofa may have been stuffed, stitched, lined, and tacked in a manner presumed authentic to the period, the possibility exists that the handsome satin upholstery fabric chosen for the sofa was an inappropriate curatorial selection, if the museum's example is to be viewed as an "American" interpretation of this Empire furniture form. Ackermann's *Repository*, it must be remembered, was a journal of English high fashion. Although its Boston readers may have admired the elegant silk damask dress sofa described and illustrated in the 1821 periodical, no firm evidence has yet been compiled to substantiate the theory that they expected their own translations of this form to be upholstered in the same manner and material. To date, none of the known Boston sofas of this type have survived with original satin or silk upholstery. Nor have any fragments of these elegant materials been retrieved from under the heads of tacks found in their wooden frames.

What has been found are fragments of what seems to be a patterned velvet material. Many of these scraps have been found, usually of red or green coloring. It therefore seems conclusive that some Boston owners of these objects had them upholstered in patterned velvet, a treatment that the writer for Ackermann's journal had recommended as an alternate material appropriate for the upholstery of a dress sofa. This also seems to be the covering of the sofa depicted in Edward Custer's painting. (*See* figure 225.) Perhaps in the future, the Museum of Fine Arts will reupholster its second Boston sofa of this particular Empire design in red or green figured velvet, offering curators, museum visitors, and professional upholsterers the opportunity to compare the high-style satin English covering with the less costly velvet dressing apparently favored by nineteenth-century Bostonians.

NOTES

1. John Hall, *The Cabinetmakers' Assistant* (Baltimore, 1840; reprint, New York: National Superior, 1944), p. 25, pl. 25, fig. 138.

2. The painting is signed: "E. L. Custer, 1872." For a brief review of Custer's career, *see* his obituary in *American Art Review*, vol. 2 (1881): 169. A similar sofa, with tufted upholstery, can be seen in a circa 1870 photograph of the music room of Rockwood, a house in Roxbury, Massachusetts. The photograph was featured in the 1984 exhibition of the Society for the Preservation of New England Antiquities, "A Photographic Intimacy: The Portraiture of Rooms."

3. Rudolph Ackermann, *The Repository of Arts, Literature, Commerce, Manufacture, Fashions, and Politics*, vol. 2, no. 61 (1821): pl. 9, facing p. 128, with full description.

4. The firm Oakley and Evans listed themselves as "Upholders, No. 8 Old Bond Street" in the 1817 London Directory. *See also* Sir Ambrose Heal, *The London Furniture Makers: From the Restoration to the Victorian Era, 1660–1890.* (London: B. T. Batsford, 1953), p. 126.

5. *Antiques* 11, no. 2 (February 1927): 83. The collection advertised is that of the dealer, Frederick Treasure of Preston, Lancashire. I am indebted to Michael K. Brown for calling this to my attention.

6. Hall, *Cabinetmakers' Assistant*.

7. Ackermann, *The Repository*, p. 28.

8. Andrew Passeri developed two slightly different patterns for the sofa pillows, in order to take into account the different lengths of the rear and side or arm pillows. (*See* figure 229.) The suggested dimensions for the arm pillow are: Length-29½ inches, width at center of pattern-18 inches, width at corner edges of pillow-24½ inches. The back or rear pillows vary from this pattern only in their overall height measurements, which were reduced by 1½ inches at the center and at the corner edges.

The A. H. Davenport Company of Boston: Notes on the Upholsterer's Trade in the Late 19th and Early 20th Centuries

Anne Farnam

PHOTOGRAPHS and paintings of interiors dating from the last decades of the nineteenth and the first two decades of the twentieth centuries suggest that the skills of the upholsterer had never been in greater demand than they were during that period. Fabric was used on virtually all surfaces, whether horizontal or vertical, within a dwelling. And not just plain fabric but fabric that had been elaborately shaped and/or trimmed.

Such well-upholstered interiors existed at virtually every economic level and in every section of the country;[1] yet, today we know little about how these interiors — and particularly, the furniture and draperies — were created. The usual sources of such knowledge — documents in the form of family and company papers, account books and receipts, and upholstered items surviving in their original condition — are hard to locate and to correlate. It is difficult, therefore, to describe and to analyze with any certainty either the upholsterer's craft practices and artistry or his economic and social role during this period of industrial expansion in America.

In spite of the numerous images of the period that confirm the overwhelming importance of the upholsterer's work, prejudice against both machine-made products and turn-of-the-century taste seems to have prevented serious scholarly consideration of this aspect of the decorative arts of that time. Now, when interest in this area is growing, those who could answer the questions about the upholstery of that period are gone. Even fifteen years ago, we could have walked into a factory that had existed during the nineteenth century and spoken to a craftsman who had been trained in the methods of that day, or whose father had been.

The A. H. Davenport Company of Boston was one of those companies from which we could have learned much. It began as the firm of Ezra Brabrook around 1841 and continued in business until the early 1970s, by which time it had become the Irving and Casson — A. H. Davenport Company. During the period from 1880 to 1906 when it was owned and operated by Albert H. Davenport as the A. H. Davenport Company, the firm was one of the most prominent of its era. The Davenport firm had showrooms in Boston and New York, in addition to a large manufacturing and importing business in East Cambridge, Massachusetts.

Although the history of furniture production at the A. H. Davenport Company has been studied in detail,[2] little consideration has been given to its upholstery work. A short review of what is known of the history of the Brabrook/Davenport company, and particularly of its upholstery business, can provide information about work practices and at the same time suggest questions that require further research.

Ezra Brabrook was the founder of the company. He is first listed in Boston city directories beginning in 1841, probably when he began in business with his father.[3] The earliest listings are for "furniture and feathers," later shortened to "furniture" or "furniture dealer." Another contemporary source, reports filed on local businesses in Boston by R. G. Dun and Company, the national credit rating company and predecessor to Dun and Bradstreet, consistently refers to Brabrook's firm as "upholsterers" at least from 1850 to 1877.[4] Did "upholsterers" mean something different from "furniture dealer" to the investor or creditor of this period? We don't know, but in any event, in 1877, after Brabrook had expanded his business and moved to a new location, Dun started to refer to the business as "furniture."

Dun's references are cryptic but suggest something of Brabrook's business affairs: ". . . is engaged in a money making business, lets furniture at large profits" (1850); "Class fair, only in quality" (1854); "Good. Never did so well as now" (1863); "Doing a handsome business and pays promptly" (1868). When post-war prosperity allowed Brabrook to enlarge his business in 1875, the Dun report noted "Has taken a store in New Washington St. and increased his expenses largely; but has money enough and is good as ever." By 1877, as noted above, Brabrook's business was referred to as "furniture" by Dun. The report stated that Brabrook was "doing a large business but not making enough to pay expenses but is not losing enough to affect him."[5] Reports of 1878 and 1879 suggest that although business was flourishing, overhead was high: ". . . his store is large and expensive and has to carry a large stock . . . Is well stocked with first class goods. Has a good trade with high toned responsible parties, gets good pieces. Is regarded by the trade as honorable and enterprising."[6]

Ezra Brabrook died in 1880. Albert Davenport, who had worked for Brabrook since 1866, took over the firm, which was then located at 96 Washington Street in Boston.

In 1879, the year before the firm was bought by Albert Davenport, one of the few advertisements that has been located for either Brabrook or Davenport appeared in the annual report of the Boston Society of Decorative Art. It described the "first class goods" offered by Brabrook.

IMPORTED FABRICS for House Decoration, including WALL PAPERS, etc., of the best colors and quality. All colors of SILK AND WOOL, WOOL AND COTTON FABRICS from MORRIS, and from the English and French Manufactories. "MADRAS" MUSLINS OF A VARIETY OF PATTERNS. FRINGES AND LACES for trimmings made to order of any design or color. Designs for Furniture and Woodwork are made by M. CHARMOIS.[7]

A newspaper account of the Brabrook establishment when it was purchased by Davenport in 1880 offers further insight into the company's business:

> . . French and Tuscan silks, intended for use as curtains and decorations for walls, arches and recesses, are sold for $18 to $40 a yard . . . The sum of $300 is often expended on a single window. . . . Oddly shaped pieces of furniture with rich carvings and velvet trimmings are frequently ordered regardless of expense, and even small articles of this class are sometimes manufactured at an expense of from $150 to $300.[8]

The U.S. Census stated that in 1878 the Brabrook firm employed some one hundred people including salesmen, designers, carvers, cabinetmakers, upholsterers, finishers, teamsters, and sewing girls. The five "principal departments" in the store were drapery and curtains, shades, furniture, carpets, and paper hangings. Both the salesrooms, arranged on four floors according to type and price of goods, and the workshops were all under one roof on Washington Street.[9] Clearly, Brabrook's was a large and diversified business, requiring many different skills and services in order to compete successfully in the marketplace.

From what little is known of Davenport's work in this period and of Brabrook's earlier work in the 1870s as well, the firm excelled in high quality goods and special commission work. In general, special commission work grew in importance during the 1880s and 1890s. Indeed, when Davenport's Boston factory building burned in 1883, R. G. Dun's report of the incident testified to the special nature of Davenport's work: ". . . opinion seems to be general that he had more property there to lose, the loss must cause considerable delay in filling orders as considerable of the stock consumed was hand work from special designs which are also destroyed."[10]

Almost immediately after the fire, Davenport purchased a factory in East Cambridge in an already established furniture manufacturing area.[11] This move separated the workmen from the showroom and the consumer, raising an interesting question: Where now would the staff designer's allegiance lie—to the factory craftsmen who interpreted his drawings or to the consumer who demanded a product with little understanding of the process? This is an area that requires further research.

From the late 1880s on, the company maintained a New York City office. This helped the firm reach an even wider array of wealthy clients as well as the biggest architectural firms in the country. Although Davenport employed its own designers, the firm also executed commission work for architects such as H. H. Richardson; McKim, Mead and White; and Peabody and Stearns, who were more and more assuming responsibility for the interior design of their buildings. By the turn of the century, Davenport's clientele was national, and the scale of its business had increased tremendously.

Albert Davenport died in 1906. In 1914, the Davenport Company merged with the firm of Irving and Casson, a Boston establishment that specialized in interior finishwork. The new firm—Irving and Casson—A. H. Davenport Company—continued in business until the early 1970s.[12]

We are fortunate to have two extraordinary sources of information about the Davenport Company's upholstery designs and techniques. One is its massive pictorial archive, and the other is the book *Practical Decorative Upholstery* written by Frank Moreland, a former employee, in which he revealed and illustrated his (and presumably his employer's) trade secrets.[13]

First, the pictorial archive:[14] Francis H. Bacon, the company's chief designer from 1884 to 1908, and an archeologist as well as a trained architect, began the archive. He assembled design ideas from the many sources available to him: art and architectural magazines published in America, Britain, and Europe, and photographs of antique furniture and buildings from every country and epoch. These photographs and drawings were pasted into scrapbooks. The result is an incomparable source for the study of design methodology and upholstery treatments in the late academic revival styles popular at that time (figs. 230 and 231).

In addition to this archive of design ideas, the company began in 1905 to keep dated photographs of its own work; this practice continued until 1930 (figs. 232–236). These too were pasted in large albums—with the designs arranged according to form and style, recording the vast range of "antique" styles promoted by the company: Jacobean, Italian, Elizabethan, Gothic, French (from Louis XII through Louis XVI), Georgian, Queen Anne, Regency, and Empire. The thousands of photographs provide important documentation of the

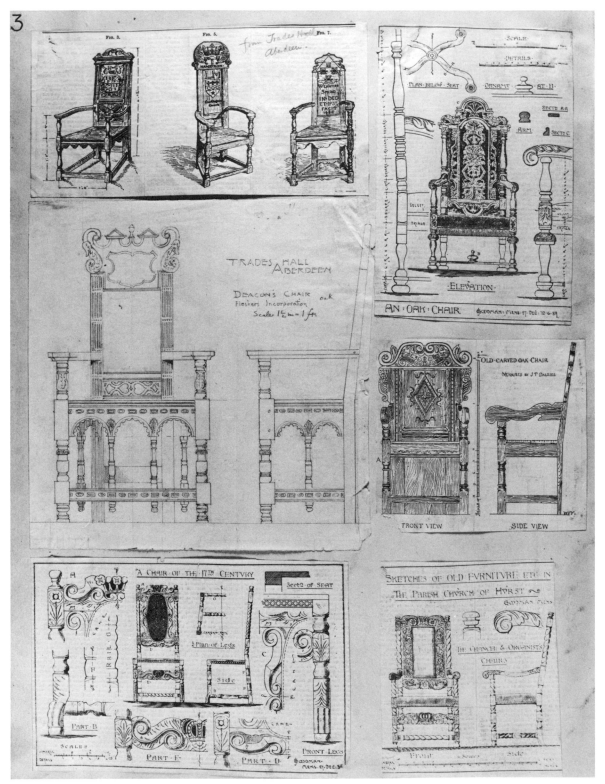

230. Page from A. H. Davenport Co. Scrapbook No. 4, "Chairs, Sofas." Probably compiled by Francis H. Bacon, 1885–1900. Drawings of antique furniture published by American and English architectural journals apparently served as primary source material. For example, the pencil drawing of the "Deacon's chair" (possibly by Bacon) is almost indistinguishable from the surrounding magazine clippings of English chairs. Courtesy, Margaret Woodbury Strong Museum. Photograph by R. Jackson Smith.

231. Page from Scrapbook No. 4. Beginning in the 1880s, photographs
of original artifacts in castles, palaces, and museums in England,
France, Switzerland, Germany, Italy, and Spain were easily available as
models for American manufacturers. Courtesy, Margaret Woodbury
Strong Museum. Photograph by R. Jackson Smith.

CARRÈRE & HASTINGS
ARCHITECTS

New Theatre Stage Curtains
also Box Curtains and Wall Covers
EXECUTED BY
A. H. DAVENPORT CO.
150 MADISON AVE.
NEW YORK

BOSTON HOUSE
96-98 WASHINGTON ST.

232. Page from Scrapbook No. 1, "Interiors." Advertisement for A. H. Davenport Co., 1909, "New Theatre Stage Curtains also Box Curtains and Wall Covers." The ability to undertake such a monumental commission (from the leading architectural firm of Carrère & Hastings) is indicative of the scale of the company's production. Courtesy, Margaret Woodbury Strong Museum. Photograph by R. Jackson Smith.

233. Page from Scrapbook No. 8, "Louis XVI chairs." Armchair in the Louis XVI style, 1916, made by Irving and Casson—A. H. Davenport Co. for F. W. Woolworth. Courtesy, Margaret Woodbury Strong Museum. Photograph by R. Jackson Smith.

company's tremendous increase in business during the early-twentieth century and illustrate vividly that the late-nineteenth and early-twentieth centuries were an era in which the upholsterer's art was much in demand.

From Frank Moreland's book, we can learn a great deal about the technical aspects of upholstery, particularly about cutting and hanging draperies. Martha Gandy Fales's essay in this volume surveys this aspect of Moreland's book and also provides a biographical sketch of Moreland. I will suggest here a few areas of interest from the point of view of the Brabrook—Davenport Company and raise questions requiring further thought and research.

Moreland joined the Brabrook Company around 1878. When he went to work there as a foreman, there were about one hundred employees, and the company was large and diversified. Moreland left the Brabrook—Davenport Company after only a year. The reasons for his leaving may never be known, although the timing suggests that it may have been because of changes made after Brabrook's death. Moreland published his book some ten years later, when he was an employee of a dry goods store that had a large upholstery and interior decoration department: Shepard, Norwell and Company.

Implicit in Moreland's "general remarks" introducing his *Practical Decorative Upholstery* are the social and economic changes occurring in the industry during this period. "Through the rapidly increasing demand for upholstery decorations, a large number of persons, as merchants, salesmen, or workmen, are brought into a business entirely new to them . . . ." There is an urgent quality in his recognition of the need for educating the workers: ". . . in this age of sharp competition it is desirable to know how to produce the best results with the least expense."[15]

Just whom he was writing for is unclear, and the possible answers to this question also reflect the societal changes that were under way at that time. He explicitly states that his book relates "entirely to practical work" and "is written for the uninitiated," but did that include the housewife with her new sewing machine and decorating ambitions or the newly affluent consumer? Or did he intend to reach a new class of semi-skilled and untrained "merchants, salesmen or workmen" now in the workforce, with whom trained professionals like himself were increasingly frustrated? Was Moreland attempting to fight an elitist system and provide professional training to future craftsmen so they could offer all aspects of upholsterer's work, while still maintaining

234. Page from Scrapbook No. 12 B, "Miscellaneous upholstered armchairs." Great stuffed chair, 1917, made by Irving and Casson— A. H. Davenport Co. for F. W. Woolworth. Courtesy, Margaret Woodbury Strong Museum. Photograph by R. Jackson Smith.

235. Page from Scrapbook No. 13, "Over stuffed furniture." Upholstered armchair with Chinese Chippendale motif, 1929, made by Irving and Casson—A. H. Davenport Co. for Henry Sleeper, a Boston interior decorator. Courtesy, Margaret Woodbury Strong Museum. Photograph by R. Jackson Smith.

236. Page from Scrapbook No. 15 A, "Miscellaneous sofas." Chair-bed, probably late 1920s, made by Irving and Casson—A. H. Davenport Co. Tufted and covered in chintz. Courtesy, Margaret Woodbury Strong Museum. Photograph by R. Jackson Smith.

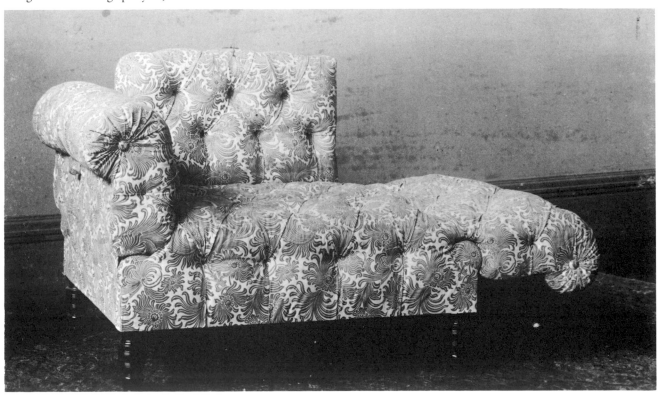

a degree of excellence in their trade? As Moreland stated,

> Apprentices have been taught, or rather allowed to learn, the other branches of the trade, but the drapery room has been a sacred precinct, a kind of blue chamber, from which the average apprentice has been excluded; and the drapery-man has usually been very unwilling to communicate what it has perhaps cost him years of experience to learn; hence the limited knowledge of the average upholsterer of what is known to the craft as "outside work."[16]

Moreland's fascinating book suggests that the upholsterer was a factory worker who was also a craftsman. He was both a technician and an artist interpreting design renderings with cloth, stuffing, and trim. To further understand his method, we must continue to collect, document, and preserve the products of his labor. We must also continue to search out company records like those of the A. H. Davenport Company, as well as public documents pertaining to labor, and manufacturing statistics regarding production, if we are to interpret the role of both upholsterers in the furniture industry at the turn of the century.

NOTES

1. *See particularly* William Seale, *The Tasteful Interlude, American Interiors Through the Camera's Eye, 1860–1917* (New York: Praeger, 1975); and Clay Lancaster, *New York Interiors at the Turn of the Century* (New York: Dover, 1976). On English interiors of the same period, *see* Nicholas Cooper, *The Opulent Eye, Late Victorian and Edwardian Taste in Interior Design* (New York: Watson-Guptil, 1977).

2. *See* Anne Farnam, "A. H. Davenport, Boston Furniture Maker," *Antiques* 109, no. 5 (May 1976): 1048–55; and Farnam, "H. H. Richardson and A. H. Davenport: Architecture and Furniture as Big Business in America's Gilded Age," in Paul B. Kebabian and William C. Lipke, eds., *Tools and Technologies, America's Wooden Age* (Burlington, Vermont: University of Vermont, 1979), pp. 80–92.

3. Brabrook was listed under various family partnerships and addresses, but he was always located in Boston's mid-nineteenth-century furniture district around Dock Square.

4. Ledgers of the Mercantile Agency, vol. 69 (Massachusetts), pp. 527, 599[tt], R. G. Dun & Co. Collection, Manuscript Division of Baker Library, Harvard University Graduate School of Business Administration.

5. Ledgers of the Mercantile Agency, vol. 69, pp. 527, 599[tt].

6. Ledgers of the Mercantile Agency, vol. 69, pp. 527, 599[tt].

7. *Annual Report of the Boston Society of Decorative Art* (Boston, 1879), p. ii. A. H. Davenport placed the identical advertisement in 1880. The identity of M. Charmois is not known. The Annual Reports can be consulted at the Boston Public Library.

8. *Malden Mirror*, May 13, 1880.

9. U.S. Census Office, *Census of the United States, Manufacturing Schedules for Massachusetts, 1880*, microfilm copy at the Massachusetts State Library.

10. Ledgers of the Mercantile Agency, volume 87 (Massachusetts), pp. 92–93.

11. *See* Farnam, "H. H. Richardson and A. H. Davenport."

12. *See* Farnam, "H. H. Richardson and A. H. Davenport."

13. F. A. Moreland, *Practical Decorative Upholstery* (Boston: F. A. Moreland, 1889). For information on this and subsequent editions, *see* the essay by Fales in this volume.

14. The archive is located at the Margaret Woodbury Strong Museum, Rochester, New York. An assortment of working drawings from the period after 1908 have been microfilmed by the Archives of American Art.

15. *The Curtain-Maker's Handbook, A Reprint of F. A. Moreland's Practical Decorative Upholstery* (New York: E. P. Dutton, 1979), p. 8.

16. *Curtain-Maker's Handbook*, p. 7.

Spring Seats of the 19th and Early-20th Centuries

Edward S. Cooke, Jr. and Andrew Passeri

SPRING SEATS were the basis of virtually all upholstered chairs and sofas during the last half of the nineteenth century. If we are to understand and recreate the shapes of the upholstered furniture of that day, we must understand such issues as when springs were first introduced, why they gained popularity, and how they—and the techniques used to install them—changed over time. This essay will survey the evolution of spring seats in the nineteenth century and discuss the techniques developed by upholsterers for handling springs effectively.

Prior to the use of spring seats, there were three main methods of making a comfortable upholstered seat. All used natural, fibrous materials to build the foundation. The easiest method of construction—"a pad seat"—involved making feather-stuffed cushions, which would then rest upon plank or cane seats. A second, more complex method—the "tight seat," a term that includes slip seats and over-the-rail upholstery—involved the layering of webbing, sackcloth, horsehair or grass, thin linen batting, and a cover material. The third technique, employed for easy chairs and sofas, combined the first two; cushion seats were set on a tight deck. This was the ultimate in eighteenth-century upholstered comfort.[1]

Upholsterers began to use springs in the eighteenth century, but only for specialized furniture, such as the exercise horse in figure 12. The advantage of these springs was their mechanical action rather than their comfortable feel. Several factors worked against the use of springs for everyday seating furniture. First of all, springs were expensive. They were made from iron, which at this time was mainly imported. In addition, the steps involved in making springs were time-consuming: First, the iron had to be drawn into wire and then the wire had to be coiled into the shapes of springs. Locally available marsh grass or horsehair provided more affordable means of stuffing furniture. The use of spring seats was also limited by the fact that they were not as comfortable as the older style upholstered seats. Both their shape—early springs were simple cylindrical coils—and their material—a soft iron—created problems with inconsistent resilience. The springs did not always return to their original shape after compression. When these early springs lost their shape, the whole seat would become lopsided and lumpy. Finally, another reason that early spring seats were not very comfortable was that upholsterers had few craft traditions to guide them in this area. They did not know how to overcome the shortcomings of springs or how to use springs to their best advantage.

In spite of these limitations, by the second quarter of the nineteenth century, springs—for reasons that are unclear—began to be used for filling seats. In America, the first use of springs for seating furniture occurred in the late 1820s. Some surviving Empire sofas made at this time have iron coil springs stapled onto board or slatted bottoms, a technique borrowed directly from the exercise horses of the eighteenth century. These sofas were not top-of-the-line or elaborately decorated examples, suggesting that their upholsterers were searching for ways of cutting costs. Springs had become more affordable due to improvements in the British iron and steel industry and, by this time, would have offered the promise of comfort and firm shape without the use of great quantities of (expensive) horsehair or the time-consuming stitching of edges. (See Jan Seidler Ramirez's essay in this volume.) In fact, it seems that springs were first widely used for public seating furniture in hotels, steamboats, and trains where durability and affordability were of great importance.[2] These concerns, along with comfort, were also very important to middle-class consumers and no doubt led to the increasing use of springs for the home, as well.

Examination of surviving spring seats from about 1820 to 1860 reveals the upholstering trade's misunderstanding of the requirements of springs. Often, as with the Empire sofas mentioned above, they used a technique borrowed directly from the exercise horses of the eighteenth century: The springs were merely stapled onto board or slatted bottoms without regard to the need for a more resilient foundation to provide comfort. Upholsterers also did not understand the importance of securing the tops of the springs in a manner that forced the springs to move together as a single, even seating platform. They seemed to have thought of springs only as a filling for a domed seat.

The chair shown in figure 237 is a good illustration of this early method, even though it was made some time between 1840 and 1860 and therefore is not a particularly early chair. Although the upholsterer in this instance did at least attach the springs to a bottom made of linen webbing, he then merely secured the tops of the springs by attaching a linen cover with only a few light stitches (fig. 238). The springs weren't tied down at all. (Interestingly, the elaborately turned and carved frame of this chair suggests that by the mid-nineteenth century springs were not just used on cheaper furniture but were being adapted for more expensive chairs such as this.)

Even those upholsterers of the 1820s and 1840s who

237. Side chair, probably Boston, Massachusetts, 1840–1860. Mahogany, mahogany veneer, chestnut. This chair features its original needlework cover. Unfortunately, the iron oxide dye used to blacken the wool stitches at the center of all the geometric designs has caused the wool to disintegrate over time, leaving colorless holes. The appearance of the chair is also adversely affected by the loss of whatever braid or tape had been used along the edges of the needlework. Nevertheless, the shape of the seat demonstrates how early springs were used simply to fill the hollow and to give the seat a domed appearance. The back was filled with hair. Courtesy, Museum of Fine Arts, Boston. Bequest of Barbara Boylston Bean.

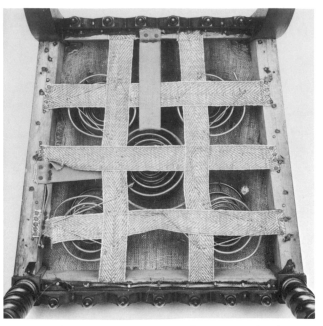

238. Detail of the underside of the chair in figure 237 showing the linen webbing and the lack of any spring tying. The covering linen sackcloth was secured with only a few stitches, one of which can be seen on the spring in the lower right-hand corner. Horsehair served as the filling for the edge and as a slight pad over the springs.

recognized the importance of tying down the springs securely almost always used a single strand of twine for the job. They would tack the twine to the rail, then simply loop it over and through the top of the coils, and then tack it to the other rail. This light tying allowed the springs to move around relatively freely, thereby allowing the springs to rub against each other and causing the twine to chafe. Eventually, the twine would part, and the unfastened springs would be free to go in all different directions. The result of all these inadequate methods was that spring seats of this period were lumpy to begin with and soon became downright uncomfortable — as each spring expanded and contracted by itself.

By the mid-nineteenth century, metallurgical developments and technological innovation in America made improved spring seats more widespread. Domestic iron ore was now in plentiful supply, largely due to newly discovered deposits around Lake Superior. New processes had been developed to transform iron to steel more efficiently and to produce steel that contained little carbon and, therefore, was stronger and more elastic. The American steel industry had expanded rapidly and could now produce great quantities of high-grade steel. Large-scale operations that emphasized increased production, mechanized working of steel, and cost efficiency became the norm. The result was a better material for springs that was better, cheaper to produce, and cheaper to form into springs.[3]

The availability of this much improved metal spurred many experiments and, during the 1850s, numerous applications for patents on new types of springs were filed with the U.S. Patent Office. Of all these innovations, the most important turned out to be the development of steel springs with biconical or hour-glass shapes.[4] The combination of the stronger metal with an hour-glass shape resulted in a much stiffer spring with a more consistent contraction and return than had ever been possible before. This type of efficient spring allowed seats to become deeper, more resilient, and more comfortable than seats upholstered in the traditional way. These improvements, in turn, led to the greater use of spring seats.

As spring seats became more common, upholsterers developed new and better techniques for handling springs, especially for tying them. These innovations included the use of double strand twine, the method of "return" tying (in which a length of twine was run through the middle of a line of coils and then brought back over the top of the same coils), the use of lashing (running twine diagonally across the springs to provide additional stability to springs already tied front to back and side to side), and the use of more effective knots, such as loop and interlocking overhand knots. (*See* figures 239 and 247.) Securing the springs firmly in this way allowed them to move together as a unified seat platform and, simultaneously, decreased problems caused by springs rubbing against one another or by the twine chafing and wearing away.

Spring seats now became the basis of most American seating furniture because, at the same time that their comfort and quality had greatly improved, there was an increased demand for upholstered furniture. By the mid-nineteenth century, America's wage-based capitalist economy had fostered the growth of a large middle class with discretionary income to spend upon consumer goods. Meanwhile, the industrialization of furniture and textile manufacturing had led to the production of affordable furniture frames and covers in a wide variety of styles. Now, with the economies and comfort offered by improved spring seats, upholstered furniture became accessible to the middle class. What had once been so expensive as to be a major symbol of wealth and status, now became an important part of American everyday life.[5]

In the last half of the nineteenth century, there were a variety of upholstery operations: from expensive custom shops that employed traditional craft methods and expensive materials to factory-type firms that used newer, cost-cutting methods and cheap coverings. In custom shops, upholsterers simply integrated springs into their existing practices. They stitched the springs to linen webbing and covered them with a second layer of sackcloth upon which they made a hair-stuffed cake with stitched edges. As a rule, their work featured strong resilient seats, elaborate contours and fillings, and rich, decorative cover fabrics. The skill and time necessary to tie the springs correctly, to compact and quilt the hair evenly, to stitch the edge tightly, and to lay out and stuff the cover properly far exceeded that required for earlier upholstering of tight seats. In addition, many of their products featured quilted, tufted, channeled, or pleated surfaces, all of which demand great skill and take considerable time.

Coexisting with the expensive custom shops were a number of what are referred to as production shops, that is middle range commercial firms in which upholsterers were more cost conscious. They often substituted jute—a cheap, inexpensive and short-lived material—for the more expensive, more durable linen webbing.[6] Burlap, a jute-related material, replaced linen for the covers used over the webbing and over the fill. Upholsterers working for this market spent less time tying springs securely. They also experimented with different ways to build a good straight seat edge that would take less time than the traditional stitched edge. They tried reed edges in the 1870s and then steel wire edges in the 1890s.

A third type of upholstery establishment, the factory operation, catered to the inexpensive market.[7] Upholsterers working in these firms performed piece work—each craftsman specialized in a specific task and had little understanding of what the whole process involved. (In custom shops, a craftsman would work on a piece from start to finish. These upholsterers therefore had to master all techniques.) Because what was under the final cover was not visible, many of these manufacturies cut corners on building proper seat foundations. They used time-saving technological developments similar to those of the middle range commercial shops but placed an even greater emphasis upon production, lower costs, and maximum profits. In addition to the use of jute, burlap, and edges stiffened by means other than stitching, they made greater use of inferior fill such as Spanish moss, seaweed, chaff, and thin spiral shavings of such woods as hickory, cedar, or yellow poplar. (These shavings were popularly referred to as "pine state hair"—and are now called excelsior.)[8] These fill materials were much less durable than horsehair or even marsh grass and usually disintegrated quickly. Springs on seats from such low-end shops were barely tied. Some of these firms owned tufting machines to make inexpensive deep buttoning on seats and backs. An operative using such a machine could perform the work of twenty-five men, but the "tufting" that the machine produced was shallow; it was also stamped indiscriminately on the seat or back and bore little relation to the lines of the chair, unlike hand-work tufting.[8]

The range of upholstery businesses continued into the early twentieth century. The custom shops continued to employ traditional techniques and materials to upholster high quality seating furniture. The middle-range production shops and the low-end factory firms continued to draw upon technological and manufacturing advantages to lower costs. They made increasing use of steel components and used the upholsterer more as a factory worker than as a craftsman. (See the essay by Ann Farnam in this volume.) Prefabricated steel component parts replaced twine-tied springs, stitched edges, and hair filling. Pre-assembled seats, known as factory units, consisted of steel straps (instead of webbing), steel conical springs, and steel wire edges. These steel parts were connected with steel clamps and covered with burlap, a thin cotton skimmer, and a cover material. These units were then simply dropped into frames.

These factory units were, by the early twentieth century, enormously popular. Even such arts and crafts proponents as Charles Limbert and Leopold and J. George Stickley raved about the advantages of pre-assembled steel spring seats with wire edges. According to furniture catalogues of the period, one of the great advantages of these spring seats was that these cushioned seats were clean and never lost their shape or resiliency.[9] (It is telling that such arts and crafts leaders, who argued so strongly for a return to handcraftsmanship, did not seem concerned about this particular displacement of craftsmen. Perhaps they did not consider traditional upholstery to be a true craft.)

In the half century since World War I, custom upholstery shops have had a difficult time competing against the inexpensive work of more commercial shops. The status of custom work has been eroded by additional changes within the upholstery craft. The most significant developments of this century have been the introduction of synthetic stuffings, such as foam rubber, rubberized hair, or plant fiber; the use of more pre-assembled fillers, such as sagless-wire springs and Marshall units (the latter are ready-made units or strips of metal springs, each sewn in its own burlap or muslin pocket); the advent of fiber glass shells; and the introduction of synthetic coverings, such as vinyl, Herculon, and Naugahyde. Indeed, Charles Eames and other mid-twentieth-century designers have produced chairs that require little or no upholstery but instead rely on the design of their molded laminate or steel wire frames to provide comfort.[10]

The following photographic essays depict three different types of spring seats. The earliest type, made in custom shops from about 1840 to 1860, utilizes many elements from the traditional upholstery methods used for over-the-rail tight seats of the eighteenth century (figs. 239–242). Only the addition of the springs is new.

The second type of spring seat, the product of a factory firm in the late-nineteenth century (figs. 243–246), uses several time-saving innovations. Steel wire defines the shape of the seat and the lines of its edges. Other cost-cutting efforts can be seen in its inadequate tying, its machine stitching and buttoning, and its cheap cover.

A final type, from the late-nineteenth or early-twentieth centuries, is a factory unit frame (fig. 248), in which steel is the dominant material. The steel springs sit upon steel spring bars with a top defined by steel edge wire and overlaid steel grid. These spring seats could be assembled from mass-produced parts, thereby simplifying and streamlining the upholstery process. They were used by a large part of the upholstery trade; only the custom shops consistently retained tied springs and stitched seats.

Custom Spring Seats

This sequence of photographs follows the reupholstering of a chair using the techniques employed by expensive custom shops working during the last half of the nineteenth century. The surviving evidence of original materials and tack marks indicates that these were the techniques originally used. The only changes were the substitution of steel biconical springs for iron cylindrical ones and the use of the more refined return tying system.

239. Side chair, probably Boston, Massachusetts, 1840–1850. Mahogany, ash. The upholsterer begins by folding one strip of linen webbing under at one end and tacking it along the underside of the front rail. He stretches it with a webbing stretcher and tacks it to the underside of the rear seat rail. After filling in the seat with two more strips of linen webbing running front to back, he interweaves webbing side to side. He places a sufficient number of springs on the webbing to fill the hollow and secures each to the webbing at four places, using heavy linen twine with continuous stitching. The upholsterer starts stitching at an outside corner of an outer spring, secures that spring at four points with loop knots, then runs the stitching along the underside of the webbing to the next closest spring. The result is a very geometric stitching pattern along the underside.

With the springs secured to the webbing, the upholsterer then ties them to ensure the proper height and straight vertical movement of the springs as a single seat platform. To do this properly requires a systematic, time-consuming sequence of steps. The upholsterer begins by securing the springs back to front and then side to side. Starting with the two springs on the right, he measures enough twine for three lengths of the back-to-front distance. Using two-thirds of this twine, he starts this return tying from a number 12 tack along the bottom of the rear rail and runs the twine to the rear part of the number 4 ring (the fourth coil down from the top coil). There he uses

a loop knot, then takes the twine and loops it around the front part of the number 1 ring of the same spring. He runs the twine to the front right spring and loops it around the back edge of the number 1 ring, loops it around the front edge of the number 4 ring, and wraps it around a protruding tack along the underside of the front rail. He then adjusts the springs to their proper height by pulling or releasing the twine. (The loop knots permit this adjustment.) When the springs are plumb, the upholsterer secures the twine by hammering down the protruding tack on the front rail.

Once the upholsterer has anchored this length of twine, he finishes the job by return tying. He takes the loose end of the twine up to the upper edge of the front rail, around a tack that is then hammered down. He next takes the twine to the number 1 ring of the front coil where he ties an interlocking overhand knot instead of the adjustable loop knot. He then secures the twine to the back edge of the same coil (around the number 1 ring), then to the front edge of the back coil (on the number 1 ring), and finally to the back edge of the other rear coil (again on the number 1 ring). All of these knots are the interlocking overhand type. He finishes with this end of the twine by tacking it to the top of the rear seat rail and then to the underside of the rail. The same procedure is used for the springs on the left side. This method of return tying is characteristic of custom work in the late nineteenth century.

When the springs are completely tied from back to front, the upholsterer then ties them from side to side. The twine is secured to the same sequence of rings and coils, but overhand knots, not loop knots, are used since the seats are already plumb.

Next, the upholsterer begins to build up the padding. With the spring arrangement shown, he adds two cross twines, one running front to back down the center and one side to side across the center, to support the covering burlap cover. These cross twines were necessary because the seat frame could comfortably accommodate only four springs and because there was, of necessity, some space between the springs; this might have allowed the seat to sag. Had the frame been slightly larger, a fifth middle spring could have been used, the closeness of the springs would have prevented any sag, and cross twines would not have been necessary. Private collection. Photograph by Richard Cheek.

front edge, then each of the side edges. He starts one inch above the tacking, pushes the curved needle in so that it emerges about one inch beyond the quilting stitch that defines the edge. He then brings the needle forward at an angle and pushes it down into the cake near the edge of the quilting stitch so that it emerges between the last two entry points on the front. He puts a double loop around the needle, and pulls tight. Then he enters the front again. (For the sake of clarity in the illustration, this figure shows the stitching of the front edge in process but without the quilting stitch on the right front edge that would normally be done first. The quilting can be seen, however, along the sides.) A skewer holds the pleated corner to the cake. (Skewers are also useful to position covers before baste-tacking.)

The upholsterer continues to use his regulator to shift and shape the filling and then stuffs any hollows on the cake with extra hair. Once this process is completed, he lays a cotton batting to prevent hair from coming through the outer cover. (This batting is not a true filling.) He then lays a muslin cover over the batting. He skewers the muslin in place, then adjusts the fit, aligning the warp and weft of the muslin with the rails. He first baste-tacks the edge of this muslin to the top of the rails and then final-tacks. He then puts on the final cover, skewers it, baste-tacks it, and final-tacks. When covering a chair that has an upholstered seat and back, the craftsman would first get the seat to the point where it is covered with muslin—and then work on the back. When the back was covered with muslin, he would put final fabric on the seat, and next on the back. Finally he would add the trimming.

240. After the springs are tied in place and the supporting cross twines secured, a linen cover is spread over them to provide an even foundation for the stuffing that is then placed upon it. The cover also prevents the filling from falling into the springs. The edges are folded under and are temporarily baste-tacked to the top of the seat rails. The cover is then stitched to the top of each spring at four points. This stitching prevents any chafing or ripping of the linen, making it a solid base for the fill.

When the linen is secured to the coils, the edges are permanently tacked along the inner edge of the upper side of the rails. As the upholsterer removes the baste-tacks one by one, he pulls the linen tight and even. He then final-tacks. Next, the upholsterer stitches a single running line all over the cover. He enters the linen approximately every four inches and covers the entire linen sackcloth with loose, long stitches in a geometric pattern. In and around this loose stitching, he tucks the horsehair filling.

Next, the upholsterer covers the fill with a second, larger linen cover, temporarily baste-tacks it to the rails, and uses his regulator—a flat-headed needle approximately eight inches in length—to adjust the horsehair fill underneath so that the center is slightly domed. (This fill does not provide resilience but eliminates the feeling of the springs and gives shape to the seat.)

The upholsterer then uses a long, double-ended straight needle in a quilting stitch to secure the fill between the linen covers. This quilting tightens and compacts the hair. The result of this quilted work is commonly called "the cake." About 3½ inches in from the front and side rails, the upholsterer uses a tighter quilting stitch to define the edge. He removes the baste-tacks along the rail and adjusts the filling between the edge and the rail, adding additional hair if necessary so that the outside roll extends slightly up above the seat and over the rail. He then baste-tacks the linen again and begins to stitch the edge with an 8-inch bow needle. Working from left to right, he stitches the

241. The back of this side chair was originally upholstered with full diamond tufting, a method of providing decorative shaping that is relatively labor intensive. The technique draws upon the traditional methods of adjusting and shifting hair-stuffed filling by the constant

use of the regulator. The deep channels and folds distinguish this form of shaping from the loop tufting of the eighteenth century or the simple buttoning or machine tufting of the late-nineteenth-century commercial shops.

The key to good diamond tufting is careful preparatory measuring and layout. This is particularly true if the large size of the frame requires that two widths of material be sewn together. The upholsterer then must cut and sew the seams so that they are hidden within the tucks and folds of the tufting, a process often needed on large sofas and deep chairs and referred to as Vandyking. This particular side chair, however, is not of sufficient size to require Vandyking.

To begin, the upholsterer tacks webbing and a linen foundation to the rabbeted inner edge of the back. (In chairs where the rabbet is too shallow for the necessary foundation and cover layers, the craftsman tacks the burlap cover and then the webbing along the inside edge of the back, using a tack strip of leather or thin wood to secure it firmly.) The upholsterer puts skewers into the burlap to lay out appropriately proportioned tufting locations. Usually there are three or four tufts along the top, following the line of the crest rail. In the illustration, the center tuft on the top row is elevated slightly above the other two tufts on that row. The upholsterer then establishes the lower row and draws diagonal lines on the linen between the tufts of the upper and lower lines. The intersections of these diagonals establish the locations for the middle row of tufts.

At each tuft location, the craftsman secures twine of about eight inches in length. Loops of twine are also stitched between each row and around the perimeter of the back to help hold the hair in place. After he tucks a good quantity of hair in place, he then marks out the tufting pattern on the muslin cover and the final cover with chalk. To account for the extra material that will be needed to cover the filling, he lays out the same pattern as on the linen, then measures the distances between buttons and between horizontal lines and adds a 1½-inch allowance between each horizontal and vertical measurement for the hair filling. These allowances may vary. When recovering a seat with its original foundation, you can determine the allowance of an old upholstery job by measuring between the tufted folds of the original fabric with calipers or a soft measuring tape.

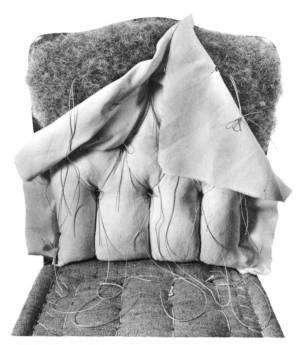

242. This photograph shows the process of stuffing, buttoning, folding, and adjusting the muslin cover to form a diamond tufted back. Each of the button loops on the lowermost row is passed through the matching marked button areas of the muslin and secured with a slipknot. This knot allows the craftsman to use the same thread for the cover, thereby ensuring the correct alignment for the cover. The upholsterer adds additional hair to fill the lower channels, pulls the lower edge of the muslin around the rail of the back, and baste-tacks it in place along the back side of the rail.

With the bottom edge secure, the upholsterer baste-tacks the muslin edge along the lower part of the rabbeted inner edge of the back posts. He then moves up to the next horizontal line, passing the second row of button twine through the cover, tucks the folds that give the pleated appearance, and adds additional fill as needed. He secures this level of tufting by tacking the muslin along the back side and continues working up the back in this manner. With the muslin in place, he puts a cotton batting on top of the muslin, allowing for the deep folds of the channeling and tufting by cutting slits in it. He also brings the button threads through very small holes in the batting.

Finally, the upholsterer puts on the final cover in a series of steps similar to those he used for the muslin. The only difference is the securing of the button twine. After passing it through the final cover and drawing the cover tight, he draws the twine tight in a double half-hitch knot. This twine is then tied to the eye of a button whose head has been covered in the chair fabric using a die press. Around the edge of the final cover, the upholsterer fastens a braid or tape finish with gimp tacks. (Contemporary upholsterers use hide glue for fastening this edging.) With the front surface of the back covered, the upholsterer turns his attention to covering the outback. After tacking a muslin or linen cover over the bare back, he simply puts on a thin cotton skimmer and then tacks on and finishes the edge of the final cover.

Factory Spring Seats

This photographic series illustrates the techniques of upholstery used by late-nineteenth-century firms that manufactured inexpensive furniture. The photographs show the processes in reverse: Rather than following the step-by-step procedures of the upholsterer, this sequence follows the step-by-step uncovering of a late-nineteenth-century chair.

The chair is similar to one illustrated in an 1897 Marshall Field and Company catalogue and described as a "Turkish-style parlor chair with full spring edges." The catalogue shows this type of chair with a fringed skirt that hung below the seat and covered the legs, and, indeed, our chair shows evidence of cover material having been cut off below the tape at the lower edge of the seat rail, suggesting that it too also originally had a fringed skirt.

The evidence from this late-nineteenth-century chair offers instructive contrast to that of the mid-nineteenth-century side chair. The upholstering techniques used on this chair reflect the continued development and use of steel upholstery materials, the introduction of new covering materials, and the compromises necessitated by large-scale production of upholstered seating forms. The upholsterer has used wire edges, minimal tying of the springs, machine stitching, and other labor-saving steps to provide an upholstered chair at an economical price.

Indeed, the upholstery on this chair is what Bostonians in the trade commonly called a "Borax job," a term used to indicate cheap work full of short cuts but with the appearance of correct work. For example, the entire seat derives its contour from steel springs and wire edges, and there is little use of any fiber materials other than jute and burlap. The covering is split leather, a cut of leather that is less expensive and not as pleasing in appearance as the top grain leather that would be used on the more expensive seating. The outback is covered with imitation leather. Other cost-cutting measures evident in the final cover are the buttoning—which gives the illusion of tufting without the necessary labor—and the machine-stitched pleated border.

This chair typifies the short cuts taken by upholstery factories. The emphasis is upon a fashionable appearance with little consideration for the upholstery foundation or the frame. Only top-of-the-line chairs had elaborate frames and custom upholstery work.

243. Parlor chair, possibly Marshall Field and Company, Chicago, 1890s. Maple, ash, and birch frame with split leather and imitation leather covering. This front view of the parlor chair shows it in "as found" condition. Unlike the case of many far older chairs upholstered with linen webbing that have survived intact, the bottom has fallen out. This is because much of the interwoven jute webbing has ripped away from the underside of the rails, taking the twine-secured springs with it. This photograph graphically illustrates the instability and limited life span of jute webbing.

The cambric bottom that was always nailed to the seat rails under the webbing to prevent dust and loose stuffing from falling to the floor is missing. This photograph also shows the deep buttoning on the chair back. The creases give the impression of the folds on real diamond tufting, but instead of using the complicated layout patterns shown in the previous essay, the upholsterer pulled the buttons tight in order to pucker the material slightly.

244. View of the rear corner of the chair in figure 243. Notice the ragged remainder of a skirt along the back. This view clearly shows the boxed cushion with its machine-pleated border. To make the boxed cushion, the upholsterer first took a length of split leather, gathered it into pleats along one edge, and machine-stitched it to one sleeve edge of a welt. He then machine-stitched this welt to a piece of split leather cut to the size of the seat. He laid this cover over the seat foundation and hand-stitched the underside of the welt's sleeve edge to the edge wire that ran around the upper edge of the seat. He put a small amount of cotton batting over the burlap that formed the side wall between the rail and the edge wire, pulled the pleated side panel over this batting, gathered pleats in the same direction along the lower edge, and tacked this edge to the top of the chair rail. A second piece of split leather with a full height pleat was then machine stitched to a second welt. The upholsterer blind-tacked the underside of the welt's sleeve to the top edge of the seat rail, making sure to cover the tacking of the edge panel. He pulled the rail cover down over the rail, put a small amount of horsehair between the rail and the cover, and then tacked the cover along the lower edge of the seat rail.

After the seat and back covers were in place, the craftsman applied the outback. On this chair, he nailed a burlap cover around the back, laid a skimmer of cotton batting on this, put on an imitation leather cover with its edges folded under (eliminating the need for finishing tape), and secured it with tacks and papier-mâché-headed nails (inexpensive substitutes for leather-covered nails), spaced further apart than those upon the more visible surfaces of the chair.

Finally, the upholsterer tacked the skirt to the lower edge of the seat rail and covered this seam with imitation leather tape and papier-mâché-headed nails.

245. Chair with split leather cover only removed. This shows that there was no muslin cover on the back and also shows how horsehair was secured to the back with twine loops before the final cover was added. When upholsterers did not put a muslin cover over the hair, as was the case with the back of this chair, they referred to the chair as "in the jacket," meaning it was only encased in its final cover. The seat, however, was not in the jacket; it did have a muslin cover underneath the split leather.

The remaining foundation layers of the seat reveal a combination of standard work and shoddy short cuts, the latter predominating. The upholsterer put a burlap cover over the springs, stitching it only to the top coil of the springs and to the edge wire, and nailing its folded edge to the top of the seat rail. This was the standard procedure for providing a solid base for the springs; as such the base rode evenly and did not allow the springs to chafe. The upholsterer, however, did not secure the burlap to each spring at four points; instead, he secured each spring at only two points, which allowed the burlap a fair amount of movement over the springs.

On top of this burlap base, he laid tow (a coarse flax or hemp fiber), a cheap substitute for horsehair. Over the tow, he placed a second layer of burlap. He skewered this in place and then ran a grid of quilting stitches to compact the tow in the middle of the seat. Near the edge, he stitched a bit more tightly to form the beginning of the edge. Then the craftsman took the shortcut of simply folding the burlap under at the wire edge, adjusting the tow around the edge, and stitching the burlap to the wire from left to right. He did not tack the edge of the burlap to the seat rail, a convention that would have provided a second layer of burlap between the wire edge and the seat rail and would have given the seat platform additional strength and stability for its up-and-down movement.

On top of this quilted burlap, the upholsterer put a thin layer of horsehair to fill hollows, a layer of thin cotton batting, and then a muslin cover. This muslin was folded over at the edges and stitched to the edge roll rather than to the wire edge or to the seat rail. Such a technique further weakened the foundation. There was no muslin layer between the wire edge and the seat rail to provide additional stability, and the stitching to the edge roll placed considerable stress on that edge.

The use of only a single burlap cover and the final cover to stretch between the wire edge and the seat and to reinforce the tying of the springs was obviously inadequate. The up-and-down movement caused by sitting placed great strain on both the burlap and split leather and, eventually, led to their ripping.

246. This shows the bare seat frame, which was assembled with dowelled and glued joints. The back was roughly sawed out with a band saw. Instead of smoothing this surface with a rasp or plane, the craftsman nailed a cardboard strip around the outside of the rear legs to provide a smooth surface for the cotton batting and split leather that would be placed on the back.

This photograph also shows how the wire edge was stapled to the rear of the side seat rails and secured by simple knots to the top rings of the springs. The most important detail to note is the cheap way of tying the springs. The craftsman used single lengths of twine to secure the springs from front to back and side to side. Because he used three springs in the first two rows and two springs in the last row, he cross-tied single lengths of twine in a diagonal way. (A stronger, more time consuming way of return tying with cross lashing is shown in figure 247.)

The condition of this spring seat demonstrates how weak single-twine tying was. Such seats lasted only for a short time before the twine chafed and broke at the rail edge or at the coil. A sharp edge along the inside of the seat rail, seen on this chair, hastened the failure of the twine. On better work, upholsterers rounded off this edge. Once a single twine broke, the springs went out of kilter and ceased to move straight up-and-down.

The back of the chair is filled with softer springs set between layers of burlap. It shows the cheap way of securing burlap to the springs with pairs of stitches and of using deep buttoning to simulate tufting. The buttoning threads have left prominent stretch holes in the burlap.

247. Model of springs properly return tied and cross lashed for maximum strength. The lashing distinguishes this from the tying seen in figure 239. To lash the springs, the upholsterer runs a twine from one edge, ties it with an overhand knot to the number 2 ring on the outside of the nearest spring, ties it at the number 1 ring on the inside, loops it around a lashing twine from the other side, ties it to the

number 1 and number 2 rings on the next spring, and tacks it to the rail. By interlooping such a series of V-shaped tyings, the craftsman provided additional firmness to the seat. Model made by Andrew Passeri. Photograph courtesy, Museum of Fine Arts, Boston.

Factory Unit Seats

The "factory unit" seat illustrated here demonstrates how upholstering became a type of metal work in the early-twentieth century. Developments in the automobile industry played a special role in the use of spring seats with steel bands and steel grids. Such cushion seats were valued for their cleanliness, comfort, and ability to keep their shape. The ease of dropping in pre-assembled inexpensive foundations (that had been put together quickly from mass-produced parts) made factory units like this ideal for mass-produced chairs. Such seats clearly show that upholstery was no longer an individualistic craft.

248. Drawing of a seat from a chair, L. & J. G. Stickley, Fayetteville, New York, 1900–1910. This cut away drawing shows a typical factory unit seat. In such prefabricated spring seats, steel spring bars replaced webbing; conical springs (less consistently resilient that biconical ones) were clipped to the bars rather than sewn to webbing. Steel wire and clamps replaced knotted twine in securing the steel edge wire and the overlaid wire grid to the top coils of the springs. No tying was necessary. An upholsterer or chairmaker, such as Stickley, purchased the steel unit from specialized manufactories. It is unclear who provided such seats for the Stickley furniture firm.

Over this metal framework, the upholsterer stretched a burlap cover that was tacked to a wooden frame. Cotton batting served as a fill; a thin cotton cover completed the seat's shape. A final cover—in this case a machine-stitched, welted leather cover—was then stretched over the padded springs and nailed along the underside of the frame. Drawing by Alice Webber.

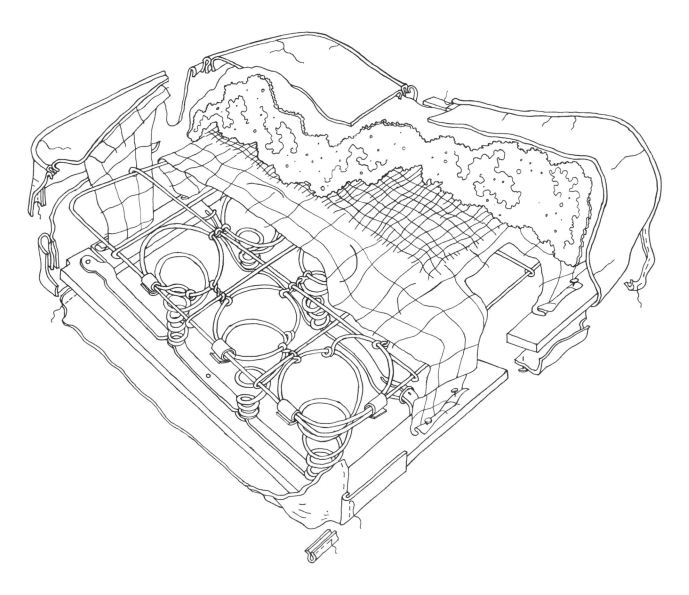

NOTES

1. *See* the essays by Peter Thornton, Robert Trent, Brock Jobe, and Morrison Heckscher in this volume.

2. On the introduction of spring seats for public furniture, *see* Katherine Grier, "Imagining the Parlor," in Gerald W. R. Ward, ed., *Perspectives on the Study of American Furniture* (forthcoming).

3. Two studies that chart the development of the iron and steel industries in nineteenth-century America are by Daniel Walkowitz, *Worker City, Company Town: Iron- and Cotton-Worker Protest in Troy and Cohoes, New York, 1855–84* (Urbana: University of Illinois Press, 1978); and David Brody, *Steelworkers in America: The Nonunion Era* (Cambridge, MA: 1960; reprint, New York: Harper Torchbooks, 1969). The connection between iron and consumer goods is explored by Ellen Snyder in "Victory over Nature: Victorian Cast-Iron Seating Furniture," *Winterthur Portfolio* 20, no. 4 (Winter 1985): 221–42.

4. *Report of the Commissioner of Patents for the Year 1858* (Washington: James B. Steedman, 1859), vol. 1, p. 582. On the development of biconical steel springs in England, *see* Dorothy Holley, "Upholstery Springs," *Furniture History* 17 (1981): 64–67.

5. Michael Ettema, "Technological Innovation and Design Economics in Furniture Manufacture," *Winterthur Portfolio* 16, no.2/3 (Summer/ Autumn 1981): 197–223; Florence Montgomery, *Textiles in America, 1650–1870* (New York: W. W. Norton & Company, 1984); Stephen Victor, "'From the Shop to the Manufactory': Silver and Industry, 1800–1970," in Barbara and Gerald Ward, eds., *Silver in American Life* (New York: The American Federation of Arts, 1979), pp. 23–32; and Catherine Lynn, *Wallpaper in America From the Seventeenth Century to World War I* (New York: W. W. Norton & Company, Inc., 1980).

6. One way to determine whether a chair was webbed with linen or jute girt is to examine the tacking marks. Most linen webbing was about 2 inches wide, so tacking patterns on the rails would be in 2-inch wide clusters. Jute webbing is often about 3½ inches wide, therefore the tacking pattern on jute-webbed chairs consists of a series of 3-inch clusters.

7. In early-twentieth-century Boston, such firms were referred to as "Borax firms" and their work considered "Borax jobs."

8. Sharon Darling, *Chicago Furniture: Art, Craft, & Industry, 1833–1983* (New York: W. W. Norton & Company, 1984), pp. 65–80.

9. Stephen Gray, ed., *The Mission Furniture of L. & J. G. Stickley* (New York: Turn of the Century Editions, 1983), p. 89; and *Charles P. Limbert Company, Cabinet Makers* (New York: Turn of the Century Editions, 1981), pp. 18–19.

10. *For example, see* John Bergen, *All About Upholstery* (New York: Hawthorn Books, Inc., 1962) and James Brumbaugh, *Upholstering* (Indianapolis: Theodore & Co., 1972). On Eames and others, *see* David Hanks, *Innovative Furniture in America from 1800 to the Present* (New York: Horizon Press, 1981), pp. 67–71, 108–15.

249. Side chair, probably Portsmouth, New Hampshire, 1760–1770. Mahogany; original green harateen upholstery. Height-37⅞ inches, width-23⅛ inches. All photographs in this essay by J. David Bohl.

Upholstery Documents in the Collections of the Society for the Preservation of New England Antiquities

Richard C. Nylander

THE Society for the Preservation of New England Antiquities (SPNEA) was founded in 1910 by William Sumner Appleton, the first person to dedicate himself full-time to the preservation of American historical architecture. Appleton established an organization committed to the preservation of "the most interesting" old buildings in New England and the acquisition and exhibition of smaller household artifacts from the region. From the beginning, he stressed an object's historical provenance as well as its aesthetic merit. Thus, for the past seventy-five years, SPNEA has acquired individual items along with their histories of ownership by New England families. Occasionally SPNEA has received an entire household including all furnishings and other objects accumulated by several generations of the same family. The result is an unusual collection of objects ranging from houses to architectural fragments, from furniture to ceramics, from wallpaper fragments to toys and even such humble items as a bar of soap made in Newburyport, Massachusetts, in the late eighteenth century. An equally important part of SPNEA's collection are the documents, photographs, and other evidence related to the individual houses and objects.[1]

SPNEA's textile collection—consisting of bed hangings, window curtains, and upholstery materials—is outstanding in its quality, diversity, and documentation. Many of the early bed hangings are illustrated and discussed in detail in *Bed Hangings: A Treatise on Fabrics and Styles in the Curtaining of Beds 1650–1850*, edited by Abbott Lowell Cummings and published by SPNEA in 1961. This volume remains the standard reference on American bed hangings. SPNEA's window curtains were first examined closely in the exhibition that was held in 1979 at Old Sturbridge Village in conjunction with the Conference on Historic Upholstery and Drapery on which this volume is based. (*See* Jane Nylander's "Drapery Documents in the Study Exhibition" in this volume.) Some early eighteenth-century upholstery materials in the textile collection are examined in Brock Jobe's essay earlier in this volume. This essay will focus on nine important SPNEA upholstery documents dating from the mid-eighteenth century to the mid-nineteenth century.

The breadth of SPNEA's collection and its emphasis on provenance has preserved not only important examples of upholstered furniture and coverings but also invaluable supporting evidence such as period documents and nineteenth-century photographs illustrating the furniture in its original context. The combination of artifacts and documentation greatly enhances our understanding of the upholstery trade and its materials and techniques between 1750 and 1870.

The Sayward-Wheeler house, an SPNEA property in York, Maine, retains most of its eighteenth-century furnishings and family records, including a number of important upholstery documents. The merchant John Sayward, upon his death in 1797, bequeathed to his second wife, Elizabeth Plummer Sayward, "six mahogany chairs seated with green" (one is illustrated in figure 249).[2] These chairs and another set of Chippendale-style chairs survive in the Sayward house. Several from each set retain the original green (now faded to blue) harateen upholstery with an impressed pattern of butterflies and flowers (fig. 44).[3]

The chair's slip seat is built up with hair over a piece of linen supported by four strips of linen webbing. During the early nineteenth century, the harateen on several of the chairs was replaced by green figured horsehair. A late-nineteenth-century photograph of the parlor documents the existence of still another covering on the chairs, which matches a surviving pair of curtains fashioned out of eighteenth-century silk dress fabric, dyed green.[4]

In 1759, Sayward received an easy chair, upholstered by Samuel Grant of Boston (fig. 59). It was shipped to Sayward by the Boston merchant John Scollay. In addition to the bill for its purchase, the chair is documented further in Sayward's will, which directs that his wife shall have, for the period of her widowhood, "The use and improvement of my Easy chair."[5] In the 1950s, the chair was reupholstered and the legs, which had been cut down in the nineteenth-century, were restored. There is some evidence that the chair was originally upholstered in the same harateen as the Chippendale-style chairs mentioned above, one of which is illustrated in figure 249. The easy chair had at least two slipcovers in the nineteenth century; one, a roller printed chintz slipcover, circa 1840, survives and is illustrated here (fig. 250). The other appears in a photograph taken early in the 1880s.

The chintz slipcover closely follows the contours of the original eighteenth-century upholstery. It consists of three elements: a cushion cover, a cover for the back and arms, and a flounce. The edges of the cushion cover are bound with striped linen tape, as are all the pieces that are joined to make up the cover for the back and arms. The covering for the outside back is one width of fabric that was pinned at the corners where it met the outsides of the wings. The flounce is fitted across the

250. Slipcover for an easy chair, c. 1840. Roller-printed chintz. Easy chair, Boston, 1759. Chair: Height-46⅛ inches, width-33⅞ inches.

front of the chair, continuing only to the arm supports. The top edge of the flounce is gathered and secured to a plain linen tape. All other edges are hemmed in the front and finished, not bound, with the striped linen tape. Thus the full width of the tape is visible.

A remarkable set of seating furniture from "The Vale" in Waltham, Massachusetts, an SPNEA property that was the elegant country seat built for the merchant Theodore Lyman in 1793, documents the use of French upholstery techniques in America during the late-eighteenth century (fig. 251). Surviving upholstery from the eighteenth century usually reflects the English upholstery tradition that was pervasive at that time. Little survives of other traditions, a fact that makes Lyman's furniture quite special. The eight armchairs and two matching settees of this set all retain the original underupholstery; one of the chairs bears the printed paper label of Adam Hains, a Philadelphia cabinet-maker. Lyman's chairs are similar to an equally remarkable set of five in the Longfellow National Historic Site, Cambridge, Massachusetts, which are known to have been upholstered for the wealthy Andrew Craigie in the same year by George Bertault, a French upholsterer working in Philadelphia.[6]

In Lyman's set, each chair seat is built up with three inches of curled hair on fine linen supported by four strips of 1⅞-inch webbing. A piece of coarser linen was placed over the hair and sewn into a rolled edge around the top. The stuffing is held firmly in place by linen thread stitched through the tops and sides. The linen thread is secured to the seat rails with rose-headed nails. Over the stuffing was placed a thin layer of hair and another piece of fine linen (not seen in the photograph). On several of the chairs, one-inch-square blue check linen was used for this covering of the stuffing. Such a use of check linen was a French convention. No trace of the final decorative covering exists. Brass shanks still in the frame indicate that it was embellished with brass nails. When the upholsterer padded the arms, he left space for the nails around the pads as well as around the arm and back supports.

The backs of the chairs were upholstered in a fashion similar to that employed for the seats, except that the basic "sackcloth" upon which the hair was placed was a cream-colored silk. This expensive cover fabric was necessary because the lack of an outback, typical of French practices at this time, left the "sackcloth" visible from the rear. On the exposed backs of the settees, a light-green worsted was used instead of the silk.

Bertault's bill to Craigie for the similar set of chairs

251. Armchairs, made by Adam Hains, Philadelphia, 1793–1797.
Mahogany; original underupholstery and (possibly) slipcovers.
Height-33¾ inches, width-23 inches, depth-19¼ inches.

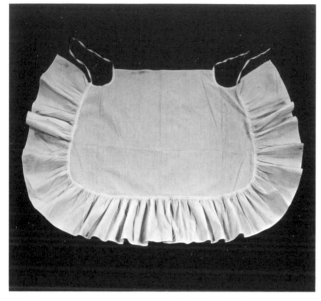

252. Slipcover for a compass-seated side chair, United States, 1810–1830. Dimity. Width-21 inches, depth-15 inches.

includes a charge for slipcovers of "fancy Chintz furniture" to protect the expensive green and white silk damask covering. For Lyman's chairs, two sets of slipcovers survive. The one illustrated in figure 251 is possibly original; it is made of plain linen and is hand-sewn. The other set, machine-sewn and made of white dimity, probably dates from 1882 when the furniture was reupholstered by the Boston firm of Leach, Annabel and Company.

Dimity was a common material for covers early in the nineteenth century. The 1815 inventory for the best room of another SPNEA house, the home of William Nickels in Wiscasset, Maine, listed "1 sofa white dimity covering" and "6 window cushions, white covering and fringe." These must have looked attractive with the un-upholstered "1 doz. white fan back chairs first quality" located in the same room.[7]

Six dimity slipcovers for chair seats, one of which is illustrated in figure 252, were given to SPNEA in 1945 with a label on which was written "6 dimity chair seat Covers of 1820's." Included with the gift were two dressing-table covers and a cover for a round stool, all made from dimity.

Each chair slipcover is made of two pieces. One piece—for the shaped seat—was completely hemmed before the second piece, the 5½-inch gathered ruffle, was attached. Strips of ¼-inch woven tape approxi-

mately 6 inches long were used for ties. The seat cover was cut in the back corners to go around the stiles of the chair, and the edges of the cutouts were reinforced with the same ¼-inch tape.

Not all slipcovers of the early-nineteenth century were as plain as these, however. Fabrics with elaborate border and filling designs suitable for slipcovers began to appear in the pattern books around 1810 and were most popular between 1815 and 1818. A chintz slipcover that covered a large couch owned by Nathan Appleton, a Boston textile merchant, featured richly printed neo-classical designs (fig. 253). Such ornament matched the Grecian style of the double parlors of Appleton's house, designed in 1818 by the Boston architect Alexander Parris.[8] SPNEA's collections also include an unused piece of the same highly glazed chintz, printed in yellow and red on a blue ground, bearing the stamp of Richard Ovey, a London linen draper of the early-nineteenth century. The design appears in the pattern books of the Bannister Hall printworks, printers of many of Ovey's designs. This design, numbered 957 and 958, was still being retailed in 1825.[9]

Another important SPNEA document that illustrates the furnishing fabrics and trimming favored by wealthy Bostonians in the first quarter of the nineteenth century are the yellow silk curtains from the drawing room of Charles Russell Codman's house at 29 Chestnut Street, Boston. A detail of these curtains, showing the star design woven in pink and the tassels, appears in figure 254. (The curtains themselves were altered from their original form in the twentieth century by Ogden Codman, a grandson of Charles Russell Codman, and therefore do not accurately depict the original style of hanging.) A copy of an 1824 letter in the Codman collection of manuscripts owned by SPNEA provides important information about these curtains. It describes in detail how the curtains and the complementary upholstery fabric were ordered.

Boston, March 5, 1824
Sam'l Welles, Esq
Paris

My dear Sir

In the right of an old friend I take the liberty to beg of you to execute a commission for me in Paris by which I hope to profit, not only by your own but of the taste of Mrs. Welles.

I am in want of the following articles of furniture for my drawing room

2 Window Curtains
2 Sofas
6 Chairs (Fauteuils)

253. Slipcover for the back of a Grecian couch, Boston, 1815–1825. Glazed chintz made by Richard Ovey, London. Height-46½ inches, width-27 inches.

254. Silk for curtains and upholstery, France, 1824. Width of border-3½ inches, length of tassels, including heading-7 inches.

The colors of my carpet are Rose color and yellow and it is not very important which of these colors you select; I think however I should prefer the former.

If the Curtains and Chairs are Rose color the fringes and lace and medallions for the chairs and sofas should be of yellow and visa versa—The drapery or inner curtain of white silk.

By the enclosed Plan you will perceive that the windows are embraced in the circle—I wish the curtains so constructed as to connect with each other at the top and to cover the top of the mirror.

As the Room is not very high the cornice, if any, should not be heavy—Mr. Sears imported some time ago, some curtains made of satin and lined which although more expensive I should prefer to silk, as I think the latter has a mesquin appearance.

The space between the Windows appears by the Plan to be greater than the windows themselves, which however is not the case—The space between the windows is 3½ feet and the windows are 5 feet wide each, including the architrave.

The height of the room is 11 feet 3 inches and the windows which are to the floor including the architrave 10 feet 3 inches, english measure.

I wish you to procure these articles to be made for me in the best style—rich but not gaudy—and to ship them to my address here or to the care of Codman Allanson & Co New York and to draw on Mr. Williams 13 Finsbury Square London for the amount, if not exceeding £–200 stg. for which I have provided. Should the articles in question cost more, I will pay the balance to your friends here.

Accept, in advance, my thanks for the trouble I am giving you and believe me very sincerely

Yr. friend

C.R.C.
(Charles Russell Codman)[10]

Codman's directions to his friend Welles make it clear that the continuous valance connecting windows was still a popular window treatment fully twenty years after it was introduced to Americans through English and French design books. The letter also shows that although Codman was relying on the taste of his friend, he had very specific ideas about the color and pattern of fabric as well as the style of drapery that he wanted to display in the best room of his house.

Samuel Welles, the recipient of Codman's letter, was a Boston merchant who lived in Paris. In 1811, Welles had shipped furnishings to his cousin John Welles of Boston. Samuel intended that his relative decorate his house in a style that the city had never seen before. The furnishings that Samuel sent back dazzled Boston and set new standards of elegance that were immediately emulated by the wealthy.[11]

Although cushions made for window seats and church furniture have not survived in great number, perhaps because they were movable, SPNEA owns several important cushions that illustrate period techniques and finish treatments. Each of the four feather-stuffed linen cushions (fig. 255) made for the window seats of the Samuel Fowler House in Danversport, Massachusetts, built in 1809, consist of a three-inch strip of linen sewn in continuous fashion to the top and the bottom pieces. The butted edges of the fabric were held fast with closely overcast stitches. The original decorative covering does not survive; however, a late-nineteenth-century photograph of the sitting room of the house shows the window seat cushions still in use, covered with contemporary fabric and embellished with a row of knotted fringe along the bottom edge of the cushion.

Another cushion (fig. 256) exhibits different fabrication and decoration techniques. Patterned red wool damask is used for the top piece and side panels; coarse linen is used as the bottom. All the edges are brought to the outside and bound in a solid red woven tape. Tufting of red wool is used in the eighteenth-century manner to stabilize the hair stuffing. The lack of linen between the wool damask and the hair stuffing suggests that these cushions were not intended for hard wear. They may have been made for pulpit furniture or for deacons' seats in a church.

This cushion was found in the attic of the Jacobs Farm in Norwell, Massachusetts. Its paper label, pasted to the bottom, reads:

MADE BY
WILLIAM HANCOCK
UPHOLSTERER
39, 41 & 45 MARKET-STREET,
BOSTON,
Where may be had all kinds of Upholstery Goods—and the business as usual attended to in all its branches.

Hancock worked as an upholsterer in Boston from 1819 to 1849 and was located at the above address between 1825 and 1829.

Later in the nineteenth century, Bostonians did not as a rule rely on local upholsterers such as William Hancock. Instead the leaders in fashion often sought the latest styles from New York decorators. An example of this practice is a set of drawing room furniture in the SPNEA collection, ordered by a Bostonian from the New York upholsterer Leon Marcotte & Co in 1869. In 1862, Ogden Codman, Sr. had re-acquired his family's former country estate in Lincoln, Massachusetts

255. Window seat cushion, New England, 1810–1820. Linen, stuffed
with feathers. Length-56 inches, width-12¾ inches, height-3 inches.

256. Cushion, made by William Hancock, Boston, 1825–1829. Red
wool damask, with curled hair and linen. Height-3 inches, width-11
inches, length-49 inches.

(Ogden's father Charles Russell Codman had sold it in 1803) and had begun to make it more stylish. He hired the Boston architect John Hubbard Sturgis to modernize it but turned to Leon Marcotte & Co. of New York to provide the furnishings. Bills and correspondence from Marcotte document the source of the curtains, wallpaper, and furniture for the newly renovated rooms.[12] At that time, drawings for chairs and sofas for the drawing room were sent from New York for Codman's approval, but when the shipments from Marcotte arrived in 1862 and 1863, no furniture for the drawing room was included. Through some misunderstanding, Marcotte had never received a specific order for this furniture.

In a letter dated July 18, 1864, Marcotte told Codman, "If you want the room furnished at once the best Plan would be to take stuffed all over furniture and to cover it with Chintz." For some reason, Codman waited until 1869 to follow this advice. Of the eight pieces of seating furniture ordered at that time, two still retain the upholstery of "garnet striped Cretonne Chintz" described on the bill. Cretonne was a popular inexpensive nineteenth-century covering fabric woven from linen or cotton and hemp and decorated with printed designs. According to the bill, the *bergère* (fig. 257), "tufted without covering," cost $70. The ten yards of chintz, seven yards of gimp, and two wool and silk "fringe rosettes" used to cover and ornament the chair cost $20.80. The "fluted flounces," which were to cover the legs, cost an extra $1.25 per chair. (These flounces were almost completely cut off at a later date.)

Although actual surviving objects are the most important documents in understanding historical upholstery, photographs too can serve as important sources for the study of materials and fabrication in the late nineteenth century. SPNEA's collection of interior views from the last half of the century is invaluable, particularly when there is corroborative evidence. For example, a photograph dated 1877 of the parlor from the James Bowdoin Bradlee house in Boston (fig. 258) can be fruitfully studied with the help of other documents—bills, correspondence, and the survival of the blue-and-white slipcovers that cover the furniture. Taken together, the evidence provides insight into the upholsterer's role in the evolution of the room's decoration and upkeep from 1848 to 1877.[13]

The first phase of the room's decoration in 1848 was supervised by G. D. Whitmore of 343 Washington Street, Boston, whose billhead states that he was a "Manufacturer of Fashionable Furniture, Upholstery,

257. *Bergère*, made by Leon Marcotte & Co., New York, 1869. Walnut, striped cretonne. Height-30 inches, width-34½ inches.

Trimmings, Curtains, Shades, Etc." He provided five new "Satin Damask Curtains *Complete*" for $80 apiece. (Later correspondence indicates these were blue.) Older curtains from Bradlee's former residence were altered, lined, and hung on new cornices in the dining room, and linen shades were put up on every window. Ten Grecian chairs were reupholstered with brocatelle, a popular nineteenth-century furniture covering comprised of cotton or linen filling with a silk relief surface. The backs of two "couches" and one "sofa" were reworked and covered with the same brocatelle. The furniture was further embellished with tassels, rosettes, gimp, and cord. "Loose covers" were made for all the pieces.

In 1856, a new sofa—that seen in the 1877 photograph—was purchased from Edward Hixon at 172 Washington Street. Although no bill exists for related chairs, Bradlee probably replaced the ten side chairs of the 1848 decoration at this same time. The striped slipcovers may also have been made at this time.

The bills from Hixon's firm for the years from 1868 to 1877 reveal the more routine aspect of the upholsterer's trade—that of refurbishment and seasonal change. Between June and July of each year, the Bradlees hired the firm to help prepare the house for summer. The

258. Interior photograph, James Bowdoin Bradlee House, 34 Beacon
Street, Boston, 1877.

wording on the year-end bill of December 28, 1868, outlined the typical work performed. On July 3, the Bradlees were charged for "Mans time taking down 14 sets of Window Curtains, brushing & putting away Do: -papering up Cornices, Chandeliers, Mirrors Etc:" (It should be noted that three quires of tissue paper, each quire consisting of twenty-four sheets, were required for the wrapping.) Between September and December, this procedure was reversed. As part of the fall housekeeping, the shades were also taken down, washed, and repaired if necessary.

The material discussed above is merely a small part of SPNEA's vast and varied holdings that relate to upholstery. Further research into its artifacts, photographs, and manuscripts should contribute significantly to the study of the upholstery trade, the identification of materials, and the understanding of techniques.

NOTES

1. Nancy Coolidge and Nancy Padnos, "William Sumner Appleton and the Society for the Preservation of New England Antiquities," and Penny Sander, "Collections of the Society," *Antiques* 129, no. 3 (March 1986): 590–605.

2. York County Register of Probate, vol. 17, p. 345, no. 16674, York County Courthouse, York, Maine. For additional information on the chairs, *see* Brock Jobe and Myrna Kaye, *New England Furniture: The Colonial Era* (Boston: Houghton Mifflin Company, 1984), pp. 400–2.

3. The design is similar to that on a set of crimson harateen bed hangings that belonged to Daniel and Sarah (Peele) Saunders of Salem, now in the Essex Institute, Salem, Massachusetts. Abbott Lowell Cummings, ed., *Bed Hangings: A Treatise on Fabrics and Styles in the Curtaining of Beds, 1650–1850* (Boston: Society for the Preservation of New England Antiquities, 1961), fig. 15.

4. Richard Nylander, "The Jonathan Sayward House," *Antiques* 116, no. 3 (September 1979): 567–77.

5. York County Register of Probate, vol. 17, p. 345.

6. Richard Nylander and Kathleen Catalano, "New Attributions to Adam Hains, Philadelphia Furniture Maker," *Antiques* 117, no. 5 (May 1980): 112–16.

7. Lincoln County Register of Probate, vol. 19, pp. 65–71, Lincoln County Courthouse, Wiscasset, Maine.

8. The seating furniture of the parlors included two pairs of couches, similarly shaped but of different sizes. The smaller pair is in the collection of the Museum of Fine Arts, Boston, and one of the larger pair is in the collection of the High Museum, Atlanta. *See* Page Talbott, "Boston Empire Furniture, Part I," *Antiques* 107, no. 5 (May 1975): 878–87.

9. Wendy Hefford of the Victoria and Albert Museum, correspondence with the author, 1981.

10. Typescript of original letter in Codman Family Manuscript Collection, SPNEA.

11. *See* Jane C. Nylander, "Henry Sargent's *Dinner Party* and *Tea Party*," *Antiques* 121, no. 5 (May 1982): 1172–83.

12. Codman Family Manuscript Collection. *See also* Richard C. Nylander, "Documenting the Interior of the Codman House: The Last Two Generations," *Old-Time New England* 121 (1981): 84–102.

13. Papers of James Bowdoin Bradlee, Codman Family Manuscript Collection, SPNEA.

Index

Page numbers in *italics* refer to captions.

A

Academy of Armory (Holme), 55, 133
Ackermann, Rudolph, 144, 181, *182*, 224, *225*, *225*, 227, 229, 230
Ackland, John, 115
aesthetic movement, *219*, *220*
Affleck, Thomas, 171
After (Hogarth), 88*n*, 89*n*
alcoves, drapery in, 198, 202
Alexander, James, 142, 166
American Woman's Home, The (Stowe and Beecher), 183
Amsden family (Suffield, England), *42*
Analysis of Drapery, An (Arrowsmith), 181, 187
Anello, Charles, 12, 97
Anonymous Boston Child (Custer), 223, *223*, 230
Apotheosis of George Washington and Benjamin Franklin pattern, *169*
Appleton, Nathan, 254
Appleton, William Sumner, 251
Appleton family (Boston, Mass.), *140*
Apthorp, Charles, 78, 80
Apthorp, James, 80
Apthorp, John, 165
archways, drapery in, 200, 202
armchairs, *237*, 252–54, *253*
   cushions for, 40
   French, 34, 122, *123*, 125, *127*, 129–30, 258, *258*
   great chairs, 30, *30*, *31*, 33, *41*, 43
   leather, *41*, 43
   slipcovers for, 33, *253*, 254
   tufting in, 36
   see also easy chairs
armrests:
   of Empire sofas, 227–28
   of French furniture, 122, 125, 129
arms, on table linens, *154*, *156*, 157, *157*, 159*n*
Arnold House, Lincoln, R.I., *140*
Arrowsmith, James, 181, 187
arts and crafts movement, 242
Assemble au concert, L' (Dequevauviller), *126*
Aston Hall, Birmingham, England, 56, *58*, 60
Atkins, Silas, 89*n*
Aubusson, 121

B

back stools, 29–30, *30*, 33, *33*, 37*n*
   armed (great chairs), *13*, 30, *30*, *31*, 33, *41*, 43
   in 18th-century England, 34
   leather, *see* leather chairs
   over-the-rail upholstering of, *90–96*, 91
   trimmings on, 33, *33*, 136–37
   Turkey-work, 39, 40–43, 44, 51–63, *51*, *52*, *56*, *57*, *58*, *60*, *61*, 136–37, 147*n*
Bacon, Francis H., 232, *233*
Baldwin, Christopher Columbus, 179
ball-and-disc turnings, *42*
ball-and-hollow turnings, *42*
Ballard, Samuel, 76
ball turnings, *38–41*, 43, *52*, *59*, *60*, 61
baluster turnings, *52*
Bannister, John, 167
banquet napkins, 155, *156*
David Barclay & Son, 142
Baroque and Rococo Silks (Thornton), 122
barrel turnings, *42*
Bass, Samuel, Jr., 78, 88*n*
baste-tacks, *244*, *245*
Baumgarten, Linda, 60
Baxter, Thomas, 71, 78
Bayou Bend Collection, Houston, Texas, 103, *111*
bay windows, 198, 200, 202
Beauvais, 121
bed covers, *18*, 128
bed hangings, 75, 76–78, *76*, *77*, 251
   American, English influence on, 137–38
   bases, bedskirts, or flounces in, 175
   crewel-embroidered, *20*, 138–39, *139*, 171, *172*
   curtain rings for, 75
   draw-up, 78
   18th-century, 19, 20, 21, 137–39, *138*, *139*, 141–42, 163, 167–71, *169–72*, 208, 209
   festoons or swags in, *171*, *174*, 175, *178*, *180*
   headcloths in, *20*, 138, 171, *172*, 175
   "heads" (rods with tassels) for, *212*
   health issues and, 175
   laundering of, 177
   mail order kits for, 136
   matching of fabrics in window curtains and, 175, 179
   Moreland's advice on, 203–4, *204*, *205*
   19th-century, 144, *145*, *174*, 175–79, *176*, *177*, *178*, 212
   printed, 141–42
   raising of, 78, 168, 171, 175
   at Rosersberg Palace, 187
   17th-century, 136, *137*

social importance of, 163
   in study exhibition of drapery documents (1979), *208–9*, 212
   tails or cascades in, *212*, *213*
   tester (canopy) cloths in, 78, 175, 176, 200, *203*–4, *204*
   textiles for, 69, 137–38, 167–71, *168*, 175, 176–79, 204
   trimmings on, 71, *135*, 136, 137–39, *137*, *138*, *139*, 141, 142, 167, 177, *177*, 179, *180*, 209
Bed Hangings (Cummings, ed.), 251
bed laces, 71
bedroom suites, French, 125–27, *127*, *128*, 129–30
bed rugs, 71
beds, 71, *74*, 75–78, *76*, *77*
   camp, field, or tent, 78, 168, 175–76, *176*
   cost of, 78, 88*n*
   dome, 168
   "French" (sofa), 176, *176*
   mattresses, bolsters, and pillows for, 35, 71, 75, 88*n*, 204
   raised, 78
   social importance of, 78
   stuffing for, 71, 76
bed screws, 89*n*
bedskirts, 175
bedsteads, 71, *74*, 75, *76*, 163
   attaching bed hangings to, 175, 177
   concealed by bed hangings, 168
   cornices or headboards of, 75, *76*, 171, 179, 200
   of late 19th century, 203–4
   painted, 177–79, *178*
   tester frames, *74*, 75, 78, 168, 175, 176
bed ticking, 71
Beecher, Catherine, 175, 183
Benge, Samuel, 114
bergères, *28*, 125, *127*, 258, *258*
Berry, Thomas, *59*, *60*, 61
Bertault, George, 252–54
Bimont, Jean-Francois, 122–25, 131
binding, *see* tape, woven
Blackfriars Hall, Norwich, England, 54
blacksmiths, 89*n*
blankets, 71
blanket stitch, 34
Blarenberghe, Louis-Nicolas van, 122
blinds, 198
blind-tacking, 228, *247*
block fringe, 144
block-printed textiles, *21*, *23*, 69, *170*, *174*, *177*, *210*, *211*, *215*
bobble fringe, 138–39, *139*

bolsters, 71, 75
"Borax jobs," *246*
bordering:
    shawl, 144, *145, 146*
    on tablecloths, 149, *158n*
Borland, Frances, 80
Boscobel, N.Y., *211*
Bosse, Abraham de, *41*
Boston, Mass.:
    bed hangings from, 138, 141, 142
    18th-century leather chairs from,
        78–79, *79,* 80, *81, 83,* 85–86, *86*
    Empire sofas from, *27, 222,* 223–30, *228,
        229*
    London fashions copied in, 40
    17th-century leather chairs from, *13, 38,
        39*–50, *39, 40, 41, 42, 44, 46, 47, 48*
    trimming makers in, 131
    Turkey work from, *14,* 60, 61, *61*
    window curtains from, 181
Boston Evening Post, 140–41
Boston Society of Decorative Art, 231–32
Boston upholstery trade, 65–89
    advertisements for, in *Practical Decora-
        tive Upholstery,* 197–98
    affluence and prestige of, 65–67
    bedding supplies stocked by, 71
    commercial and craft aspects inter-
        mingled in, 67, 75
    A. H. Davenport Company in, 231–38
    establishing one's own business in, 67
    Grant's activities in, 75–81
    hardware used by, 72–75
    leather used by, 69–71
    Moreland in, 197, 232, 236
    needlework supplies stocked by, 71–72
    pieces attributed to specific 18th-cen-
        tury craftsmen in, 80–83, *81, 82, 83*
    subdivision of tasks in, 75, 76–78, *88n,*
        232
    trimmings stocked by, 71, 139
    upholstery fabrics imported by, 67–69
    upholstery practices of, 83–86, *84, 87*
Boteler, Lady Alice Apsley, *42*
Böttinger, John, 58
bottom linen, *83, 84,* 226, 227
    in 18th-century American easy chairs,
        98, *98*
    in leather chairs, 43–44, *45*
    in over-the-rail upholstery, *91–93*
Boulard, Jean-Baptiste, *127*
Bourn, William, 78
Bowdoin, Elizabeth, Lady Temple,
    177–79
Bowdoin, James, 80, 176

Bowman, Jonathan, *83*
Brabrook, Ezra H., 197, 206n, 231–32
James Bowdoin Bradlee House, Boston,
    Mass., 258–60, *259*
braid, 121, 131, 133, 137, 139–42, 144
    on bed hangings, 138, *138,* 141, 142
    none-so-pretties, 140–41
    printed, 141
    on seating furniture, 139–40, 141
    tacking and gluing, 227, 228, 229
    on window curtains, 195
brasilwood dyes, 46
brass upholstery nails, 72, *72,* 73, 144
    in Anglo-American vs. Iberian tradi-
        tion, 48
    casting of, 72
    in double and triple nailing, 47–48
    in 18th-century sofas, 108, 110, 112–13
    in over-the-rail upholstery, 85, 96
    rectilinear and curving nailing patterns
        with, 36
    trimmings secured with, 137, 139
Brick Store Museum, Kennebunk,
    Maine, 197
Bright, George:
    employed by Grant, 75, 78, *88n*
    side chairs attributed to, 80, 81–83, *82,
        83*
brocade, 121
brocatelle, *25,* 198, *215*
Bromley Hall, *209*
Brooklyn Museum, Brooklyn, N.Y.:
    bed hangings at, *139*
    easy chairs at, *16,* 97, 98–103, *99, 102, 105,*
        139
    Turkey-work chairs at, 61, *63n*
Brown, Nelson H., 198
John Brown family (Providence, R.I.),
    208
Brunschwig & Fils, *211,* 226, 227
Buccleuch, Duke of, 54, *63n*
Buckman, Sarah, 136
bullion fringe, 133
bullions, 48, *49*
Bulman, Mary, 171
Burd, James, *213*
burlap, 241, *247–48*
Burnham family (Newburyport, Mass.),
    142–44
Burr, Brown & Company, 198
Sir William Burrell Collection, Glasgow,
    Scotland, 60
buttoning, 35, 144, *245*
    in spring seats, 242, *246*

C
*Cabinet-Maker and Upholsterer's Drawing-
    Book, The* (Sheraton), 37
*Cabinet-Maker and Upholsterer's Guide,
    The* (Hepplewhite), 142, 167–68
Cabinetmakers' Assistant, The (Hall), *222,*
    223, 224
Cadwalader, John, 105, 165, 170–71
Cadwalader, Williamina, 114
"cake,"*244*
Calef, Joseph, *88n*
calendered textiles, *19,* 138, *138*
"calf" leather, 46
Callows, Mr., 108
Camelot, J. A. J., *34*
campaign fringe, 133, *135,* 137
camp beds (tent or field beds), 78, 168,
    175–76, *176*
Campbell, Robert, 65, *88n, 134*
canapes, 120, 122, 125
caning, 33, *34,* 55, 121, 239
canopy beds, *see* tester frames
canopy cloths, *see* tester cloths
canvas, needlework, 71–72
Capin (*tapissier*), 127, 129
capiton, 35
Carl XIII, King of Sweden, 187
Carl Johan XIV, King of Sweden, 187
carpets, 150, 205
    Turkey-work, 54, 58, 62
Carrère & Hastings, *235*
cascades, *see* tails
casters, 78, 107, 203
*Catalogue of a Loan Exhibition of English
    Chintz,* 209
ceiling screws, *89n*
chaff, 241–42
chairs:
    bergères, 28, 125, *127,* 258, *258*
    caning in, 33, *34,* 55, 121, 239
    exercising ("chamber horses"), 36, *37*
    fauteuils, 34, 121, 122, *127*
    "French," 34, 36
    great, *13,* 30, *30,* 31, 33, *41,* 43
    invalid, *29,* 32
    rush-seated, 33
    with spring seats, 36, *38n,* 239–42, *240,*
        243–49, *250n*
    tall-backed, 40, 56, *56*
    voyeuses, 125, *127,* 129, *129, 130n*
    see also armchairs; back stools; easy
        chairs; leather chairs; side chairs
"chamber horses," 36, *37*
Charles I, King of England, 51

Charles II, King of England, 32, *44*, 51, 63*n*
Charlotte, Queen of England, 142
Chartard (gilder), 127
Chase, Persis F., 179
à chassis, 122
checked fabrics, 123, 252
   in bed hangings, *170*, 171, *171*, *179*, *208*
   Boston upholsterers' use of, 69
   in window curtains, 165, 179
cheney, *19*, 67, 69, *69*, 138, 166
chinoiserie, *24*, 122, 142, 170, 171, *212*
chintz, *168*, 202, 203, 258
   bed hangings, 170, 177–79
   slipcovers, 251–52, *252*, 254, *255*
   window curtains, 181, *213*, *215*
Chippendale, Thomas, 65, 75, 76, 86*n*, *96*, 131, 163
Chippendale style, 97, 168, *237*
   easy chairs, *96–108*, *97–108*
   precise contours in, 85–86, 108
   side chairs, *15*, 108, *250*, 251
   sofas, 108–10, *109*, *110*, 112–13, *113*
Choiseul, Duc Etienne-Francois de, 122
Christ Church College, Oxford, England, 54
church furniture, 256
Civil War, U.S., 52
Clifford and Lawton, 206*n*
close-nailing, 36
"close stools," 107–8, *108*
clothing, *165*
   trimmings on, 131, 133, 137
Codman, Charles Russell, 254–56, 258
Codman, Ogden (20th century), 254
Codman, Ogden, Sr. (19th century), 256–58
   Charles Russell Codman house, Boston, Mass., 254–56
Coit, Job, 78
Collection of Designs for Household Furniture and Interior Decoration, A (Smith), 181, 187
colonial America:
   bed hangings in, 136, 137–39, *138*, *139*, 163, 167–71, *169*, *170*, *171*, *172*
   English influence on, 137–38, 163
   trimmings in, 136, 137–39, *138*, *139*
   Turkey-work covers and carpets exported to, 58–60
   window curtains in, *162*, 163–67, *164*, *167*
   see also Boston, Mass.; Boston upholstery trade; Philadelphia, Pa.

Colonial Williamsburg, Williamsburg, Va., *70*, 150
   beds and bed hangings at, *74*, *75*, *77*, 171
   leather chairs at, *40*, *47*
   reupholstering of back stools and chair at, *90–96*, *91*
   Turkey-work chairs at, 60–61, 63*n*
color:
   Chippendale's views on, 163
   of French furniture coverings, 121, 122
columnar turnings, 43, *58*
commodes, 107–8, *108*
Company of Merchants of the City of Edinburgh, 54, 63*n*
Compleat Treatise on Perspective, A (Malton), 168
Conference on Historic Drapery and Upholstery (1979), 11–12
   drapery documents exhibited at, 207, *207–21*, 251
Connelly, Henry, 114, 115, 117–19
Connelly, John, 114, 117–19
Connoisseur, 86
Consolation de l'absence, La (Delaunay), *126*
Cooper-Hewitt Museum, New York, N.Y., 144
Copley, John Singleton, *64*, 65, 97, 108, 110, 142, *143*
copper pin nails, *73*
copperplate-printed fabrics, 69, 165
   bed hangings, *141*, *142*, *169*, 170–71, *209*
   slipcovers, *70*, 71
cord (line), 71, 131, *132*
   French, 135, 139
   gimp, 131, *132*, 135
   for window curtains, *162*, 179, 201
Cordonnier, Le (Bosse), *41*
cornices:
   bed, 75, *76*, 171, 179, 200
   window, 181, 183, 205
"cosey corners," 198
Costume of Colonial Times (Earle), 138
cottage curtains, 202
cotton, 165, 204
   linings, 43, 44
cotton, printed:
   bed hangings, 167–71, *168*, *169*, *174*, 177–79, *177*, *180*, *209*
   in French furniture, 121, 122
   window curtains, *21*, *24*, 210–14, *216*
cotton batting, 226, 227, 228
   in spring seats, *244*, *245*, 247
couches:
   in 18th-century Boston, 79

slipcovers for, 254, *255*
   Turkey-work, *14*, *59*, 60, 61, 137
   see also settees; sofas
counterpanes, 175
coverlets, 71
Cowper, William, 11
cradles, 80, *81*
Craigie, Andrew, 252–54
crepine, 136
cretonne, 200, 202, 203, 204, 205, 220, 258, *258*
crewels, 71–72, 103, *209*
   bed hangings, *20*, 138–39, *139*, 171, *172*
   easy-chair slipcovers, 139–40
   fringe, 137
   trimmings used with, 138–40, *139*, 141
Croeser, Nicolaes Pietersz, *154*
"Cromwellian chairs," 63*n*
Crown and Cushion, 75
Cullick, John, 42
Cummings, Abbott Lowell, 87*n*, 251
curled hair, 83, *84*, 93–94, 98, *99*, 252
Curtain-Maker's Handbook, 196, 206*n*
curtain pins, *217*
curtain rings, 72, 75
curtain rods, 181–83, 202, 205
   French, 163, 165, 179, *212*
   at Rosersberg Palace, 187, 193–95
curtains, *see* bed hangings; draperies; window curtains
Curwen family (Salem, Mass.), *174*, *176*
cushions, 33
   on easy chairs, 98, 100, *102*, 103
   on French furniture, 122, 125
   on leather chairs, 40, *41*
   trimmings on, 133, 139, *140*, *141*
   Turkey-work, 54, 62
   window seat, 256, *257*
   see also pillows
Custer, Edward, 223, *223*, 230
custom shops, spring seats made by, 241, 242, *243–45*
cutting:
   of leather edges, 48
   of window curtains, 187, 189, *189*, *191*, 193, *194*, 195, 199, 200

D
damask:
   bed hangings, 176–77
   as covering for Empire sofas, 224
   silk, in French furniture, 121–22
   silk and wool, 167, *167*
   table linens, 149
   window curtains, 165, 179, *216*, *218*, *221*
   worsted, 67

damas lampas, 126–27
Davanzati Palace, Florence, Italy, 58
Davenport, Albert H., 231, 232
A. H. Davenport Company, 231–38
   history of, 231–32
   Moreland as employee of, 232, 236–38
   pictorial archive of, 232–36, *233–37*
Davis, Samuel, 89*n*
daybeds, 35
Decorative Arts Society, forum organized
   by (1979), 11–12
   drapery documents at, 207, *207–21*
Delany, Mrs. (English diarist), 142
Delaunay, Nicolas, *124, 126*
Dequevauviller, Francois-Nicolas-
   Barthélemy, *126*
Des Granges, David, 136
design and pattern books, 36, *37*, 142
   bed hangings and window curtains in,
      163, 166, 167–68, 187, 256
   by Chippendale, 65, 75, 76, 86*n*, 96, 163
   Empire sofas in, *222, 223, 224, 225*, 230
   trimmings in, 131
diamond tufting, *244–45*
diapering:
   of leathers, *40, 46, 46*
   of table linens, 149, 151, *152*, 157, *157*, 158*n*
*Dictionnaire de l'Ameublement et de la
   Décoration Depuis le XIIIe siècle jusqu'à
   nos jours* (Harvard), *29*
Diderot, Denis, 65, *66*, 73, 77, 88*n*, 115, 131,
   132, 133, 134
C. T. Dillingham, 206*n*
dimity, 165, *165*
   bed hangings, *135*, 167, *178, 179*
   slipcovers, 204, 254, *254*
   in window curtains, *212*
dining rooms, draperies in, 198–99
Distichlis spicata (spike grass), 44, *45*
   see also marsh grass
documentation sources, 36, 258
   see also inventories
Dolbear, Benjamin, 89*n*
dome beds, 168
double loop stitches, 226, 227, *244*
double nailing, 47–48
double-stuff stitching, 43, 44, *45*, 48
down, 32, 129
   seat cushions filled with, 41, 98
   see also feathers
Downe, William, 67, 78
drab style, 142
draperies:
   in alcoves and "cosey corners," 198, 202
   in archways, 200, 202

   in dining rooms, 198–99
   dressing-table, 202–3, *203*
   mantel, 202, *203*
   portières, 199, 202, *219*
   see also bed hangings; valances; win-
      dow curtains
drapery documents, exhibit of (1979),
   207, *207–21*
draw-up curtains, 78
dressing-table drapery, 202–3, *203*
driving-bolts, *73*
Duddings' Furniture, 211
Dudley, Joseph, 89*n*
Dudley, Robert, Earl of Leicester, 54
R. G. Dun and Company, 231, 232
Dunblane, England, 54
Dutch furniture, 29, *42*
   double-stuff stitching in, 44
   leather chairs, 48, *49*
E. P. Dutton, 206*n*

E
Eames, Charles, 242
Earle, Alice Morse, 138, 140
East Hampton Historical Society, East
   Hampton, N.Y., *42*
Eastlake, Charles Locke, 198
easy chairs, *68*, 239
   attributred to Grant, 80–81, *82*
   commodes or "close stools," 107–8, *108*
   cost of, 105–7
   cushions for, 98, 100, *102, 103*
   18th-century upholstery techniques
      for, *96–108*, 97–108
   Irish-stitch, 72, *100, 101, 103*
   linings in, 44
   from New England, *16, 17*, 80–81, *82*, 96,
      97–105, *97–103*
   original function of, 107–8
   padding on inner vs. outer surfaces of,
      100
   from Philadelphia, *104*, 105–8, *106, 107,
      108*
   17th-century, 30–33, *32, 34*
   slipcovers for, *70*, 105, 139–40, *141*,
      251–52, *252*
   trimmings on, *71*, 139
edge treatments:
   blind-tacking in, 228
   in Empire sofas, 226
   French edges, 85, *92–93, 95, 96*, 125, *139*,
      226
   in French furniture, 125, 129
   leather cutting, 48
   rolled, 85, *92–93, 95, 98, 99*, 100, 252

   in spring seats, 241, *244, 246, 248*
   squared, in 17th century, 33, 34
   trimmings in, 33, 131, 133–35, *139*, 140,
      140, 251, 252
   wire, 241, *246, 248*
Eldredge, Mr. and Mrs. James, 163
Peter W. Eliot Collection, New York,
   N.Y., *104*, 105
Ellery, Esther, 181
Elliott, John, 105–7
Elyas, Isaac, *150*
embassy gimp, 131, *135*
embroidery, 121, 138–40, *139*
   marks of ownership, 155–57, *157*
   see also crewels; needlework
Emery, Sarah Anna, 177
Emery family (Boston, Mass.), 217
Empire sofas, *27*, 144, *222*, 223–30, *225*
   armrests of, 227–28
   arm supports of, 228, *228, 229*
   attribution of, 223–24, 230
   back panels of, 227, *229*
   carved features of, 223
   covering fabrics for, 224, 226–27, 230
   decorative pillows for, 229–30, *229*
   reupholstering of, 225–30, *228, 229*
   seats of, 225–27
   with spring seats, 239
   trimmings on, 224, 227, *228*
Empire style, 144, 198
   Rosersberg draperies, *186*, 187–95,
      188–94
Encyclopedia (Loudon), 144, 175, *183*
Encyclopedia of Domestic Economy, An
   (Webster and Parkes), 179, *180*, 181
Encyclopédie, L' (Diderot), 65, *66*, 73, 77,
   88*n*, 115, 131, *132, 133, 134*
Endicott, John, 147*n*
Endicott, Zerubbabel, great chair owned
   by, *41, 43*, 44, *45*, 50, 137
England:
   American taste influenced by, 40,
      137–38, 163, 175
   textiles for bed hangings in, 170
   upholstery trade in, 65
English furniture:
   back stools, 29–30
   caning in, 33
   "chamber horses," 36, *37*
   double and triple brass nailing in, 47,
      48
   double-stuff stitching in, 44
   18th-century upholstery treatments in,
      33–36, *35*
   "French chairs," 34, 36

over-the-rail upholstery in, *90–96*, 91
springing in, 36, 38*n*
trimmings in, 133, 136–37, *137*
tufted, 35–36, *36*
Turkey-work chairs, 51–63, *51, 52, 56, 57, 58, 60, 61*
turned elements in, 43
webbing in, 98, 122
engravings, as documentation, 36
Erskine, Margaret, 54
Essex Institute, Salem, Mass., 85, 166, 197, *219,* 260*n*
   bed hangings at, *19,* 138, *138, 174*
   braid-trimmed panel at, *134,* 142
   Turkey-work couch at, *14, 59,* 60, 61, *137*
   window curtains at, *213, 216, 221*
Essex Institute Historical Collections, 197
excelsior, 241–42
exercise horses, 239
exercising chairs, 36, *37*
eyelet stitch, 157

F
fabrics, *see* textiles
factory operations, spring seats made by, 241–42, *246–49*
factory unit seats, 242, *249*
Fales, Martha Gandy, 236
"farthingale chairs," 37*n,* 54
   see also back stools
fauteuils, 34, *127*
   de cabinet, 121
   à la Reine, 122
feathers, 71, 75, 78, 204
   down, 32, 41, 98, 129
Federal-style easy chairs, 107–8, *108*
Felletin, 121
Fenaille, Maurice, 121
festoons (swags), 142, *212,* 221
   in bed hangings, *171, 174,* 175, *178, 180*
   on chairs, 137
   in French drapery, 179, *180,* 181, *182,* 199–200
   Moreland's advice on, 198, 199–200, *201,* 205
   narrow, 200
   in Rosersberg draperies, 187–89, *188, 191,* 193–94
   in window curtains, *24,* 163, *164,* 165, *174, 176,* 179, 181, *182,* 187–89, *188, 191,* 193–94, 198, 199–200, *201,* 205
festoon shades, 202
field beds (camp or tent beds), 78, 168, 175–76, *176*
Fitch, Thomas, 67, 71, 75, 86*n,* 87*n,* 138

flax stuffing, 83
Fleeson, Plunket, 105, 114, 170–71
Flemish furniture, 29, *30, 42*
flounces, 175, 200, 251–2
Fogg Art Museum, Cambridge, Mass., *126*
Fontainebleau, Francce, 126
foundations:
   of Empire sofas, 225–26
   of leather chairs, 43–44, *45*
   in over-the-rail upholstery, 85, *91–95*
   of slip seats, 83–85, *84*
   of spring seats, 239–40, *240,* 241–42, *243–49*
   see also bottom linen; horsehair stuffing; padding; stiches, stitching; stuffing; top linen or canvas; webbing
four-post beds, 168
   see also tester frames
Samuel Fowler House, Danversport, Mass., 256
frames:
   of leather chairs, 39–43
   of Turkey-work chairs, 54, 56
   see also bedsteads
France:
   interior design in, 121
   New England draperies influenced by, 175, 177, 179–81, *180, 182, 183*
   textiles for bed hangings in, 170
   see also French furniture
Franklin, Benjamin, 170
Franklin, William, 167
Freake, John, 137
Freeman, Jonathan, 89*n*
"French (sofa) beds," 175, *176*
"French chairs," 34, 36
French cord (applied cord edging), 135, 139
French curtain rods, 163, 165, 179, *212*
French drapery, 175, 177, 179–81, *180, 182,* 183
   basic elements of, 179
   Moreland's advice on, 198, 199–200, *199,* 202
French edges, 85, *92–93, 95, 96,* 125, 139, 226
French furniture, *120,* 121–30
   American upholstery techniques influenced by, 252
   bergères, 28, 125, *127,* 258, *258*
   caning in, 33, *34*
   chair backs in, 123–25, 129
   colors of, 121, 122

   distorted by reupholstering, 121, 125, 129–30
   edge treatments in, 125, 129
   fauteuils, 34, 121, 122, *127*
   high-backed chairs, 40
   importance of upholstery in, 121
   silk coverings in, 121–22, *127,* 129
   summer vs. winter coverings for, 121–22
   tapestry coverings in, 121
   thickness of padding and cushioning in, 125, 129
   Thierry's bedroom suite, 122, 125–27, *127, 128,* 129–30
   trimmings on, 121
   tufting in, 35–36
   upholstery techniques for, 122–25, *123*
   voyeuses from St. Cloud, 125, 129, *129,* 130*n*
   webbing in, 98, 122, 123, *123*
French rolls, 85, *92–93, 95*
French seams, 135, 139, 140, 204
fringe, 131, 133, *246*
   on bed hangings, 167, 177, *177,* 179, *180, 209*
   block, 144
   bobble, 138–39, *139*
   bullion, 133
   campaign, 133, *135, 137*
   crewel, 137
   18th-century, *70, 71,* 121, *135,* 138–39, *139,* 142–44, 163, 165, 167, *167, 177, 180*
   making of, *134,* 142
   19th-century and after, 144–46, 177, 179, 256
   17th-century, *33, 42,* 136–137, *137*
   thread, 133, *135,* 142
   trellis, 136, *137*
   on window curtains, 163, 165, *167,* 179, 187, 189, *190, 191, 192,* 195, 200, 202, *210,* 216–21
fringe looms, *134,* 142

G
galloon (*galon*), 131–33, 136, 137
   making of, *132, 133*
Garde Meuble, 121, 122, 125, 129
Genesee Country Museum, Mumford, N.Y., *220*
Gentleman and Cabinet-Maker's Director, The (Chippendale), 65, 75, 76, 86*n, 96,* 163
George IV, King of England, 63*n*
German furniture, springing in, 36, 38*n*
gimp, 131, *132, 135, 177, 180, 210, 218*
   heading, 142, 167

glass curtains, 198, 202
Glover, Widow, 136
goat skin, 71
Gobelins, 121
Godey, Louis Antoine, 183
Golding, Timothy, 167
Jeff Goldthwait & Company, 198
Good Housekeeper, The (Hale), 175
Gould, Robert, 89*n*
Gragg, Samuel, *178*
Grandmother's Bedroom (Kilbourne), *184*
Grant, Elizabeth, 88*n*
Grant, John, 75, 88*n*
Grant, Samuel, Jr., 80, *81*
Grant, Samuel, Sr., 67, 69, 71, 72, 75–81, *81, 82,* 86*n*–87*n*, 88*n*, 105, 139, 251
grass stuffing, *see* marsh grass
Gray, Abigail, 176
Gray, Harrison, 65
Gray, John, 65
great chairs, 30, *30, 31*
    leather, *13, 41, 43*
    with slipcovers, 33
"Great Heeles," *51, 52,* 53
grillwork, in window treatments, 198–99, 200
Gusler, Wallace, 12

H
Hains, Adam, 252, *253*
haircloth (horsehair seating), 69, *71,* 224
hair hides, *42*
Hale, Sarah Josepha, 175
half-tester beds, 168
Hall, John, *222, 223,* 224
Ham House, Richmond, England, 138
Hamilton Palace, Lanarkshire, Scotland, 55
hammers, *73*
Hancock, John, 67, *68,* 171
Hancock, Thomas, 88*n,* 138
Hancock, William, 256, *257*
hand towels, 151–55, *154, 157,* 160*n*
    dimensions of, 153–55
    use of, 151–53
harateen, 67, 69, *69,* 138, 166, *167, 250,* 251
hardware, 78
    ceiling screws, 89*n*
    curtain rings, 72, 75
    iron bed screws, 78
    iron upholstery tacks, 47–48, 72, *72, 73,* 175
    see also brass upholstery nails; curtain rods

Hardwick Hall, Derbyshire, England, 58, 60, 153
Harlot's Progress, The (Hogarth), 88*n*
Harriman, Jean, 197
Harris, Stephen, 78
Hartssdörfer, George Philipp, *153*
Harvard, Henry, *29*
Haven, Maria Tufton, *210*
Hawks, Elkanah, 89*n*
headboards, cloth-covered, *75, 76*
headcloths, *20,* 138, *171, 172,* 175
Headley, Mac, 91
"heads," *212*
Heath, William, 89*n*
Heaton, Herbert, 165
hems, of table linens, 155
Hepplewhite, George, 131, 142, 167–68
Heurtaut, Nicholas, *123*
high-backed chairs, 40, 56, *56*
High Museum, Atlanta, Ga., 260*n*
Hinckley, David, 176, 179
History of British Carpets, The (Tattersall), 54
Hixon, Edward, 258–60
Hoar, Leonard, 136
Hogarth, William, 88*n,* 89*n*
Holker, John, *165, 166, 167,* 170
Holme, Randall, 55, 133
Holyroodhouse, Edinburgh, Scotland, *42*
    history of, 51–53
    inventories of, 53
    rebuilding and expansion of, 53
    Turkey-work chairs of, 51–63, *51, 52*
honeycomb weave tapes, 138, 139, *140, 141,* 142
Hooper, Silas, 138
horsehair seating (haircloth), 69, *71,* 224
horsehair stuffing, *29, 32, 44, 92,* 239, 256
    in Empire sofas, 226, *227*
    in French furniture, 122, *123, 125*
    in spring seats, 241, *244, 245, 247, 248*
Howard, Abraham, 75
Howard, Lord William, 155
Hurd, Nathaniel, *67*

I
inbacks, in French furniture, 123–25, *129*
indigo blue resist prints, 142, 170
inkle, 138
interlocking overhand knots, 241, *243*
invalid chairs, *29, 32*
inventories:
    of bed hangings and window curtains, 163, 176, 181
    of French furniture, 121

of Holyroodhouse, 53
from 17th-century Boston, 60
of sofas and settees, 108
of table linens, 149, 151, 153–55
trimmings listed in, 136, 139
of Wevill's upholstery business, 114–15, 117–19
Irish stitch easy chair, 72, *100, 101,* 103
iron bed screws, 78
iron upholstery tacks, 47–48, 72, *72, 73,* 175
irregular drapery, 200, *200*
Irving and Casson—A. H. Davenport Company, *221, 231, 232, 236, 237*
Italian furniture, *29*

J
"in the jacket," *247*
Jacob, Georges, 129, *129*
Jacobs Farm, Norwell, Mass., 256
James I, King of England (James VI of Scotland), 51
James II, King of England, 53
javelins, window curtains draped over, *187, 195*
Jefferson, Thomas, 181
Journal du Garde-Meuble, 121
jute webbing, 43, 241, *246,* 250*n*

K
Kemble, Elizabeth, 76, 88*n*
Kennedy, David, 115
Kilbourne, M. J., *184*
Kindig, Joe, III, 105
Kip, Richard, 168, *168*
kits, mail order, 136
Knole, Kent, England, 136
knots, in spring-seat furniture, 241, *243*
Kunstindustrie Museum, Oslo, Norway, 58

L
labor costs, 76–78
lace (braid), 133, 136
lace curtains, 183, 198, *199,* 200, 202
Ladd, Alexander, *210*
Ladys Book, 183
lambrequins, *25,* 183, *214, 215, 216,* 220
Lammertijn, Paschier, *156*
lampas, 26, 121, 126–27, *129,* 130*n, 215, 216*
Lasalle, Philippe de, *129*
lashing, 241, *248–49*
Lauderdale, John Maitland, Earl of, 53, 55
laundering, of draperies, 177, 202
Lavreince, Nicolas, *124, 126*
Leach, Annabel and Company, 254

Lear, Tobias, *86*
leather, 46–47, 69–71
    cradle, 80, *81*
    dehydration of, *39*
    diapered, *40*, 46, *46*
    in French furniture, 121
    "neat" or "calf," 46
    "New England," 69–71
    "Russia," *38*, *44*, 46, *46*, 69
    slipcovers, 53
    split, *246*
    Turkey-work chairs reupholstered
        with, 56
leather chairs, 29, 54
    Anglo-American vs. Iberian, 48, *49*
    attaching leathers to frames in, 47–48
    conservation of, 50
    "Cromwellian chairs," 63*n*
    cusions on, *40*, *41*
    dark green lacquer applied to, 47
    dyed, 88*n*
    from 18th-century Boston, 78–79, *79*,
        80, *81*, *83*, 85–86, *86*
    foundations in, 43–44, *45*
    frames of, 39–43
    great chairs, *13*, *41*, 43
    key compositional elements of, 39
    with large, high back panels, 40
    measurements of, 39–40, *49*
    with open outbacks, 48, *48*
    ornamental nailing finishes in, 47–48
    ornamental turnings on, *see* turnings,
        ornamental
    17th-century, *38*, 39–50, *39*, *40*, *41*, *42*, *44*,
        46, *47*, *48*, *49*
    with spring seats, *246–49*
Lee and Shepard, 206*n*
Leicester, Robert Dudley, Earl of, 54
Leighton, Robert, 54
Lely, Sir Peter, 53
Leverett, John, *59*, *60*, *61*
Lewis house, Gorham, Maine, 142
Limbert, Charles, 242
line, *see* cord
line and tassel treatment, 142
linen, 121, 165, 204, 252
    bed hangings, *20*, 167–68, *170*, 171, *171*,
        172, 179, *208*, *209*
    webbing, 241, *246*, 250*n*
    see also bottom linen; top linen or
        canvas
linings:
    in leather chairs, 43, 44
    of window curtains, 181, *182*, 198

Litchfield Historical Society, Litchfield,
    Conn., 165
Lockwood, Luke Vincent, 63*n*
Logan, James, 171
LoNano, Ernest, 12
London Furniture Gazette, 204
London Tradesman, The (Campbell), 65,
    134
Longfellow National Historic Site,
    Cambridge, Mass., 252–54
looms:
    fringe, *134*, 142
    galloon, *132*
    tape, 139, *140*
looped drapery, 200, 201, *201*
looped tufting, *96*, 113, *245*
loop knots, 241, *243*
loop stitches, double, 226, 227, *244*
Lords of Session (Scotland), 52–53
Los Angeles County Museum of Art,
    Los Angeles, Calif., *64*
Loudon, J. C., 144, 175, *183*
Louis, le Grand Dauphin, 29, *32*
Louis XIV, King of France, 40
Louis XIV style, 198
Louis XV style, 198
Louis XVI style, *216*, *236*
Lyinbg-in, The (Naiveu), *31*
Lyman, Theodore, 252–54
Lyon, John, second Earl of Kinghorne
    and tenth Lord Glamis, 54

M
McFarlin's China Parlor, 198
McGann, T. F., 198
McKim, Mead and White, 232
madras, 202
mail order kits, for bed hangings, 136
Maitland, John, Earl of Lauderdale, 53, 55
Malbone, Godfrey, 105
Malton, Thomas, 168
mantel drapery, 202, *203*
Marblehead Historical Society,
    Marblehead, Mass., *80*
Leon Marcotte & Co., *28*, 256, 258, *258*
Mare, John, 165
marks of ownership, on table linens, *154*,
    155–57, *157*, 158
Marot, Daniel, 34
Marshall, Henry, 78
Marshall Field and Company, *246*
Marshall units, 242
marsh grass, 44, *45*, *48*, 56, 78, 83, *84*, *93*,
    98, 239, 242

Mary and Elizabeth Royall (Copley), 142,
    143
Mason, David, 65, 78
mass production:
    of spring seats, 241–42, *246–49*
    of trimmings, 144
mattings, 205
mattresses, 35, 204
    feather, 71, 75
    two used together, 88*n*
Maule, Elizabeth, 54
Merchant Haiden Hospital, Edinburgh,
    Scotland, 54
metal trim, 144
Metropolitan Museum of Art, New
    York, N.Y., *36*, *86*, *124*, 130*n*, 165, 171
    camel-back sofa at, 110
    easy chairs at, *17*, *96*, *97*, *97*, 98–103, *100*,
        101, *102*, *103*, *105*, 107–8, *108*, 139
    Turkey-works chairs at, *60*, *60*, *61*
Mifflin, Mr. and Mrs. Thomas, 142
Mrs. Freake and Baby Mary, 137
modern upholstery, *95*
Moffatt, Samuel, 67
Moffatt-Ladd House, Portsmouth,
    N.H., *210*
mollet, 136
Montgomery, Florence M., 179
Monticello, Charlottesville, Va., 181
moreen, 67–69, 87*n*, 103, 105, 177
Moreland, Benjamin P., 197
Moreland, F. A., 197–206, 232, 236–38
    on bed hangings, 203–4, *204*, *205*
    biography of, 197, 236
    on carpets, 205
    on "cosey corners" and alcoves, 198,
        202
    on dining rooms, 198–99
    on dressing-table drapery, 202–3, *203*
    on lace and glass curtains, 202
    on mantel drapery, 202, *203*
    on parlors, 198
    on poles, cornices, traverse rods, and
        shades, 205
    on portières, 199, 202
    on slipcovers, 204, *205*
    on social and economic changes,
        236–38
    on wall coverings, 204
    on window curtains, *196*, 197, 198–202,
        199, *200*, *201*
Moreland, Sarah Pitman, 197
Mortimer, Hamilton, *70*
Mt. Zion Works, Radcliffe, England, *213*
Musée des Arts Decoratifs, Paris, France,
    165, 166, *167*

Musée du Louvre, Paris, France, *34, 127*
Musée Historique des Tissus, Lyon,
  France, 122
Museum of Fine Arts, Boston, Mass., 12,
  18, 126, 139, *143,* 240, 260*n*
  embroidered easy-chair slipcover at,
    139–40, *141*
  Empire sofas at, *27, 222,* 223–30, *228, 229*
  French furniture at, *123,* 125–30, *127, 128,
    129*
  leather chairs at, *13, 39, 41, 45, 46, 48,* 137
  reupholstered 17th-century chair at, *42,*
    137
  Turkey-work chair at, *56*
muslin, 202, 203
  undercurtains, 181, 183

N
nailing patterns, 29, 47–48
  original, determining of, 36, 48
nails:
  copper pin, *73*
  see also brass upholstery nails
Naiveu, Mathys, *31*
napkins, 151, *152, 153,* 159*n*
  banquet, 155, *156*
  dimensions of, 151, 153
  hems of, 155
  marks of ownership on, 155–157, *157*
National Gallery of Art, Washington,
  D.C., 122, *164*
National Societies of the Colonial
  Dames of America, *22, 79, 170,* 210
"neat" leather, 46
needlework, 71–72, 240
  Irish stitch easy chair, 72, *100, 101,* 103
  see also crewels; embroidery
neoclassical style, 125, *127,* 144, 227, 254
  French drapery, 179–81, *180, 182,* 183
Netherlands:
  Turkey work produced in, 54
  see also Dutch furniture
netted canopies, 176
New Cookbook (Rumpolt), 149–50
New England:
  18th-century easy chairs from, *16, 17,*
    80–81, *82, 96, 97–105, 97–103*
  French influence in, 175, 177, 179–81,
    180, 182, 183
  19th-century bed hangings from, *174,*
    175–79, *176, 177, 178*
  19th-century window curtains from,
    179–83, *180, 182, 183*
  see also Boston, Mass.; Boston up-
    holstery trade

New England Historic Genealogical
  Society, Boston, Mass., *68*
"New England" leather, 69–71
New York:
  leather chairs from, 47
  upholstery trade in, 256–58
New-York Historical Society, New York,
  N.Y., 166
New York Public Library, New York,
  N.Y., *168*
New York State Education Department,
  Albany, N.Y., *61*
Nicholas, Lewis, 115
William Nickels House, Wiscasset,
  Maine, 254
Noddles Island, Mass., 78
none-so-pretties, 71, 140–41
Nordiska Museum, Stockholm, Sweden,
  56–58
North Andover Historical Society,
  North Andover, Mass., *44*
Norway, turkey work exported to, 56–58
Norwich, as turkey-work center, 54
Nye, Alvan Crocker, *174, 176*

O
Oakley and Evans, 224
Old Saybrook Historical Society, Old
  Saybrook, Conn., *42*
Old Sturbridge Village, Sturbridge,
  Mass., 12
  bed hangings and window curtains at,
    23, 24, 174, 183, 184
  drapery documents exhibited at
    (1979), 207, *207–21,* 251
  window curtains at, *211, 212, 213, 214*
Old York Gaol, York, Maine, *171*
Oliver, Andrew, 80
Oliver, Mrs. Mercy, 47–48
Ossun, Marquis d', 122
Osterley Park, England, 135
"Osterly" pattern, *211*
Ourt, Mary, 115
Ourt, Rosanna, 115
outbacks, 252
  of French furniture, 125, 129
  of leather chairs, 48, *48*
  of spring-seated furniture, *245, 246, 247*
over-the-rail upholstery, 85, 239, 242
  pictorial essay on, *90–96,* 91
Ovey, Richard, *140,* 254, *255*
Oyestad Church, Norway, 58

P
padding:
  of armrests, 227–28
  of 18th-century English furniture, 34
  of French furniture, 125, 129
  securing of, 29, *29, 30*
  of spring seats, 241, *243*
  see also stuffing
Paddock, Samuel, 89*n*
pad seats, 239
Paine family (Boston, Mass.), 217
paintings, as documentation, 36
paneled fabrics, trimmings and, 136
Parable of Lazarus and the Rich Man, The
  (van Rijck), *154*
Parkes, Mrs. William, 179, *180,* 181
parlors, *41,* 198
Parris, Alexander, 254
Parson, Nathaniel, 177
Party, A (Elyas), *150*
passementerie, 121, 131
Passeri, Andrew, 12, 225–30
pattern books, *see* design and pattern
  books
Peabody and Stearns, 232
Peabody Museum, Salem, Mass., 197
pelmets, 181
Period Furnishings, 197
Perkins, Edmund, Jr., 75
Perkins, Edmund, Sr., 75
Perkins, Henry, 75, 78
Perkins, John, 75, 78
Perkins, William, 75, 89*n*
Pernon, 129
Philadelphia, Pa.:
  bed hangings from, 163
  businesses started by craftsmen in, 114
  18th-century easy chairs from, *104,*
    105–8, *106, 107, 108*
  upholstery trade in, 114–19, 252–54
  window curtains from, 163, 165
photographs, as documentation, 258
pillows, 71, 75, 110
  decorative, for Empire sofas, 229–30,
    229
  see also cushions
pincers, *73, 83, 85*
pine state hair, 241–42
Pingree House, Salem, Mass., *221*
piping, 33, 131, 133–35, 137, *140*
la piqure à l'Angloise, 125
Platt, Jeremiah, 165
pleats:
  in bed hangings, 204
  in dressing-table drapery, 203

in machine-stitched borders, *246, 247*
in skirting, *32*
in window curtains, 181, 183, *183,* 199,
    201–2
plush, 202
Pocumtuck Valley Memorial Association,
    Deerfield, Mass., *42*
poles, for window curtains, 205
portières, 199, 202, *219*
Portland, Duchess of, 142
Portrait of Marquis de Mirabeau
    (Camelot), *34*
Practical Decorative Upholstery (More-
    land), *196,* 197–206, *199, 200, 201, 203, 204,
    205,* 232, 236–38
    advertisements of Boston firms in,
        197–98
    publishing of, 206*n*
    see also Moreland, F. A.
Pratt, Samuel, 38*n*
Principes de l'art du Tapissier (Bimont),
    122–25, 131
printed textiles, 69, *70, 140,* 141–42
    in bed hangings, *21,* 167–71, *168, 169, 174,*
        177–79, *177, 180, 209*
    block-, *21, 23,* 69, 141, 170, *174, 177, 178,
        210, 211, 215*
    copperplate-, 69, *70,* 141, 142, 165, *169,*
        170–71, *209*
    in French furniture, 121, 122
    roller-, *183,* 212, *213, 214,* 251–52, *252*
    in slipcovers, 251–52, *252*
    trimmings, 141, 142, 144
    in window curtains, *23,* 24, 165, *183,*
        210–16
Privy Council of Scotland, 52–53, *52,* 55
production shops, spring seats made by,
    241, 242
Public Record Office, London, England,
    166, *166*
public seat furniture, 239
punches, *73*
Colonel Daniel Putnam Association,
    Brooklyn, Conn., 103–5

Q

Queen Anne style, 79, 85, 97, 171
    easy chairs, *96–108,* 97–108
    side chairs, 108
    sofas, 108–10, *109, 110*
Qu'en dit l'Mobé? (Delaunay), *124*
quilting, in foundations, 29, *29,* 34–35, *94,
    123, 226, 244*
quilts, 71

R

raised beds, 78
raised drapery, 200, *201*
raw wool stuffing, 83
Louis Reboul, Fontebrune et Cie, 127, *128*
rectilinearity, 33, *34,* 85–86
    in French furniture, 125, 129
*Recueil de Planches, sur les Sciences, les Arts
    Libéraux, et les Arts Méchaniques*
    (Diderot), 65, *66, 73, 77,* 88*n,* 115, 131, *132,
    133, 134*
reel-and-ball turnings, *42*
reel and twist turnings, *43*
regulators, *45,* 244, *245*
*Repository of Arts, Literature, Commerce,
    Manufacture, Fashions and Politics, The,*
    144, 181, *182,* 224, 225, *225,* 227, 229, 230
resist dying, 142, 170
return tying, 241, *243*
reupholstering:
    determining original nailing pattern
        in, 36, 48
    determining original tufting pattern
        in, 36
    of 18th-century American easy chairs,
        97–108, *97–108*
    of 18th-century French furniture, 121,
        125, 129–30
    of Empire sofas, 222, 225–30, *228, 229*
    of late 18th-century sofas, 112
    over-the-rail, pictorial essay on, *90–96,
        91*
    preserving remaining material in, 108,
        110
    sources of information in, 36–37
    standard museum practice of, in past, 11
    see also specific topics
revival styles, 232–36, *233, 234*
Rhode Island Historical Society, Provi-
    dence, R.I., *208, 209*
Rhymes for the Nursery, 176
Richardson, H. H., 232
Ridgely, Ann, 114, 115
Ridgely, Williamina, 144
Ridgeway, Samuel, 89*n*
Rijksmuseum, Amsterdam, Netherlands:
    canapé at, *120,* 122, 125
    table linens at, 149, *152, 157*
Robbins family (Arlington and
    Lexington, Mass.), 138
Rockwood, Roxbury, Mass., 230*n*
rococo style, 125
rods, *see* curtain rods
Rogers, Nabby, 176

rolled edges, 252
    French, 85, *92–93,* 95
    straw, 98, *99,* 100
roller-printed fabrics, 24, *183,* 212, *213, 214,*
    251–52, *252*
Rosersberg Palace, Sweden, draperies at,
    187–95
    in council room, *190*
    cutting out of, 187, 189, *189, 191, 193, 194,*
        195
    in green antechamber, 187, *192,* 193–95,
        193, 194
    hanging of, *186,* 187–89, 193–95
    in queen's bedroom, *186,* 187–89, *188, 189*
    in yellow antechamber, 187, 189–93, *190,
        191*
rosettes:
    in Empire sofas, *228, 229, 230*
    in window curtains, *182, 195,* 200, *201*
Royal Ontario Museum, Toronto,
    Canada, 62
Royal Scottish Museum, Edinburgh,
    Scotland, 61
ruffles, 200, 204, 254
Rumpolt, M., 149–50
Rundlett-May House, Portsmouth,
    N.H., 181
running stitch, 227, *244*
rush-seated chairs, 33
russels, 166
Russia leather, *38, 44,* 46, *46,* 69

S

Sack, Albert, 108
sackcloth, 43–44, *45,* 48, 252
saddlers, *42*
saddle stitch, *93*
St. Cloud, France, *voyeuses* from, 125, 129,
    129, 130*n*
Salem Towne House, Sturbridge, Mass.,
    174
Saltonstall Family, The (Des Granges), 136
*Sargeant-at-Arms Bonfoy, His Son, and
    John Clementson, Sr.* (Mortimer), *70*
Sargeant Family, The, 164
sateen, 202
satin, 121, 168
    as covering material for Empire sofas,
        224, 226–27, 230
    lampas, 126–27, *129,* 130*n*
    tacking of, 227
Saunders, Daniel and Sarah, 260*n*
Savonnerie carpeting, 121
Sayward, Elizabeth Plummer, 251
Sayward, John, 251

Sayward, Jonathan, *69*, 80–81, *82, 208*
Sayward-Wheeler House, York, Maine, *208*, 251
Scalamandre Silks, 228
Scale Drawings of Colonial Furniture (Nye), *174, 176*
Scandinavian furniture, 44
Scollay, John, 251
Scollay family (Boston, Mass.), 72
Scott, Dorothy Quincy Hancock, 142, *177*
Scott, George, 69
screws, 122
screw-wrenches, *73*
sealskins, *42*, 46, 71
seams:
　French, 135, 139, 140, 204
　trimmings in finishing of, 100–103, *100, 101*, 131, 135, 136, 139
seasonal changes, 258–60
　in French furniture, 121–22
seat furniture:
　canapés, *120*, 122, 125
　Grant's manufacture of, 78–81
　public, 239
　settees, 108–10, 252
　in 17th and 18th-century Europe, 28–39
　spring seats in, 36, 38*n*, 239–42, *240, 243–49*, 250*n*
　see also armchairs; back stools; chairs; couches; easy chairs; Empire sofas; leather chairs; side chairs; sofas
seaweed, 241–42
Sené, Jean-Baptiste-Claude, 127, *127*
settees, 252
　18th-century American upholstery techniques for, 108–10
　see also couches; sofas
set-work, 63*n*
　see also Turkey work
Seventeenth-Century Interior Decoration in England, France and Holland (Thornton), 136
Sewall, Judith, 138
Sewall, Samuel, 136, 138, 166
shades, 205
shawl bordering, 144, *145, 146*
shell gimp, 131, *135*
Shepard, Norwell and Company, 197, 206*n*, 236
Sheraton, Thomas, *37*, 131, 175, 224
Shippen, Dr., 115
Shirley, William, 79–80
shutters, 198
side chairs:
　cushions for, 40

18th-century Boston leather chairs, 78–79, *79, 80*, 81, *83*, 85–86, *86*
　Queen Anne and Chippendale, *15*, 108, *250*, 251
　slipcovers for, 83, *254, 254*
　with spring seats, *240, 243–45*
　see also back stools
side webbing, *91, 92, 95*
sieges courants, 123
sieges meublants, 123
silk, 168
　bed hangings, 204
　damask, 137, *167, 167*
　dressing-table drapery, *202, 203*
　Empire sofas covered with, 224
　French furniture covered with, 121–22, 127, 129
　fringe, 137
　mantel drapery, 202
　patterned, 165
　tacking of, 227
　window curtains, *26*, 165, 176–77, *179*, 198, *199–200*, 202, *215, 216*
skewers, *244, 245*
Skillin, Simeon, 75
skirting, pleated, *32*
Skutans, Albert, 12
Sleeper, Henry, *237*
slipcovers, 81
　for armchairs, 33, *253, 254*
　check, 69
　for couches, 254, *255*
　for easy chairs, *70*, 105, 139–40, *141*, 251–52, *252*
　for great chairs, 33
　leather, 53
　Moreland's advice on, 204, *205*
　for side chairs, 83, *254, 254*
　trimmings on, 135, 139–40, *141*, 144
slip seats, 122, 239, 251
　upholstery of, 83–85, *84*
Smith, George, 181, 187
Smith, Isaac, 89*n*, 141
societal changes:
　Moreland on, 236–38
　and organization of upholstery trade, 241–42
Society for the Preservation of New England Antiquities (SPNEA), *15*, 28, 69, 86, 89*n*, 251–60
　bed hangings at, *21*, 137, 138, 141, 142, *177, 178*, 180, *208, 209*
　cushions at, *140*, 141, 256, *257*
　18th-century Boston upholstered furniture at, 80–83, *81, 82, 83*

library of, *66, 73*, 132, *133, 134*
William Nickels House and, 254
photograph collection of, 258, *259*
provenance emphasized by, 251
Sayward-Wheeler house and, 251–52
tape loom at, *140*
trimmings at, *135*, 136, *145*
"The Vale" and, 252–54
window curtains at, *25, 26*, 144, *146, 210, 212, 215–19*, 254–56
sofa ("French") beds, 175, *176*
sofas, 35, 237, 239
　canapés, *120*, 122, 125
　Chippendale, 108–10, *109, 110*, 112–13, *113*
　Empire, *see* Empire sofas
　pillows on, 110
　17th-century, 32–33, *32*
　trimmings on, 144
　see also couches; settees
Somerville, James, 53
Spanish furniture:
　leather chairs, 48, *49*
　quilted padding in, 29
Spanish moss, 241–42
spike grass (*Distichlis spicata*), 44, *45*
　see also marsh grass
Spitalfields, London, England, 165
split leather, *246*
Spring, Marshall B., 181
spring seats, 239–42, *240, 243–49*, 250*n*
　and affordability of upholstered furniture, 241
　from custom shops, 241, 242, *243–45*
　edge treatments in, 241, *244, 246*, 248
　from factory operations, 241–42, 246–49
　first uses of, 36, 38*n*, 239–40
　limitations of, 239
　metallurgical developments and, 240–41
　pre-assembled, 242, *249*
　from production shops, 241, 242
　securing tops of springs in, 239–40, 241, *243*, 248
　trimmings on, 144
　upholstery techniques for, 239–40, *240*, 241–42, *243–49*
squabs, 33, *34*, 35
s-scroll carving, *56*
Stanhope family (Yorkshire, England), 54
State House, Hartford, Conn., 163
Stengel, W., 36, 38*n*
Stenton Mansion, Germantown, Pa., *170*, 171, *171*
Stickley, J. George, 242, *249*
Stickley, Leopold, 242, *249*

stitches, stitching:
  blanket, 34
  double loop, 226, 227, *244*
  double-stuff, 43, 44, *45, 48*
  of edges in Empire sofas, 226
  eyelet, 157
  of French edges, 85, 92–93, *95, 96*, 125,
    139, 226
  quilting, 29, *29*, 34–35, *94*, 123, 226, *244*
  running, 227, *244*
  saddle, *93*
  of spring seats, 239, 240, 241, *243–48*
  see also crewels; embroidery; nee-
    dlework; tufting
Stone, Nathaniel, 89*n*
Stowe, Harriet Beecher, 183
Strahan, William, 167
Strangers Hall Museum, Norwich,
  England, 54
straw roll edging, 98, *99*, 100
stuffing, 43, 44, *45*, 78
  in Chippendale sofas, 110
  curled hair, 83, *84, 93–94*, 98, *99*, 252
  down, 32, 41, 98, 129
  in 18th-century American easy chairs,
    97–100, *99*
  feathers, 71, 75, 78, 204
  flax, 83
  inferior, in factory operations, 241–42
  marsh grass, 44, *45, 48*, 56, 78, 83, *84, 93*,
    98, 239, 242
  in over-the-rail upholstery, *92–94*
  in pillows, 230
  raw wool, 83
  secured by quilting, *94*, 123, 226, *244*
  synthetic, 242
  tow, 44, *248*
  see also horsehair stuffing; padding
Sturgis, John Hubbard, 258
Svenska Slöjdföreningens Mönsteralbum,
  186, 190, 192
swags, *see* festoons
Swan, James, 126
Swan, T. F., 197–98
Sweden:
  Turkey work exported to, 56–58
  royal draperies from, *186*, 187–95, *188–94*
Symonds, R. W., 55
synthetics, 242

T
à tableau, 125
tablecloths, *148*, 149–50, 158*n*
  dimensions of, 149, 158*n*
  hems of, 155

table linens, 149–61
  banquet napkins, 155, *156*
  dating of, 158
  diapered, 149, 151, *152*, 157, *157*, 158*n*
  hand towels, 151–55, *154*, 157, 160*n*
  hems of, 155
  inventories of, 149, 151, 153–55
  marks of ownership on, *154*, 155–57, *157*,
    158
  napkins, 151, *152, 153*, 155, 159*n*
  social importance of, 149
  tablecloths, *148*, 149–50, 155, 158*n*
tables, laying, 149–50
tacking, 227
  baste, *244, 245*
  blind, 228, *247*
tails (cascades), *24*, 179, *180*, 212, *213, 221*
  Moreland's advice on, 199, 200
  of Rosersberg draperies, *186*, 187–89,
    188, 191
tall-backed chairs, 40, 56, *56*
tape, woven (binding), 71, 131–33, 138–42,
  138–41, 254
  on bed hangings, *177*, 179, *180*
  in crewels, 171, *172*
  on 18th-century easy chairs, 100–103,
    100–103, 105
  on Empire sofas, 227
  galloon, 131–33, *132, 133*, 136, 137
  honeycomb, 138, 139, *140, 141*, 142
  none-so-pretties, 71, *140–41*
  printed, 141, 142
  resist borders, 142
  seams covered with, 100–103, *100, 101*
  on slipcovers, 251, 252
  see also braid
tape looms, 139, *140*
tapestry:
  as covering material in French furni-
    ture, 121
  in window curtains, 198, 199
"Task, The" (Cowper), 11
tassels, 121, 131
  on bed hangings, 71, *209*
  18th-century, 71, *135*, 142, *144*, 165, *209*
  on Empire sofas, 224, 228
  17th-century, 137
  on window curtains, 71, 165, 179, 183,
    201, *217*, 254, *255*
Tattersall, C. E. C., 54
Taylor, J., 224
Taylor-Barry House, Kennebunk,
  Maine, 197
tent beds (camp or field beds), 78, 168,
  175–76, *176*

ter Borch, Gesina, *30*
tester (canopy) cloths, 78, 175, 200,
  203–4, *204*
  netted, 176
tester (canopy) frames, *74, 75*, 78, 168, 175,
  176
textile mills, of Philadelphia, 115–16
textiles, 137, 138
  for bed hangings, 69, 137–38, 167–71,
    168, 175, 176–79, 204
  brocade, 121
  brocatelle, *25*, 198, *215*
  calendered, *19*, 138, *138*
  cheney, *19*, 67, 69, *69*, 138, 166
  crepine, 136
  cretonne, 200, 202, 203, 204, 205, *220*,
    258, *258*
  for Empire sofas, 224, 226–27, 230
  English, American importation of,
    163, 165, 177
  French covering materials, 121–22,
    126–27, 129
  on front vs. sides of New England easy
    chairs, 103
  harateen, 67, 69, *69*, 138, 166, *167, 250*, 251
  horsehair seating (haircloth), 69, *71*,
    224
  imported by Boston upholstery trade,
    67–69
  lace, 183, 198, 199, 200, 202
  lampas, *26*, 121, 126–27, 129, 130*n*, *215*
  matching of, in rooms, 175, 179
  moreen, 67–69, 87*n*, 103, 105, 177
  resist-dyed, 142, 170
  tapestry, 121, 198, 199
  velour, 199, 202
  velvet, 121, 137, 167, 168, *219*, 224, 230
  watered, 69, 166
  for window curtains, 165–67, *166, 167*,
    176, 177, 178, 198, 199–200, 202, 254,
    255
  see also checked fabrics; chintz; crewels;
    damask; dimity; embroidery; linen;
    printed textiles; satin; silk; table
    linens; trimmings; wool; worsted
Thayer, Turrell, 78
Thayer, Ziphion, 67–75, *67*, 87*n*, 131
Thierry de Ville d'Avray, Marc-Antoine,
  bedroom furniture made for, 122,
    125–27, *127, 128*, 129–30
Thornton, Peter, 86, 122, 136
thread fringe, 133, *135*, 142
tiebacks, 163, *217*
tight seats, 239, 241
toiles-de-Jouy, 170

tools, *73*, 83, *85*
top linen or canvas, 226, 227
  in 18th-century Boston upholstery
    practice, 83–85, *84*
  in 18th-century easy chairs, 98, *99*, 100
  in French furniture, 122, 123, 125
  in over-the-rail upholstery, *94–95*
  in slipcovered easy chairs, 105
  in spring seats, 239, *240*, 241, *244*, *245*, 247
tow, 44, *248*
Townsend, Gertrude, 141
trade cards, 131, 168, *168*
  of Boston upholsterer, 67–75, *67*, 87*n*
  textile samples on, 166, *166*
traverse rods, 205
Treatise on Domestic Economy (Beecher),
  175
trellis fringe, 136, *137*
trimmings, 131–47
  on bed hangings, 71, *135*, 136, 137–39, *137*,
    138, *139*, 141, 142, 167, 177, *177*, 179, *180*,
    209
  cord, 131, *132*, *135*, *162*, 179, 201
  costume, 131, 133, 137
  for crewels, 138–40, *139*, 141
  on cushions, 133, 139, *140*, *141*
  early 19th-century, 131, *135*, 144
  on easy chairs, 71, 139
  in edge treatments, 33, 131, 133–35, 139,
    140, *140*, 251, 252
  18th-century, 131, *135*, 137–44, *138*, *139*
  on Empire sofas, 224, 227, 228
  French, 121
  galloon, 131–33, *132*, *133*, 136, 137, *210*
  gimp, 131, *132*, *135*, *177*, *180*, *210*, 218
  leather strips, 47
  making of, 131, *132*, *133*, *134*, 136, 139, *140*,
    142, 144
  mid-19th century and after, 131, 144–46,
    145, *146*
  none-so-pretties, 71, 140–41
  paneled effect created by, 136
  piping, 131, 133–35, 137, 140
  printed, 141, 142, 144
  ruffles, 200, 204, 254
  scarcity of information on, 131
  in seam finishes, 100–103, *100*, *101*, 131,
    135, 136, 139
  17th-century, 131, 136–37, *137*
  shawl bordering, 144, *145*, *146*
  on slipcovers, 135, 139–40, 141, 144
  sold by Boston upholstery trade, 71
  terminology for, 131–35
  on Turkey-work chairs, 136–37, 147*n*

on window curtains, 142–44, *145*, 163,
  165, *167*, 179, 181, 183, 187, 189, *190*, *191*,
  192, 195, 200, 202, 210, 216–21
  see also braid; fringe; tape, woven;
    tassels
Trinity College, Hartford, Conn., *49*
triple nailing, 47
tufting, 35–36, *36*, *246*, 256
  on chair backs, 98, *111*
  diamond, *244–45*
  looped, *96*, 113, *245*
  machine, 242
  trimmings and, 133–35, 144
  see also buttoning
Tufts, George A., 179
Turkey work, 29, 54
  carpets, 54, 58, 62
  couches, *14*, *59*, 60, 61, 137
  dated or documented covers and
    cushions, 62
  defined, 51
  fine vs. heavy weave in, 54
  incorrectly attributed to amateurs, 54
  period of production, 51, 54–55
  as weaving vs. needlework, 54
Turkey-work chairs, 39, 40–43, 51–63, *51*,
  52, *56*, *57*, *58*, *60*, *61*
  dating of, 51, 53–54
  design of, 60–62
  exported covers for, 56–60
  frames of, 54, 56
  linings in, 43, 44
  measurements of, 62
  prices of, 53, 55
  trimmings on, 136–37, 147*n*
  at Whitehall, 53, 55–56
turnings, ornamental, 43
  ball, *38–41*, 43, *52*, *59*, *60*, *61*
  ball-and-disc, *42*
  ball-and-hollow, *42*
  baluster, *52*
  barrel, *42*
  columnar, 43, *58*
  reel-and-ball, *42*
  twist, *44*, *51*, *56*
  vasiform, *38*, *42*, 43
turnscrews, *73*
twine, 226, 227
  in 18th-century American easy chairs,
    98
  in spring seats, *240*, 241, *243*, *245*, 247, *248*
twist turnings, *44*, *51*, *56*
"Tyger" pattern, *209*

U
undercurtains, muslin, 181, 183
Unidentified Woman (Copley), *64*, 65
University Museum, Pittsburgh, Pa., 130*n*
upholstery trade:
  affluence and prestige of, 65–67
  in Boston, *see* Boston upholstery trade
  commercial and craft aspects inter-
    mingled in, 67, 75
  concentrated in urban areas, 65
  custom shops in, 241, 242, *243–45*
  factory operations in, 241–42, *246–49*
  mercantile activities of, 75, 114–15
  in Philadelphia, 114–19, 252–54
  production shops in, 241, 242
  setting up business in, 67
  subdivision of tasks in, 75, 76–78, 88*n*,
    115–16, 232
  trimmings sold by, 71, 131, 139
  in 20th century, 242

V
valances:
  in bed hangings, *19*, *21*, 71, 137–39, *137*,
    138, *139*, 142, *169*, 171, 175, *177*, 179, *208*,
    209
  blue resist, 142
  flat, 183, 200–202, *201*
  in French drapery, 179, 181
  lambrequins, 183, *214*, *215*, *216*, 220
  pleated, 181, 201–2
  trimmings on, 137–39, *137*, *138*, *139*,
    142–44
  in window curtains, 142–44, 163, *167*,
    179, 181, 183, 198, 200–202, *201*, 204,
    210, *214–20*, 256
"The Vale," Waltham, Mass., 252–54
Vallois (carver), 127
Vandyking, *245*
van Rijck, Cornelius, *154*
van Senten, Magteld, *154*
vasiform turnings, *38*, *42*, 43
velour, 199, 202
velvet, 121, 137, *167*, 168, *219*
  Empire sofas covered with, 224, 230
Venetian window curtains, *162*, 163–65
Victoire, Madame, 36
Victoria, Queen of England, 51
Victoria and Albert Museum, London,
  England, *30*, *33*, *35*, 211
  fringed back stool at, 137
  Turkey-work chair at, 61, 62
Victorian period, 65, 144, 197
  top linen in, *95*
Vincent, Clement, 75, 78, 82

Vollstandig und Von Neuem Vermehrtes Trineir Buch (Hartssdörfer), *153*
voyeuses, 125, *127*, 129, *129*, 130*n*

W
Wadham, Dorothy, 54
Wadham College, Oxford, England, 54
Wadsworth Atheneum, Hartford, Conn., *49*, 103, 163
wall coverings, 204
wall hangings, *18*, *128*
Wanton, Joseph, *49*
Wanton, William, *49*
watering, 69, 166
webbing, 72, 98, *98*, 252
    in 18th-century easy chairs, 98, *98*
    in Empire sofas, 225–26, 227
    English vs. French, 98, 122
    in French furniture, 98, 122, 123, *123*
    jute vs. linen, 43, *246*, 250*n*
    in over-the-rail upholstery, *91*
    in 17th-century Boston chairs, 43, 44, *45*
    side, *91*, *92*, *95*
    in slip seats, 83, *84*
    in spring seats, 239, *240*, 241, *243*, *245*, *246*, 250*n*
Webster, John, 165
Webster, T., 179, *180*, 181
Welles, John, 256
Welles, Samuel, 256
Welting, 105
    tape sewn over, *102*, 103
Werken van D. Marot, 162
Wevill, Ann, 115
Wevill, George, 115
Wevill, Richard, 114–19
    employees of, 115
    inventory of, 114–15, 117–19
    mercantile activities of, 114–15
    multiple locations of, 115
Wevill & Nicolas, 115
Wharton, Isaac, 115
John Hall Wheelock Collection, East Hampton, N.Y., *42*
Wheelwright, Theodore, 72
white curtains, 183, *184*, 212
Whitehall, London, England, Turkey-work chairs at, 53, 55–56
whitework marks, 157
Whiting, Flora E., 97
Whitmore, G. D., 258
William III, Prince of Orange and King of England, 34, 151
William V, Stadtholder of Holland and Prince of Orange, 155

William-and-Mary-style leather chairs, 85
Williams, Henry Howell, 89*n*
window curtains:
    American, English influence on, 137–38
    attaching to window frames, 181
    curtain pins for, *217*
    curtain rings for, 72, 75
    cutting out of, 187, 189, *189*, *191*, 193, *194*, 195, 199, 200
    draw-up, 78
    18th-century, *21*, 142–44, *162*, 163–67, *164*, *167*, 210
    festoons or swags in, 163, *164*, 165, *174*, *176*, 179, 181, *182*, 187–89, *188*, *191*, 193–94, 198, 199–200, *201*, 205
    with flat valances or lambrequins, *25*, 183, 200–202, *201*, *214*, *215*, *216*, 220
    flounces in, 200
    French, 175, 177, 179–81, *180*, *182*, 183, 198, 199–200, *199*, 202
    glass, 198, 202
    irregular, 200, *200*
    lace, 183, 198, 199, 200, 202
    laundering of, 202
    linings of, 181, *182*, 198
    looped, 200, 201, *201*
    with massive exposed rods, 181–83
    matching of fabrics in bed hangings and, 175, 179
    measuring house for, 199
    Moreland's advice on, *196*, 197, 198–202, *199*, *200*, *201*
    muslin undercurtains for, 181, 183
    with narrow festoons, 200
    19th-century, *22–26*, 144, *145*, 179–83, *180*, *182*, *183*, 210–20, 254–56, *255*
    pleated, 181, 183, *183*, 199, 201–2
    poles and accessory supports for, 195
    proper length for, 201
    raised, 200, *201*
    raising of, 78, *162*, 163–65
    from Rosersberg Palace, *186*, 187–95, *188–94*
    social importance of, 163, 179, 183
    straight hanging, 163
    in study exhibition of drapery documents (1979), 208–9, *210–18*
    tails or cascades in, 179, *180*, *186*, 187–89, *188*, *191*, 199, 200, *221*
    textiles for, 165–67, *166*, *167*, 176, 177, 178, 198, 199–200, 202, 254, *255*
    trimmings on, 142–44, *145*, 163, 165, *167*, 179, 181, 183, 187, 189, *190*, *191*, *192*, 195, 200, 202, *210*, *216–21*
    20th century, *221*

two or more windows unified with, 181, *182*, 256
    Venetian, *162*, 163–65
    white, 183, *184*, 212
    see also curtain rods; valances
window seat cushions, 256, *257*
Winslow, Edward, 147*n*
Winterthur Museum, Wilmington, Del., *38*, *70*, *162*, *167*, *168*
    bed hangings at, *20*, 138, 142, *169*, 171, *172*
    easy chairs at, 97–98, *98*, *99*, 103
wire edges, 241, *246*, *248*
women workers:
    in Boston upholstery trade, 76
    in trim production, 131, *134*
wool, 44
    bed hangings, 176, 177
    and silk damask, *167*, *167*
    window curtains, *22*, 165–66, *167*, *167*, *210*, 218
    see also worsted
Woolworth, F. W., *237*
Worcester Art Museum, Worcester, Mass., *67*, 137
Workwoman's Guide, The, 135, 163–65, 175, 183
worsted, 67, 137, 138, *208*
    fringe, 137
    patterned, 166
    watered, 69
    window curtains, 165, 166–67, *166*, *167*

Y
Yale Center for British Art, New Haven, Conn., *70*

Z
Zoffany, John, 34

DATE DUE
